D0939255

Owens River Gorge Climbs

The Climbing Guide to the Owens River Gorge

10th Edition

Central Gully Approach greeting. ©*Marty Lewis Photo.*

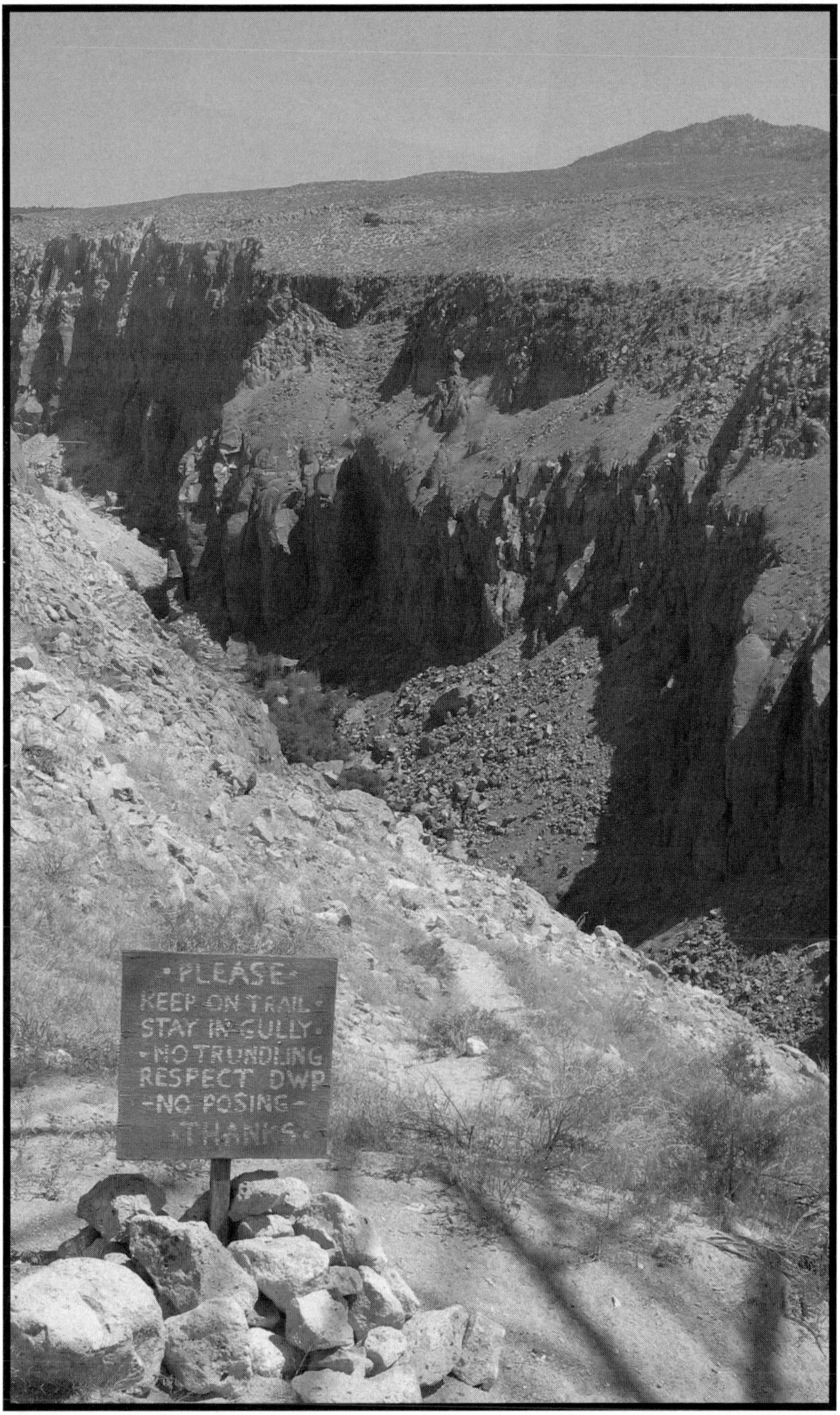

OWENS RIVER GORGE CLIMBS

The Climbing Guide to the Owens River Gorge

BY MARTY LEWIS

10TH EDITION

EASTERN SIERRA CLIMBING GUIDES VOL. 1

MAXIMVS PRESS

Owens River Gorge Climbs 10th Edition

The Climbing Guide to the Owens River Gorge

by Marty Lewis

EASTERN SIERRA CLIMBING GUIDES VOL. 1

Maximus Press
P.O. Box 1565
Bishop, CA 93515
Phone & Fax: 760-387-1013
E-mail: smlewis@qnet.com
Website: maximuspress.com

Copyright © 2005 Maximus Press
October 2005 Tenth Edition
ISBN 0-9676116-8-7

Printed in Canada.

Notice of Rights—All rights reserved under the International and Pan-American Copyright Conventions. No part of this book, including maps, photographs and topos, may be reproduced or transmitted in any form or by any means, electronic or mechanical, including photocopying, recording, or by any information storage or retrieval system except as may be expressly permitted by the 1976 Copyright Act or in writing from the publisher.

Front Cover Photo: Peter Croft on **Wooly Bugger** 12d*****. ©*Kevin Calder Photo.*
Back Cover Photo: Chad Shepard on the **Towering Inferno** 11b*****. ©*Aaron Black Photo.*

MAXIMVS PRESS

Notice of Liability—The information in this book is distributed on an "As Is" basis, without warranty. While every precaution has been taken to make this guide as accurate as possible, neither the author nor Maximus Press shall have any liability to any person with respect to any loss or damage caused by the information contained in this book.

Warning—Rock Climbing is an inherently dangerous sport in which severe injuries or death may occur. The user of this book accepts a number of unavoidable risks. It should be assumed that information could be erroneous. Please examine the rock carefully before climbing it. Use your own judgement to determine whether you are up to a particular route or not.

The authors, editors, publishers, distributors and land owners accept no liability for any injuries incurred from using this book.

Acknowledgments

This guide would not have been possible without the information and ideas provided by the following people: Louie Anderson, Scott Ayers, Greg Barnes, Fred Berman, Kevin Calder, Kelly Cordner, Tom Costa, Peter Croft, Nils Davis, Mike Forkash, Todd Graham, Marek Hajek, Tom Herbert, John & Annie Hoffman, Eric Kohl, Bruce Lella, Lance Lewis, Tony Puppo, Joe Rousek, Mick Ryan, Steve Schneider and Gary Slate. A special thanks to my wife, Sharon, for her understanding and support.

New Route Information and Comments

I would like to hear from you. Please e-mail, call or send any comments, errors, criticisms, opinions on ratings, new route information, or anything else in connection with this guide to Marty Lewis. Your feedback will help perfect future editions of this guide.

Marty Lewis
P.O. Box 1565
Bishop, CA 93515
E-mail: smlewis@qnet.com
Phone & Fax: 760-387-1013

About Climbing Guides

There are very few facts in a guidebook. Climbing guides are simply collections of personal opinions. At best the information is based on a broad consensus, but it can also be just the experience of the author or even hearsay.

The moment a guidebook comes out it begins a slow downward slide in accuracy. Holds break, routes get added, routes get removed, bolts fail, government policies change, roads close, prices go up, businesses close and acts of god occur. What you find in the real world takes precedence over anything found in a guidebook. Use your own judgement.

While most art can be easily thrown away and forgotten, the art that a first ascensionist busts out on our public lands can last for generations. So it is important that we have the freedom to critique these creations. If you write a guidebook, you're guaranteed to ruffle some feathers. Thankfully, in this great country the freedom to express these opinions is guaranteed.

The thing to keep in mind is that guidebooks are personal, subjective works of opinion. Try not to take them too seriously. And if you want a perfect guidebook, you'll have to write it yourself!

—Marty Lewis

©2005 Maximus Press.

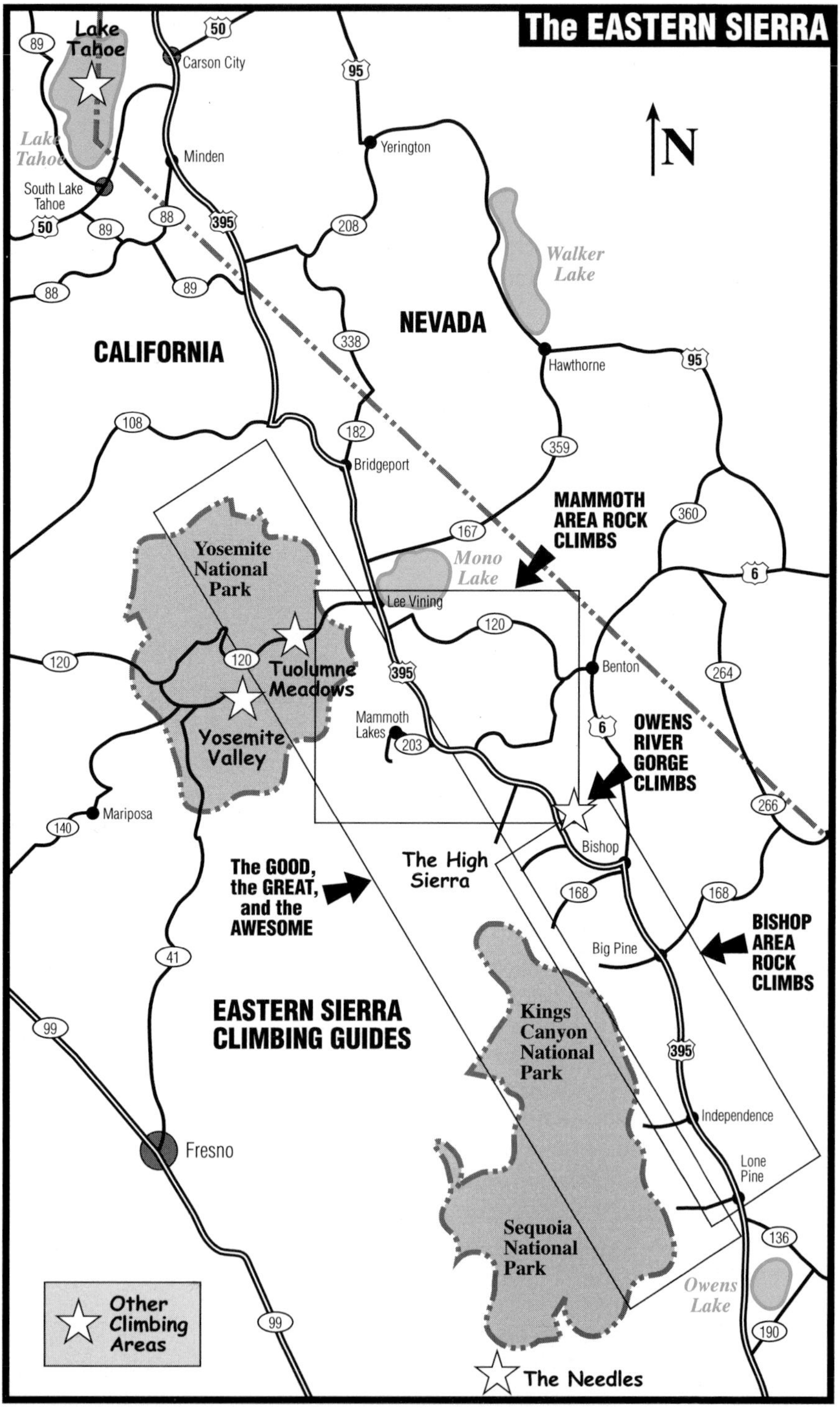

EASTERN SIERRA CLIMBING GUIDES

The Eastern Sierra is located on the edge of three major biogeographic regions: the Sierra Nevada Mountains, the Great Basin Desert and the Mojave Desert. Elevations in the Eastern Sierra range from 3,500 ft. to 14,500 ft., creating one of the most beautiful, diverse and dramatic landscapes imaginable. The area has tremendous contrasts. In the Owens Valley, Bishop is one of the driest cities in the country, with a short mild winter and a long hot summer—while 45 miles away in the High Sierra, Mammoth Lakes has a long cool winter averaging 25 feet of snow, and a short mild summer.

Within this region you will find world-class bouldering, diverse sport climbing, great traditional cragging, long alpine rock climbs and quick access to Yosemite—making this area quite possibly, one of the best rock climbing locations in the world. On the coldest days of winter you may be climbing on south facing volcanic boulders at 4,000 ft., or during the hottest days of summer you may be alpine cragging on north facing granite at 10,000 ft. Either way you can almost always find excellent conditions.

maximuspress.com

Vol. 1—
Owens River Gorge Climbs
by Marty Lewis

Featuring 700 fantastic climbs at California's premier sport climbing area.

Vol. 2—
Mammoth Area Rock Climbs
by Marty Lewis and John Moynier

Great summer cragging and bouldering in the cool Sierra around Mammoth Lakes, California.

Vol. 3—
Bishop Area Rock Climbs
by Peter Croft and Marty Lewis

A guidebook to the four season cragging and world-class bouldering in the Bishop, California area.

Vol. 4—
The Good, the Great and the Awesome
by Peter Croft

The Guidebook to the top 40 High Sierra Rock Climbs.

MAXIMUS PRESS BOOKS

ACCESS: It's every climber's concern

The Access Fund, a national, non-profit climbers organization, works to keep climbing areas open and to conserve the climbing environment. Need help with closures? land acquisition? legal or land management issues? funding for trails and other projects? starting a local climbers' group? CALL US!

Climbers can help preserve access by being committed to leaving the environment in its natural state.

- **ASPIRE TO CLIMB WITHOUT LEAVING A TRACE** especially in environmentally sensitive areas like caves. Chalk can be a significant impact – don't use it around historic rock art. Pick up litter, and leave trees and plants intact.

- **DISPOSE OF HUMAN WASTE PROPERLY** Use toilets whenever possible. If toilets are not available, dig a "cat hole" at least six inches deep and 200 feet from any water, trails, campsites, or the base of climbs. *Always pack out toilet paper.* On big wall routes, use a "poop tube."

- **USE EXISTING TRAILS** Cutting switchbacks causes erosion. When walking off-trail, tread lightly, especially in the desert on cryptogamic soils. "Rim ecologies" (the clifftop) are often highly sensitive to disturbance.

- **BE DISCRETE WITH FIXED ANCHORS** *Bolts are controversial and are not a convenience* – don't place 'em unless they are *really* necessary. Camouflage all anchors. Remove unsightly slings from rappel stations.

- **RESPECT THE RULES** and speak up when other climbers don't. Expect restrictions in designated wilderness areas, rock art sites, caves, and to protect wildlife, especially nesting birds of prey. *Power drills are illegal in wilderness and all national parks.*

- **PARK AND CAMP IN DESIGNATED AREAS** Some climbing areas require a permit for overnight camping.

- **MAINTAIN A LOW PROFILE** Leave the boom box and day-glo clothing at home.

- **RESPECT PRIVATE PROPERTY** Be courteous to land owners. Don't climb where you're not wanted.

- **JOIN THE ACCESS FUND** To become a member, make a tax-deductible donation of $25.

The Access Fund
Your Climbing Future
PO Box 17010
Boulder, CO 80308
303.545.6772
www.accessfund.org

A deadly bolt more than 20 years old ... one of several thousand on popular climbs throughout the United States.

A new bolt rated to over 5,000 pounds. The ASCA wants to replace the bad bolt above with one of these.

Bad Bolts Kill

We need YOUR help. The American Safe Climbing Association has helped replace more than 4,500 bolts throughout the country. We estimate that there are more than 20,000 bad bolts remaining on popular climbs today. Your $50 donation will make at least one route safe . . . and that one route could be the next one you climb. The ASCA would like to get there before you do.

Does your crag need re-bolting? Please contact us.

asca
American Safe Climbing Association

❑ $25 Supporter ❑ $50 Contributor ❑ $100 Advocate ❑ $500 Lifer

Name ______________________
Address ______________________

E-Mail/Phone ______________________

All contributors receive the ASCA newsletter.
Make checks payable to: ASCA, 2 Bradford Way, Mill Valley, CA 94941
or donate online at www.safeclimbing.org

The American Safe Climbing Association is a 501(c)3 organization and contributions are tax-deductible.

Table of Contents

Foreword 12
Preface 13

Chapter 1

Introduction 15
- Where is the Owens River Gorge? 17
  - Driving Times 17
- Climate 19
- Camping 21
- Getting There 23
- Approaches 25
- Amenities - Bishop 27
- Amenities - Mammoth Lakes 29
- Access Information 31
- Environmental Concerns 31
- Brief History 32
- First Ascent Ethics 40
- Climbing in the Owens River Gorge 42
  - Conduct 42
  - The Rock 42
  - Equipment 43
  - Anchors 43
  - Projects 43
  - Retrobolting 43
- Safety Concerns 44
- How to Use this Guide 46
  - Maps 46
  - Approach Instructions 46
  - Difficulty Ratings 47
  - Quality Ratings 47
  - Route Descriptions 47

Chapter 2

Sub Gorge 49
- Sub Gorge Basics 51
- Silent Pillar Wall 54
- Volcanic Meltdown Cliff 55
- Old Fart's Formation 55
- Splashdown 55
- Inyo Mono Line Tower 56
- Truck Tire Graveyard Tower 56
- Slander Crag 57
- Mental Ward 57

Chapter 3

Lower Gorge 59
- Lower Gorge Basics 61
- Big Tower 62
- Pink Face 63
- Grey Wall 64
- Diamond Face 65
- Blocky Top Wall 66
- Dead Crow Buttress 66
- Greenhouse Wall 67
- Warning Signs Wall 69
- Pitstop 70
- Powerhouse Wall 71
- Penstock Rock 73

Chapter 4

Central Gorge 75
- Central Gorge Basics 77
- L. Alien Wall 81
- Banana Belt 83
- High Tension Towers 85
- Pub Wall 87
- Riverside Island 91
- Social Platform 95
- Negress Wall 97
- Warm Up Wall 98
- Pop Tart Towers 99
- Faulty Tower 103
- Attila the Hun Wall 104
- Health Club 105
- Mystical Tricks Cliff 106
- Roadside Boulders 107
- Great Wall of China - Overview 109
  - Great Wall of China - Right Side 110
  - Great Wall of China - Center 113
  - Great Wall of China - Left Side 115
- Solarium 119
- Emergency Room 121
- Shaded Wall 123

Chapter 5

Inner Gorge 125
Inner Gorge Basics 127
Staying Power Towers 129
Weird Corner 131
DMZ 133
Eldorado Roof - Overview 135
Eldorado Roof - Towering Inferno 137
Eldorado Roof - Right Side 139
Eldorado Roof - Left Side 143
Land of the Giants 145
Mothership Cliff 147
Fun House 149
Dilithium Crystal 153
Crystal Corridor 154
Rob's Rock 155
Megalithic 157
Local Trivia Tower 157
Narrows West 159
Narrows East 161
P.T. Barnum Wall 162
Monkey to Monk Cliff 163
Supreme Wizard Formation 165
McCracken Wall 166

Chapter 6

Upper Gorge 169
Upper Gorge Basics 171
Lower Elbow Room - Left 174
Lower Elbow Room - Right 175
Joe's Garage 176
Gorgeous Towers 179
Triple Play Cliff 181
Holy Trinity Wall 183
Staging Tower 183
Flavin Haven 184
Middle Elbow Room 187
Upper Elbow Room 188
Warm Out Wall 189
Failsafe Wall 191
ICBM Tower 192
Trestle Wall 195
Underground Cliff 196
Junior Wall 197
Mini Buttress 197
All You Can Eat Cliff 199
Franklin's Tower 200
Gotham City 203
Cracked Towers 207
Dihedrals 211
Sanitarium 212

Chapter 7

North Gorge 215
North Gorge Basics 217
Savage Garden 218
Organ Pipes 218
El Pollo Grande 219
Chuckwalla Wall 221
Last Frontier 221

Chapter 8

Appendix 223
Hot Springs - North 224
Hot Springs - South 226
Players 227
Routes by Rating 228
Further Reading 236
Guide Services 236
Advertisements 237
Index 242
About the Author 251
About Maximus Press 252

FOREWORD

The first time I visited the Gorge I was *not* impressed. It looked like a very big hole to me, dry and crumbly like a quarry. In fact, it seemed like someone had found a swell spot for some underground nuclear testing.

But that was before the river came back and since then the restoration has been practically magical. Trees, real ones, have grown up and the vegetation in some sections borders on Amazonian. All sorts of creatures are flourishing here as well. On quiet mornings one can see herons and hawks, fishermen and squirrels, behaving like animals by the rivers edge.

But most of us don't go there for nature walks. We go there to look manly, or at least not too cowardly. And there's plenty for everyone: The Warm Up Wall, where just about everyone looks manly; the almost downtown atmosphere at the Great Wall of China, where herbal tea may not be enough and most people wear padded harnesses; and the very steep Eldorado Roof, where just hanging out at the base makes you look and feel like Charlton Heston.

The first time I met Marty I *was* impressed. Who wouldn't be? He seems much bigger than his six-foot-six due to his redwood-sized arms and shoulders. His appetite for climbing seems endless and his appetite for food *is* endless. He eats chocolates like other people breathe air and has an otherworldly appreciation of cheese. Most impressive, though, is his enthusiasm for the Gorge. He's climbed there pretty much since the beginning and has put up more classics, built more bridges, placed more anchors and groomed more trails than anyone else. To call it a labor of love may sound hokey but I can think of no better way to describe it. An incident that occurred a few years ago illustrates his deep feelings for the place.

We were climbing with some friends at a crag near Mammoth when I casually mentioned to Marty that even he would have to admit the Gorge was a pretty ugly place. This was before the river returned and at the time it seemed like a fairly innocent remark. In the pregnant pause that followed the blood drained from Marty's face and the horrible magnitude of my dumb-ass remark dawned on me. The emotional outburst that followed floored me far better than any knuckle sandwich and I promised myself to be more careful in the future.

Having done some new routes with Marty, I welcomed the arrival of the new guidebook with the same enthusiasm as Steve Martin celebrating the new phone book in "The Jerk." "The new guidebook's here! The new guidebook's here! I'm Somebody now!!!"

For those of you who would simply climb here—if this doesn't help you nothing will. For those of you who would compete with Marty's awesome first ascent record—read it and weep. And for those of us lucky enough to climb with him—hey, look at us, we're winning!

—Peter Croft

Preface

In 1985 Kevin Calder and I had briefly visited the Gorge. We climbed a forty-foot crack, looked around, and decided that it wasn't a very good place for climbing. The rock seemed too steep, too loose, and devoid of clean cracks. During the summer of 1989, I heard that people were putting up routes in the Gorge. I was skeptical; I thought I knew what was down there.

Soon after, Gary Slate talked me into returning. After a twenty-minute scramble, we came upon a vertical arete with a slight bulge at the top. Anguish came over me, but Gary assured me the arete was only 5.9+. And the route was sprinkled with shiny new 3/8" bolts. Having completed "Gorgeous" with quite a pump, I immediately became obsessed with the positive-hold, endurance climbing that makes up the Owens River Gorge.

In the fall of 1989, Mike Strassman and Scott Ayers put together a "Rock & Ice Guide" to the 120 routes in the Gorge. New routes were being completed at a furious pace; so almost as soon as the guide came out, it was in need of an update. I decided to put my computer to use, compiling a list of the routes for friends and local climbers. From that point on, the whole project snowballed. After hundreds of hours, tons of feedback, and personally field testing over six hundred routes, you now have it: the "Owens River Gorge Climbs" guidebook.

It has been absolutely amazing to see the fifteen-year transition of the Gorge: from a rarely visited, bone dry, semi-industrial area—to the return of the river, a riparian environment and people; from bushwacking to buffed-out trails; from a small obscure climbing area to a world-class sport climbing area. I'm damn proud of what we've done to this place.

Over the years I've climbed at quite a few of the best crags around the West. So I know it's easy to come up with negatives when comparing the Owens River Gorge. But, even after logging more than a thousand days in that ditch—when I just want to have a good time cragging with good company—the Gorge is simply my favorite place.

I would like to thank all the people who have invested so much time, sweat, and money, making the Owens River Gorge a climbers' paradise. I would also like to thank Mono County District Attorneys George Booth and Stan Eller along with the L.A.D.W.P. for their diligent efforts in returning water to the Gorge. And I'd like to thank the Access Fund, Dean Rosnau, James Wilson, Tony Puppo and the L.A.D.W.P. for their efforts establishing the toilets.

—Marty Lewis

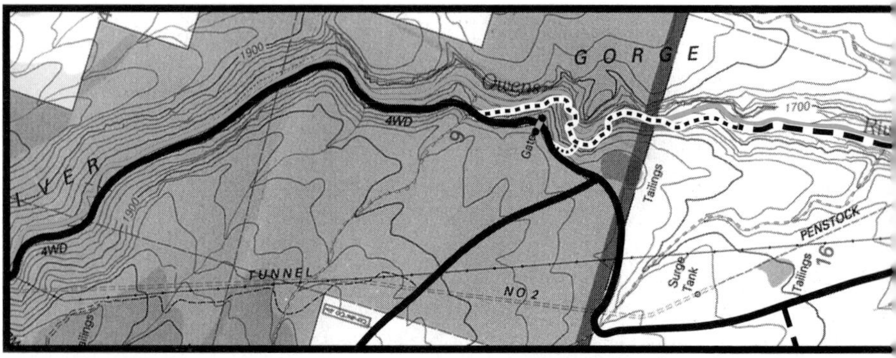

The Owens River Gorge. ©*Kevin Calder Photo.*

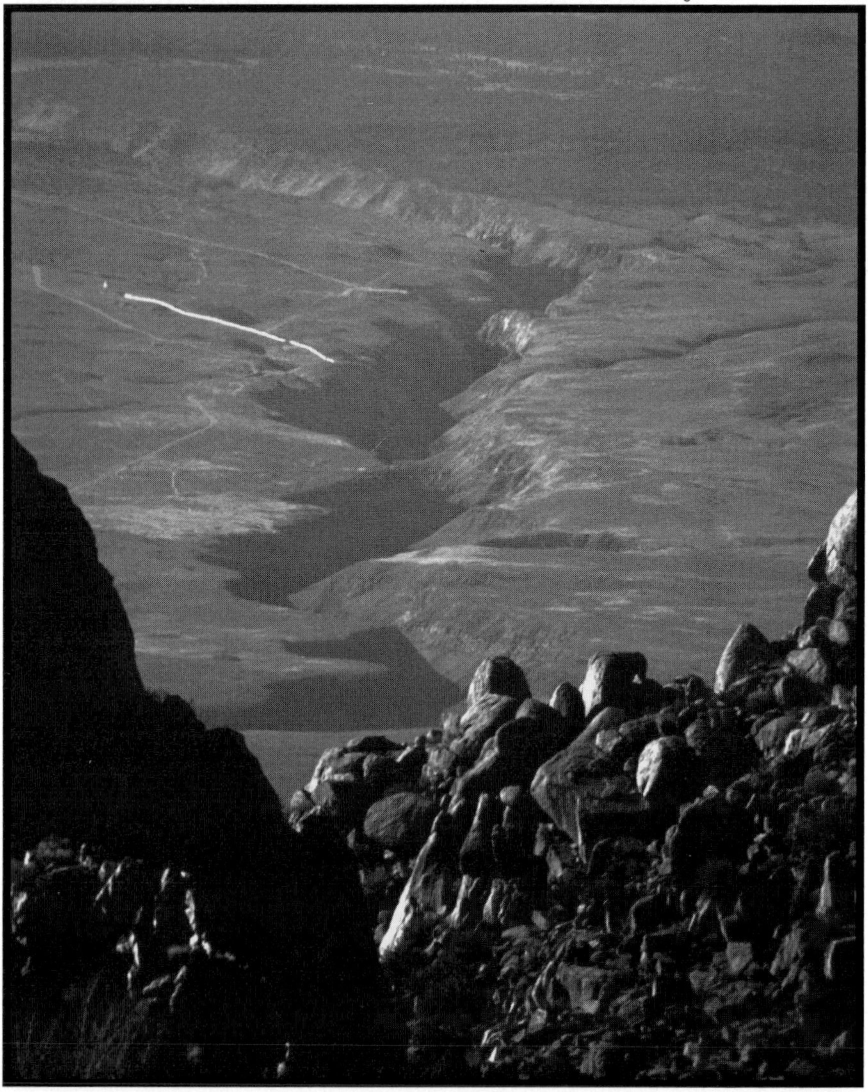

Adapted from the U.S.G.S. 1:24,000 Casa Diablo Mtn. and Rovana Quadrangles.

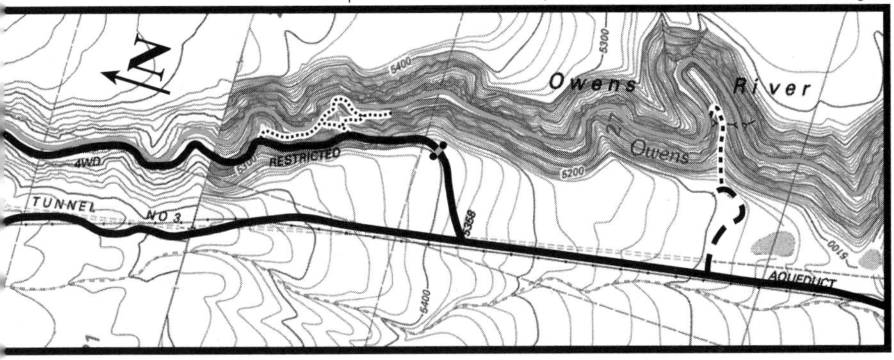

CHAPTER 1

Where is the Owens River Gorge? .... pg 17
Climate .... pg 19
Camping .... pg 21
Getting There .... pg 23
Approaches .... pg 25
Amenities - Bishop .... pg 27
Amenities - Mammoth Lakes .... pg 29
Access Information .... pg 31
Environmental Concerns .... pg 31
Brief History .... pg 32
First Ascent Ethics .... pg 40
Climbing in the Owens River Gorge .... pg 42
Safety Concerns .... pg 44
How to Use This Guide .... pg 46

INTRODUCTION

©2005 Maximus Press.

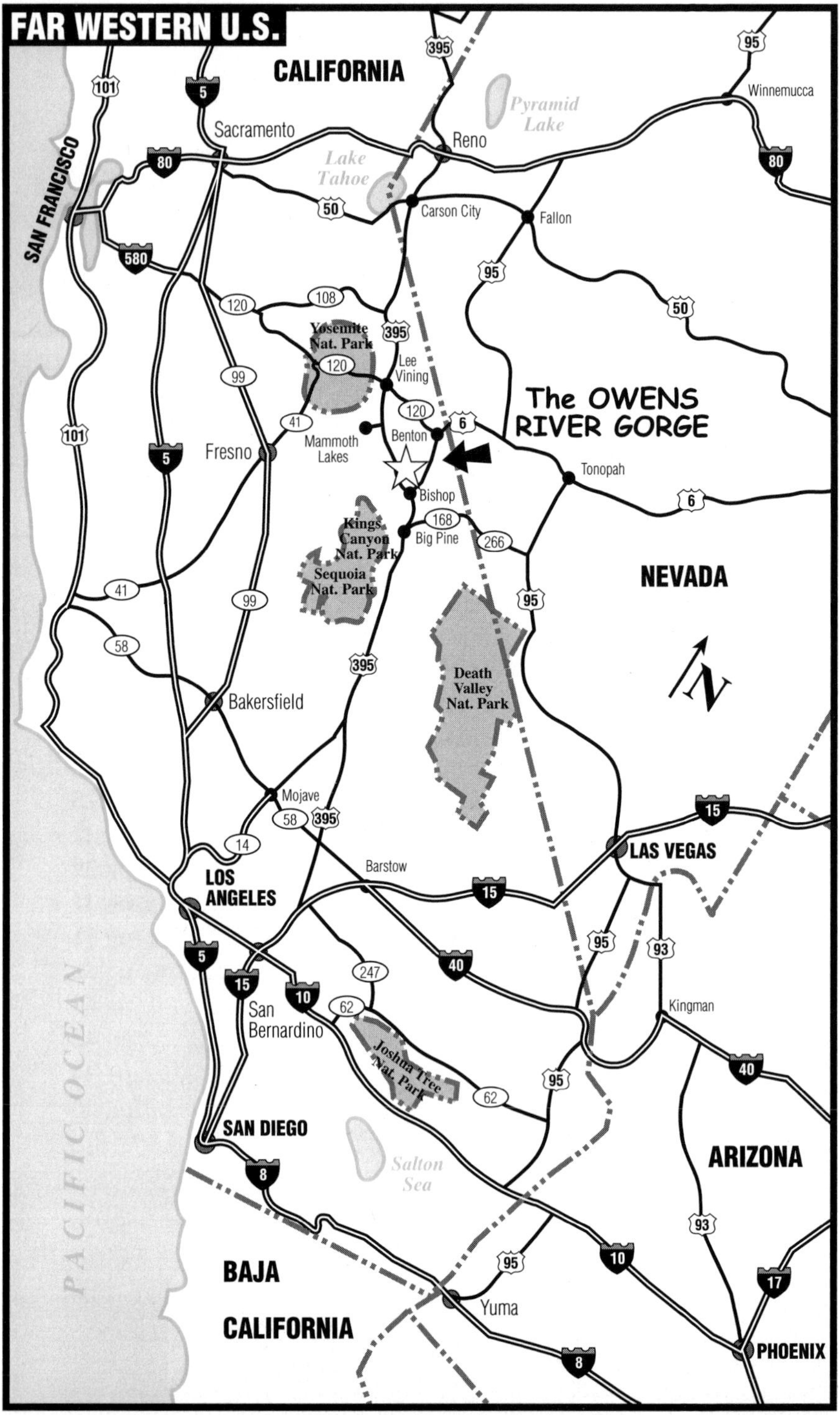

INTRODUCTION

Owens River Gorge Details

Environment: Dry high desert gorge, that holds a river in a riparian corridor.
Elevation: 4,900 to 5,900 ft.
Rock Type: Volcanic Tuff.
Sport Climbs: 544 routes, 5.5 to 13c.
Gear Climbs: 158 routes, 5.4 to 12d.
Approach: 10 to 20 minutes.

Congratulations! You are examining the latest edition of the original guide devoted to the Owens River Gorge. This book has been painstakingly researched for your enjoyment. This is the guide that all future guidebook authors will use as a reference. The reader will find this book to be one of the most organized and accurate climbing guides ever. Before jumping straight into the climbing routes you should *read the entire introduction*. It is your responsibility to know the ins and outs before climbing here.

The Gorge is located on private property and is very popular. Because of this we must follow the access guidelines and try to minimize our impacts within the Gorge.

Situated in the rain shadow of the Sierra Nevada, the Owens River Gorge has a dry, benign climate. The volcanic rock is usually vertical to gently overhanging with lots of holds that are smooth yet positive. Rounded edges, crimps, pockets and plates are the norm. Climbs will be found on every kind of feature imaginable. Routes are concentrated along an easily-traveled gorge. First ascensionists have a liberal attitude about placing bolts and anchors. A solid selection of routes are found in the grades ranging from 5.7 to 5.13b. These factors contribute to make the Owens River Gorge a sport climbing paradise.

On top of all this there is a smattering of mixed climbs, gear climbs and aid climbs; so you can fiddle with gear 'til the cows come home. In other words, stacks of diverse routes should keep you climbing to your heart's content.

Where is the Owens River Gorge?

The Owens River Gorge is located in East-Central California, just east of Yosemite National Park, situated between the towns of Bishop and Mammoth Lakes off of U.S. Hwy. 395.

Driving Times (in hours):

Los Angeles 5	Yosemite Valley 3*	Tuolumne Meadows 1.5*
Reno 3.5	Salt Lake City 8	Joshua Tree 6
Las Vegas 5	Sacramento 5.5	Smith Rock 10

*Tioga Pass (Hwy. 120) is usually closed from November through May. This makes Yosemite Valley an epic 8-hour drive. Tuolumne Meadows becomes accessible only by ski touring.

©2005 Maximus Press.

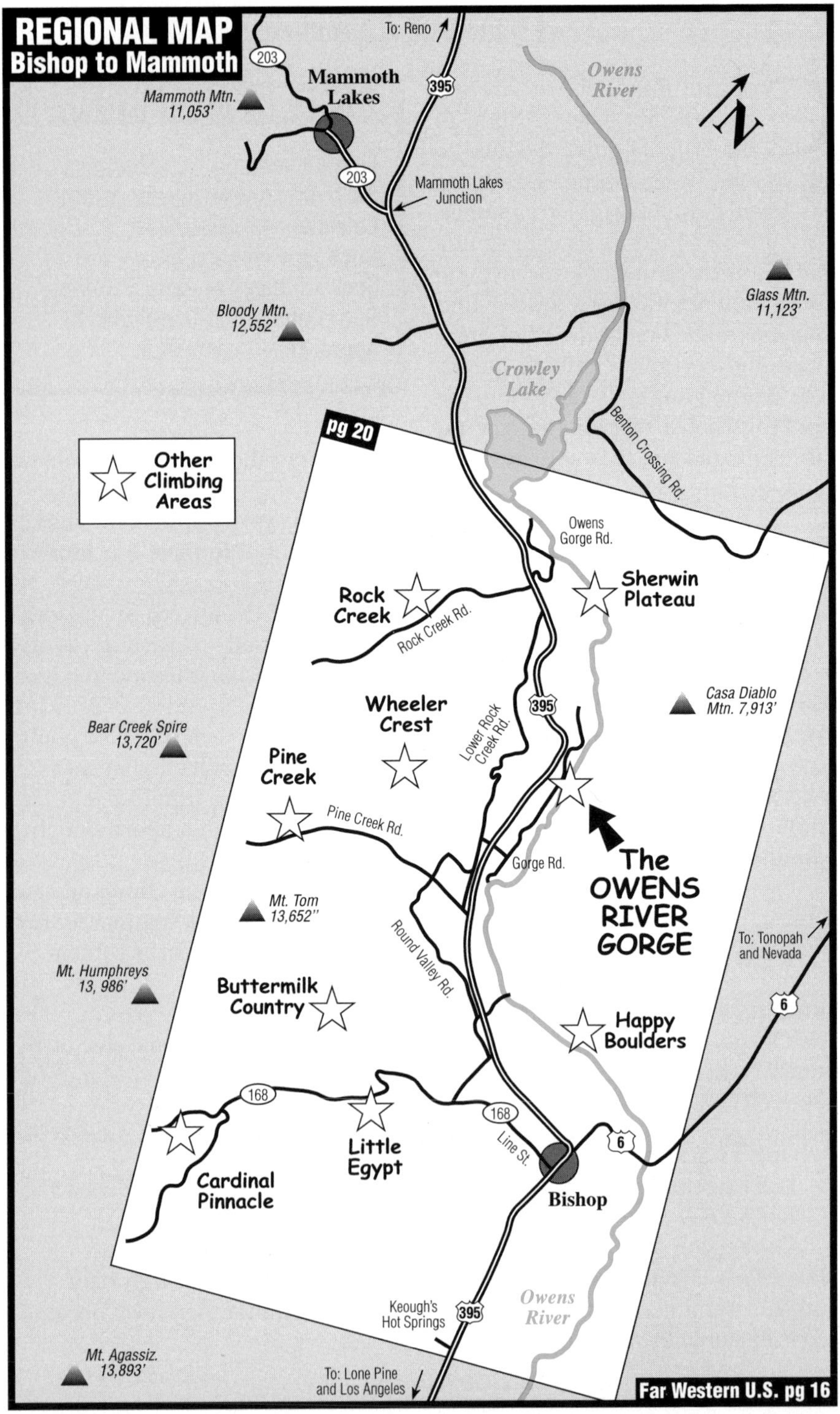
REGIONAL MAP
Bishop to Mammoth
To: Reno
203
395
Mammoth Lakes
Mammoth Mtn. 11,053'
Owens River
N
203
Mammoth Lakes Junction
Glass Mtn. 11,123'
Bloody Mtn. 12,552'
Crowley Lake
Benton Crossing Rd.
pg 20
Other Climbing Areas
Owens Gorge Rd.
Rock Creek
Sherwin Plateau
Rock Creek Rd.
Wheeler Crest
Casa Diablo Mtn. 7,913'
395
Lower Rock Creek Rd.
Bear Creek Spire 13,720'
Pine Creek
Pine Creek Rd.
Gorge Rd.
The OWENS RIVER GORGE
Mt. Tom 13,652''
Round Valley Rd.
To: Tonopah and Nevada
Mt. Humphreys 13, 986'
Buttermilk Country
6
Happy Boulders
168
168
Line St.
6
Little Egypt
Cardinal Pinnacle
Bishop
Keough's Hot Springs
395
Owens River
Mt. Agassiz. 13,893'
To: Lone Pine and Los Angeles
Far Western U.S. pg 16

Climate

The Owens River Gorge is located in the Great Basin Desert at an elevation of 5,500 ft. This climate is generally dry. Temperatures can vary drastically.

Spring and fall are the best times to climb in the Gorge, with pleasant days (50°F to 80°F) and cool nights.

Summer temperatures are usually in the high 80°F's to low 100°F's, so the climbing is limited to shady walls in the early morning or late afternoon. By 4 P.M. the entire Gorge goes into the shade, and a light breeze usually picks up, making conditions excellent until dark.

Winter is cold to mild, with minimal sun penetration. Highs are usually in the 40°F's to 50°F's, and lows are in the twenties. During high pressure periods climbing in the sun can be glorious. About half the winters can have one or two major snow events that can produce up to two feet of snow in and around the Gorge.

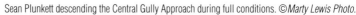

Sean Plunkett descending the Central Gully Approach during full conditions. ©*Marty Lewis Photo.*

©2005 Maximus Press.

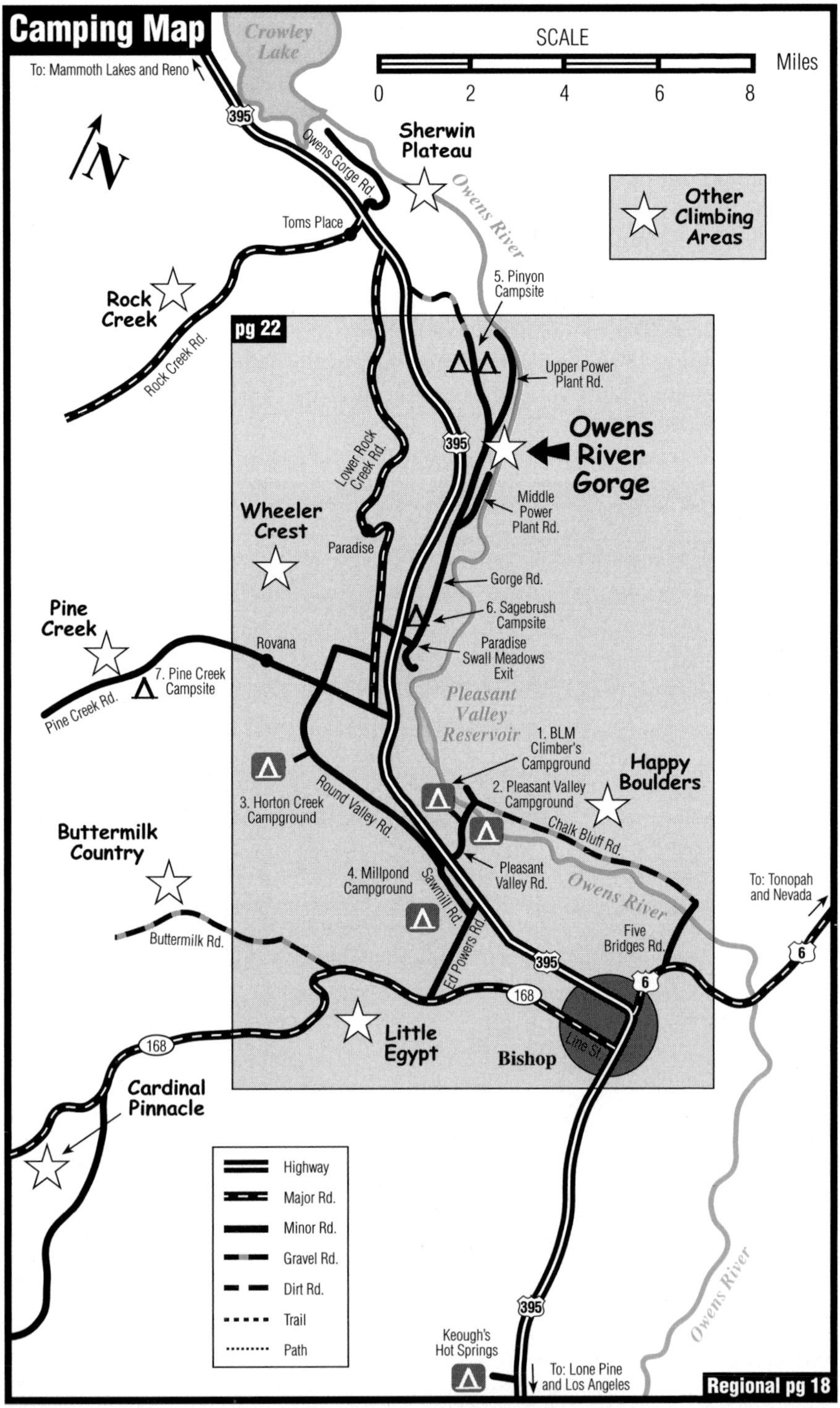
Camping Map
To: Mammoth Lakes and Reno
Crowley Lake
SCALE
0 2 4 6 8
Miles
N
395
Owens Gorge Rd.
Sherwin Plateau
Owens River
Other Climbing Areas
Toms Place
Rock Creek
Rock Creek Rd.
5. Pinyon Campsite
pg 22
Upper Power Plant Rd.
Owens River Gorge
Lower Rock Creek Rd.
Middle Power Plant Rd.
Wheeler Crest
Paradise
Gorge Rd.
6. Sagebrush Campsite
Pine Creek
Rovana
Paradise Swall Meadows Exit
7. Pine Creek Campsite
Pine Creek Rd.
Pleasant Valley Reservoir
1. BLM Climber's Campground
Happy Boulders
2. Pleasant Valley Campground
3. Horton Creek Campground
Round Valley Rd.
Chalk Bluff Rd.
Buttermilk Country
Pleasant Valley Rd.
4. Millpond Campground
Sawmill Rd.
To: Tonopah and Nevada
Five Bridges Rd.
Buttermilk Rd.
Ed Powers Rd.
6
168
Little Egypt
Bishop
Line St.
Cardinal Pinnacle
Highway
Major Rd.
Minor Rd.
Gravel Rd.
Dirt Rd.
Trail
Path
Keough's Hot Springs
To: Lone Pine and Los Angeles
Regional pg 18

Camping

The climbing routes in the Owens River Gorge are located on private property owned by the City of Los Angeles Department of Water and Power. Historically, the L.A.D.W.P. has allowed recreation on their land. However, camping is not permitted on L.A.D.W.P. property. Do not camp, bivouac, or park overnight in the Gorge, on the rim of the Gorge, or in the parking areas. Illegal camping will cause an access problem.

Campgrounds

1. BLM Climber's Campground

Open all year, the fee is $1. Pit toilets, no water, elev. 4,400 ft.
☎ (760) 872-4881.

Directions: Drive South on U.S. 395 to the Pleasant Valley exit. Turn left here and drive 0.9 miles to a dirt road on the left before a power line. Follow this dirt road a half mile into the campground (an old quarry).

2. Pleasant Valley Campground

This campground is located on the Owens River. Open all year, the fee is $10 per vehicle. Picnic tables, piped water, pit toilets, elev. 4,200 ft.
☎ (760) 878-0272.

Directions: Drive South on U.S. 395 to the Pleasant Valley exit. Turn left here; the campground is 2 miles ahead.

3. Horton Creek Campground

Open May through October, the fee is $5. Picnic tables, no potable water, pit toilets, elev. 5,000 ft. ☎ (760) 872-4881

Directions: To get there, drive South on U.S. 395 until reaching the Pine Creek exit. Turn right and drive 2 miles to Round Valley Road. Turn left here; drive 2 miles and turn right. The campground is 2.5 miles ahead.

4. Millpond Campground

Open March through October, the fee is $17 per vehicle. Picnic tables, piped water, showers, flush toilets, elev. 4,000 ft.
☎ (760) 872-6911.

Directions: Drive South on U.S. 395 to the Sawmill Road exit. Turn right here. The campground is 1 mile ahead.

Primitive Camping

5. Pinyon Campsite

This site offers primitive camping on Inyo National Forest land five minutes from the Gorge. You may camp wherever you like for up to 28 days. Available all year, there is no fee. No water, elev. 6,700 ft.

Directions: To get there drive north on the Gorge Road. Right before the North Parking Area is a paved road that branches left (north). Follow this; after 1.5 miles a pinyon forest is reached. Campsites are found on either side of the road.

6. Sagebrush Campsite

This site offers primitive camping on Bureau of Land Management land five minutes from the Gorge. You may camp wherever you like for up to 14 days. Available all year, there is no fee. No water, elev. 4,800 ft.

Directions: To get there drive north on the Gorge Rd. Follow this for 0.4 miles then turn left on a dirt road, a ruin of a rock house will be seen.

7. Pine Creek Campsite

This site offers primitive camping on Inyo National Forest land in a beautiful canyon. You may camp wherever you like for up to 28 days. Available all year, there is no fee. No potable water, elev. 6,500 ft.

Directions: Drive South on U.S. 395 and turn right at the Pine Creek/Rovana exit. Follow Pine Creek Rd. 6 miles up the canyon. Campsites are on the left along the creek.

©2005 Maximus Press.

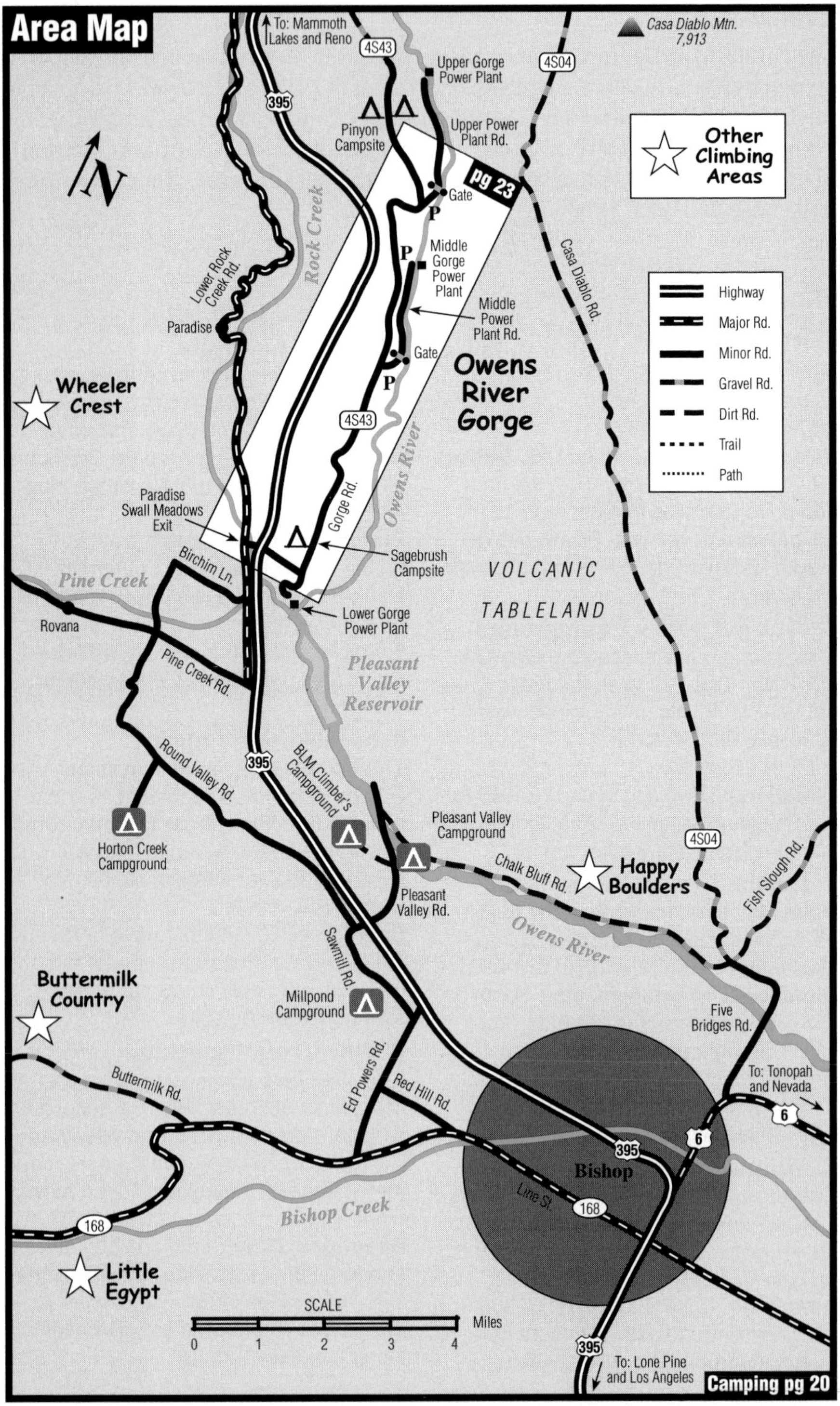
Area Map
To: Mammoth Lakes and Reno
4S43
Casa Diablo Mtn. 7,913
4S04
Upper Gorge Power Plant
395
Pinyon Campsite
Upper Power Plant Rd.
Other Climbing Areas
N
pg 23
Gate
P
Rock Creek
Middle Gorge Power Plant
Casa Diablo Rd.
Highway
Major Rd.
Minor Rd.
Gravel Rd.
Dirt Rd.
Trail
Path
Lower Rock Creek Rd.
Paradise
Middle Power Plant Rd.
Gate
Owens River Gorge
Wheeler Crest
4S43
Owens River
Gorge Rd.
Paradise Swall Meadows Exit
Sagebrush Campsite
Birchim Ln.
VOLCANIC TABLELAND
Pine Creek
Rovana
Lower Gorge Power Plant
Pine Creek Rd.
Pleasant Valley Reservoir
395
Round Valley Rd.
BLM Climber's Campground
Pleasant Valley Campground
4S04
Horton Creek Campground
Chalk Bluff Rd.
Happy Boulders
Fish Slough Rd.
Pleasant Valley Rd.
Owens River
Sawmill Rd.
Buttermilk Country
Millpond Campground
Five Bridges Rd.
Ed Powers Rd.
Red Hill Rd.
Buttermilk Rd.
To: Tonopah and Nevada
6
6
395
Bishop
Line St.
168
Bishop Creek
168
Little Egypt
SCALE
0
1
2
3
4
Miles
395
To: Lone Pine and Los Angeles
Camping pg 20

Getting There

From Bishop: Drive 14 miles north on U.S. 395. After passing the Rovana Exit turn right (east) at the Paradise/Swall Meadows Exit. Drive up a steep hill for 0.7 miles until reaching the Gorge Rd. Turn left (north) on the Gorge Rd. You will come to the paved South Parking Area turnoff after 3.3 miles. The dirt Central Parking Area turnoff is at 4.8 miles. The North Parking Area is 6.4 miles up the Gorge Rd.

From Mammoth Lakes Junction (U.S. 395 and Hwy. 203): Drive 26 miles south on U.S. 395—do not exit at the "Toms Place/Owens Gorge Rd." sign! Descend a long grade past an "Elevation 5,000 ft." sign and an "Inyo County Line" sign. Soon after turn left (east) at the Paradise/Swall Meadows Exit. Drive up a steep hill for 0.7 miles until reaching the Gorge Rd. Turn left (north) on the Gorge Rd. You will come to the paved South Parking Area turnoff after 3.3 miles. The dirt Central Parking Area turnoff is at 4.8 miles. The North Parking Area is 6.4 miles up the Gorge Rd.

The three parking areas provide access to all the climbs in the Owens River Gorge. Use the South Parking Area for routes in the Sub Gorge and Lower Gorge. Cyclists can use this parking area for the Lower, Central, and Inner Gorge. The Central Parking Area provides quick access to the Central and Inner Gorge. The North Parking Area accesses climbs in the Inner, Upper and North Gorge.

©2005 Maximus Press.

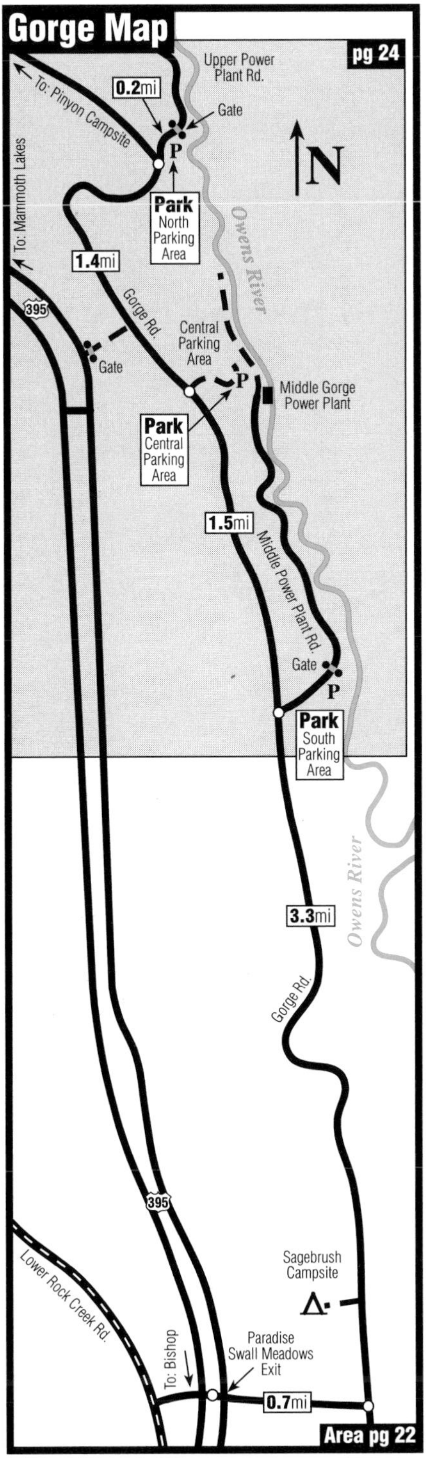

Adapted from the U.S.G.S. 1:24,000 Casa Diablo Mtn. and Rovana Quadrangles.

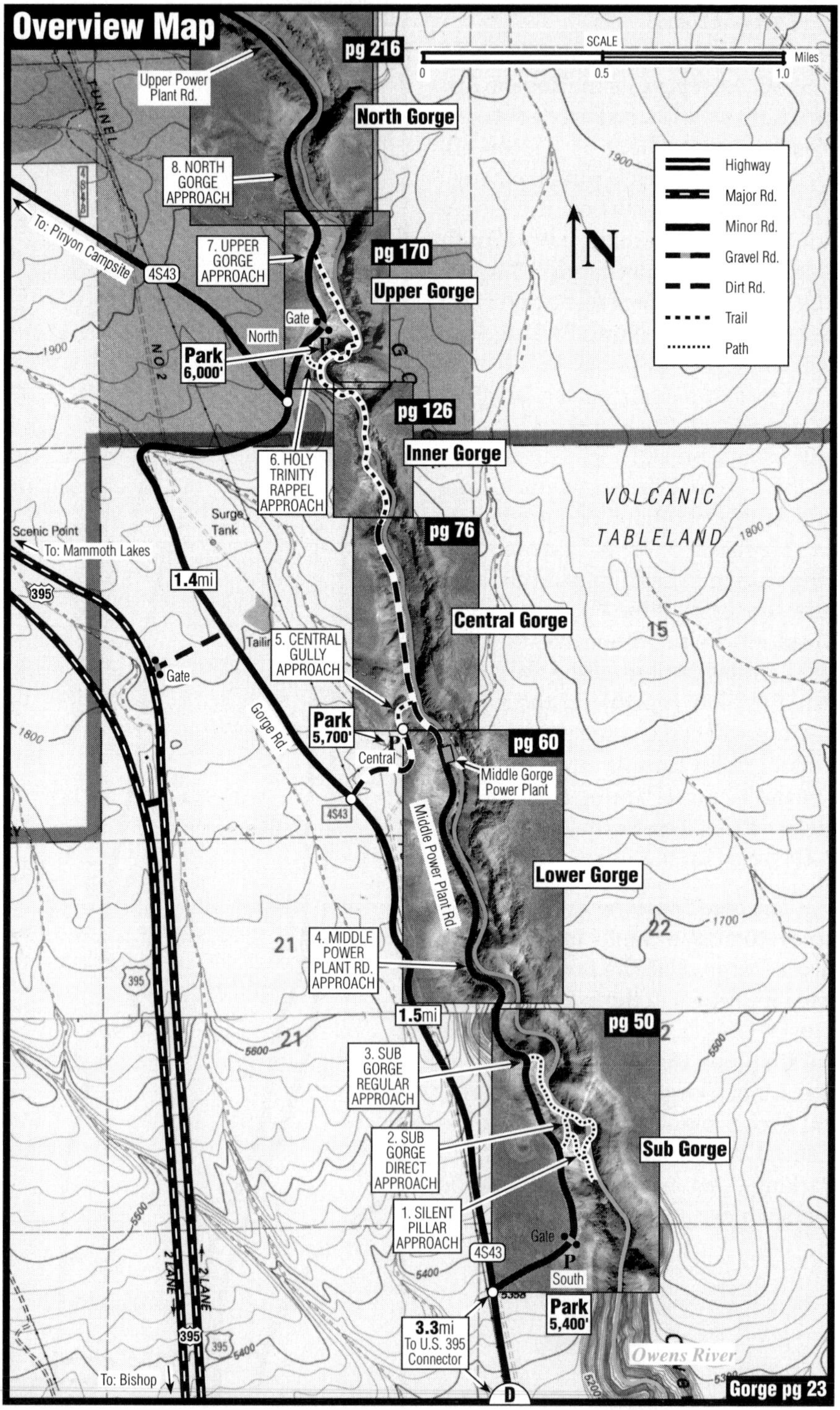
Overview Map
SCALE
0
0.5
1.0
Miles
Highway
Major Rd.
Minor Rd.
Gravel Rd.
Dirt Rd.
Trail
Path
N
pg 216
North Gorge
Upper Power Plant Rd.
8. NORTH GORGE APPROACH
To: Pinyon Campsite
4S43
7. UPPER GORGE APPROACH
pg 170
Upper Gorge
Gate
North
Park 6,000'
pg 126
Inner Gorge
6. HOLY TRINITY RAPPEL APPROACH
Surge Tank
Scenic Point
To: Mammoth Lakes
1.4mi
395
VOLCANIC TABLELAND
pg 76
Central Gorge
15
5. CENTRAL GULLY APPROACH
Gate
Gorge Rd.
Park 5,700'
Central
pg 60
Middle Gorge Power Plant
Middle Power Plant Rd.
Lower Gorge
21
22
4. MIDDLE POWER PLANT RD. APPROACH
1.5mi
pg 50
3. SUB GORGE REGULAR APPROACH
2. SUB GORGE DIRECT APPROACH
Sub Gorge
1. SILENT PILLAR APPROACH
Gate
South
Park 5,400'
3.3mi To U.S. 395 Connector
2 LANE
To: Bishop
Owens River
Gorge pg 23

Approaches

Yield to L.A.D.W.P. vehicles.

South Parking Area

The South Parking Area is 0.3 miles east of the Gorge Rd. on the paved Middle Power Plant Rd. Park on the east side well before the gate.

1. Silent Pillar Approach

From the parking area, walk the Middle Power Plant Rd. 0.2 miles (5 min.) beyond the gate. Head east down a short scree section past some talus blocks. Where a ridge wishbones contour right (south) on a loose slope, then skirt diagonally down under a small cliff band to a notch with a cairn. From here loose scree leads down to the river. This point is just north of the Silent Pillar Wall in the Sub Gorge. Class 2; 20 minutes.

2. Sub Gorge Direct Approach

From the parking area, walk the Middle Power Plant Rd. 0.2 miles (5 min.) beyond the gate. Head east down a short loose section and follow a sharp north-trending ridge. From here, head southeast down steep exposed ledges to the Gorge bottom. This point is just south of the Inyo Mono Line Tower in the Sub Gorge. Class 4; 15 minutes.

3. Sub Gorge Regular Approach

From the parking area, follow the Middle Power Plant Rd. 0.5 miles (10 min.) beyond the gate to a sweeping left-hand turn with an obvious turnout. From here, head east 100 ft. to a saddle, then immediately drop down a south facing gully to the Gorge bottom. This point is just south of the Slander Crag in the Sub Gorge. Class 2; 15 minutes.

4. Middle Power Plant Road Approach

From the parking area, follow the paved Middle Power Plant Road 0.9 miles beyond the gate. This point is just across the river from the Big Tower where the road changes from downhill to uphill. Class 1; 20 minutes. Bicycles can be used for this approach.

Central Parking Area

The Central Parking Area is just east of the Gorge Road on a dirt road where a power line drops into the Gorge. The turnoff is 1.5 miles north of the South Parking Area. 0.2 miles down this dirt road is a transmission tower. Park there.

5. Central Gully Approach

Be very careful not to dislodge rocks—climbs are right below. From the transmission tower, follow a trail north about 100 ft. Scramble down 2nd class blocks about 30 ft. From here, head north through a notch until reaching a steep 3rd class gully. Drop down the gully a few hundred feet to the Gorge bottom. This point is between the Negress Wall and the Social Platform in the Central Gorge. Class 3; 10 minutes.

North Parking Area

The North Parking Area is on the Upper Power Plant Rd., 3.1 miles north of the South Parking Area. Park on the east side before the gate. Make sure large D.W.P. vehicles can pass through.

6. Holy Trinity Rappel Approach

From the parking area, traverse southwest down a loose slope (3rd class). Head into a notch and down climb a 4th class chimney until reaching a rappel station. Rappel 25m/80' to the Gorge bottom. This point is between the Holy Trinity Wall and the Staging Tower in the Upper Gorge. Class 5; 10 minutes.

7. Upper Gorge Approach

Follow the paved Upper Power Plant Rd. 0.2 miles (5 min.) beyond the gate. From here, drop down a steep eroding slope just a few feet until encountering a south-trending gully. Follow it (3rd class) to a good trail. The first crag encountered is the All You Can Eat Area in the Upper Gorge. Class 3; 10 minutes.

8. North Gorge Approach

Follow the paved Upper Power Plant Rd. 0.4 miles beyond the gate. This point is directly across from the Organ Pipes in the North Gorge. Class 1; 15 minutes. Bicycles can be used for this approach.

©2005 Maximus Press.

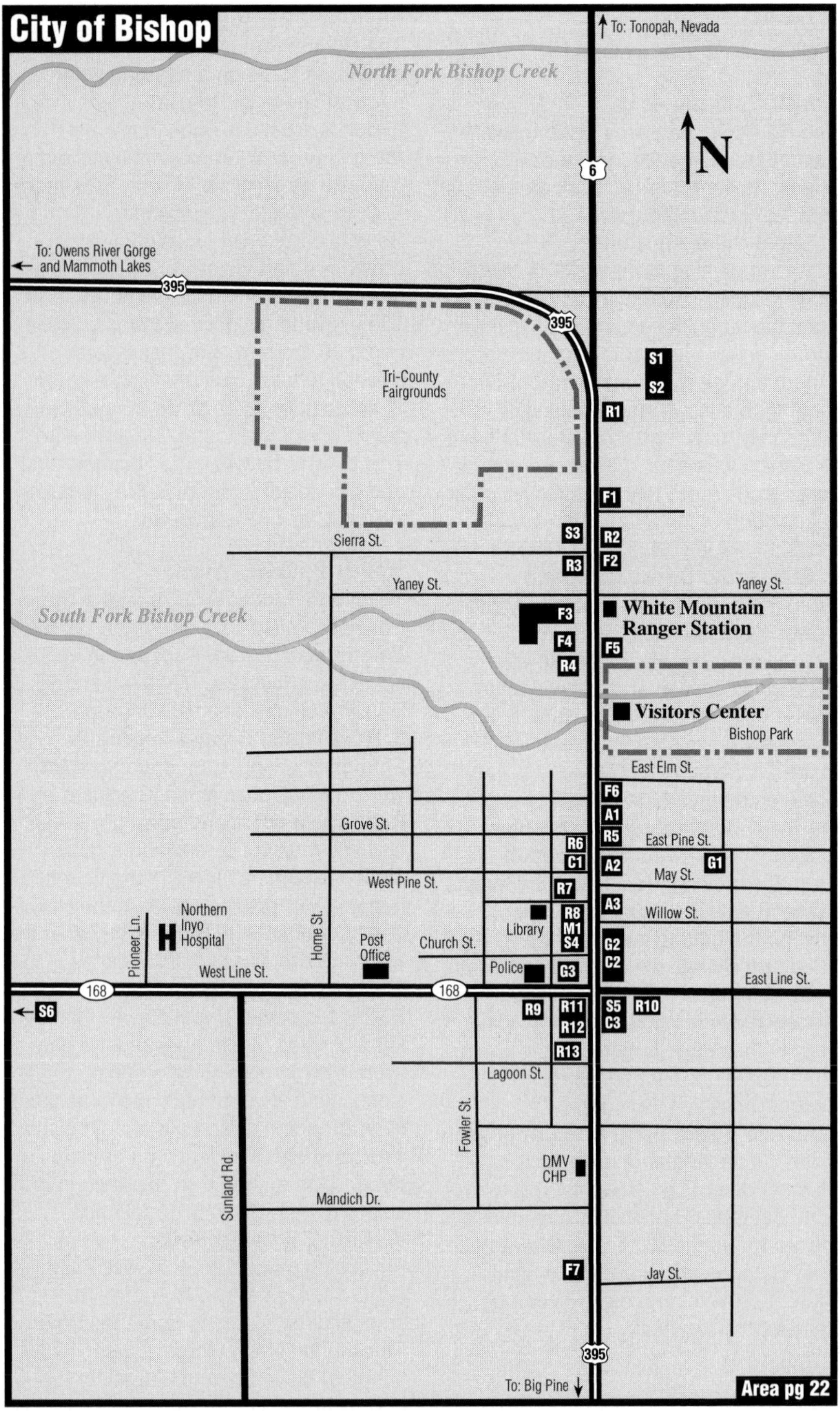

Amenities - Bishop

Twenty minutes south of the Gorge is the city of Bishop, offering most necessities.

ATMs/Banks

A1. Bank of America

A2. Washington Mutual

A3. Union Bank of California

Coffee

C1. Looney Bean
Internet cafe. ☎ 872-2326.

C2. Kava Coffee & Cybercafe
Climber's hang. ☎ 872-1010.

C3. Spellbinders Books & Coffee
Bookstore also. ☎ 873-4511

Fast Food

F1. Kentucky Fried Chicken

F2. Taco Bell

F3. Subway

F4. Burger King

F5. Carl's Junior

F6. McDonalds

F7. Jack in the Box

Gear/Gyms

G1. Sierra Flex Gym
Weight lifting gym. ☎ 872-5550

G2. Wilson's Eastside Sports
A great climbing and outdoor shop. An Eastside tradition. ☎ 873-7520.
See advertisement on page 238.

G3. The Rubber Room
The best rock shoe resoles on the planet. ☎ (888) 395-ROCK.
See advertisement on page 240.

Movie Theaters

M1. Bishop Twin Theatre
Two screens. ☎ 873-3575

Restaurants

B=Breakfast, L=Lunch, D=Dinner.

R1. Upper Crust Pizza (LD)
Great Pizza. ☎ 872-8153

R2. Western Kitchen (BLD)
Thai food, local's favorite. ☎ 872-3246.

R3. Sizzler (LD)
Buffett style steak house. ☎ 873-6821.

R4. Erik Schat's Bakery (BL)
Fresh baked goods, fantastic sandwiches. ☎ 873-7156.

R5. Whiskey Creek (LD)
Steakhouse, bar and microbrews. Breakfast on the weekend. ☎ 873-7174.

R6. Jack's Waffle Shop (BLD)
Breakfast and waffles. ☎ 872-7971.

R7. Inyo Country Store (BL)
Casual breakfast place. ☎ 872-2552

R8. Amigo's (LD)
Excellent authentic mexican food and cervezas. ☎ 872-2189.

R9. Nik-n-Willies Pizza (LD)
Pizza and sandwiches. ☎ 872-2410.

R10. Taqueria las Palmas (LD)
Mexican food, cervezas. ☎ 873-4337.

R11. La Casita (LD)
Mexican food and a bar. ☎ 873-4828.

R12. Bar B-Q Bills (LD)
Country cooking. ☎ 872-5535.

R13. Great Basin Bakery (BL)
Fresh baked goods. ☎ 873-9828.

Shopping

S1. Super K

S2. Vons
Giant supermarket with pharmacy.

S3. Napa Auto Parts

S4. Joseph's Market
Nice downtown market.

S5. Mountain Light Gallery
Incredible photography. ☎ 873-7700.

S6. Manor Market
Unique market, excellent wine cellar and gas, local's favorite.

©2005 Maximus Press.

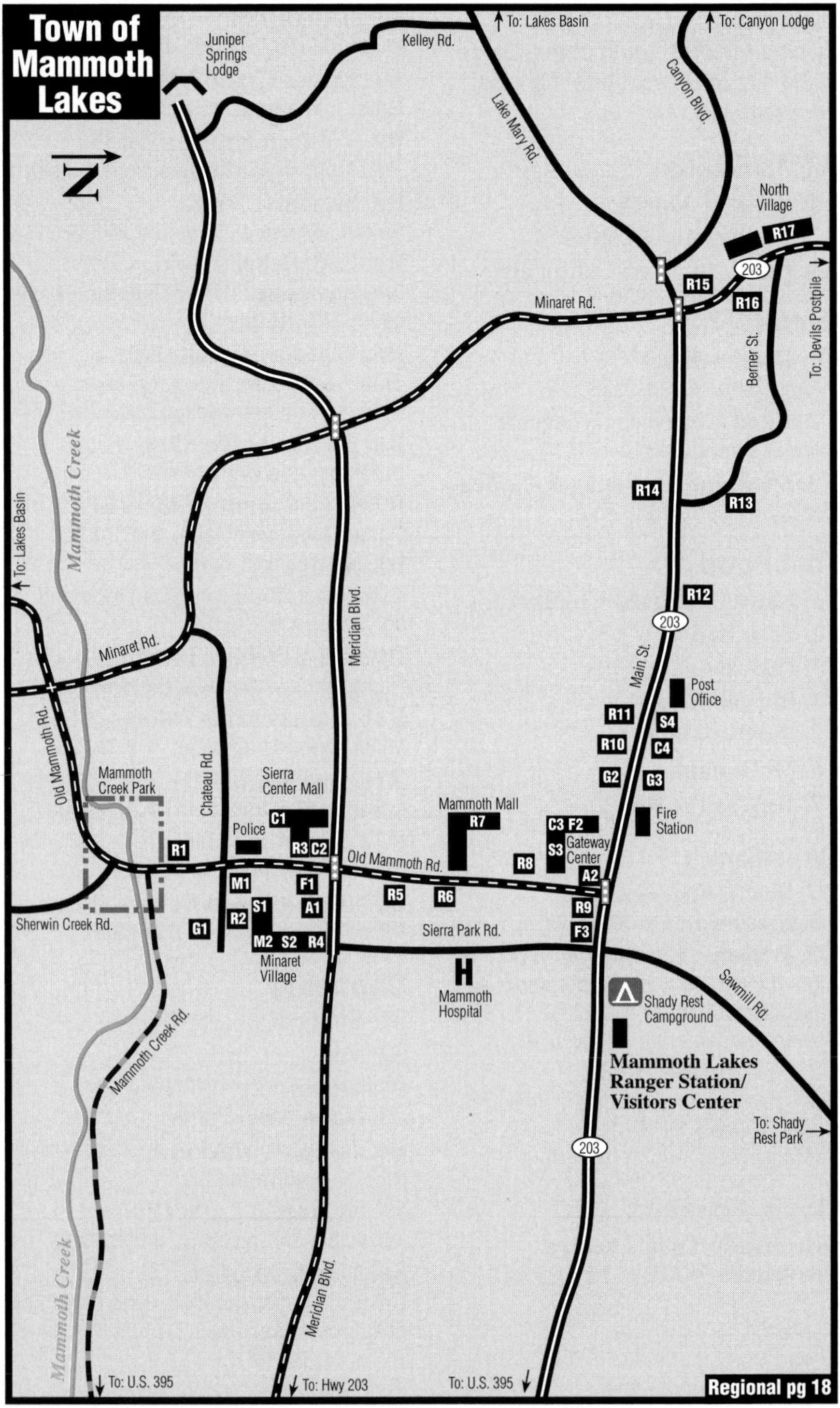

Regional pg 18

Amenities - Mammoth Lakes

Forty minutes north of the Gorge is the resort town of Mammoth Lakes.

ATMs/Banks

A1. Union Bank

A2. Bank of America

Coffee

C1. Sierra's Best Coffee
☎ 934-7408.

C2. Starbucks

C3. Looney Bean
☎ 934-1435.

C4. Stellar Brew
☎ 924-3559.

Fast Food

F1. Carls Jr.

F2. Subway

F3. McDonalds

Gear/Gyms

G1. Body Shop
Weight lifting and climbing. ☎ 934-3700.

G2. Mammoth Mountaineering Supply
Awesome climbing shop. ☎ 934-4191. See advertisement on page 237.

G3. Kittredge Sports
General sport shop and climbing gear. ☎ 934-7566.

Movie Theaters

M1. Plaza Theater
☎ 934-3131.

M2. Minaret Cinemas
☎ 934-3131.

Restaurants

B=Breakfast, L=Lunch, D=Dinner.

R1. Stove (BLD)
Country Cookin'. ☎ 934-2821.

R2. Skadi (D)
Fine dining, great atmosphere and awesome views. ☎ 934-3902.

R3. Shogun (D)
Japanese cuisine, awesome sushi. ☎ 934-3970.

R4. Giovanni's (LD)
Gourmet pizza and Italian food. ☎ 934-7563.

R5. Grumpy's (LD)
Sports bar/ restaurant. ☎ 934-8587.

R6. Roberto's Cafe (LD)
Authentic Mexican food. ☎ 934-3667.

R7. Good Life (BL)
Wholesome, healthy food. ☎ 934-1734.

R8. Nik-n-Willies (LD)
Great sandwiches, pizza, takeout. ☎ 934-2012.

R9. Breakfast Club (BL)
Breakfast and bakery. ☎ 934-6944.

R10. Paul Schat's Bakery (BL)
Fresh baked goods. ☎ 934-6055.

R11. Base Camp Cafe (BLD)
Good food, reasonable prices, mountaineering decor. ☎ 934-3900.

R12. Angel's (LD)
Hearty homestyle cooking. ☎ 934-7427.

R13. Gomez's (LD)
Great Mexican food. ☎ 924-2693.

R14. Matsu (LD)
Asian cuisine, eat in or take out. ☎ 934-8277.

R15. Whiskey Creek (D)
Steakhouse, bar and microbrews. ☎ 934-2555

R16. Bergers (LD)
Great burgers and sandwiches. ☎ 934-6622.

R17. The Pita Pit (BLD)
Awesome pita sandwiches. ☎ 924-7482

Shopping

S1. Vons
Large supermarket with pharmacy.

S2. Booky Joint
Books, Music, DVDs. ☎ 934-3240.

S3. Rite-Aid
Pharmacy and general store.

S4. Napa Auto Parts

©2005 Maximus Press.

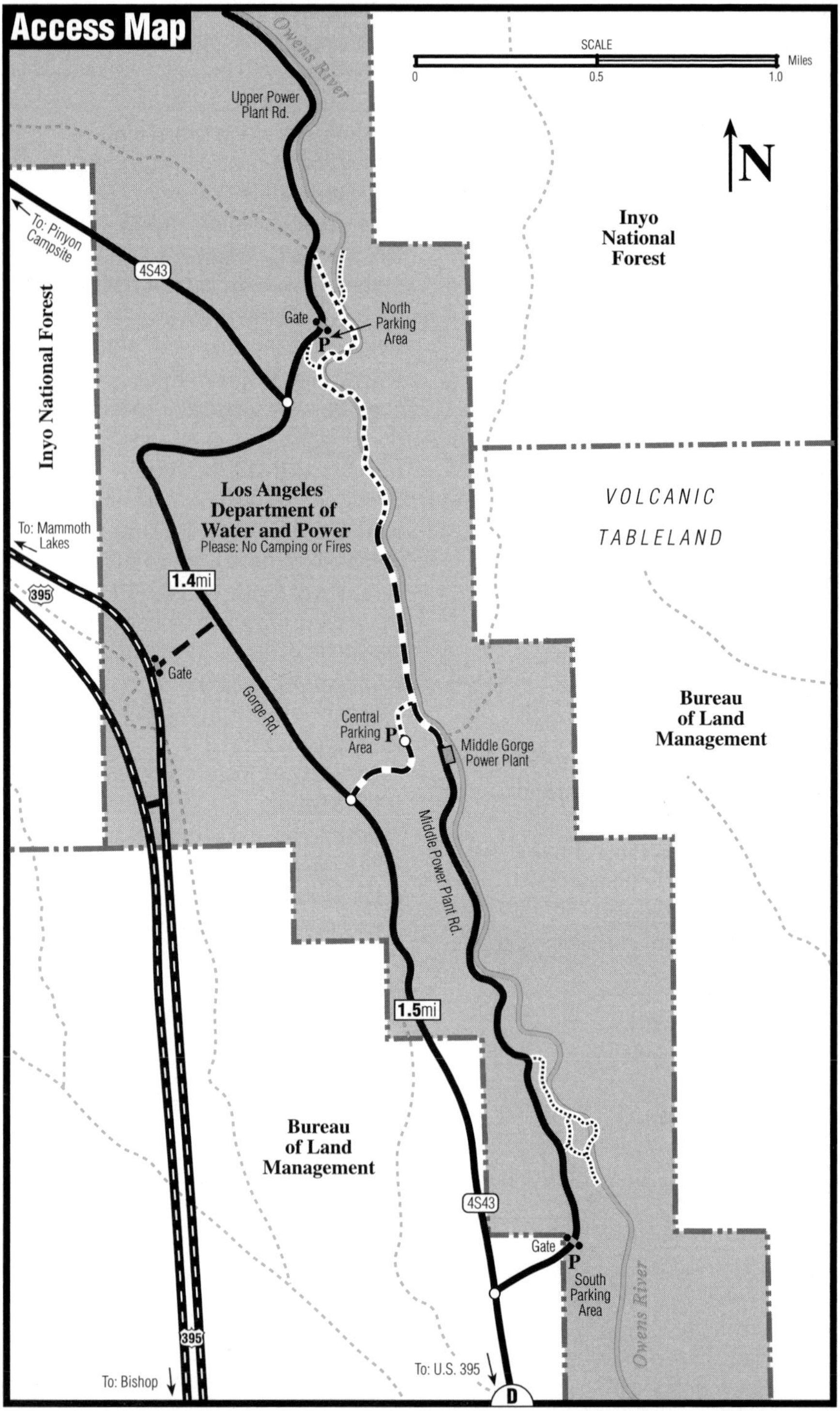
Access Map
SCALE
0
0.5
1.0
Miles
N
Owens River
Upper Power Plant Rd.
To: Pinyon Campsite
4S43
Inyo National Forest
Gate
North Parking Area
P
Inyo National Forest
Los Angeles Department of Water and Power
Please: No Camping or Fires
VOLCANIC TABLELAND
To: Mammoth Lakes
395
1.4mi
Gate
Gorge Rd.
Central Parking Area
P
Middle Gorge Power Plant
Bureau of Land Management
Middle Power Plant Rd.
1.5mi
Bureau of Land Management
4S43
Gate
P
South Parking Area
Owens River
395
To: Bishop
To: U.S. 395
D

Access Information

The climbing routes in the Owens River Gorge are located on private property owned by the City of Los Angeles Department of Water and Power. Historically the L.A.D.W.P. has allowed recreation on their land, but they don't recommend climbing. You do so at your own risk. There are no entry fees and no rangers. But we still must use the Owens River Gorge in a responsible manner. If we become a problem, we could be denied access to the Gorge. If you have any questions concerning the Owens River Gorge please call Wilson's Eastside Sports at (760) 873-7520 or Maximus Press at (760) 387-1013.

Guidelines

- ☞ Be respectful and courteous to L.A.D.W.P. personnel.
- ☞ Do not camp on L.A.D.W.P. property. This includes the parking areas.
- ☞ Do not block or park near the entrance gates.
- ☞ No motorized vehicles beyond the gates.
- ☞ Yield to L.A.D.W.P. vehicles on their roads.
- ☞ Stay away from L.A.D.W.P. equipment.
- ☞ Clean up trash, even if it's not yours. This includes cigarette butts.
- ☞ Do not throw trash in the toilets, pack it out.
- ☞ No graffiti anywhere.
- ☞ Maintain a low profile. Be on your best behavior!
- ☞ Climbing in the Gorge is a privilege, not a right.

Environmental Concerns

Sanitation

The water in the Owens River Gorge is a domestic supply for the City of Los Angeles. Maintaining the quality of this water is a major concern. Whenever possible, try to relieve yourself before entering the Gorge. When in the Gorge, use the toilets provided or go at least 150 ft. from the river or the base of any routes. Please pack out or bury toilet paper. Do not relieve yourself in the narrow riparian corridors between the river and the routes; instead go up the talus slopes.

Erosion

An excellent system of trails and paths exists in the Gorge. Minimize erosion by using them. When there is more than one path, pick the most traveled route. Don't thrash up and down vegetated slopes; stay on the trails.

The Owens River

For fifty years the Owens River Gorge was dry. The water instead flowed through a penstock for power generation. Due to an historic agreement in the mid-1990s, water has now been returned to the Gorge. The river has been stocked with Brown Trout to restore the fishery. The river flow will be increased each year. This welcome improvement has a small downside; some routes will no longer be climbable due to flooding and a few of the river crossings are becoming quite hazardous.

Brief History

Native Americans have lived in this area for 6,000 years. They existed by hunting and gathering, and left a legacy of beautiful petroglyphs on the volcanic tableland east of the Gorge. As with the rest of the United States, there was friction when the European Americans arrived in great numbers, and battles were fought. Native Americans still live in this region, many at the Bishop Paiute Indian Reservation.

The first European Americans settled this area in the mid 1800s. The settlers established ranches, farms, and mining areas. The Owens River Gorge was mined (for what I don't know). One will find mine shafts, rock structures, bottles, cans, lumber, and an abandoned trestle from this era.

In the late 1800s trout were introduced to local streams and rivers, just about wiping out the native Tui Chub (now an endangered species). The trout flourished and became a staple in the local settlers' diets. The Owens River Gorge was known for some of the best fishing in the Eastern Sierra.

In the early 1900s two low-tech power plants were built along the Owens River in the Gorge. The ruins are found below the Warning Signs Wall and below the DMZ. Nine plant operators and their families lived adjacent to the power plants in attractive living quarters, complete with lawns, flower gardens, vegetable gardens and chicken coops.

During this time the Los Angeles Department of Water and Power began buying up ranches and water rights in the Eastern Sierra (including the Gorge). The federal government encouraged this activity so that Los Angeles would have the water required to become an economic power. An aqueduct, considered an early engineering marvel, was constructed down the Owens Valley and through the hostile Mojave Desert.

In the 1940s, the L.A.D.W.P. constructed a pipeline on the rim of the Gorge and three modern high pressure power plants within the Gorge. The entire Owens River flowed through this enclosed system. The Gorge became a dry desolate place. The fishery died and the birds left.

Fifty years later an historic agreement was reached between the L.A.D.W.P. and Mono County. Water was returned to the Gorge. Over the next few years the river flow will be increasing in an effort to determine the optimum level required to restore the fishery. The return of water and a riparian environment has greatly improved the atmosphere in the Gorge.

Power plants and employee housing in the 1930s. *Photos courtesy of Community Printing.*

Kevin Calder on the first ascent of **Not Proud Enough to Name** 8** (1985) at the Dihedrals. ©*Marty Lewis Photo.*

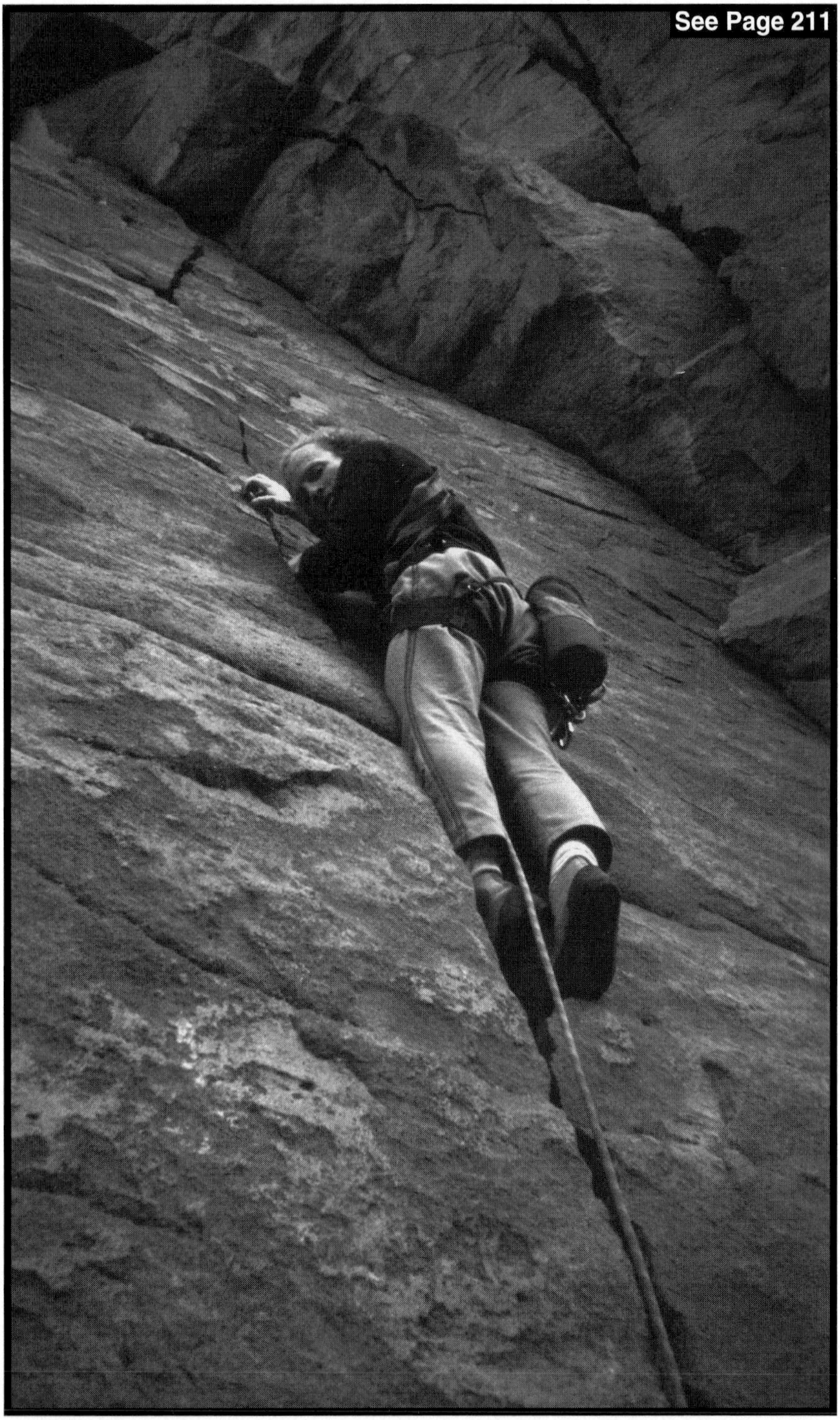

Climbing History

During the 1970s the few climbers that ventured into the Gorge declared the place a total choss pile. But by 1978 Eastside hardman Bob Harrington climbed the crack "Swamp Thing" (9). Even back then, Bob found it necessary to place a bolt to back up the sketchy gear placements. He also placed the first bolted anchor to descend. During the mid 1980s a few scattered cracks were climbed: Bob Harrington's *Bob & Eric Crack* (10a), Hank Levine's *Hotcake Flake* (10a) and Kevin Calder's *Not Proud Enough to Name* (8). Climbers remained less than impressed by the Gorge.

In 1987 Gary Slate stance-drilled two bolts on the mixed route *Soul Music* (10b). In 1988 visionary Yosemite climber, John Bachar, using skyhooks to place bolts, put up the amazing face route *Pick Pocket* (11a). Thus, a staunch "traditionalist" put up the first all bolt climb in the Gorge. In May of 1989 Joe Rousek and Tony Puppo ground-up bolted *Orange Peel* (10c). The sustained, technical climbing required tightly spaced bolts. Arguably, the first true sport climb was born. Climbers were sold on the Gorge's potential and the rush was on.

Joe Rousek on the first ascent of **Orange Peel** 10c**** (1989) at the Social Platform. ©*Tony Puppo Photo.*

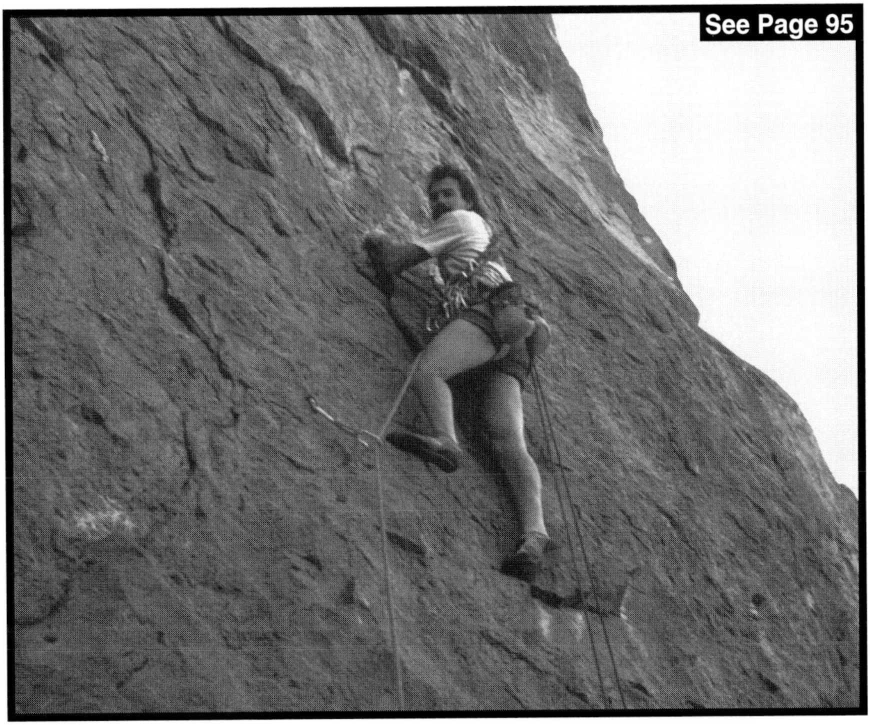
See Page 95

Steve Schneider on the first ascent of **Please Baby, Baby, Baby, Please** 12c** (1989). ©*Marty Lewis Photo.*

See Page 183

John Bachar free soloing **Enterprise** 12b***** (1990) at the Dilithium Crystal. ©*John McDonald Photo.*

See Page 153

In the summer of 1989 the development went full tilt. Bold traditional climbers put up many early classics ground-up, using assortments of bolts, pitons and natural gear. It wasn't about sport climbing in 1989. Gear was used whenever possible. However, some of the routes ended up being sport climbs out of necessity. Eastern Sierra climbers were operating in the Lower and Central Gorge, and their highlights include: Kevin Leary's bold *Tumbling Dice* (10d, mixed), Tony Puppo's *One Holer* (10b, mixed), Joe Rousek's *Z Dong* (10a, gear) and *Hip Pockets* (11a, mixed), Steve Schnieder's *D.W.P.* (11c, sport) and *Flashflood* (12b, sport), Gary Slate's *Darshan* (12b, sport) and Todd Vogel's *Feudal Beerlords* (10d, gear). Arizonan Scott Ayers was hard at work in the Upper Gorge, his highlights include: *Gorgeous* (10b, sport), *O.R.G. asm* (11a, mixed), *Sex* (11d, sport), *Sex Packets* (12a, sport) and *Failsafe* (12a, mixed).

By 1990 climbers who had visited Smith Rock, City of Rocks and other sport climbing venues came armed with a new vision of what the Gorge should be. Ground-up "traditionalists" began putting gear in the pockets and horizontal cracks, then drilling protection bolts next to the gear to make their routes sport climbs. Top-down bolting also made its appearance, but it was far from accepted. Tom Herbert, 20 years old, brash and talented, soon was rappel-bolting many classic routes. His best are the "E" quartet of *Excelsior* (12d), *Enterprise* (12b), *Escapade* (11a) and *Expressway* (11b). Once, he boasted of rap-bolting three routes in one day. This really irked the methodical ground-up guys. Soon it was realized that it was all about quality routes, regardless of the style of the first ascent. Instead of rushing around for quantity, the pace slowed down to yield finely-crafted routes. 1990's highlights include: Scott Ayers' *Phasers on Stun* (12c), Joe Rousek's *Sendero Luminoso* (10b), and Todd Vogel's *Warning Signs* (10d).

During this time John Bachar would be seen roaming around the Gorge carrying a huge ghetto blaster. He would prop up the stereo facing a difficult climb, crank some funky hip-hop music, and then proceed to free solo the route. His circuit included *Bloody Pawprints* (11d), *Flashflood* (12b), *Darshan* (12b) and *Enterprise* (12b).

1991-1994: Climbers began attempting chossier and chossier lines. The funny thing is, many of these became some of the most fun, popular and buffed-out routes in the Gorge. Highlights include: Louie Anderson's *Left for Dead* (11b), Fred Berman's *From Chocolate to Morphine* (11d), Todd Graham's *Gravitron* (12d), Eric Kohl's *Drill Rig* (11c), Marty Lewis' *Flex Your Head* (11c), Tony Puppo's *Black Hole* (12b) and Gary Slate's *Hungover* (11b).

After a couple of years of putting bolts next to horizontal cracks and pockets, and with the rising popularity of these sport routes, it was time to breach the next ethical level: Bolts next to vertical crack placements. Why would climbers do this? If you bolted the crack section, the route would be repeated constantly, making it a buffed-out classic—if the route required gear it would rarely be climbed and remain a choss pile. Not to mention the fact that the Gorge, being owned by a power company, seemed like the perfect arena to experiment with relaxed sport climbing ethics. Examples of this new thinking include: Bruce Lella's face to crack *Hardly Wallbanger* (10c), Tony Puppo's face to crack *Focus* (11b), Marty Lewis' crack to face *Ya Shoulda Killed Me Last Year* (11c) and Tom Addison's visionary dihedral *Gape Index* (12c).

By this time the Gorge had caught on in a big way, and climbers were coming from all over to check it out. Legendary grovelers "Alf" and "the Scrutinizer" took up residence in the Central Parking Area. When climbers arrived they would be greeted by camping gear, trash and clothing strewn all about. This really pissed off a lot of locals and showed a total lack of respect for L.A.D.W.P. authority. Luckily they moved on to the next "hot" area before it became a problem.

In Alf's brief stay he did manage to recruit Marty Lewis to finish off an abandoned giant roof project which became *Loony Binge* (12c). This intimidating line had a thirty foot roof with a detached flake halfway out. Marty did some pullups on the flake, declared it bomber and continued bolting to the finish. This route, in addition to Eric Kohl's *Brewtalized* (12d) and Tom Addison's *Gape Index* (12c) made the Eldorado Roof a hardman's dream. These routes could all be considered bolted cracks—but you'd have to have a death wish to place gear behind the loose flakes and detached blocks found under there.

With the increase in popularity came the need for local climbers to become pro-active addressing the problems of erosion, sanitation and dangerous river crossings. Tony and Nan Puppo constructed the terraces at the base of the Gorgeous Towers. Teachers Steve and Barbara Elia, their Bishop High School

Construction of the Negress Wall staircase. ©*Kevin Calder Photo.*

Social Platform bridge. ©*Kevin Calder Photo.*

students, and climbers built the giant staircase from the Negress Wall to the Warm Up Wall. Dean Rosnau and climber volunteers in partnership with the Access Fund, CRAG, and the L.A.D.W.P. constructed the toilets. Burly bridges were built to the Social Platform, Great Wall of China and the Staying Power Towers.

The late 1990s came and most climbers felt the Gorge was climbed out. Kelly Cordner arrived on the scene and felt otherwise. High on motivation, Kelly sprayed bolts at a pace not matched since the go-go years of 1989 and 1990, making some folks a little nervous. When the dust settled, he ended up making quite a contribution. His standouts include *Cinderella* (9), *Fender Strat* (10a), and *Pumpkin* (11c). Greg Barnes made an amazing clean-crack discovery when developing the two-pitch mixed classic *Jesus Built My Tri-cam* (10a).

Kevin Calder and Marty Lewis were also productive by climbing ignored features such as *Dr. Evil* (10a), *Superfly* (10c) and *Grindrite* (11b). With a brief introduction on power drilling from Kevin and Marty, longtime Gorge climber Peter Croft got the first ascent bug. The three of them completed a five-pitch sport climb above the Eldorado Roof: the *Towering Inferno* (11b). Peter also realized that the Eldorado Roof was only partially done, and that many of the routes ended prematurely. He soon went on a first ascent binge, coming up with the best hard climbing yet seen in the Gorge. These routes include the *Sniveling* (13a), *Loony Tunes* (13b) and *Sneak* (13c). Kevin Calder got into the act with the *Billion Million* (12d).

During the late 1990s the Gorge became a ghost town—there were a few diehards—but everybody else was busy bouldering. The turn of the century came and climbers became repsyched on the Gorge. It is now a busy place again, with a great group of core devotees.

2000-2005: One amazing thing is that great lines are still being developed; a few of these are some of the best hard routes yet reported. These include Mike Melkonian and Bruce Lella's *Aurora* (13a), Robert Miller and Todd Graham's *Fight Club* (13b), Peter Croft and Andrew Stevens' *Wooly Bugger* (12d) and Lonnie Kauk's *Ascension* (13b).

The great choss climbing experiment known as the Owens River Gorge will no doubt continue to mature, getting better and better every year.

First Ascent Ethics

Every climbing area has different ethics; there is no grand unifying theme. The ethics come about based on a variety of conditions: the era that the crag was primarily developed, the type of rock, the quality of the rock and most importantly the cast of characters that developed it. The following "rules and ethics" are based on a consensus of Gorge regulars and first ascensionists. Please respect them.

Bolts Vs. Gear

During the early development of the Owens River Gorge, natural gear was used whenever possible. Even pure face climbs utilized the many horizontal pockets for gear. Soon thereafter if a route required just a few pieces of natural gear—the route would be made a sport climb. Eventually first ascensionists even dared to put bolts next to vertical crack placements. Sport Climbing became king. Virtually every sport climb in the Gorge has bolts next to potential gear placements. This ethic has been accepted at the Owens River Gorge.

Ground-Up

Half of the routes were done ground-up using hooks, gear, or stances to place bolts. Ground-up climbers have the option of placing bolts when and where they feel they need them. Future ascent parties will have to climb at the same level of boldness as the first ascensionists. This is a tradition of the sport.

Top-Down

Half of the routes were bolted on rappel. The only reason to place bolts on rappel is to create perfect sport climbs. Rappel-bolted routes should be well protected. Clip stances should be well thought out.

If you want to put up routes that are runout, have sketchy pro, no pro, or are adventure climbs, they should be pure ground-up ascents (no previewing). Dangerous rappel routes are a hypocrisy. Bold routes should be created ground-up, the way future climbers will experience them.

Cleaning

On the chossy rock often encountered in the Gorge, aggressive cleaning is usually required. Hammers, crowbars, wire brushes and whisk brooms are all used to remove loose rock and surface detritus. There is a fine line between cleaning and chipping—cleaning is removing loose and chossy rock, chipping is creating holds on blank rock.

Radical Tactics

Although there have been a few incidents of gluing and chipping in the Gorge, these tactics are not an accepted practice. To my knowledge less than ten routes in the entire Gorge have been glued or chipped, almost all of which are 5.12 or 5.13.

Squeeze Jobs

Because of the nature of the rock in the Owens River Gorge, just about any piece of rock can be climbed. Does this mean we should grid-bolt all the formations? No! Squeeze jobs detract from the beauty of the original lines. Please don't bolt lines of strength that closely parallel existing routes.

- ☞ If your proposed route would share numerous holds with a preexisting route it is a squeeze job.
- ☞ If a climber on your proposed route would interfere with a climber on an adjacent route it is a squeeze job.
- ☞ If bolts on your proposed route can easily be clipped from the adjacent route it is a squeeze job.

Anchors

Mussy Hook Anchor System.

Sling wads, chains and coldshuts are no longer appropriate anchors. After years of experimentation there is an anchor system that is quickly becoming the standard for the Eastern Sierra. Most first ascensionists, CRAG and the ASCA have all agreed to use these anchors exclusively on Eastside crags. The anchor consists of a quick link and tow hook on a conventional bolt hanger. This system is known as a "Mussy Hook" and can be purchased from Fish Products (see advertisement on page 241) or from Maximus Press (see page 253).

First Ascent Guidelines

- ☞ Bolts should be 3/8" or larger in diameter.
- ☞ Bolts placed in overhanging rock should be 1/2" in diameter.
- ☞ No fixed pitons; use a bolt.
- ☞ Use "Mussy Hooks" on all anchors.
- ☞ Don't put up squeeze jobs.
- ☞ The first ascent party has the option of using bolts or natural gear.
- ☞ Do not chip, glue, or manufacture holds.
- ☞ Keep the number of projects to a minimum. Trying to grab too much real estate might encourage other climbers to try your projects.
- ☞ The rock is a limited resource. Think before you drill.
- ☞ If you put up a route—you may get a bunch of high fives from your bros—but from others you may be criticized. Try not to take it too personally, it's part of the game.

Climbing in the Owens River Gorge

The Owens River Gorge is like a lot of popular sport climbing areas. Busy walls can have an almost circus-like atmosphere. While five minutes away at a less obvious spot, you can find solitude and climb by yourself all day.

Conduct

Your style of climbing is your own business. However, please operate within these simple rules when in the Owens River Gorge:

- ☞ If you retreat off a route before the anchors, leave a carabiner behind. Leaving a retreat sling is ugly, dangerous, and considered bad style.
- ☞ Please don't leave chalk graffiti on the crags. This includes giant tick marks, arrows, X's, ratings and words.
- ☞ Please brush (only with a toothbrush) chalk-caked holds on popular routes, especially after hangdogging and top-roping sessions.
- ☞ You may use quickdraws found on existing routes. Never remove them.
- ☞ Rather than clipping a bolt and hypocritically spraying that you could have gotten a piece of gear in, it would be way prouder to actually carry gear and place it.
- ☞ Don't attempt to redpoint other people's projects (these are usually marked with a red tag on the first bolt or a fixed rope).
- ☞ Gear and ropes found on projects are not booty. The equipment belongs to people who are working hard creating routes for your enjoyment. Thieves will be flogged, drawn and quartered.

Is this really necessary? Crag hieroglyphics.

The Rock

The Owens River Gorge has multitudes of excellent climbing routes on volcanic tuff. Most of these involve endurance climbing up vertical and gently overhanging faces with incredible square cut edges, buckets, and incut pockets for holds. The few slabs in the Gorge tend to be very thin and polished. There are a few clean cracks in the Gorge, but many are lined with a grotty substance that makes natural gear less than 100% reliable. Most of the crack routes utilize combinations of jamming and face holds.

The rock can be very friable. Holds occasionally break. Belayers should be prepared for falling rock and falling climbers. New routes are especially suspect. It takes hundreds of ascents before routes become "buffed."

Important Note: There are stacks of small, shallow pockets in the Gorge—usually they are not used because there is something better. On the cruxes of harder routes these small pockets become mandatory to use, causing some climbers to make the false assumption that the pockets are drilled!

Equipment
Ropes that are 70m/230′ long are convenient for lowering off the many long pitches found in the Gorge. A rope bag is recommended as most routes start in the dirt. Over 540 routes in the Gorge can be done with just a rack of quickdraws. Over 150 gear routes require standard racks of camming units and wired nuts. The Gorge is not a good area to learn to place gear. The rock can be friable, and skill is required in using the often devious placements.

Anchors
The anchors in the Gorge are heavily used and take a tremendous beating. To help reduce wear and tear, use quickdraws at the anchors; especially for extended top-roping sessions. Donations for anchor replacement can be made to the local organization CRAG at Wilson's Eastside Sports (see advertisement on page 238) or at the Rubber Room (see advertisement on page 240). A portion of the profits from this guidebook are spent on anchor maintenance.

Projects
Tragically, some lazy opportunists use the truism "no one owns the rock" to poach other climber's first free ascents. Route developers may not own the rock, but when they put up a route, they own the privilege of naming it and free climbing it! That is what motivates them.

The climbers that might have the ability (and lowhanded buggeryness) to steal routes rarely have an inkling of what is required to put up a route. New routing is a long and difficult process. Those who indulge in it spend a lengthy and humbling apprenticeship perfecting that process. Comparing it to, say plumbing, gives some idea of what the new router must endure. Pioneering a single bolted pitch requires more equipment, more knuckle scraping, at least ten times as much labor and probably an equal amount of dealing with poop (in this case bird and bat) as fixing a broken toilet. A plumber makes, what, $50 an hour—so do the math.

After the developers have done all this work, climbed the route (with aid) and then headed home exhausted—these thieves want to jump out of the bushes and steal the icing on the cake: the first free ascent! So if you want to move in on someone's project, do the right thing, ask nicely. And write a fat check; $500 should probably cover it.

Retrobolting
The extremely controversial act of adding bolts to an existing route is known as Retrobolting. There are generally two situations that warrant this; one is to eliminate potentially hazardous situations on popular "sport climbs," the other is to facilitate sport climbs that cross obscure gear routes. If you are not a Gorge regular with a giant consensus—do not retrobolt!

Also remember, it is extremely important, that we as climbers preserve the classic historical gear climbs and mixed testpieces of the day.

Safety Concerns

While climbing in the Gorge may seem inherently safer than many climbing situations, there is a surprising number of serious accidents every year. Unfortunately, many of these accidents end up involving the L.A.D.W.P. **Climbing is dangerous, think safety!**

Prevention

Ninety percent of the accidents in the Gorge can be attributed to poor judgment. The top five ways to get seriously injured or killed are:

#1. Climber dropped by belayer. Many of the routes in the Gorge are rope stretchers. Get in a habit of tying a knot in the end of the rope. Communicate with your belayer when getting lowered. The belayer should watch for the end of the rope.

#2. Climber failed to tie in properly. Get in the habit of checking your knot before you step off the ground, when the climbing gets tough, and before lowering.

#3. Bicycle accidents. Please ride bikes conservatively. The roads are steep and narrow. Obstacles include: L.A.D.W.P. vehicles, climbers, fisherman, dogs, kids, and sharp rocks. Go somewhere else for adventure cycling.

#4. To boldly go where no man has gone before. Unclimbed rock in the Gorge is very loose and dangerous. If you don't see chalk, bolts, or anchors, chances are, you are off route. Please use the established approaches and exits. Pioneering new ways into and out of the Gorge can cause massive rockfall and injury.

#5. Dropping loose rock. Even on popular routes holds will occasionally break. Don't hang out under climbers.

Objective Hazards

In the summer you should watch out for rattlesnakes. During high winds or wet weather, there can be rockfall from the unstable scree slopes that lie above the cliffs. Many sections of the river are lined with stinging nettles.

In Case of an Accident

In the event of a serious injury, you should telephone for emergency help by dialing 911.

Cellular phones don't work in the Gorge, but if you hike up to the rim they will usually function. The nearest telephone is at the Mill Creek Station, six miles south of the South Parking Area at the Mill Creek exit off of U.S. 395. There is also an emergency phone on the chain link fence that surrounds the Middle Power Plant. This phone is connected to an L.A.D.W.P. office; use it only in a dire emergency.

Important Note: When discussing your location with emergency personnel, describe your position in relation to either the Middle Power Plant, the Middle Power Plant Rd. or the Upper Power Plant Rd. Using the names of the Gorge sections or the cliff names may cause confusion.

Three emergency litters are available to facilitate self-rescue in the Gorge. The litters are located:

☞ at the toilet, below the Negress Wall in the Central Gorge.
☞ at the toilet, below the DMZ, in the Inner Gorge.
☞ on the west side of the main trail, between the Flavin Haven and the Warm Out Wall in the Upper Gorge.

Please return the litters to their respective locations when finished.

Medical Care is available at:
Northern Inyo Hospital
150 Pioneer Ln.
Bishop
☎ (760) 873-5811.

To get there, drive south on U.S. 395 until reaching Bishop. Turn right at the first light onto Barlow Lane and follow it one mile. At a light turn left onto Line St. (CA 168). After one mile the hospital will be seen on the left.

Climbing in the Gorge is not risk free—a standard Owens River Gorge injury. ©*Kevin Calder Photo.*

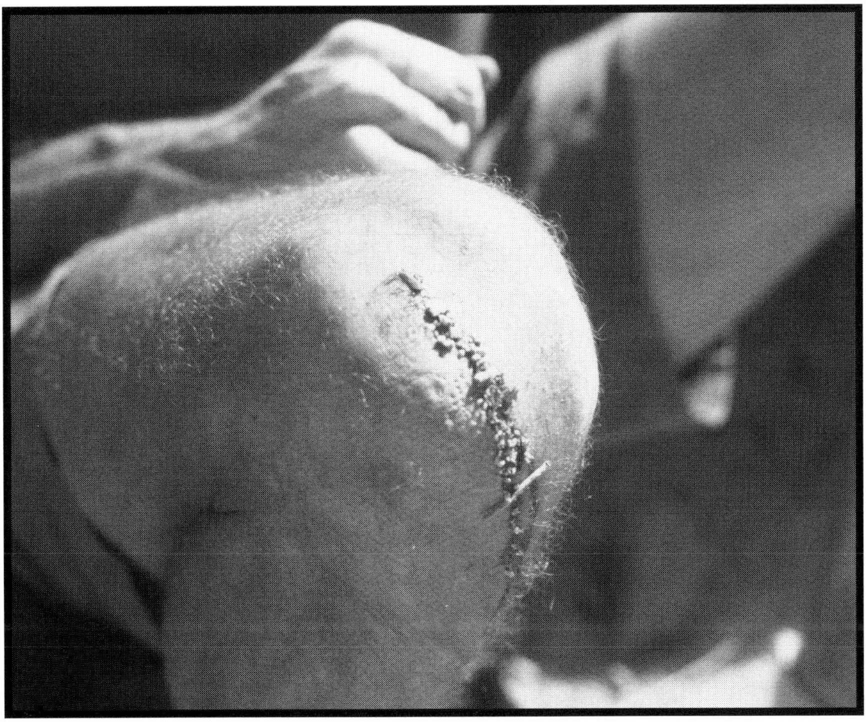

How to Use This Guide

The Owens River Gorge is a compact chasm that drains north to south. The individual cliffs are arranged south to north as they would appear traveling along the Gorge bottom. Major cliffs usually have both a photo diagram of the best routes and a detailed topo. Minor cliffs usually will have either a photo diagram (showing the bolts) or a topo. For convenience the Gorge has been divided into six sections (see page 24). At the beginning of each chapter, there is a map showing the location of the various crags and the page number those crags will be found on.

Maps

Sub Gorge50
Lower Gorge60
Central Gorge76
Inner Gorge126
Upper Gorge170
North Gorge216

Approach Instructions

Approach instructions will be found at the beginning of each section. There is also an approach overview located on page 25.

Map Legend

	Highway
	Major Rd.
	Minor Rd.
	Gravel Rd.
	Dirt Rd.
	Trail
	Path
210	Interstate Hwy.
395	U.S. Hwy.
203	State Hwy.
3S43	Forest Rd.
● ● ●	Cities, Town
P ●—●	Parking, Gate
△	Campground
Λ	Primitive Camp
	National Park
▲ ▲ ▲	Mountains
	Lake
	River
	Creek
	Drainage
	Cliff
▽ ● ▽	Boulders
○ ○ ○	Trees
D	Start of Drive
○—1.5mi—○	Distance in Miles
☆ ☆S	Climbing, Sport
☆G ☆B	Gear, Bouldering
Ⓐ B,C	Climbing Routes
↑N	North

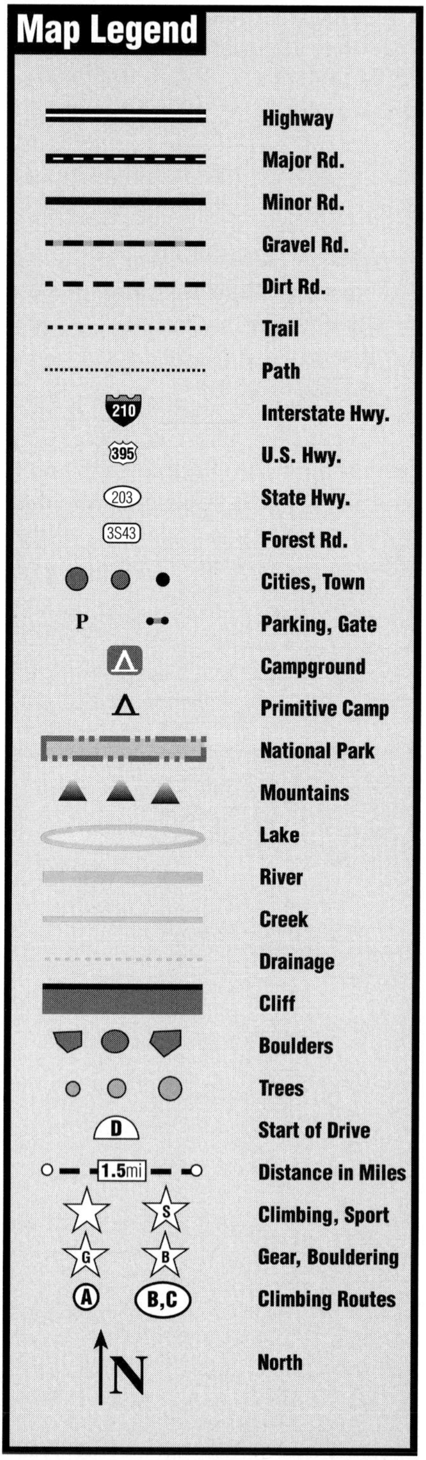

Important Note—Difficulty Ratings and Quality Ratings are not facts. These systems are subjective and based on a consensus of opinions.

Difficulty Ratings

Pitches have been rated according to the Yosemite Decimal System. The 5th class prefix has been dropped for simplicity. Difficulty ratings should be comparable to routes found at other sport climbing areas.

Quite a few of the difficulty ratings found in this book have been raised over previous editions. It might be that I'm getting weaker, causing the routes to feel harder. But there are other factors at work. One is trying to address obvious sandbags—routes that climbers have been complaining about for years. The other is the problem of holds polishing and crumbling. Years of high volume traffic can change holds that had a nice bite into slippery horrors. Over time the outside edge of an incut can crumble away turning it into a rounded open-handed hold.

Quality Ratings

Quality ratings have been assigned based on the following factors: the amount of sustained climbing, the aesthetics of the moves, pump factor, exposure, location and rock quality. Squeeze jobs, contrived lines and poorly equipped routes subtract from the quality rating.

*****	Owens River Gorge Classic
****	Awesome
***	Great
**	Good
*	Mediocre
•	Poor

Following the quality rating an (r) indicates a runout route.

Route Descriptions

First off, the name of the route and the difficulty and quality ratings are listed. The second line contains a description of the gear that is required, followed by a brief description of the route. Descent information is then listed, pitches longer than 25m/80′ are noted.

The following line is the first ascent party. The first climber listed completed the first redpoint of the route. Subsequent climbers contributed to the route in some fashion. At the most, they may have done half the work and may have redpointed the route immediately. At the least, they may have spent many tedious hours belaying. Following the date of the first ascent is the style of route preparation: GU=Ground-Up, TD=Top-Down.

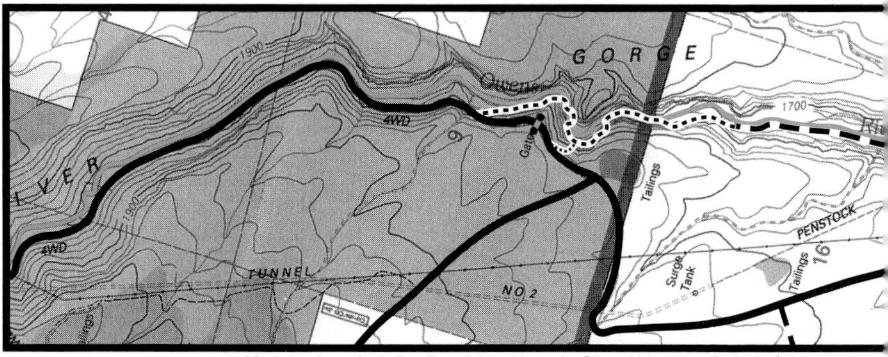

Marty Lewis on **Left For Dead** 11b**** at the Silent Pillar Wall. ©*Kevin Calder Photo.*

See Page 54

Adapted from the U.S.G.S. 1:24,000 Casa Diablo Mtn. and Rovana Quadrangles.

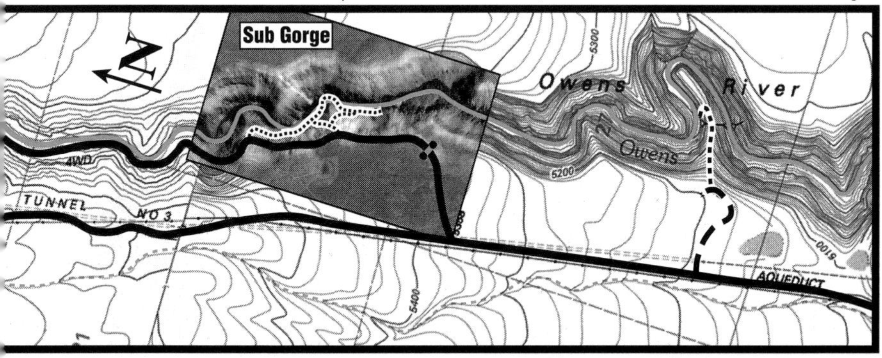

CHAPTER 2

Sub Gorge Basics .... pg 51
Silent Pillar Wall .... pg 54
Volcanic Meltdown Cliff .... pg 55
Old Fart's Formation .... pg 55
Splashdown .... pg 55
Inyo Mono Line Tower .... pg 56
Truck Tire Graveyard Tower .... pg 56
Slander Crag .... pg 57
Mental Ward .... pg 57

SUB GORGE

©2005 Maximus Press.

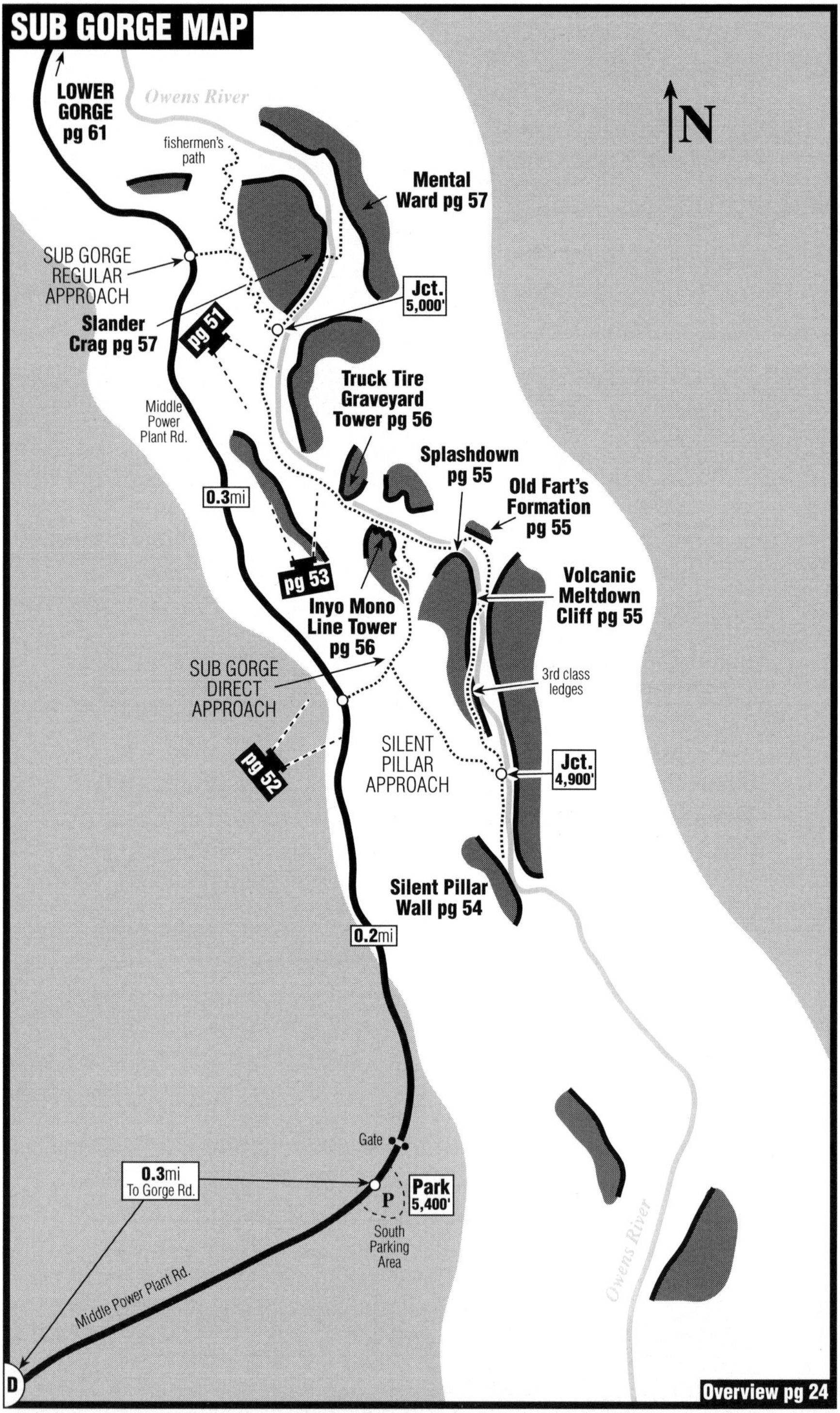

SUB GORGE MAP
LOWER GORGE pg 61
Owens River
fishermen's path
Mental Ward pg 57
N
SUB GORGE REGULAR APPROACH
Slander Crag pg 57
pg 51
Jct. 5,000'
Truck Tire Graveyard Tower pg 56
Middle Power Plant Rd.
Splashdown pg 55
Old Fart's Formation pg 55
0.3mi
pg 53
Inyo Mono Line Tower pg 56
Volcanic Meltdown Cliff pg 55
3rd class ledges
SUB GORGE DIRECT APPROACH
pg 52
SILENT PILLAR APPROACH
Jct. 4,900'
Silent Pillar Wall pg 54
0.2mi
Gate
0.3mi To Gorge Rd.
P
Park 5,400'
South Parking Area
Middle Power Plant Rd.
Owens River
D
Overview pg 24

SUB GORGE BASICS

The Sub Gorge is the southernmost area. It is small and rarely visited. The area is wild, pristine and untouched by industry. Most of the travel is on talus and scree slopes. The adventurous climber will encounter secluded and uncrowded moderate climbing routes. The best of which will be found on the concentrated Silent Pillar Wall.

Sub Gorge Details

Elevation: 4,900 to 5,000 ft.
Sport Climbs: 21 routes, 5.9 to 11d.
Gear Climbs: 1 route, 5.9.
Approach: 15 minute talus scramble with a 500 ft. descent.

South of the Old Fart's Formation the cliffs are accessible by wading across the river, or better, by utilizing the Silent Pillar Approach.

The Approach: From U.S. 395, take the Paradise/Swall Meadows Exit east. Drive up a steep hill for 0.7 miles until reaching the Gorge Rd. Turn left (north) and drive 3.3 miles. Turn right on the paved Middle Power Plant Rd. After 0.3 miles you will come to the South Parking Area. Park on the east side well before the gate.

©2005 Maximus Press. *Marty Lewis Photo.*

©2005 Maximus Press. *Marty Lewis Photo.*

©2005 Maximus Press. *Marty Lewis Photo.*

Silent Pillar Approach: From the South Parking Area, walk the Middle Power Plant Rd. 0.2 miles (5 min.) beyond the gate. Head east down a short scree section past some talus blocks. Where a ridge wishbones contour right (south) on a loose slope, then skirt diagonally down under a small cliff band to a notch with a cairn. From here loose scree leads down to the river. This point is just north of the Silent Pillar Wall in the Sub Gorge. Class 2; 20 minutes.

Sub Gorge Direct Approach: From the South Parking Area, walk the Middle Power Plant Rd. 0.2 miles (5 min.) beyond the gate. Head east down a short loose section and follow a sharp north-trending ridge. From here, head southeast down steep exposed ledges to the Gorge bottom. This point is just south of the Inyo Mono Line Tower in the Sub Gorge. Class 4; 15 minutes.

Sub Gorge Regular Approach: From the South Parking Area, follow the Middle Power Plant Rd. 0.5 miles (10 min.) beyond the gate to a sweeping left-hand turn with an obvious turnout. From here, head east 100 ft. to a saddle, then immediately drop down a south facing gully to the Gorge bottom. This point is just south of the Slander Crag in the Sub Gorge. Class 2, 15 minutes.

©2005 Maximus Press. *Marty Lewis Topo.*

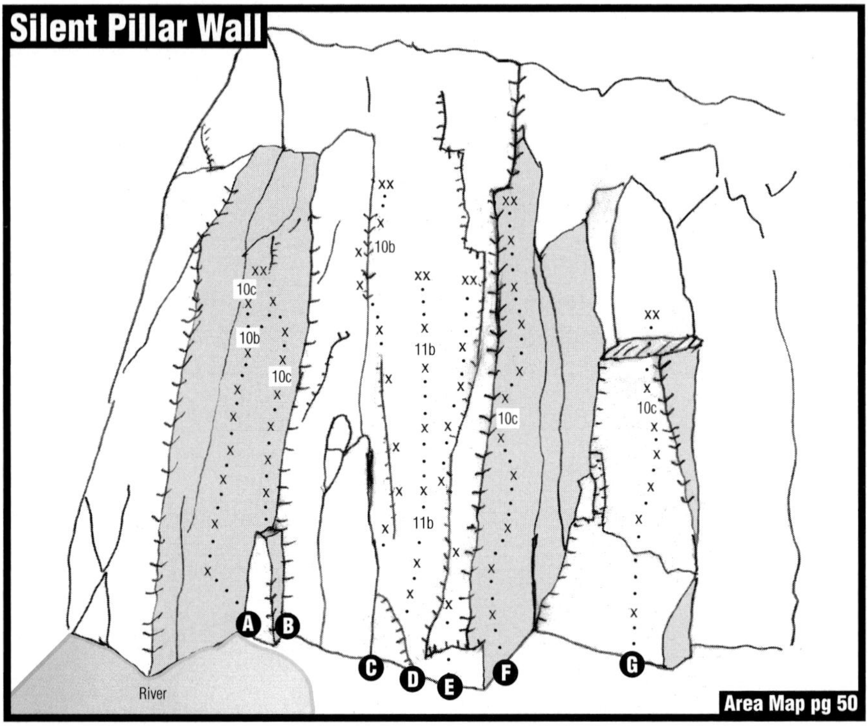

Silent Pillar Wall

This large wall on the west side is the furthest cliff south that has been developed. Superb climbing on excellent rock.

A. Nicely Displayed But Wrappers Weren't Included 10b***

8 bolts. Face. Lower off.

Variation: 10c*. 8 bolts. Go left at the 7th bolt for a slightly harder contrived finish. Lower off.

FA: John Hartman, Gabe Acosta, Bill Trethewey, 1990, GU.

B. Incorncentric 10c**

7 bolts. Face. Lower off.

FA: John Hartman, 1992, GU.

C. Life in Electric Larvae Land 10b****

8 bolts. Dihedral to Arete. 30m/100' lower off.

FA: John Hartman, Gabe Acosta, Merlin Fortner, 1992, GU.

D. Left for Dead 11b****

6 bolts. Sustained technical face. Lower off.

➤ Photo page 48.

FA: Louie Anderson, Todd Miller, 8/1991, TD.

E. Right for Life 10c***

6 bolts. Dihedral to face. Lower off.

FA: John Hartman, Gabe Acosta, Merlin Fortner, 1992, GU.

F. Buried Treasure 10c*****

10 bolts. Face. 30m/100' lower off.

FA: Mark Blanchard, Phil Green, 1990, GU.

G. Safety in Numbers 10c**

6 bolts. Arete. Lower off.

FA: Mark Blanchard, 1990, GU.

This climb is found 50 feet north of Safety in Numbers on the opposite side of the Gorge. Wade across the river to access.

Don't Nuke Nevada 11b*

9 bolts. Climb a face past a ledge, then finish on slab. Lower off.

FA: John Hartman, Gabe Acosta, Merlin Fortner, 1992, GU.

©2005 Maximus Press. *Marty Lewis Photo.*

Volcanic Meltdown Cliff

Short wide cliff band on the west side.

A. Slab Metrical Illusions 10d**

Wade to the base. 7 bolts. Slab to face. Lower off.

FA: John Hartman, Mike Thompson, Merlin Fortner, 1990, GU.

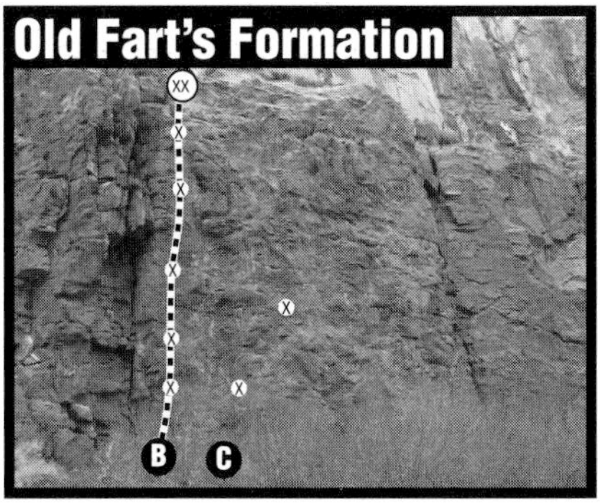

Old Fart's Formation

Short face on the east side. The main path squeezes between the brush and the cliff here.

B. Head Banger 10c**

5 bolts. Face. Lower off.

FA: Bill Trethewey, John Hartman, 1990, GU.

C. Open Project

2 bolts. Face.

P: Errett Allen.

Splashdown

A tower on the west side where the river runs into the cliff.

D. Splashdown 11d****

8 bolts. Steep face. Lower off, when lowering keep a swing going, so that you don't end up in the river.

FA: Eric Kohl, 4/1994, GU.

©2005 Maximus Press. *Marty Lewis Topo.*

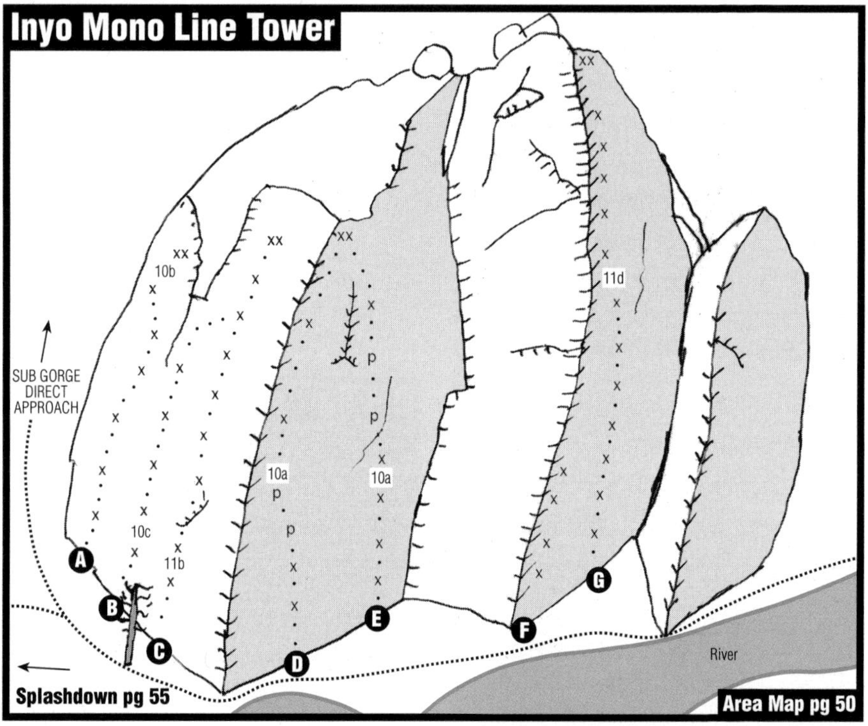

Inyo Mono Line Tower

North facing pinnacle on the west side. It's actually about 2.5 miles north of the county line.

A. Praying Mantle 10b***

6 bolts. Face. Lower off.
FA: John Hartman, Mike Thompson, Merlin Fortner, 1990, GU.

B. Fixings For a Sandwich 10c*

7 bolts. Start behind a tree, face to slab. Lower off.
FA: John Hartman, Bill Trethewey, 1990, GU.

C. Flashing With Jeckyl Juice 11b**

8 bolts. Face to slab. Lower off.
FA: John Hartman, Gabe Acosta, 1990, GU.

D. Scratch 'n Sniff 10a***

4 bolts, 2 pitons. Face to arete. Lower off.
FA: Errett Allen, Karen Young, 1990, GU.

E. Three Stooges 10a***

5 bolts, 2 pitons. Face. Lower off.
FA: Errett Allen, Bill Serniuk, Corey Hicks, 1990, GU.

F. Open Project

4 bolts. Red hangers.
P: Bruce Lella.

G. Pick a Finger 11d***

12 bolts. Face to arete. 40m/130' rappel or scramble off.
FA: Bruce Lella, 1990, TD.

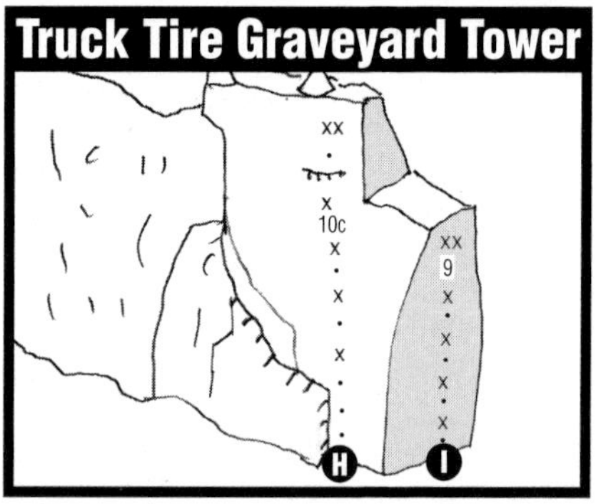

Truck Tire Graveyard Tower

Small tower on the east side where the river goes under a talus field.

H. Michelin Man 10c**

4 bolts. Face, kind of sporty. Lower off.
FA: Bill McChesney, 2/1990, GU.

I. 20/20 9**

4 bolts. Face. Lower off.
FA: Sondra Utterback, Tom Herbert, 1/1990.

©2005 Maximus Press. *Marty Lewis Photo.*

Slander Crag

Long cliff on the west side.

To access these climbs you must wade across the river.

A. Open Project

4 bolts. Face.
P: Errett Allen.

B. Open Project

1 bolt. Face.

C. Open Project

1 bolt. Face.

D. Slander Session 10b*

4 bolts. Starts left of a corner, climb a narrow face, then move left around an arete. Lower off.
FA: Errett Allen, Bill Serniuk, Corey Hicks, 1990, GU.

E. Open Project

1 bolt. Face behind a tree.

©2005 Maximus Press. *Marty Lewis Photo.*

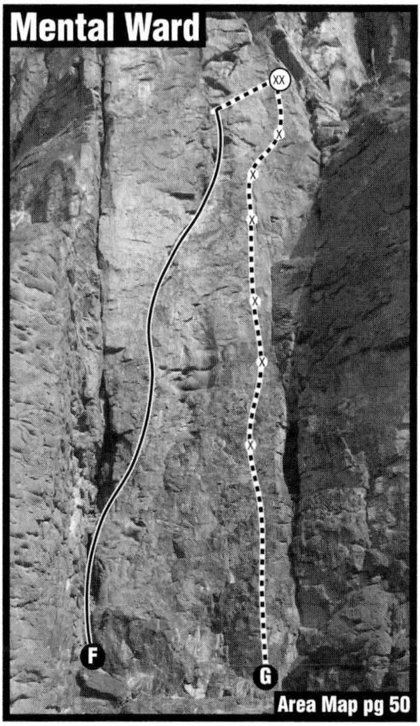

Mental Ward

Tower on the east side.

F. I'm Like This Because I Live in My Van 9**

Gear to 3". Flake/crack. Lower off.
FA: Bill Trethewey, Glenn Johnson, 1992, GU.

G. Too Crazy to Be Gripped 10b**

6 bolts. Face. Lower off.
FA: Bill Trethewey, Glenn Johnson, 1992, TD.

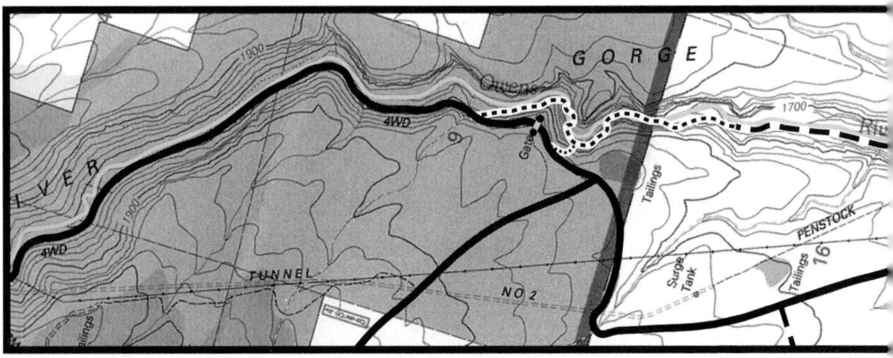

Neil Rankin on **Warning: Laser Beam** 8*** at the Warning Signs Wall. ©*Marty Lewis Photo.*

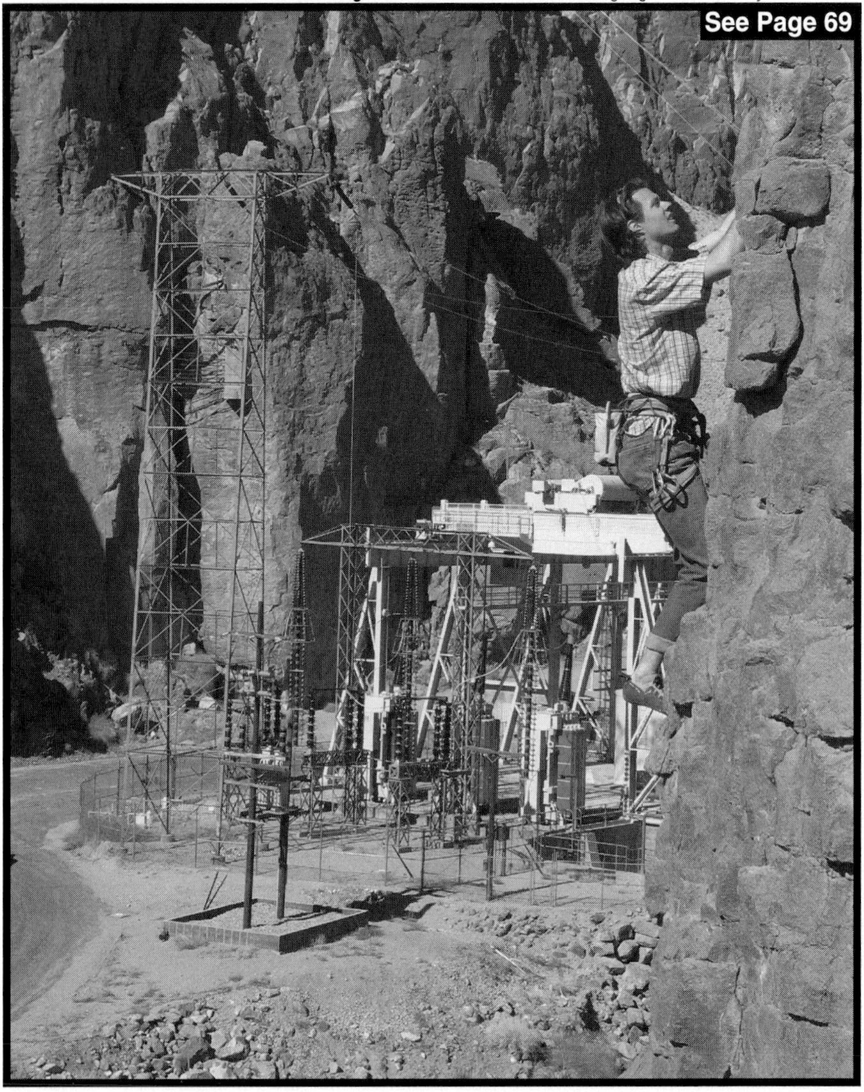

Adapted from the U.S.G.S. 1:24,000 Casa Diablo Mtn. and Rovana Quadrangles.

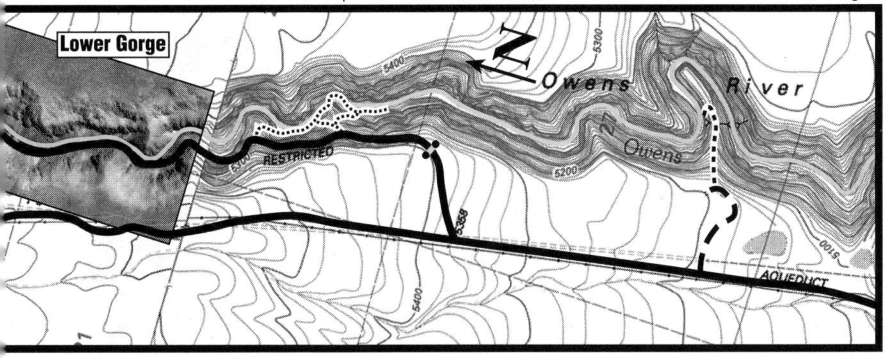

CHAPTER 3

Lower Gorge Basics .... pg 61
Big Tower .... pg 62
Pink Face .... pg 63
Grey Wall .... pg 64
Diamond Face .... pg 65
Blocky Top Wall .... pg 66
Dead Crow Buttress .... pg 66
Greenhouse Wall .... pg 67
Warning Signs Wall .... pg 69
Pitstop .... pg 70
Powerhouse Wall .... pg 71
Penstock Rock .... pg 73

LOWER GORGE

©2005 Maximus Press.

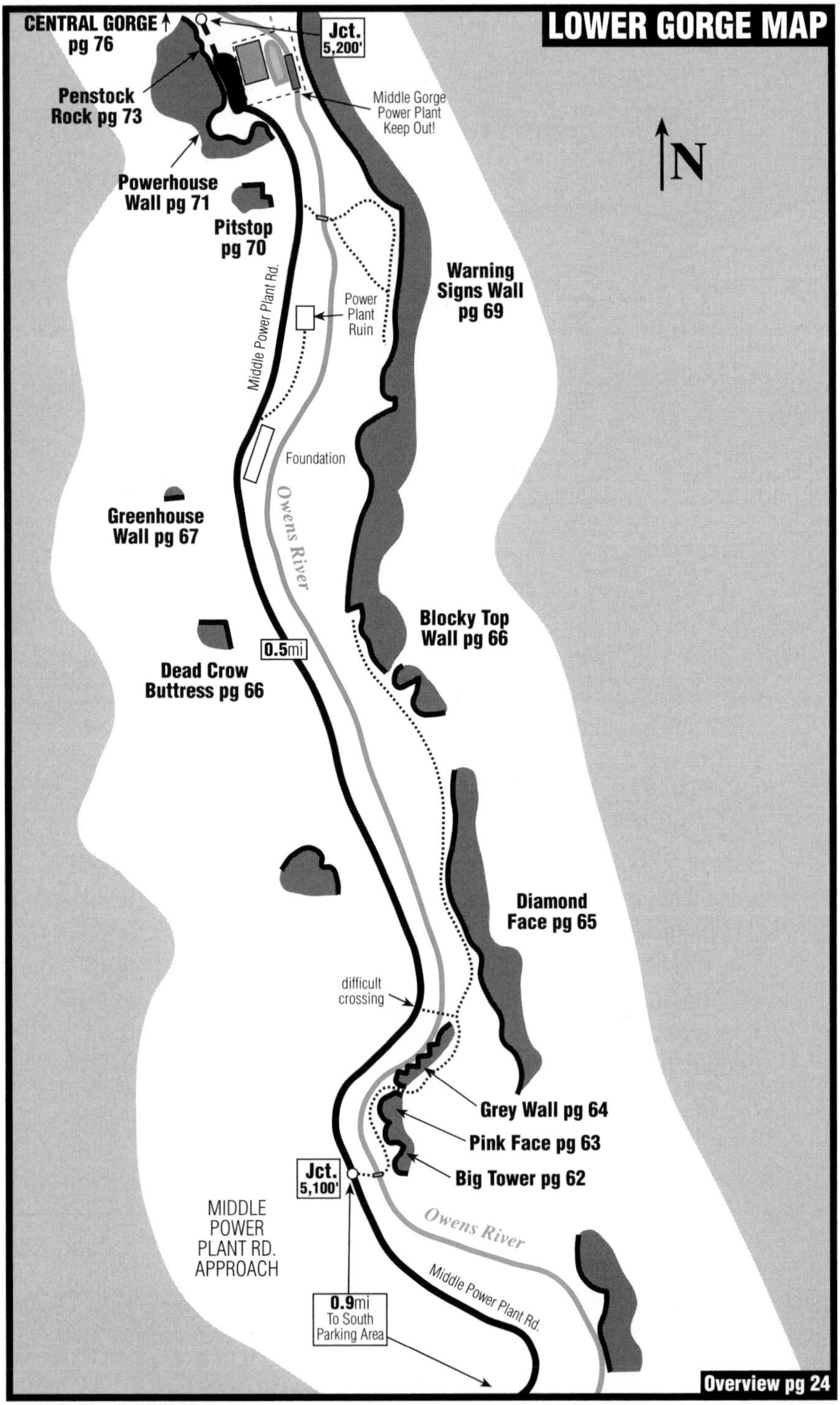

LOWER GORGE MAP
CENTRAL GORGE pg 76
Jct. 5,200'
Penstock Rock pg 73
Middle Gorge Power Plant Keep Out!
Powerhouse Wall pg 71
Pitstop pg 70
Warning Signs Wall pg 69
Middle Power Plant Rd.
Power Plant Ruin
Foundation
Owens River
Greenhouse Wall pg 67
Blocky Top Wall pg 66
0.5mi
Dead Crow Buttress pg 66
Diamond Face pg 65
difficult crossing
Grey Wall pg 64
Pink Face pg 63
Big Tower pg 62
Jct. 5,100'
MIDDLE POWER PLANT RD. APPROACH
Owens River
Middle Power Plant Rd.
0.9mi To South Parking Area
Overview pg 24

LOWER GORGE BASICS

Lower Gorge Details

Elevation: 5,100 to 5,200 ft.
Sport Climbs: 48 routes, 5.5 to 12d.
Gear Climbs: 26 routes, 5.4 to 11d.
Approach: 20 minute paved walk with a 300 ft. descent.

The Lower Gorge starts where the Middle Power Plant Rd. reaches the bottom of the Gorge and continues 0.5 miles to the Middle Gorge Power Plant.

Because of the ease of access (before the river) some of the earliest route development took place in the Lower Gorge. During this era climbers were trying to use gear whenever possible—so there are many mixed routes. After the discovery of the Central Gully Approach the Central Gorge became the main focus.

The routes in the Lower Gorge are spread over many towers and are easily accessed via a paved road. However, crossing the river can sometimes be problematic. The first cliffs encountered are the Big Tower and the Pink Face, which offer great easy and moderate climbing, accessed by a log river crossing. Further up canyon the Warning Signs Wall has a sturdy suspended beam crossing that leads to an awesome collection of moderate routes.

The Approach: From U.S. 395, take the Paradise/Swall Meadows Exit east. Drive up a steep hill for 0.7 miles until reaching the Gorge Rd. Turn left (north) and drive 3.3 miles. Turn right on the paved Middle Power Plant Rd. After 0.3 miles you will come to the South Parking Area. Park on the southeast side well before the gate.

Middle Power Plant Road Approach: From the South Parking Area, follow the paved Middle Power Plant Rd. 0.9 miles beyond the gate. This point is just across the river from the Big Tower where the road changes from downhill to uphill. Class 1; 20 minutes to the Big Tower, 30 minutes to Penstock Rock. Bicycles can be used for this approach. Yield to D.W.P. vehicles.

From the Central Gorge: You can also park at the Central Parking Area and take the Central Gully Approach; then head south down the Gorge. Class 3; 15 minutes to Penstock Rock, 25 minutes to the Big Tower. See page 77.

©2005 Maximus Press. *Marty Lewis Photo.*

Big Tower

The tower located on the east side where the road changes from downhill to uphill. Cross the river just downstream from Anonymous Bolter under some trees.

A. Brief Intermission 10a*
3 bolts. Arete. Lower off. ☞ Let's see—what's the easiest way to get my name in a guidebook?
FA: Marty Lewis, Charlie Johnson, 3/1990, GU.

B. Held Over 10c***
7 bolts. Sustained off-vertical face. Lower off.
FA: Sean Greer, Dave Focardi, 12/1989, GU.

C. Bust a Move 12a**
5 bolts. Pass a roof, move right then back left to an arete. Lower off.
FA: Tom Herbert, Tom Kleinfelter, Sean Greer, Bruce Pottenger, 3/1990, TD.

D. Exit Stage Left II 10a**
4 bolts. Clip the first 2 bolts of *Big Screen* then move up and left to the arete. Lower off.
FA: Bruce Pottenger, Jeff Neer, 1/1990.

E. Big Screen 10b**
6 bolts. Face. Lower off.
FA: Bruce Pottenger, Jeff Neer, 10/1989, TD.

F. Little Crack 5*
Gear to 3". Crack. Lower off.

G. Bonus Features 7**
3 bolts, gear to 0.5". Thin crack to a ledge, then face. Lower off.
FA: Eric Sorenson, 3/2005, GU.

H. Coming Attractions 8***
7 bolts. Off-vertical face. Lower off.
FA: Dave Focardi, Mike Robinson, Grant Schumacher, 1/1990, GU.

I. Anonymous Bolter 5***
4 bolts. Narrow face. Lower off.

J. Sneak Preview 9*
This route faces south and is 100 ft. south of *Coming Attractions*. 3 bolts. Face. Lower off.
FA: Sondra Utterback, Tom Herbert, 1/1990, TD.

Located on a square block 100 feet up scree, on the west side of the Gorge directly opposite the Big Tower.

Guns & Poses 11d*
2 bolts. Steep face. Lower off.
FA: Tom Addison, Eirik Austlid, Doug Nidever, 1990, TD.

©2005 Maximus Press. *Marty Lewis Photo.*

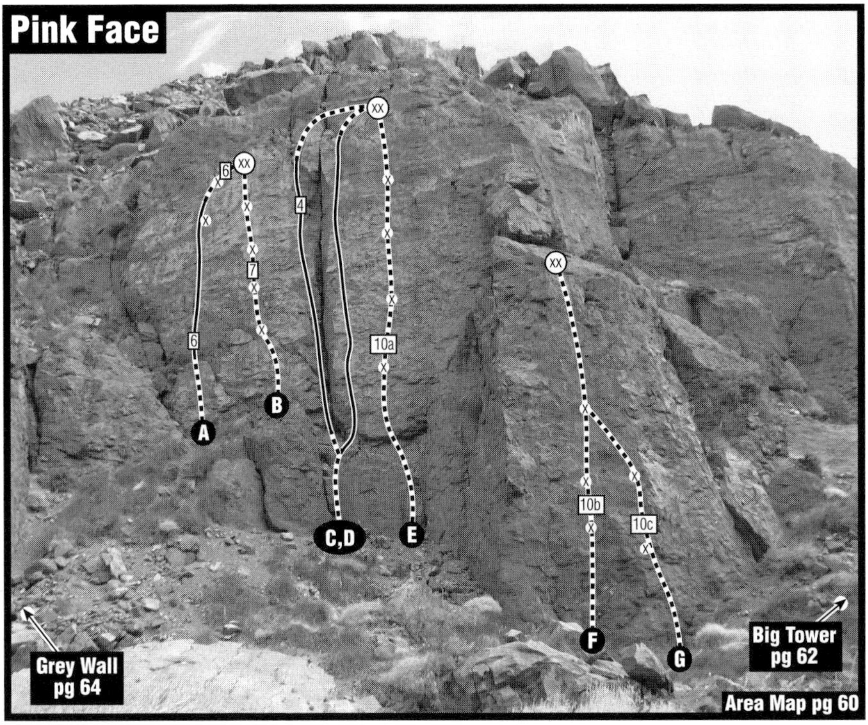

Pink Face

Northwest facing pink rock just left of the Big Tower. Use the river crossing below the Big Tower.

A. Natural Lite 6**

2 bolts, gear to 4.5". Crack to face. Lower off.

FA: Eric Sorenson, 4/2003, GU.

B. Rapscallion 7**

4 bolts. Pink face. Lower off.

FA: Eric Sorenson, Jody Martin, 4/2003, TD.

C. Leave No Trace 4*

Gear to 4". Chimney/double crack, then traverse right to anchor of *Wowie Zowie*. Single rope rappel.

FA: Eric Sorenson, 3/2005, GU.

D. Mile High Crack 8***

Gear to 3.5". Crack. Lower off.

FA: Tom Kleinfelter, Bruce Pottenger, 1989, GU.

E. Wowie Zowie 10a***(r)

4 bolts. Cool pink face. Lower off.

FA: Steve Schneider, Rob Henderson, 1989, GU.

F. Shell of a Man 10b*

3 bolts. Face. Lower off.

FA: Bruce Pottenger, Jeff Neer, 3/1990, TD.

G. Naked Gun 10c*

3 bolts. Face. Lower off.

FA: Bruce Pottenger, Jeff Neer, 11/1989, TD.

©2005 Maximus Press. *Marty Lewis Topo.*

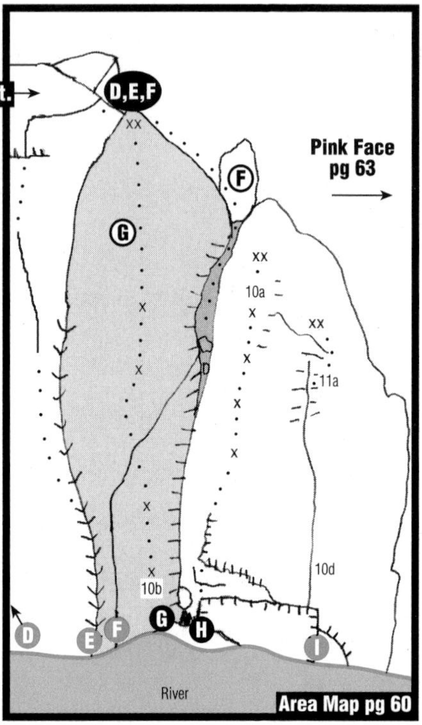

Grey Wall

A series of north facing dihedrals on the east side marked by four cottonwoods. Most of the routes found here have been swallowed by the river—no great loss!

A. Flash or Splash 9*

Flooded. 3 bolts. Face. Lower off.
FA: Tom Kleinfelter, Sean Greer, 3/1990.

B. Whirlpool 10d*

Flooded. 4 bolts. Face. Lower off.
FA: Bruce Pottenger, Jeff Neer, Tom Kleinfelter, Sean Greer, 3/1990.

C. Bot's Folly 11a•

Flooded. Gear to 3". Thin crack. One bolt lower off.
FA: Scott Ayers, Tom Kleinfelter, 10/1990, GU.

D. Grey Hair 7•

Flooded. Gear to 3". Nebulous cracks. Single rope rappel.
FA: Mike Strassman, Erin Stoffels, 1989, GU.

E. Moat 8*(r)

Flooded. Gear to 3". An arete leads to cracks. Single rope rappel.
FA: Bruce Pottenger, 1989, GU.

F. Bad Light 7•

Flooded. Gear to 3.5". A right leaning hand crack, cross *Gunnin' For a Heart Attack*, climb a chimney, then back left to the anchor. Single rope rappel.
FA: Bruce Pottenger, 8/1989, GU.

G. Gunnin' For a Heart Attack 10b**

Wade to the base. 4 bolts, gear: 1.25" piece. Face. Lower off.
FA: Bruce Pottenger, 1989, TD.

H. Grey Scale 10a***

Wade to the base. 4 bolts, gear: 1" piece. Face. Lower off.
FA: Mike Strassman, Bruce Pottenger, Tony Puppo, 8/1989, TD.

I. Half Tone 11a**(r)

Flooded. Gear to 2.5". Hand crack to sporty seam. Lower off.
FA: Dave Turner, Mike Strassman, 1990, GU.

©2005 Maximus Press. *Marty Lewis Photo.*

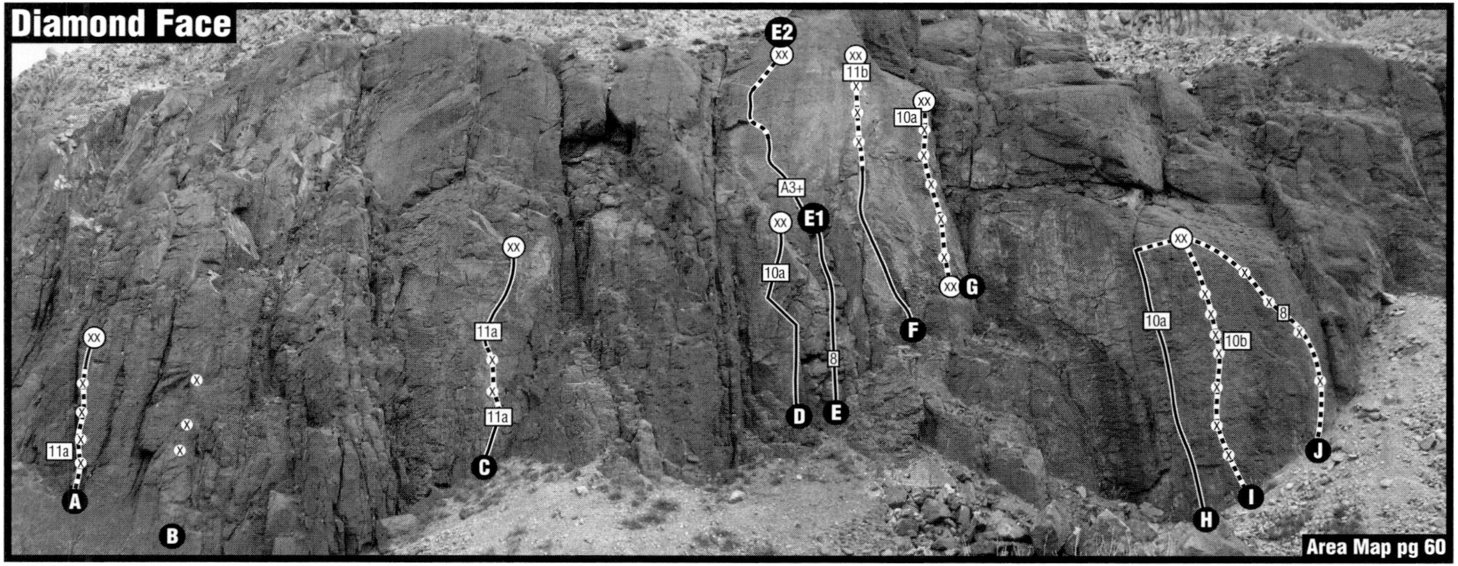

Diamond Face

A wide west facing wall on the east side.

A. Look Out Below 11a**

4 bolts, opt. gear: 0.5" piece. Face to dihedral. Lower off.
FA: Charlie Johnson, Sue Farley, 1990, GU.

B. Open Project

3 bolts. Face.

C. Daughters of a Coral Dawn 11a**

2 bolts, gear to 1.5". Face to crack. Lower off.
FA: Robert Parker, 1990, GU.

D. Zig Zag 10a**

Gear to 3". Dihedral. Lower off.
FA: Sue Farley, Charlie Johnson, 4/1990, GU.

E. Titty Twister 8 *A3+***

Gear to 3", heads, rurps, beaks, pins, hooks.
Pitch 1: 8•. Climb broken cracks. Gear anchor.
Pitch 2: A3+***. Flake systems. Single rope rappel to *Zig Zag.*
FA: Mike McGrale, 12/2000, GU.

F. Mickey Mantle 11b**

3 bolts, gear to 2". Dihedral to face. 30m/100' lower off.
FA: Dave Turner, Robert Parker, 1990, GU.

G. Uncontrollable Urge 10a**

5 bolts. Face. Lower off.

H. Bob & Eric Crack 10a**

Gear to 2.5". Crack, step right to *Mad Cat* anchor. Lower off.
FA: Bob Harrington, Eric Hein, 1984, GU.

I. Mad Cat 10b**

7 bolts. Vertical face. Lower off.
FA: Dan Haughelstine, Debbie Haughelstine, 1990, GU.

J. Dirt Pile 8*

4 bolts. Face. Lower off.
FA: John Hartman, Merlin Fortner, 1990, GU.

©2005 Maximus Press. *Marty Lewis Photo.*

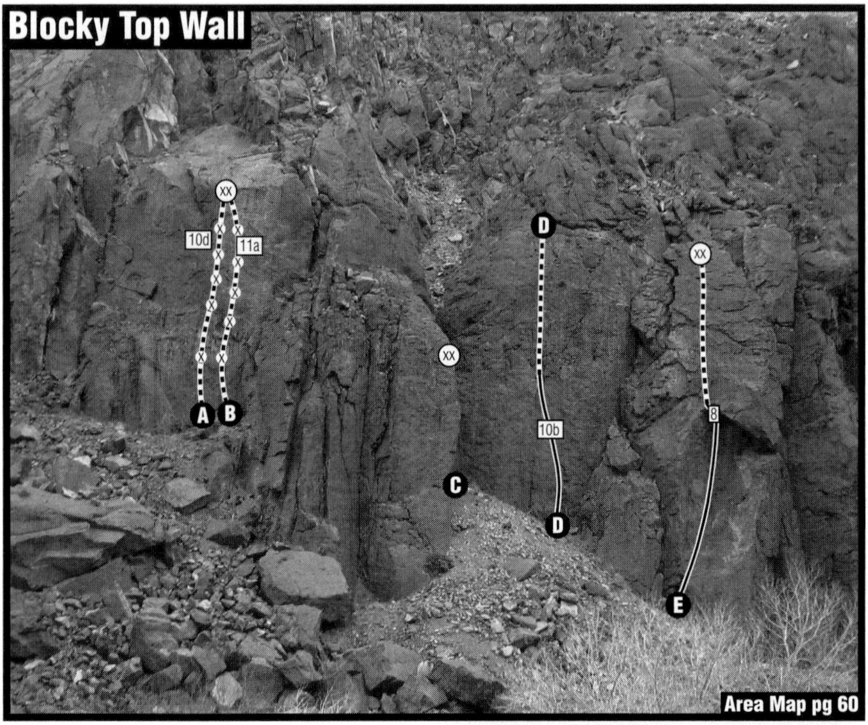

Blocky Top Wall

Wall on the east side. Currently it is difficult to cross the river.

A. Subdivisions 10d*

5 bolts. Face. Lower off. ☞ A little too close for comfort.
FA: Bruce Pottenger, Jeff Neer, 5/1990, TD.

B. Membership Has its Privileges 11a***

5 bolts. Blunt arete. Lower off.
FA: Sean Greer, Jeff Neer, Bruce Pottenger, 2/1990, TD.

C. Short Cake 11d**

On a south facing mini tower. 4 bolts, crux 2nd to 3rd. Face. Lower off.
FA: Tom Herbert, 1/1990, TD.

D. Death By Mudhen 10b•

Gear to 2". Crack to face. Gear anchor, scramble off left, then head down a rotten 4th class chimney.
FA: Mike Strassman, Austin Hearst, 1989, GU.

E. Blocky Top 8**(r)

Gear to 4". Climb a dihedral, turn a roof, then up a runout slab. Lower off.
FA: Dave Focardi, Robert Parker, 1989, GU.

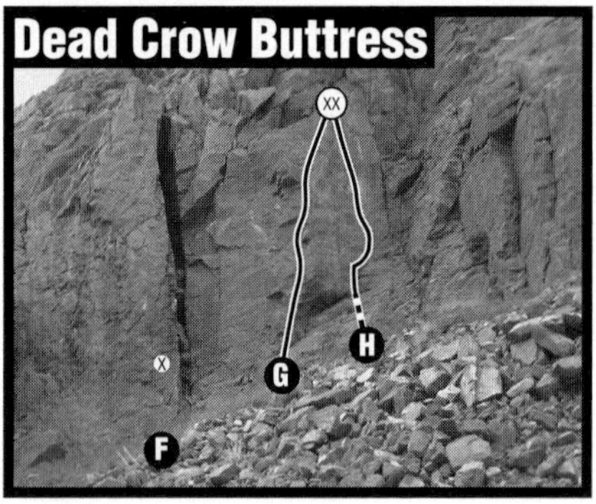

Dead Crow Buttress

Northeast facing pinnacles on the west side.

F. Open Project

1 bolt. Arete.

G. Hireaeth 10a*

Gear to 3". Right slanting crack. Lower off.
FA: Robert Parker, Andy Selters, 1990, GU.

H. Corvus Mortis 6•

Gear. Flake system with large loose blocks. Lower off.
FA: Robert Parker, Andy Selters, 1990, GU.

Bill Kerwin on the first ascent of **Global Warming** 10c*. ©*Andy Selters Photo.*

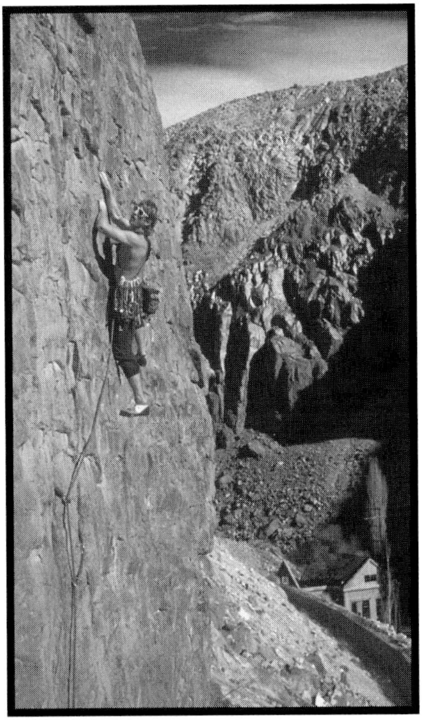

Greenhouse Wall

Southeast facing pink rock on the west side, about 100 feet up.

I. Global Warming 10c*

Gear to 2". Follow seams to a face finish. Gear anchor, scramble off right. ➤ Photo this page.

FA: Bill Kerwin, Robert Parker, 1990, GU.

©2005 Maximus Press. *Marty Lewis Photo.*

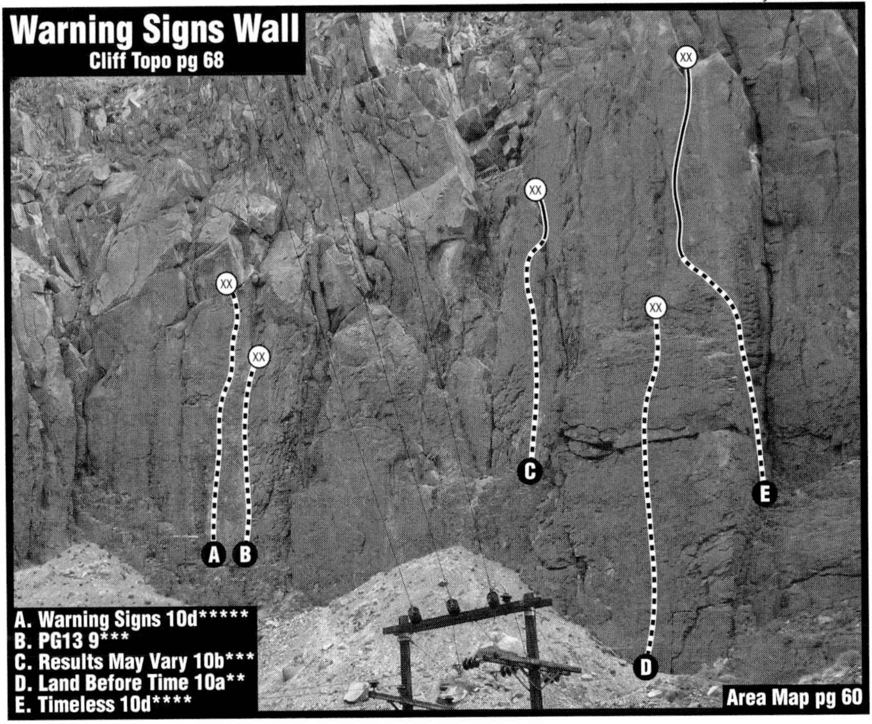

©2005 Maximus Press. *Marty Lewis Topo.*

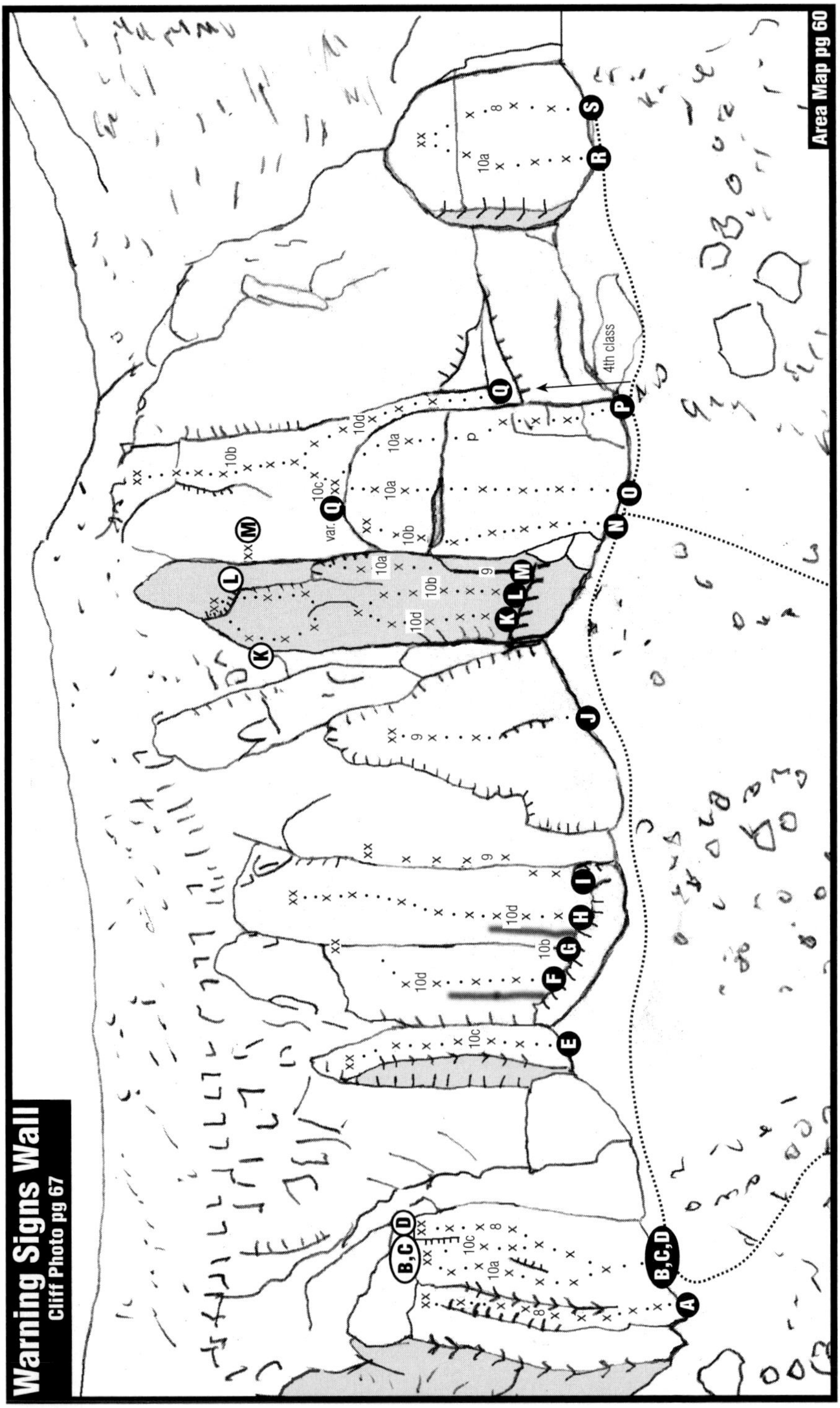

Warning Signs Wall

A long wall up talus on the east side above a prominent ruin. Cross the river on a long beam directly below the Pitstop. This cliff recieves the last sun of the day in winter. An excellent alternative to the busy Great Wall of China.

A. Warning: Laser Beam 8***
8 bolts. Arete. Lower off. ➤ Photo page 58.
FA: Marty Lewis, Kevin Calder, 2/2002, TD.

B. Boating Prohibited 10a***
6 bolts. Face. Lower off.
FA: Dave Focardi, Sean Greer, 1990, GU.

C. Batting Cage 10c*
5 bolts. Squeezed in face. Lower off.
FA: Dave Focardi, 1990, TD.

D. Watch for Rocks 8***
6 bolts. Clip the first 3 bolts of *Batting Cage* then step right up a flake system. Lower off.
FA: Eric Sorenson, Jody Martin, 3/2005, GU.

E. Red Circle With a Slash 10c**
5 bolts. Arete. Lower off.
FA: Dave Focardi, Grant Schumacher, 9/1991, GU.

F. No Lifeguard on Duty 10d**
4 bolts, optional gear: 0.75" piece. Face to crack. Lower off.
FA: Todd Vogel, Dave Focardi, 1991, GU.

G. Power Surge 10b**
Gear to 2". Seam to crack. Lower off.
FA: Todd Vogel, Dave Focardi, 1991, GU.

H. Warning Signs 10d*****
8 bolts. Sustained vertical face on perfect rock. Lower off.
➤ Photo this page.
FA: Todd Vogel, Dave Focardi, 10/1990, GU.

I. PG13 9***
6 bolts. Climb the seam. Lower off.
FA: Marty Lewis, Charlie Johnson, 1/1991, TD.

J. Sharptooth 9**
2 bolts, gear to 2". Flake to face. Lower off.
FA: Alan Bartlett, Katie Wilkinson, 1990, GU.

K. Enter at Your Own Risk 10d***
8 bolts. Off-vertical face. Lower off.
FA: Todd Vogel, Dave Focardi, 10/1990, GU.

L. Results May Vary 10b***
8 bolts. Face to arete (6th bolt shared with *Enter at Your Own Risk*). Lower off.
FA: Dave Focardi, Todd Vogel, 1/1991, TD.

M. Surgeon General 10a*
2 bolts, gear to 3.5". Crack to face to a crack through a bulge. Lower off.
FA: Eric Sorenson, 1/2004, GU.

N. R.P. #4 10b**
6 bolts. Face. Lower off.
FA: Mike Strassman, Scott Loomis, Cameron Guthrie, 1991, GU.

O. Land Before Time 10a**
5 bolts, gear: 2" piece. Face. Lower off.
FA: Bruce Pottenger, Jeff Neer, 12/1989, TD.

P. Time Will Tell 10a*(r)
4 bolts, 1 piton. Face, a bit loose. Lower off.
FA: Mike Strassman, Dana Drucker, 1991, TD.

Q. Timeless 10d****
Approach via a short 4th class scramble to a belay ledge. 11 bolts, optional gear to 2". Climb a vertical face then traverse left to a crack, continue up flakes in a dihedral, sustained and exposed. 35m/115' lower off or do a short rappel to the top of *Land Before Time*.

Time Variation: 10c***. 7 bolts, optional gear to 2". Start at the top of *Land Before Time*. Lower off.
FA: Charlie Johnson, Mike Yost, 1/1991, TD.

R. Wonka 10a**
4 bolts. Face. Lower off.
FA: Mike Yost, Charlie Johnson, 1990, GU.

S. Oompa Loompa 8**
3 bolts. Face. Lower off.
FA: Charlie Johnson, Mike Yost, 1990, GU.

Steve "Roadie" Seats on **Warning Signs** 10d*****. ©*Marty Lewis Photo.*

Marty Lewis on **Flashflood** 12b***** at Penstock Rock. ©*Bill McChesney Photo.* See Page 73

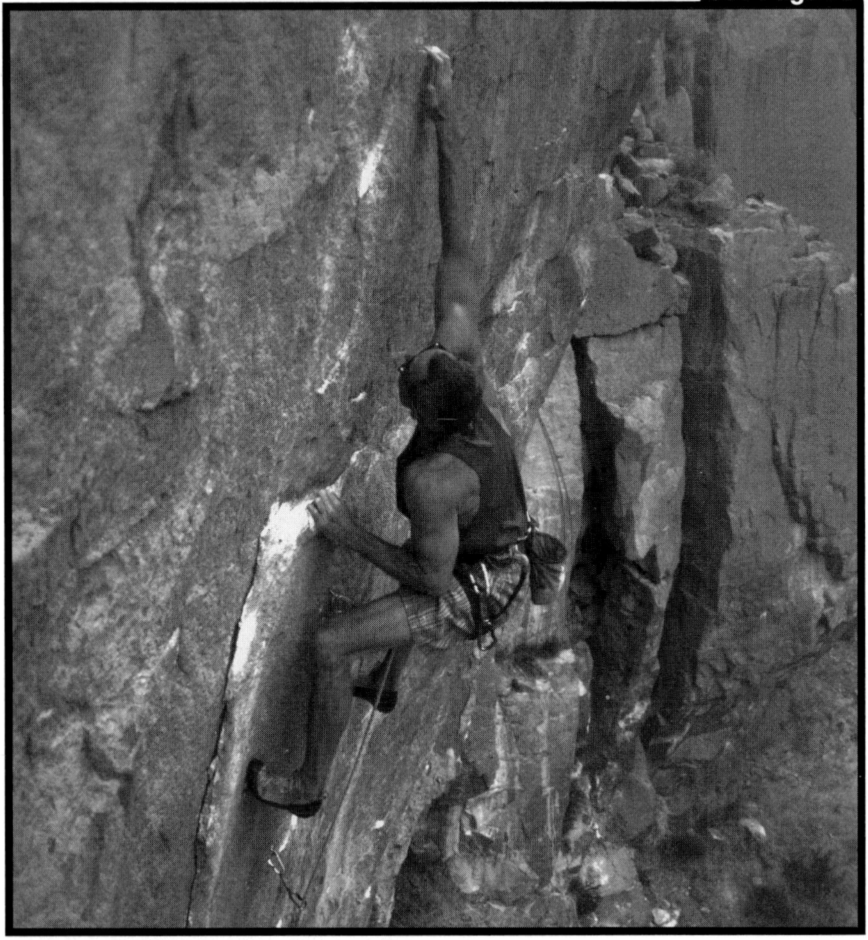

©2005 Maximus Press. *Marty Lewis Topo.*

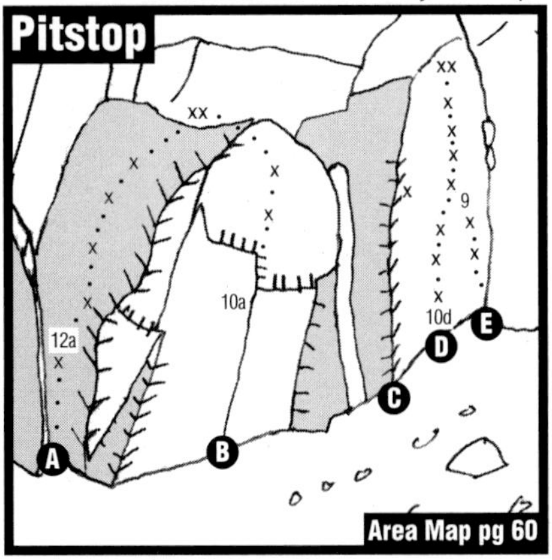

Pitstop

Pinnacle on the west side.

A. Pitstop 12a**

5 bolts. Face to slab. Lower off. ☞ Possible sandbag.

FA: Tom Herbert, Sean Greer, Dave Focardi, 1/1990, TD.

B. Late for Work 10a**

2 bolts, gear to 3.5". Crack to face. Lower off.

FA: Dave Focardi, Sean Greer, 1990, GU.

C. Open Project

1 bolt. Arete.

D. High Octane 10d**

7 bolts. Boulder problem start into *Low Octane.* Lower off.

FA: Malcolm Jolley, Alan Hirahara, 1992, TD.

E. Low Octane 9***

6 bolts. Face. Lower off.

FA: Malcolm Jolley, Alan Hirahara, 1992, TD.

©2005 Maximus Press. *Marty Lewis Topo.*

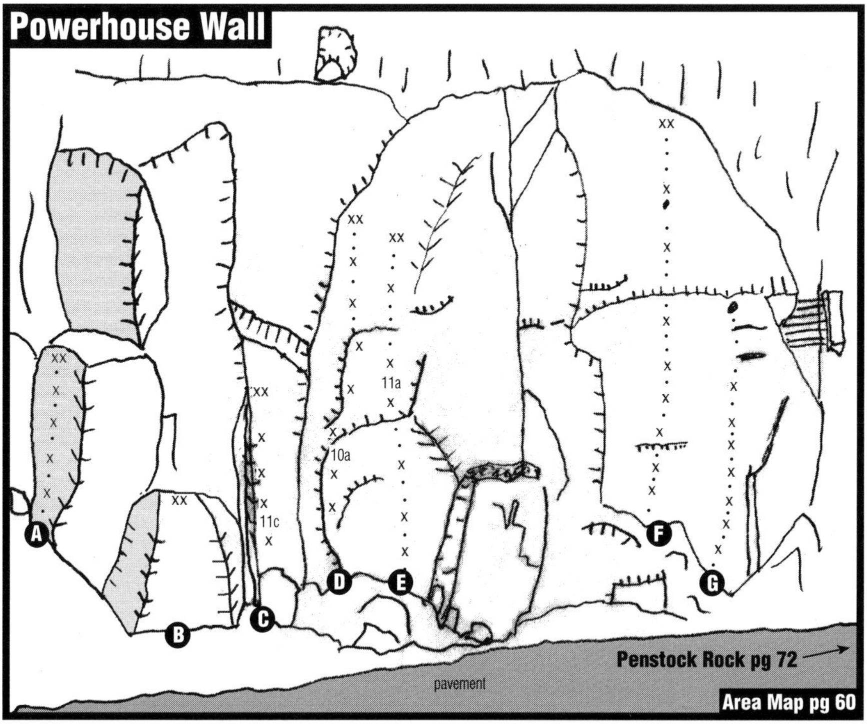

Powerhouse Wall

On the west side at the power plant.

A. L.A. is Burning 9*

4 bolts. Face. Lower off.
FA: James Scheh, 1992, TD.

B. Open Project

Anchors on a mini tower.

C. Some Kind of Wonderful 11c**

4 bolts. A bouldery start leads to tricky arete climbing. Lower off.
FA: Tom Herbert, 10/1990, TD.

D. Valley 5.8 10a****

7 bolts. Dihedral to face. Lower off. ☞ After John Bachar climbed this route he exclaimed, "that would be 5.8 in the valley." Once a 2 bolt mixed climb.
FA: Marty Lewis, Charlie Johnson, Mike Cann, 2/1991, GU.

E. If I Told You I'd Have to Kill You 11a***

6 bolts. Great edging, pass a roof, more edging. Lower off.
FA: Bruce Pottenger, Jeff Neer, 1/1990, TD.

F. Thing That Wouldn't Leave 12d**

8 bolts. Face. Lower off. ☞ When a guest wouldn't leave his home it reminded Steve of a Saturday Night Live skit of the same name.
FA: Steve Schneider, 3/1990, GU.

G. Electric Vex 12c**

7 bolts. Arete to face, oh so thin. Lower off, old industrial works are the top anchor.
FA: Jeff Schoen, 1990, GU.

©2005 Maximus Press. *Marty Lewis Photo.*

©2005 Maximus Press. *Marty Lewis Topo.*

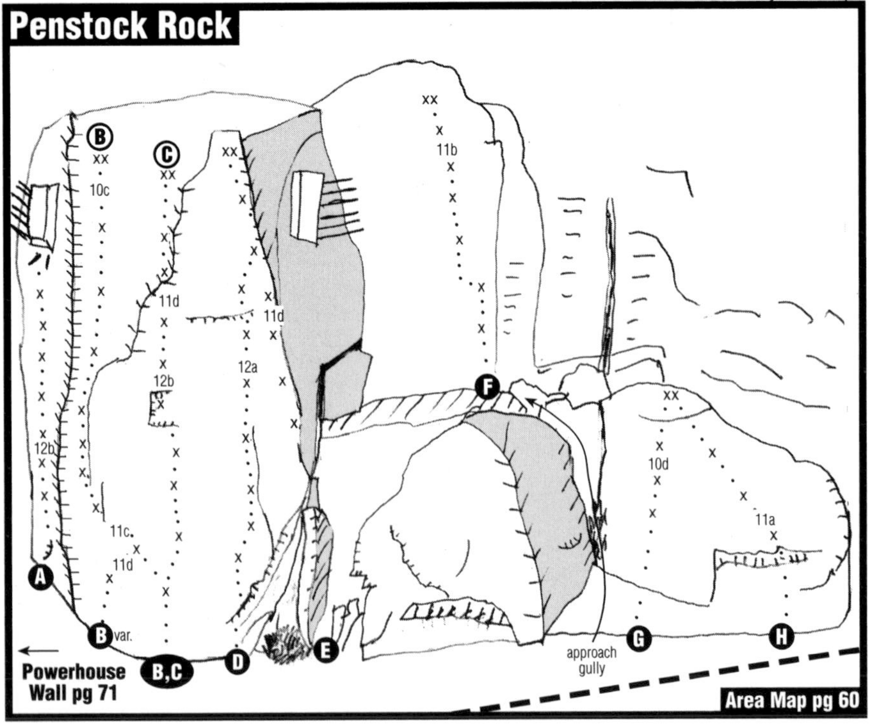

Penstock Rock

On the west side, where the pavement ends at the power plant. Superb climbing in an industrial vibe.

A. Cement Overshoes 12b**

7 bolts. Vertical technical face. Lower off, old industrial works are the top anchor.
FA: Steve Schneider, 1/1990, GU.

B. D.W.P. 11c*****

9 bolts. A technical face leads to an exciting arete. 27.5m/90' lower off.
FA: Steve Schneider, Bill Russell, 10/1989, GU.

Variation: 11d***. The left hand boulder problem start.

C. Flashflood 12b*****

9 bolts. Awesome edging and side pulls lead up the gently overhanging face. Lower off. ➤ Photo page 70.
FA: Steve Schneider, 12/1989, GU.

D. Pumping Groundwater 12a*****

9 bolts. A steep finger crack leads to a reachy crux followed by a technical arete. Lower off.
FA: Bill Russell, Steve Schneider, 12/1989, GU.

E. Save Mono Lake 11d•

6 bolts, gear 3" piece. Scramble up, a short hand crack leads to a blunt arete. Lower off.
FA: Steve Schneider, Mike Strassman, 1990, GU.

F. Funky Cole Patina 11b***

6 bolts. Sustained vertical face. Lower off.
FA: Steve Schneider, Scott Cole, Bill Russell, 12/1989, GU.

G. Penstock Slab 10d*

3 bolts. Slab. Lower off.
FA: Bruce Pottenger, Jeff Neer, 11/1989, TD.

H. Stress Puppet 11a*

3 bolts, gear: 0.6" piece. Roof to slab. Lower off.
FA: Scott Cole, Mike Strassman, 2/1990, GU.

©2005 Maximus Press. *Marty Lewis Photo.*

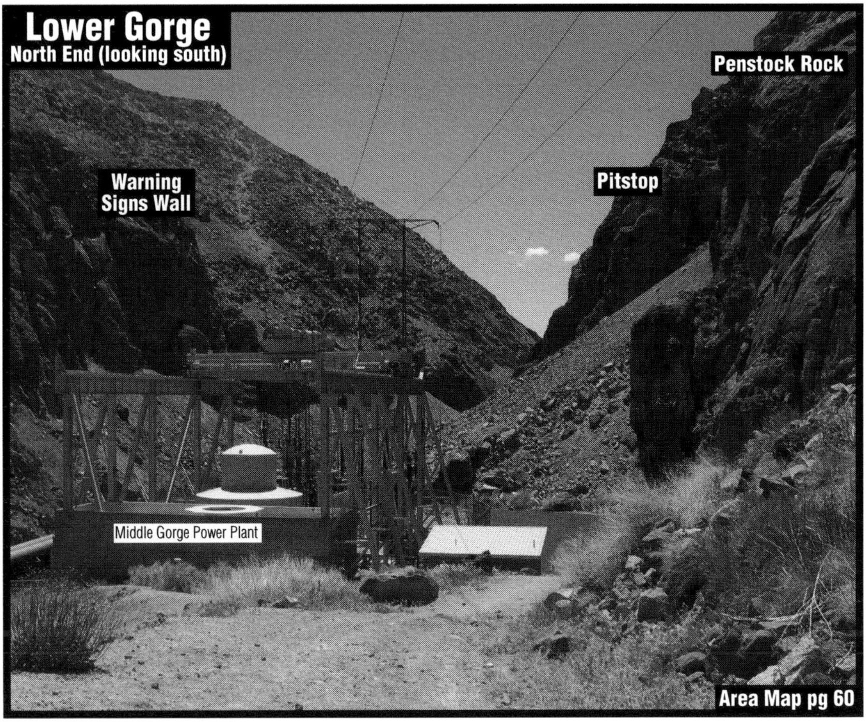

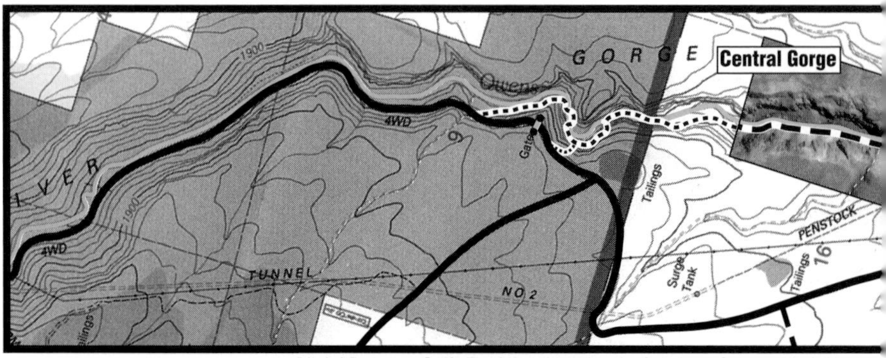

Dimitri Barton on **Split Decision** 11a*** at the Solarium. ©*Aaron Black Photo.*

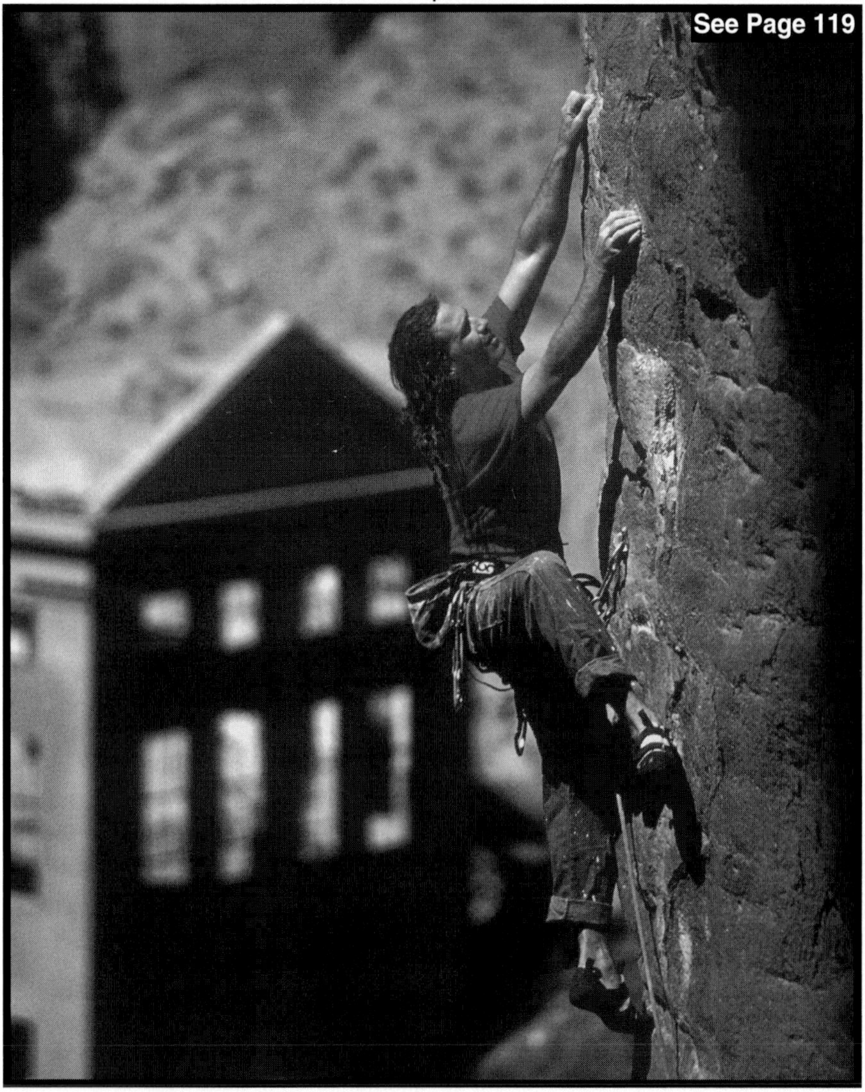

Adapted from the U.S.G.S. 1:24,000 Casa Diablo Mtn. and Rovana Quadrangles.

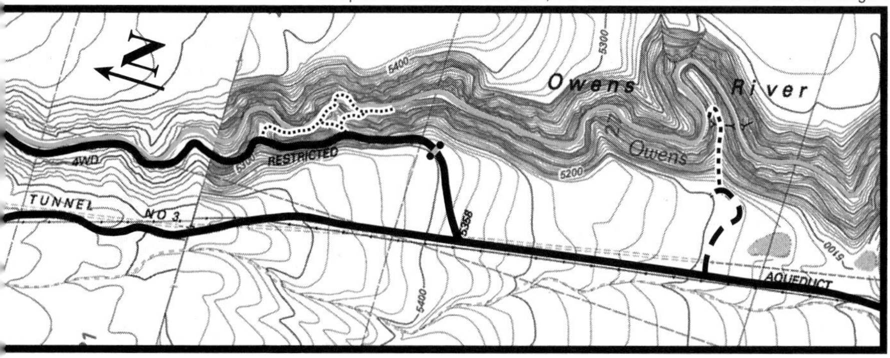

CHAPTER 4

Central Gorge Basics .... pg 77
L. Alien Wall .... pg 81
Banana Belt .... pg 83
High Tension Towers .... pg 85
Pub Wall .... pg 87
Riverside Island .... pg 91
Social Platform .... pg 95
Negress Wall .... pg 97
Warm Up Wall .... pg 98
Pop Tart Towers .... pg 99
Faulty Tower .... pg 103
Attila the Hun Wall .... pg 104
Health Club .... pg 105
Mystical Tricks Cliff .... pg 106
Roadside Boulders .... pg 107
Great Wall of China - Overview .... pg 109
Great Wall of China - Right .... pg 110
Great Wall of China - Center .... pg 113
Great Wall of China - Left .... pg 115
Solarium .... pg 119
Emergency Room .... pg 121
Shaded Wall .... pg 123

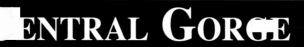

CENTRAL GORGE

©2005 Maximus Press.

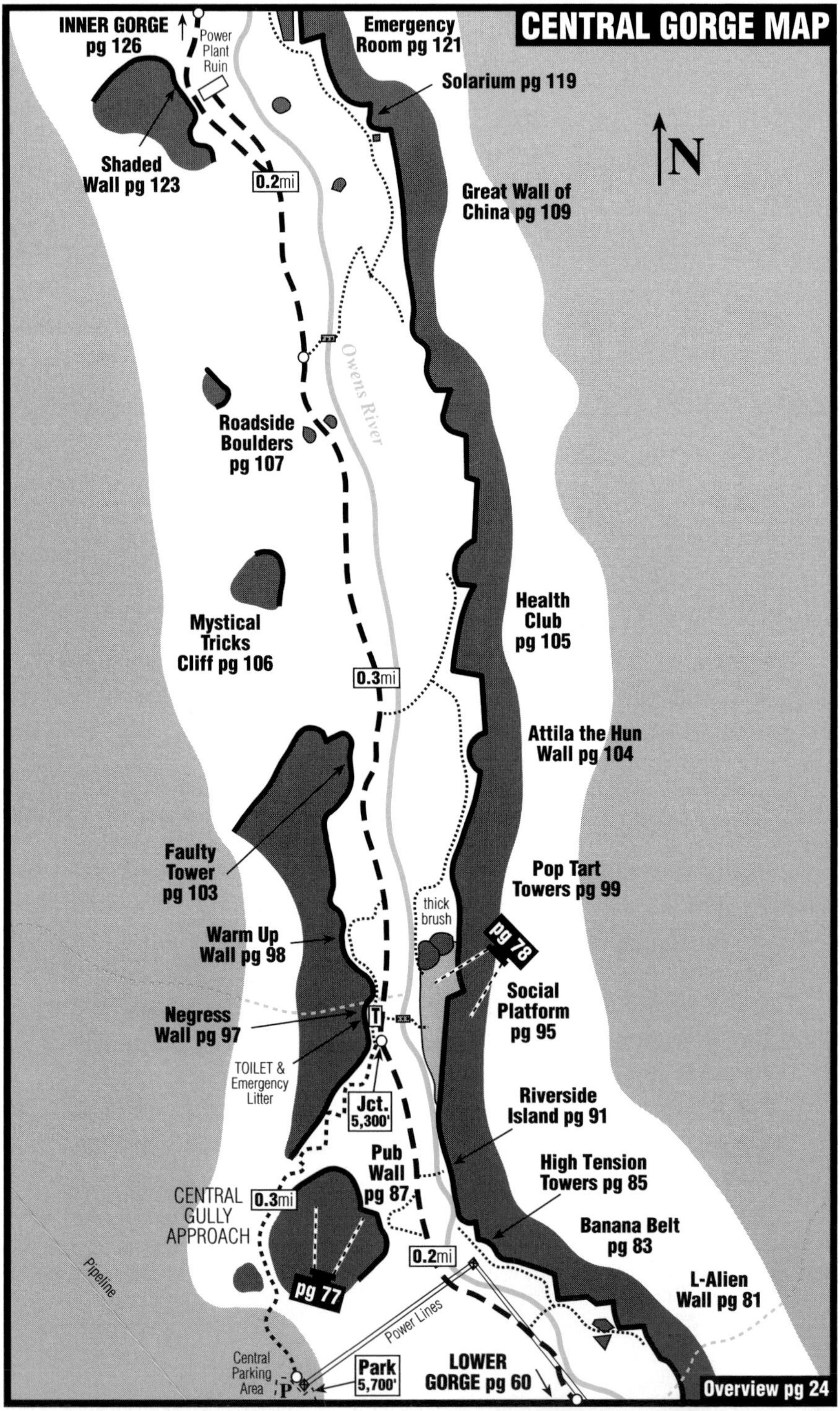
CENTRAL GORGE MAP
INNER GORGE pg 126
Power Plant Ruin
Emergency Room pg 121
Solarium pg 119
N
Shaded Wall pg 123
0.2mi
Great Wall of China pg 109
Owens River
Roadside Boulders pg 107
Health Club pg 105
Mystical Tricks Cliff pg 106
0.3mi
Attila the Hun Wall pg 104
Faulty Tower pg 103
Pop Tart Towers pg 99
thick brush
pg 78
Warm Up Wall pg 98
Social Platform pg 95
Negress Wall pg 97
T
TOILET & Emergency Litter
Jct. 5,300'
Riverside Island pg 91
Pub Wall pg 87
High Tension Towers pg 85
CENTRAL GULLY APPROACH
0.3mi
Banana Belt pg 83
0.2mi
pg 77
Pipeline
L-Alien Wall pg 81
Power Lines
Central Parking Area
P
Park 5,700'
LOWER GORGE pg 60
Overview pg 24

CENTRAL GORGE BASICS

This section starts just past the Middle Power Plant and follows a dirt road until it ends at some ruins.

The Central Gorge is the "main area." Climbs are highly concentrated on both canyon walls. Quality routes abound. On busy weekends and holidays many of these cliffs can become quite crowded.

Central Gorge Details

Elevation: 5,200 to 5,400 ft.
Sport Climbs: 166 routes, 5.6 to 13b.
Gear Climbs: 51 routes, 5.6 to 12a.
Approach: 10 minute talus and scree gully with a 400 ft. descent.

The two most popular moderate cliffs are found in the Central Gorge: the Warm Up Wall and the Great Wall of China. These two cliffs are on opposite sides of the canyon, so when one is sunny the other is in shade.

Please note the location of the toilet at the base of the Negress Wall and use it if necessary.

The Approach: From U.S. 395, take the Paradise / Swall Meadows Exit east. Drive up a steep hill for 0.7 miles until reaching the Gorge Rd. Turn left (north) and drive 4.8 miles. Turn right on a dirt road where a power line drops into the Gorge. 0.2 miles down this dirt road is a transmission tower. Park here.

©2005 Maximus Press. *Marty Lewis Photo.*

©2005 Maximus Press. *Marty Lewis Photo.*

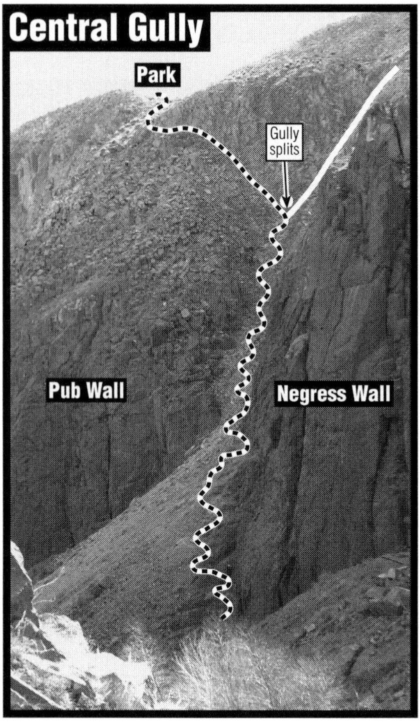

Central Gully Approach: Be very careful not to dislodge rocks—climbs are right below. From the transmission tower at the Central Parking Area, follow a trail north about 100 ft. Scramble down 2nd class blocks about 30 ft. From here, head north through a notch until reaching a steep 3rd class gully. Drop down the gully a few hundred feet to the Gorge bottom. This point is between the Negress Wall and the Social Platform in the Central Gorge. Class 3; 10 minutes to the Negress Wall, 15 minutes to the Banana Belt, 20 minutes to the Solarium.

Important Note: When climbing back up the gully, about halfway up, the chute splits in two. Take the left hand branch. The right hand branch is loose and dangerous 4th class that ends up a long way from the Central Parking Area.

From the Lower Gorge: You can also park at the South Parking Area and take the Middle Power Plant Rd. Approach; then head north up the Gorge. This approach is long; the only advantage being that it is on a paved road and that the road is plowed when snowy. Class 1; 30 minutes to the Banana Belt, 45 minutes to the Solarium. Bicycles can be used for this approach. Yield to D.W.P. vehicles. See page 61.

From the Upper Gorge: You can also park at the North Parking Area and take the Upper Gorge Approach; then head south down the Gorge. Class 3; 35 minutes to the Solarium, 50 minutes to the Banana Belt. See page 171.

©2005 Maximus Press. *Marty Lewis Photo.*

Barb Howe on **Sendero Luminoso** 10b***** at the Solarium. ©*Kevin Calder Photo.*

Mike Martyr on the **Dynamite Face** 11d*. ©*Andy Selters Photo.*

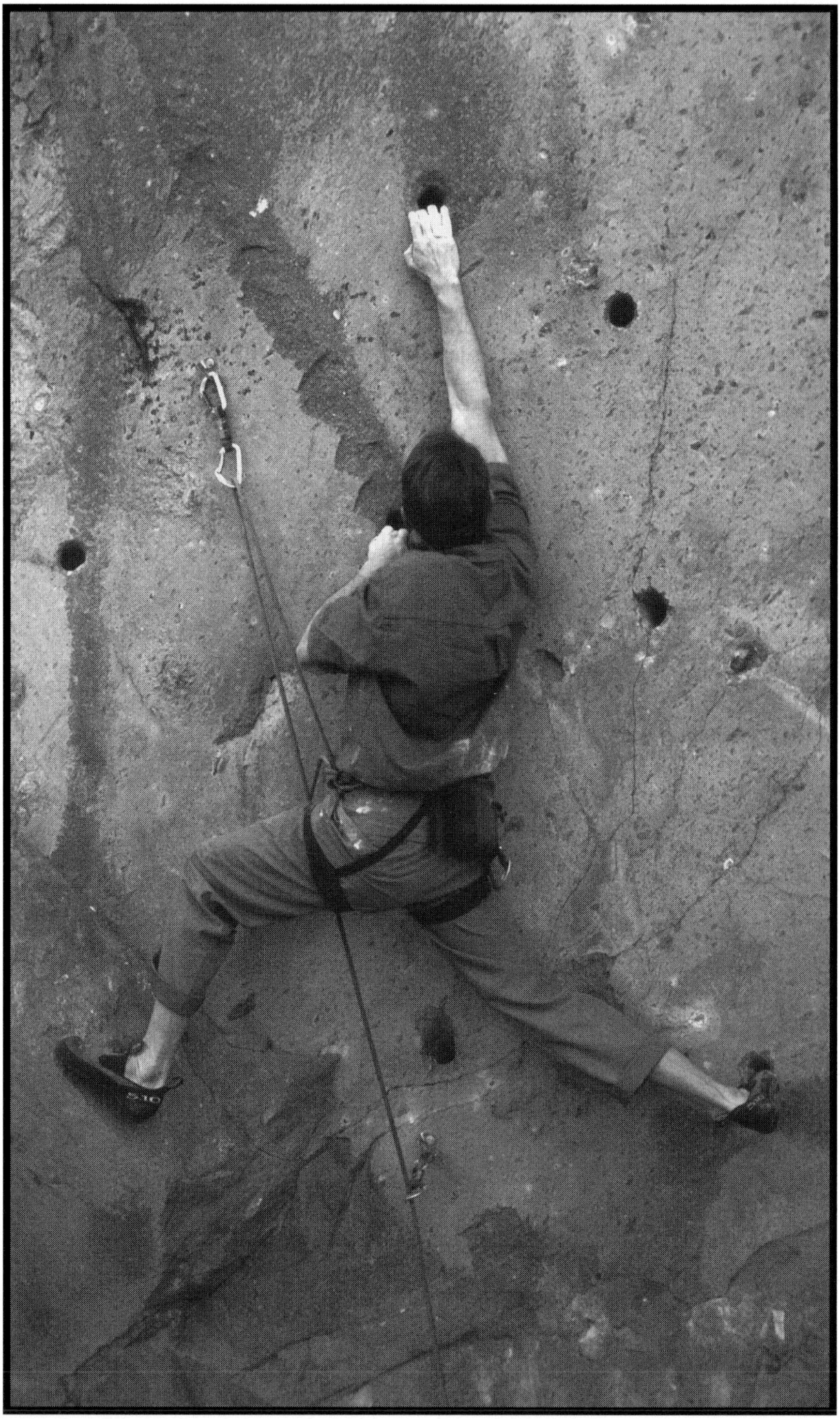

©2005 Maximus Press. *Marty Lewis Topo.*

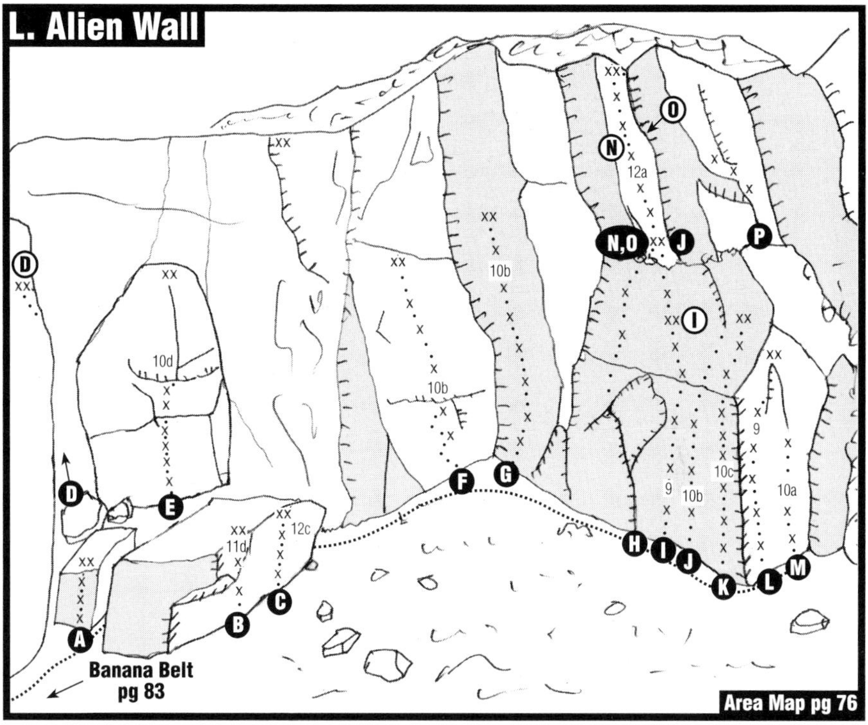

L. Alien Wall

Pink slabs and dihedrals on the east side. Cross the river at the Banana Belt.

A. Idol Maker 12a*

3 bolts. Sideways holds on a fallen block. Lower off.
FA: Steve Schneider, 1990, GU.

B. Dynamite Face 11d*

2 bolts. Steep face. Lower off. ☞ The L.A.D.W.P drilled many holes in this boulder in an effort to blow it up and remove it; but it's hangin' tough. ➤ Photo facing page.
FA: Steve Schneider, Marty Lewis, 1990, GU.

C. Custom Made 12c*

3 bolts. Steep face. Lower off. ☞ Tom drilled pockets too.
FA: Tom Herbert, 1991, TD.

D. Shout Around 11d*(r)

On the east face of a tower. 3 bolts. Face. Lower off.
FA: Steve Schneider, 1/1990, GU.

E. Spare Change 10d***

6 bolts, gear to 0.5". Face to slabby crack. Lower off.
FA: Mark Blanchard, 3/1991, GU.

F. Dollar Three Ninety Eight 10b***

5 bolts. Slab. Lower off.
FA: Mark Blanchard, Jessica VanBriesen, 1991, GU.

G. Upwardly Mobile 10b***

7 bolts. Vertical face. Lower off.
FA: Kelly Cordner, John DiAnnibale, 5/1997, TD.

H. Electric Launderland 8**

2 bolts, gear to 2". Dihedral to slab. 35m/115' lower off.
FA: Mike Strassman, Moira Smith, 1990, GU.

I. Positive Approach 9***(r)

5 bolts. Face to slab. Lower off.
FA: Jeff Schoen, Will Johnson, 1990, GU.

J. Approach Pitch 10b**(r)

3 bolts, gear to 1.5". Face to slab. 40m/130' rappel.
FA: Steve Schneider, Scott Cole, 1990, GU.

K. Cadillac Desert 10c***

8 bolts. Vertical face to slab. Lower off.
FA: Marty Lewis, Sean Plunkett, 3/1996, TD.

L. Humjob 9***

5 bolts. Face. Lower off.
FA: Scott Cole, Errett Allen, 1990, GU.

M. Humdinger 10a**

3 bolts, gear to 1.5". Face to seam. Lower off.
FA: Mark Blanchard, John Dittli, Scott Croll, 1991, GU.

N. Go Back Where You Came From 12a**

5 bolts. Slab. Lower off.
FA: Steve Schneider, Tom Herbert, 1/1990, TD.

O. Worst Enemy 9•

Gear to 3". Dihedral, then traverse left. Lower off.
FA: Steve Schneider, GU, 1/1990, GU.

P. Open Project

3 bolts. Slabby dihedral.
P: Scott Cole.

©2005 Maximus Press. *Marty Lewis Photo.*

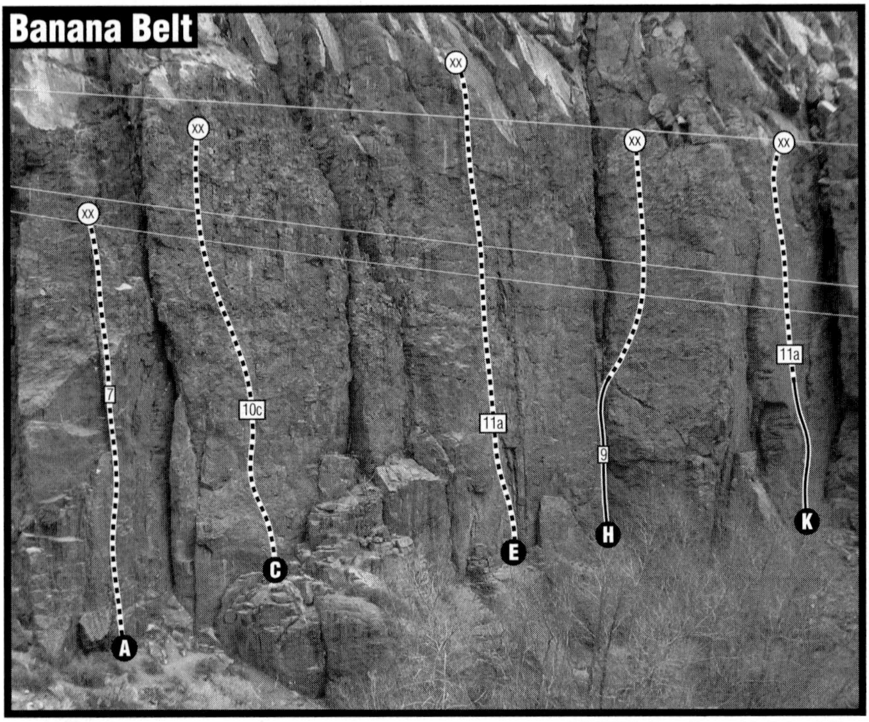

©2005 Maximus Press. *Marty Lewis Topo.*

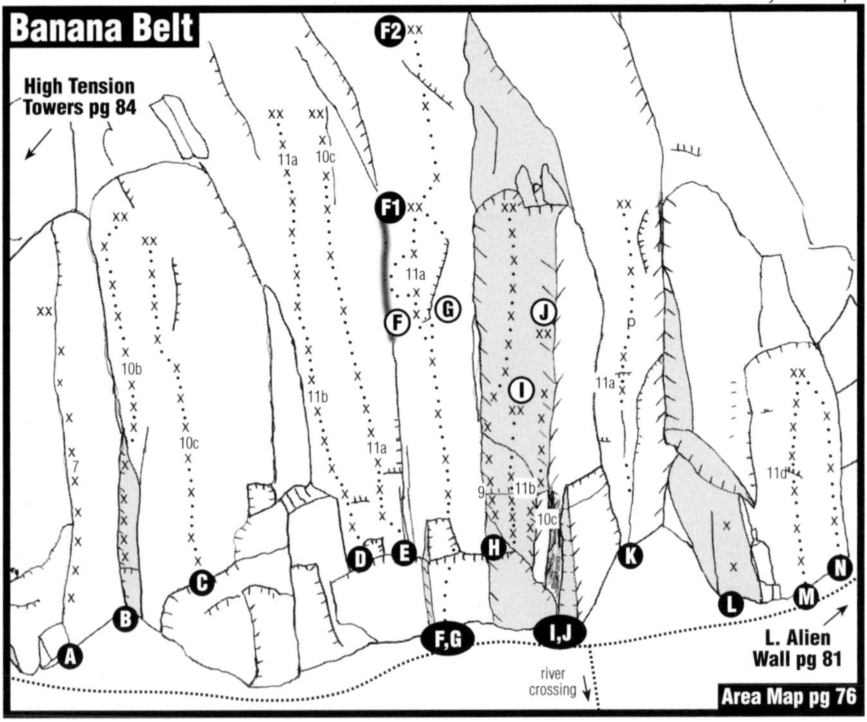

Banana Belt

Massive south facing wall just north of the power plant on the east side.

A. Northern Lite 7****

9 bolts. Climb a seam to an arete/dihedral, then continue up face. Lower off. ☞ First led on gear.
FA: Heather Culbert, Greg Barnes, 11/2001, GU.

B. Wedge-O 10b***

12 bolts. A pinnacle leads to a bulge, finish on exposed face climbing. 30m/100' lower off. ☞ "If the runout don't get you the choss will"—Mike Strassman. In a giant improvement, this once loose and dangerous route has had 6 bolts added by the first ascensionist.
FA: Mike Strassman, Eric Ellis, 2/1991, TD.

C. Environmental Terrorist 10c****

10 bolts. Slab to vertical face. Lower off. ☞ Originally this runout and circuitous line went right up a crack and then way back left to *Wedge-O*. It improved considerably when bolts and an anchor were added and it was realigned.
FA: Eric Ellis, Mike Strassman, 2/1991, TD. Realignment: Gary Slate, Marty Lewis.

D. Love Over Gold 11b***

13 bolts. Vertical face to bulge. 35m/115' lower off to ledge system, or do a 40m/130' rappel to the ground.
FA: Todd Graham, Bruce Lella, Steve Plunkett, 11/1990, TD.

E. Love Stinks 11a*****

11 bolts, optional gear to 1.5". Technical face climbing leads to a runout moderate section, then finish up a strenuous bulge. 35m/115' lower off to ledge system, or rappel 40m/130' to the ground. ☞ Once a "mixed" classic; it soon became apparent that it was easier to run it out than to fiddle gear into the pockets. ➤ Photo this page.
FA: Joe Rousek, Tony Puppo, 2/1990, GU.

F. Rim Job 11a**

Pitch 1: 11a***. 7 bolts. Face to bulge, the crux can be avoided by traversing left to a chossy area. 35m/115' lower off or climb 2nd pitch.
Pitch 2: 10b•. 2 bolts, gear to 1.5". Face. Lower off.
Can be done as one pitch.
FA: Steve Schneider, Mike Strassman, 1990, GU.

G. Butt Wipe 10a*

4 bolts, gear to 3". Start *Rim Job*, but at the 5th bolt head right up a right slanting weakness. 35m/115' lower off.
FA: Mike Strassman, 1990, GU.

H. Paradise 9****

12 bolts. Climb a right facing corner, then move right up a long beautiful face. 35m/115' lower off to ledge system, or a 30m/100' lower off to the anchor of *Monsters of Rock*.
FA: Greg Barnes, John Aughinbaugh, 4/2001, GU.

I. Monsters of Rock 11b**

4 bolts, optional gear: 0.75" piece. Face.
FA: Sean Greer, Bruce Pottenger, 4/1990, TD.

J. Range of Light 10c**

6 bolts. Scramble up a ways to reach the 1st bolt then climb the arete. Lower off. ☞ This route once had a giant runout to the top of the pinnacle, requiring a double rope rappel. In a controversial move I put an anchor in at 25m/80' up, never imagining that ropes would get longer!
FA: Mike Strassman, 1990, TD.

K. Hip Pockets 11a****

3 bolts, 1 piton, gear to 2". Seam to awesome pocketed face. 30m/100' lower off. ☞ An old school mixed classic.
FA: Joe Rousek, Tony Puppo, 1989, GU.

L. Open Project

2 bolts.
P: Bill McChesney.

M. Bloody Pawprints 11d***

6 bolts. Technical off-vertical face. Lower off.
FA: Scott Cole, Bill McChesney, 1990, GU.

N. Quest 10c*(r)

3 bolts. Arete. Lower off.
FA: Louie Anderson, Cory Zinngrabe, 9/1991, GU.

John Bachar on **Love Stinks** 11a*****.
©Andy Selters Photo.

©2005 Maximus Press. *Marty Lewis Photo.*

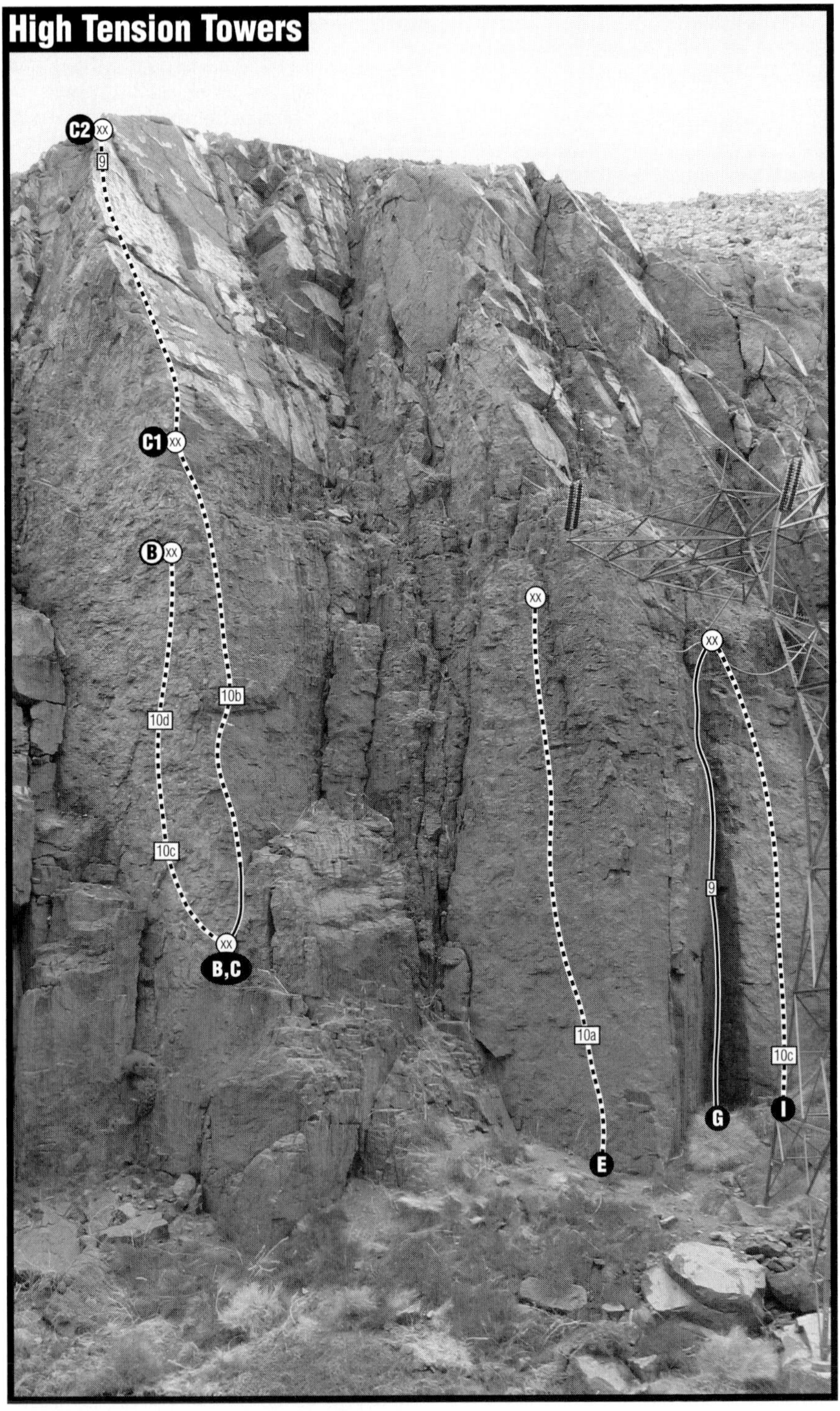

©2005 Maximus Press. *Marty Lewis Topo.*

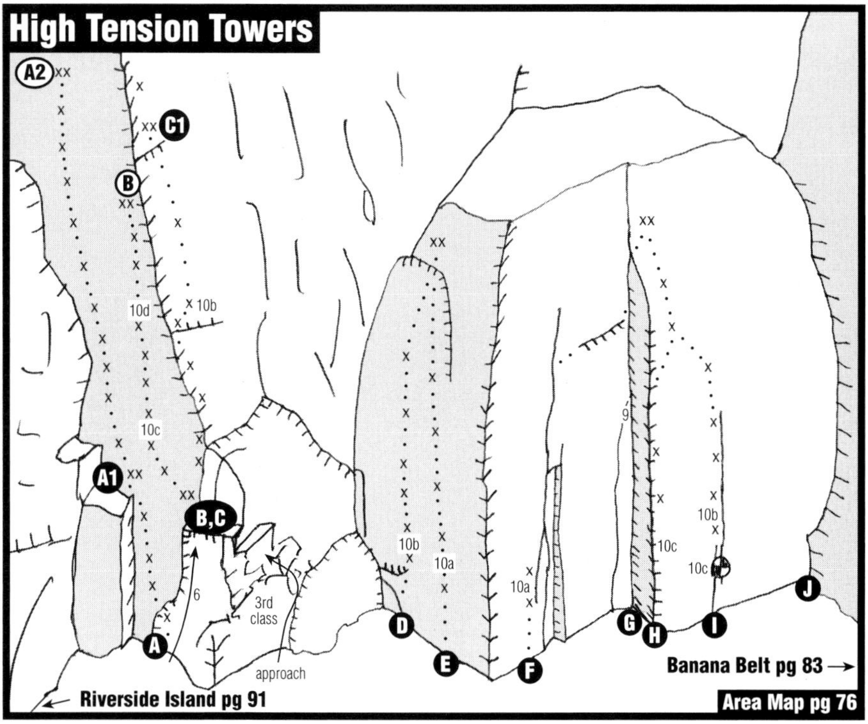

High Tension Towers

Buttress on the east side behind a transmission tower.

A. Sparky Does Power Tower 10b***

Pitch 1: 7*. 4 bolts. Face/dihedral. Climb the 2nd pitch or lower off.

Pitch 2: 10b***. 10 bolts. Climb the vertical face past three bulges. Lower off.

Can be done as one 35m/115' pitch.

FA: Jacques Rutschman, Laurie Chow, 3/1999, TD.

B. Brothers in Arms 10d****

8 bolts. Exposed vertical face, a little sporty. Lower off.

FA: Joe Rousek, Gary Slate, Tony Puppo, Marty Lewis, Dave Focardi, 1989, GU.

C. Scorpion 10b***

Pitch 1: 10b**. 7 bolts. Crack to arete to roof to face. Climb 2nd pitch or lower off 25m/80' to ledge or lower off 35m/115' to ground.

Pitch 2: 9***. 9 bolts. Exposed arete and slab. 30m/100' lower off to 1st anchor.

FA: Greg Barnes, Barry Hutten, John Aughinbaugh, 4/2001, GU.

D. Hatchett Job 10b**

6 bolts. Face. Lower off.

FA: Dave Hatchett, 1991, TD.

E. Black Chicks in Heat 10a***(r)

5 bolts. Technical face. Lower off. ☞ Good route, offensive name.

FA: Kevin Leary, Joe Rousek, 1989, TD.

The next four routes all finish surprisingly close to a high voltage power line. If you are an excellent conductor you may want to avoid these routes.

F. Just Under the Wire 10a**

2 bolts, gear to 2.5". A tricky slab leads to a finger crack, then traverse right to a dihedral. Lower off.

FA: Tony Puppo, Richard Leversee, 1989, GU.

G. Electric Kachina 9***

Gear to 3". Steep crack in a corner, awkward and physical. Lower off.

FA: Mike Strassman, Moira Smith, 1990, GU.

H. Double Insulated 10c*(r)

4 bolts, gear to 2". Arete. Lower off.

FA: Richard Leversee, Tony Puppo, 1989, GU.

I. C.L.O.T. 10c***

7 bolts. A bouldery start up a tenuous seam to finish on face. Lower off.

FA: Tony Puppo, Richard Leversee, 1989, GU.

J. Peligro 6•

Gear to 2". Brushy loose dihedral. Unknown anchor.

FA: Mike Strassman, 1990, GU.

©2005 Maximus Press. *Marty Lewis Photo.*

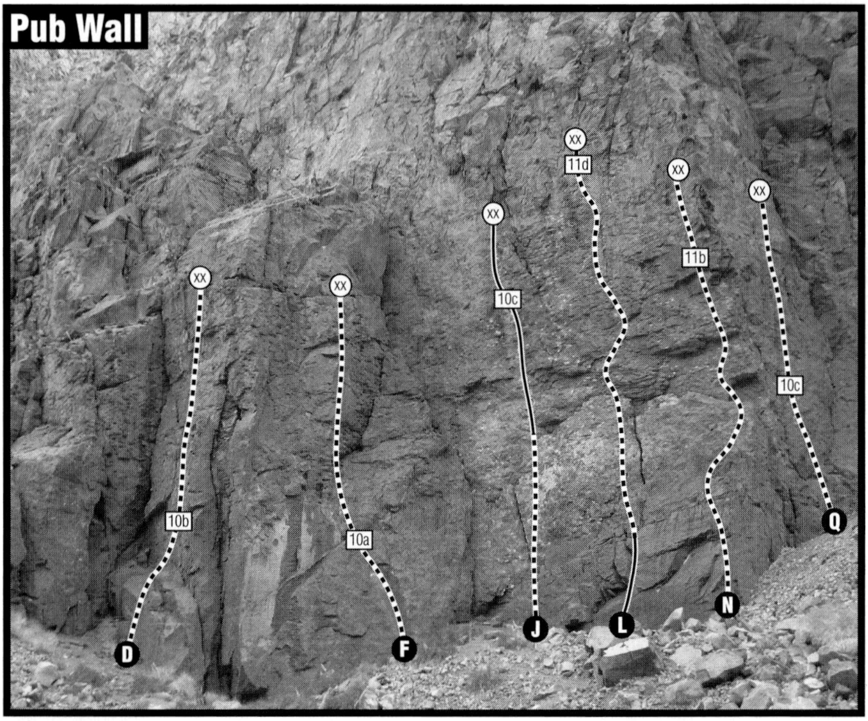

©2005 Maximus Press. *Marty Lewis Topo.*

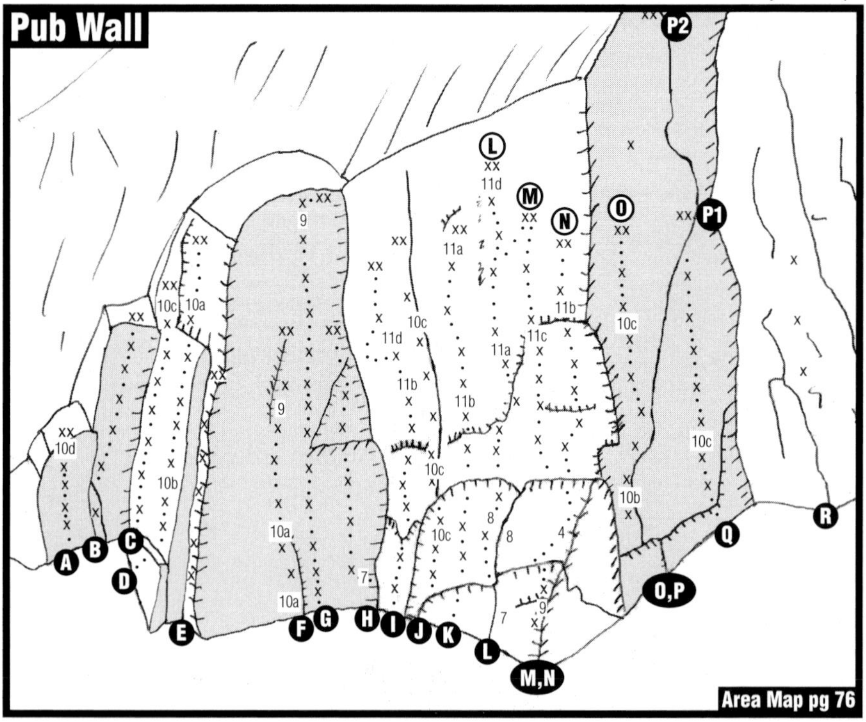

Pub Wall

A large buttress on the west side, below power lines. A great collection of gently overhanging 5.11's. The main wall was the sight of frequent accidents when belayers dropped their partners! Now that most people carry longer ropes the problem has been alleviated.

A. Wonderbar 10d**

4 bolts. Sustained little face. Lower off.
FA: Tony Puppo, Grant Schumacher, 6/1992, TD.

B. Alotarot 11a•

6 bolts. Climb the loose and chossy blunt arete. Lower off.

C. Somerot 10c*

7 bolts. Face. Lower off.

D. Gary Gray 10b***

7 bolts. Technical face to juggy roof. Lower off.
FA: Mike Strassman, Paul Linaweaver, Scott Ayers, Austin Hearst, 9/1991, TD.

E. Gringuita 13a**

5 bolts. Arete. Lower off. ☞ A long-standing open project finally sent.
FA: Kevin Thaw, 1999, TD.

F. Abitarot 10a****

6 bolts. A bouldery dihedral leads to a killer jug haul, kind of sporty. Lower off. ☞ Once known for "a bit of rot", this route has really cleaned up nicely.
FA: Joe Rousek, 10/1990, GU.

G. Abitafun 9****

13 bolts. Face climbing leads to a steep headwall, finish in a bulging corner. 32.5m/105' lower off.
FA: John Hoffman, Annie Hoffman, Jock VanPatten, 5/2005, TD.

H. Not Too Stout 7**

5 bolts. Face. Lower off.
FA: Todd Graham, 4/2002, GU.

I. Homebrew 11b*** or 11d***

9 bolts. Gently overhanging face. Going left at the 8th bolt is 11b, going straight up is 11d. Lower off.
FA: Marty Lewis, Fred Berman, 3/1993, TD.

J. Hardly Wallbanger 10c*****

9 bolts. Face to crack, sustained, the steepest 10c in the Gorge. 27.5m/90' lower off. ☞ First led onsight on gear. Please feel free to emulate the challenge (use the wide crack left of the first 3 bolts). Keep in mind that if it wasn't for the traffic caused by the bolts this would be a loose dangerous chosspile.
FA: Bruce Lella, Marty Lewis, Fred Berman, 11/1992, GU.

K. Hungover 11b*****

8 bolts. Face to roof to steep face. 27.5m/90' lower off.
FA: Gary Slate, Charlie Johnson, Marty Lewis, 5/1991, GU.

L. High Ball 11d****

10 bolts. Steep flake to face. 30m/100' lower off.
FA: Todd Graham, Bruce Lella, 6/1991, TD.

High Sobriety Variation: 11a****. Go right at the 8th bolt to the anchors of *Menace to Sobriety*. 27.5m/90' lower off.

The following two routes can be started either by climbing a 5.7 wide crack then moving right up 4th class ledges, or by a bolted start at the toe of the buttress.

M. Menace to Sobriety 11c****

8 bolts. Steep face to a small roof. 27.5m/90' lower off.
FA: Eric Kohl, 7/1995, TD. New start: John Hoffman.

N. Hammered 11b****

8 bolts. Steep, exposed, pumpy jug hauling through roofs. 27.5m/90' lower off.
FA: Fred Berman, Marty Lewis, 3/1992, TD. New start: John Hoffman.

O. Set Free 10c***

8 bolts. Seam to exposed bulge. Lower off.
FA: Tony Puppo, Joe Rousek. 2/1994, TD.

P. Tempest 10b**

Pitch 1: 10b**. 4 bolts, gear to 2.5". Climb the seam past 4 bolts, then move right up the crack. Climb the 2nd pitch or lower off. ☞ Originally a gear lead with tricky pro, the bolts were added to facilitate the route *Set Free*, please feel free to skip them.

Pitch 2: 10a*. Gear to 2.5". Crack. Lower off.
FA: Tony Puppo, Joe Rousek, 1989, GU.

Q. Light Within 10c*****

7 bolts. Sustained vertical face, clipping the 1st bolt can be reachy. Lower off.
FA: Joe Rousek, Gary Slate, Jim Stimson, 11/1990, TD.

R. Open Project

3 bolts. On the tower right of *Light Within*.
P: Joe Rousek.

John Bachar on **Hard Copy** 12a*** at the Riverside Island. ©*John McDonald Photo.* **See Page 91**

Jason Lakey on **Feudal Beerlords** 10d**** at the Social Platform. ©*Shawn Reeder Photo.* See Page 95

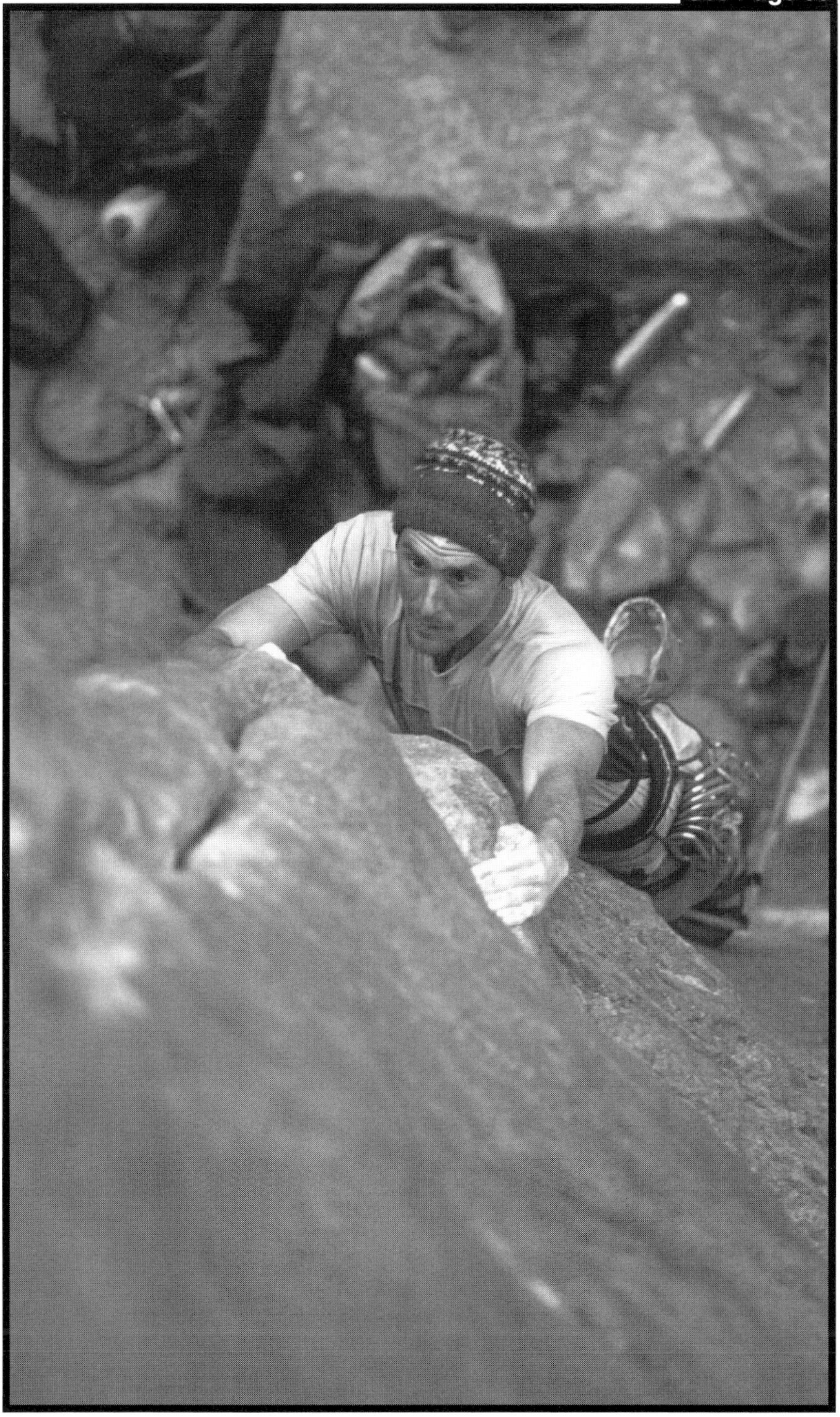

©2005 Maximus Press. *Marty Lewis Photo.*

©2005 Maximus Press. *Marty Lewis Topo.*

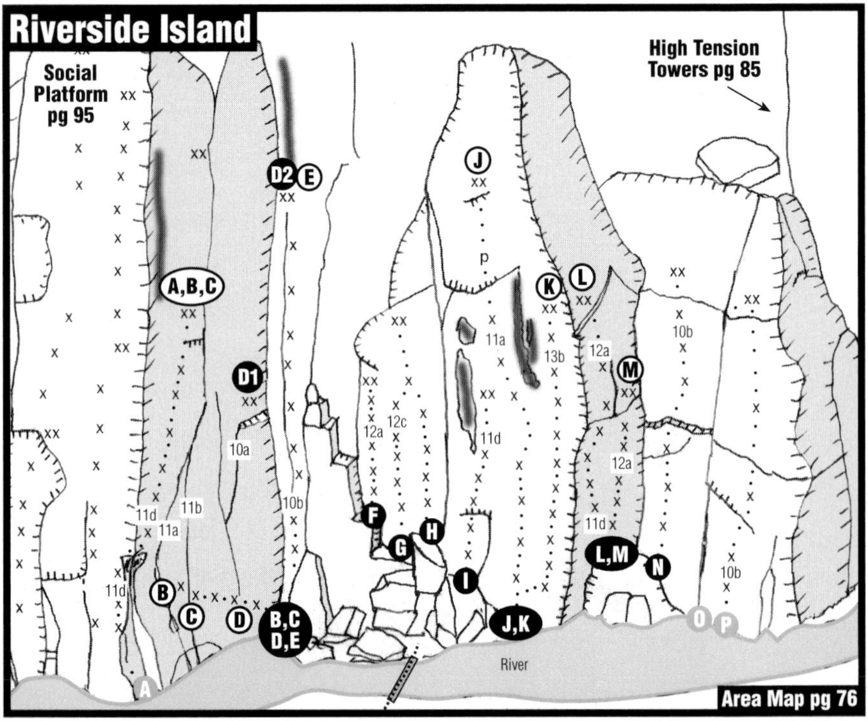

Riverside Island

Monolithic towers on the east side right on the river.

A. Unbearable Lightness of Beans 11d***

Flooded. 9 bolts. Seam to off-vertical face. Lower off.
FA: Bruce Lella, Todd Graham, 1990, TD.

B. Noble Mouse 11a**

5 bolts, gear to 2.5". Traverse left past bolts to the left vertical thin crack. Lower off. ☞ After the base of this route was flooded the traverse was added.
FA: Bruce Lella, Gary Slate, 1990, GU.
Traverse bolts: Greg Barnes, Karin Wuhrmann.

C. King Rat 11b***

5 bolts, gear to 2.5". Traverse left past bolts to the right vertical thin crack. Lower off. ☞ After the base of this route was flooded the traverse was added.
FA: Jay Smith, Joe Bentley, 6/1989, GU.
Traverse bolts: Greg Barnes, Karin Wuhrmann.

D. Ratso 10a*

Pitch 1: 10a**. 2 bolts, gear to 2". Crack. Climb 2nd pitch or lower off.
Pitch 2: 10a*. Gear to 2". Dihedral. Lower off.
Can be done as one 30m/100' pitch.
FA: Jay Smith, Joe Bentley, 6/1989, GU.
Traverse bolts: Greg Barnes, Karin Wuhrmann.

E. Old & in the Way 10b**

9 bolts. Thin crack along a dihedral. 30m/100' lower off. ☞ Thinking they were doing a first ascent this gear climb was inadvertently retrobolted.
FA: Bruce Lella, Mike Carr, 1990, GU. Retrobolts: Alan Hirahara, Joe Rousek.

F. Me So Horny 12a***

5 bolts. Small positive edges up a vertical face. Lower off.
FA: John Bachar, Rick Cashner, 1989, GU.

G. Skin Tight 12c***

6 bolts. Vertical face. Lower off.
FA: John Bachar, 1989, GU.

H. Going Back to Cali 12a**

5 bolts. Face to offwidth, then back left. Lower off.
FA: Steve Schneider, 1990, GU.

I. Oceanside 11d***

5 bolts. Crimpy technical face. Lower off.
➤ Photo this page.
FA: Tom Herbert, Sondra Utterback, 11/1990, TD.

J. Malibu 11a***(r)

7 bolts, 1 piton, optional gear: 3" piece. Sporty face. 35m/115' lower off.
FA: Jay Smith, Bob Gaines, Joe Bentley, 6/1989, GU.

K. Conquistadors Without Swords 13b***

10 bolts. Face to steep headwall. The base is flooded; start on *Malibu* then go right. Lower off.
FA: Tom Herbert, 1990, TD.

The next three routes were once quite popular. At this point in time one must wade to get to them.

L. Embrace This 12a***

7 bolts. Vertical arete to slabby crux. Lower off.
FA: Tom Herbert, Bruce Pottenger, Bob Gaines, 1/1990, TD.

M. Hard Copy 12a***

5 bolts. Continuous steep edging. Lower off.
➤ Photo page 88.
FA: Tom Herbert, 11/1989, TD.

N. George Bush 10b****

6 bolts. Vertical face. Lower off.
FA: Bob Gaines, Bruce Pottenger, 5/1989, GU.

O. Barbara Bush 8*

Flooded. Gear to 4". Wide crack, then move right to belay of *Right Wing*. Lower off.
FA: Bruce Pottenger, Tom Kleinfelter, 6/1989, GU.

P. Right Wing 10b**

Flooded. 4 bolts, gear: 1.25" piece. Face. Lower off.
FA: Bob Gaines, Bruce Pottenger, 6/1989, GU.

Mark Blanchard on **Oceanside** 11d***.
©Marty Lewis Photo.

Sylvia Mireles on **Darshan** 12b***** at the Social Platform. ©*Greg Epperson Photo.*

See Page 95

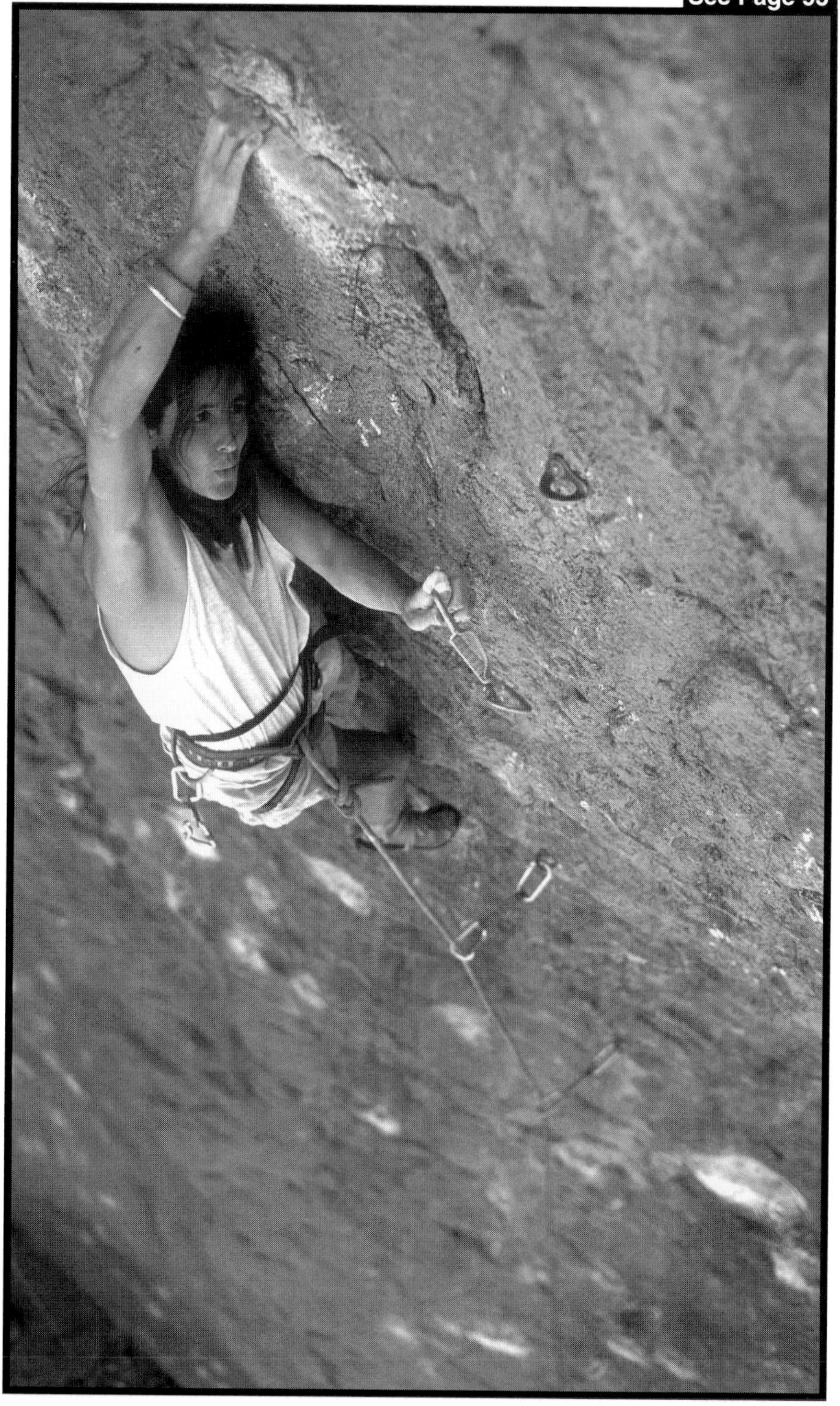

Joi Gallant on **Nirvana** 10a*** at the Social Platform. ©*Shawn Reeder Photo.* **See Page 95**

©2005 Maximus Press. *Marty Lewis Photo.*

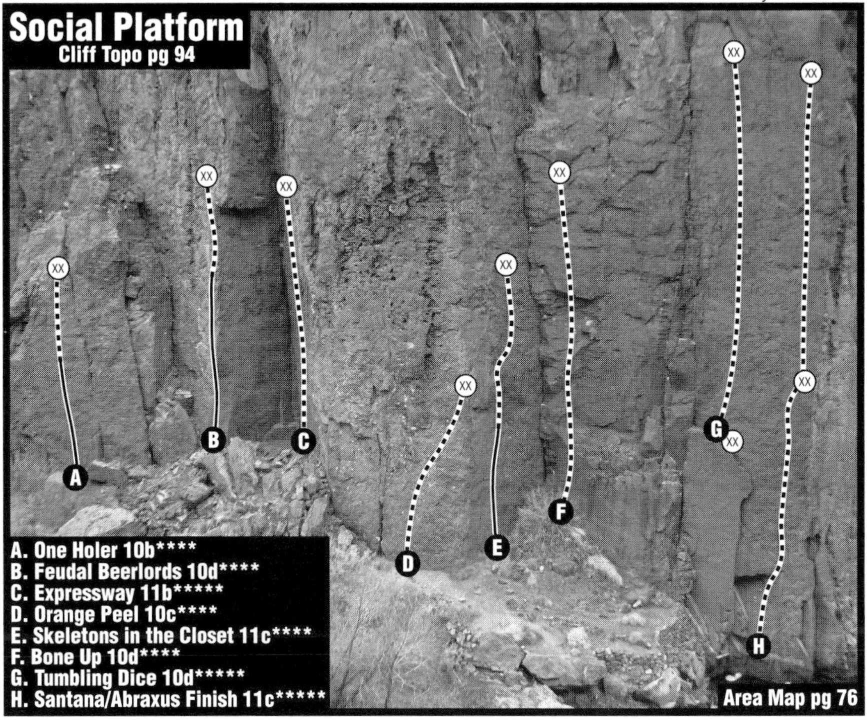

©2005 Maximus Press. *Marty Lewis Topo.*

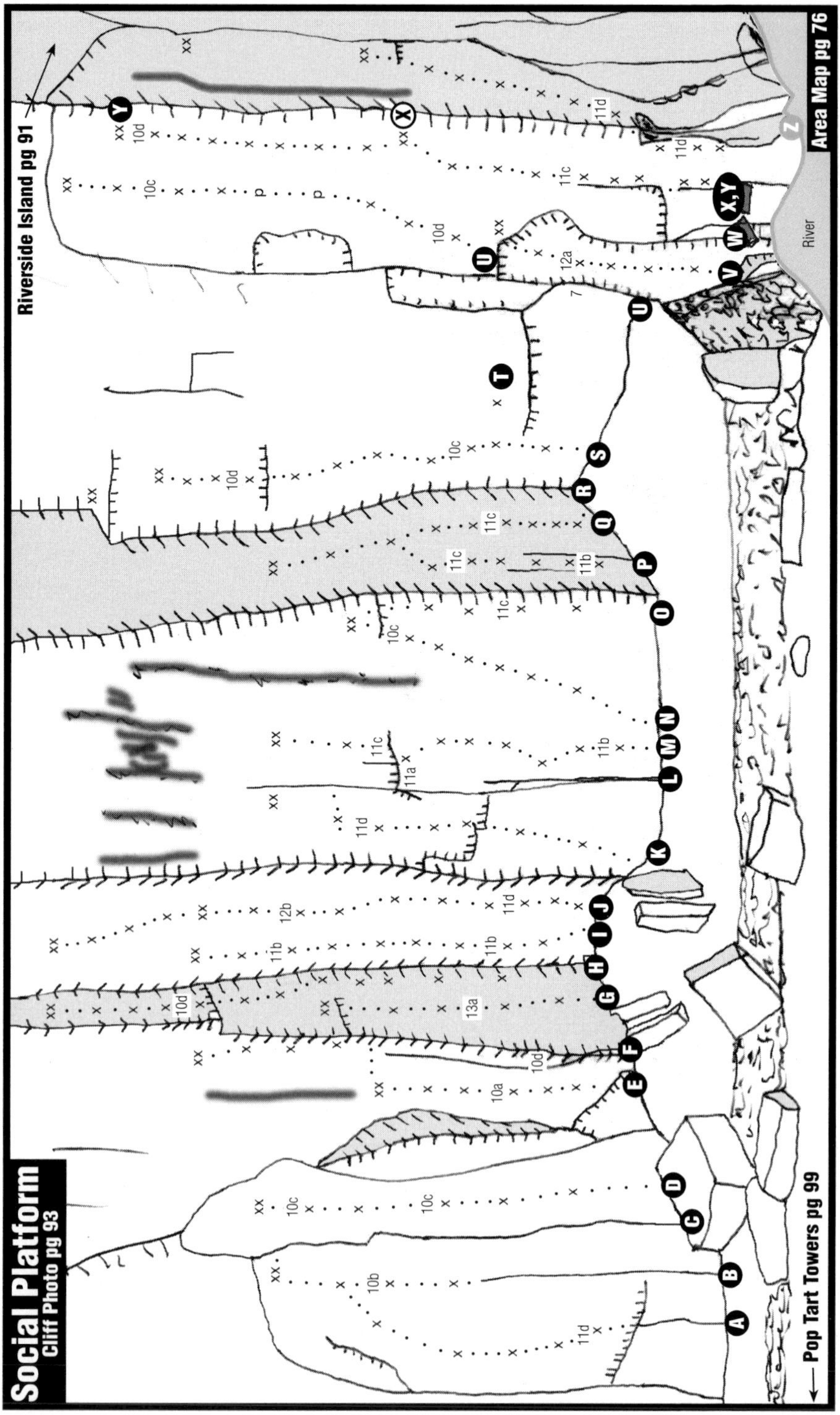

Social Platform

The towers above a platform built of stones on the east side. A popular spot.

A. Unrepentant Sinner 11d**(r)
6 bolts, gear to 2.5". Roof to face. Lower off.
FA: Kevin Leary, Joe Rousek, 1989, TD.

B. One Holer 10b****
3 bolts, gear to 1". Vertical thin crack to face, sustained with tricky gear placements. Lower off.
FA: Tony Puppo, Bruce Pottenger, Joe Rousek, 4/1989, TD.

C. Butterknife 8***
Gear to 5". Wide crack. Lower off.
FA: Tony Puppo, Bruce Pottenger, Tom Kleinfelter, 6/1989, GU.

D. Fork it Over 10c**(r)
5 bolts. Face. Lower off.
FA: Bruce Pottenger, Tony Puppo, 7/1989, TD.

E. Nirvana 10a***
5 bolts. Face with flakes. Lower off. ➤ Photo page 93.
FA: Louie Anderson, Ripley Casdorph, 10/1991, GU.

Variation: 10a***. 9 bolts. Climb *Nirvana* then traverse right to the arete and finish on *Feudal Beerlords*, be mindful of rope drag.

F. Feudal Beerlords 10d****
3 bolts, gear to 2.5". Sustained awkward finger crack on an arete, then continue on face. Lower off. ➤ Photo page 89.
FA: Todd Vogel, Fred Lifton, Chris Iverson, 1989, GU.

G. Roadkill 13a**(r)
4 bolts. Face with micro holds, poorly bolted. Lower off.
FA: Tom Herbert, Tom Kleinfelter, 1990, TD.

H. Offramp 10d***
11 bolts. Chimney to roof. 35m/115' lower off.
FA: Bruce Lella, Rob Stockstill, 6/1995, TD.

I. Expressway 11b*****
8 bolts. Technical edging to a pumpy bulge, polished and slippery. Lower off.
FA: Tom Herbert, Sean Greer, Todd Vogel, 6/1990, TD.

J. Darshan aka Ripoff 12b*****
9 bolts. Technical edging to a pumpy bulge. Lower off. ☞ A climber proudly called this route *Ripoff* after stealing this project. ➤ Photo page 92.
FA(Aid): Gary Slate, Joe Rousek, Kevin Leary, 10/1989, GU. FA(Free): Stolen.

K. Ned Guy's Proud Pearl Necklace 11d****
6 bolts. Face through a roof to a technical section into a giant jug, then traverse right to a crack. Lower off. ☞ A few bolts were moved, making this a much better climb.
FA: Mark Blanchard, Bill McChesney, 1990, GU. Realignment: Todd Graham.

L. Spinal Fracture 11a***
Gear to 2". Steep thin crack. Lower off.
FA: Jay Smith, Joe Bentley, 6/1989, GU.

M. Chillin' at the Grill 11c***
8 bolts. A nebulous start leads to technical face followed by a committing bulge. Lower off.
FA: Erik Eriksson, Bill McChesney, Bill Russell, 1990, GU.

N. Orange Peel 10c****
6 bolts. Slippery edging up an off-vertical face. Lower off. ☞ Known as "Banana Peel"—guess why. ➤ Photo page 35.
FA: Joe Rousek, Tony Puppo, 5/1989, GU.

O. Fresh Squeezed 11c*
4 bolts. Arete, a bit contrived, a bit squeezed. Lower off.
FA: Tom Herbert, Tom Kleinfelter, Bruce Pottenger, 4/1990, TD.

P. Skeletons in the Closet 11c****
8 bolts. Technical seam to a tricky bulge. Lower off.
FA(Aid): Mike Strassman, Tony Puppo, Tom Kleinfelter, 1989, TD. FA(Free): Stolen.

Q. Scrutinized 11c***
8 bolts. Vertical face. Lower off.
FA: Marty Lewis, Scott Ayers, 2/1991, TD.

R. Book of Bones 9*
Gear to 5". Loose dihedral. 35m/115' lower off.
FA: Mike Strassman, Chris Lindel, 1989, GU.

S. Bone Up 10d****
10 bolts. Technical face to a crank through a roof. 27.5m/90' lower off.
FA: Mike Strassman, Paul Linaweaver, 9/1991, TD.

T. Open Project
1 bolt. Face.
FA: Bruce Lella.

U. Tumbling Dice 10d*****(r)
Climb a 5.7 dihedral to a ledge with a belay to approach this climb. 6 bolts, 2 pitons, gear to 1". Incredible stimulating face. 30m/100' lower off to ledge.
FA: Kevin Leary, Joe Rousek, Tony Puppo, 1989, GU.

V. Return to Forever 12a**
5 bolts. Thin off-vertical face. Lower off.
FA: Kevin Leary, 8/1989, TD.

W. Hotcake Flake 10a**
Gear to 6". Start on a wooden platform, climb the dihedral. Lower off.
FA: Hank Levine, 1984, GU.

X. Santana 11c****
8 bolts. Start on a wooden platform, pass a roof to a sustained off-vertical face. Lower off.
FA: Gary Slate, Joe Rousek, 3/1990, TD.

Y. Abraxas Finish 11c*****
16 bolts. Exposed vertical face continuation of *Santana*. 27.5m/90' rappel to the *Hotcake Flake* belay.
Can be broken into two pitches.
FA: Perry Beckham, Becky Bates, 1994, TD.

Z. Unbearable Lightness of Beans 11d***
Flooded. 9 bolts. Seam to off-vertical face. Lower off.
FA: Bruce Lella, Todd Graham, 1990, TD.

©2005 Maximus Press. *Marty Lewis Photo.*

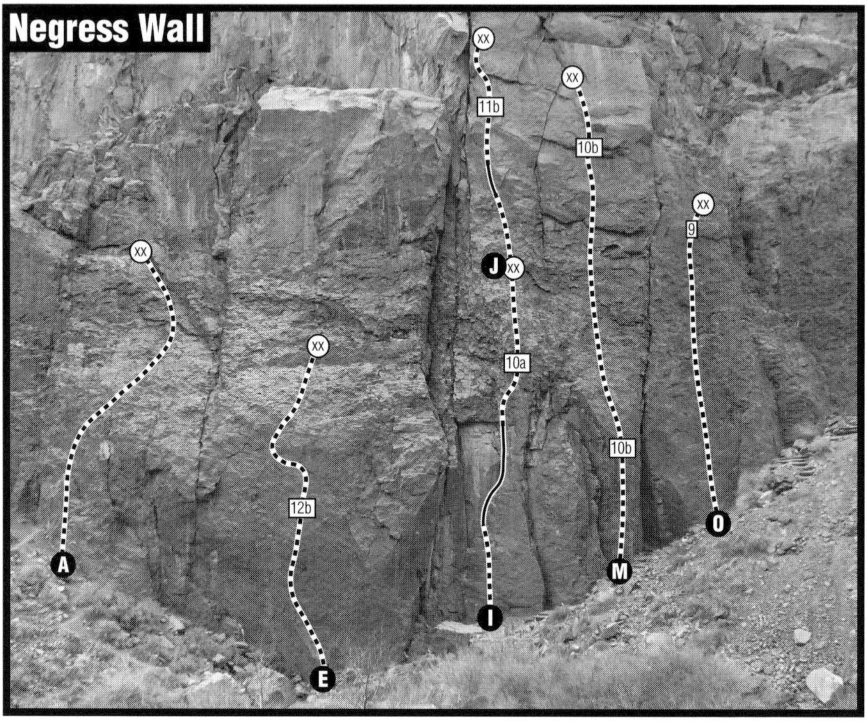

©2005 Maximus Press. *Marty Lewis Topo.*

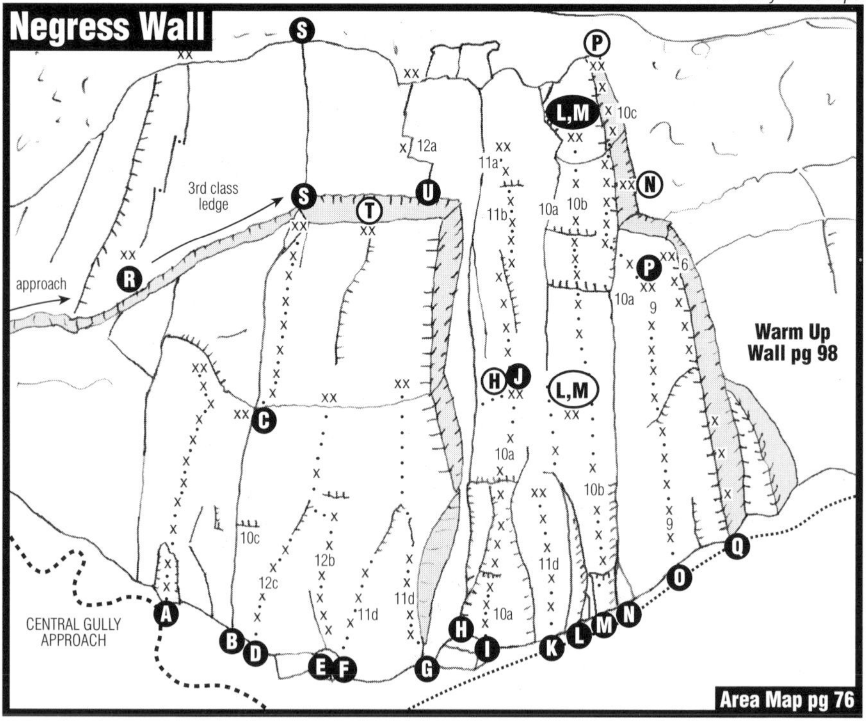

Negress Wall

A polished dark wall on the west side right above the toilet.

A. Imprisoned Behind Lies 6***

10 bolts. Pillar to face. Lower off.
FA: Greg Barnes, Barry Hutten, 3/1997, TD.

B. Black Ice 10c***

Gear to 1.5". Slick thin crack. Lower off.
FA: Tony Puppo, Joe Rousek, 1989, GU.

C. Sidewinder 9**

7 bolts. Face. Lower off.
FA: Kelly Cordner, Alan Hirahara, 5/1997, TD.

D. Smoothie 12c**

5 bolts, optional gear: 1.25" piece. Teflon face. Lower off.
FA: Tom Herbert, 1991, TD.

E. Malcolm X 12b***

7 bolts. Off-vertical face, so thin. Lower off.
FA: Erik Eriksson, John Bachar, Bill McChesney, 1992, GU.

F. Broken Battery 11d**

3 bolts, gear to 2". Face to flakes. Lower off.
FA: John Bachar, 1989, GU.

G. Chocolate City 11d**

4 bolts, gear to 1.5". Arete to crack. Lower off.
FA: Scott Cole, Bill Russell, 1990, GU.

H. Botswana Baby 9*

Gear to 2.5". Finger crack in a dihedral, then traverse right to the belay of *Fear of a Black Planet*. Lower off.
FA: Wendy Borgerd, Phil Green, 8/1989, GU.

I. Fear of a Black Planet 10a***

9 bolts. Bouldery face leads to a steep dihedral, then pass a bulge. 27.5m/90' lower off. ☞ Also a ground-breaking 1990 release from the hip-hop band Public Enemy. What's the flavor Flavor Flav?
FA: Kevin Calder, Marty Lewis, 10/1991, TD.

J. James Brown 11b****

9 bolts. Killer flake to tenuous slab climbing. Lower off. ☞ The "Wheat Thin" of the Gorge.
FA: Marty Lewis, Dave Focardi, Kevin Calder, 2/1992, TD.

Fear of a Black Planet/James Brown Link-up: 11b****. 19 bolts. Be mindful of rope drag.

K. Mandela 11d*

4 bolts. Contrived face, the further left you move the easier it gets. Lower off.
FA: Louie Anderson, Chris Murray, 4/1992, TD.

L. Z Dong 10a****

1 bolt, gear to 2.5". Climb a short dihedral, pass a bolt to an easy runout face, then climb an awesome right leaning rattly finger crack. Two single rope rappels or a 37.5m/125' rappel.
Can be broken into two pitches.
FA: Joe Rousek, Tony Puppo, 1989, GU.

Variation: Approach by climbing either *Fear of a Black Planet* or *Ambassadors of Funk*, then enter the crack, avoiding the runout face.

M. Ambassadors of Funk 10b****

11 bolts. Blunt arete to face through roofs. Two single rope rappels or a 37.5m/125' rappel.
Can be broken into two pitches.
FA: Marty Lewis, Fred Berman, Todd Vogel, 3/1992, TD.

N. Sweet & Sour 10a**

Gear to 3.5". Dihedral that seams out at the top. 30m/100' lower off.
FA: Joe Rousek, Kevin Leary, 1989, GU.

O. Welcome to the Gorge 9***

9 bolts. Wandering slippery climbing leads to great edges up a face. Lower off.
FA: Scott Ayers, Eden Masters, Elizabeth Gorin, 1992, GU.

P. Pulp Friction 10c**

9 bolts. Cross *Sweet & Sour* then climb the slab to an arete. Lower off.
FA: Kelly Cordner, Randy Jacobs, 4/1997, TD.

Q. Clip Jr. 6****

7 bolts. Pillar to arete. Lower off.
FA: Kelly Cordner, Briant Phillips, Scott Ayers, 4/1997, TD.

R. Under the Knife aka Sport This A3****

Gear to 1", knifeblades. Nail up the seams. 27.5m/90' lower off. ☞ Whatever guy.
FA: Mike McGrale, Jeff Snedden, 1992, GU.

S. Mouth T. Dung 10c*

Gear to 2". Crack. Gear anchor, walk off left.
FA: Bill Kerwin, Andy Selters, 1990, GU.

T. Project

Anchor.

U. Z Crack 12a*

1 bolt, gear to 4". The Z shaped crack. Lower off.
FA: Steve Schneider, Doug Englekirk, 1990, GU.

©2005 Maximus Press. *Marty Lewis Photo.*

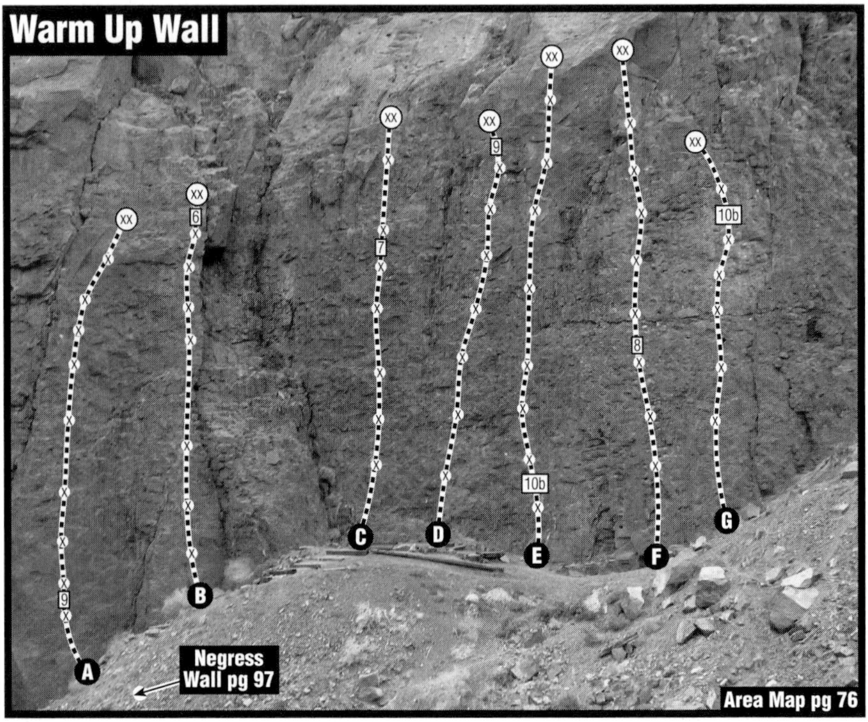

Warm Up Wall

Small dark wall on the west side, up and right from the Negress Wall. Please use the excellent stepped trail that leads up from the Negress Wall to get here.

A. Welcome to the Gorge 9***

9 bolts. Wandering slippery climbing leads to great edges up a face. Lower off.

FA: Scott Ayers, Eden Masters, Elizabeth Gorin, 1992, GU.

B. Clip Jr. 6****

7 bolts. Pillar to arete. Lower off.

FA: Kelly Cordner, Briant Phillips, Scott Ayers, 4/1997, TD.

Because the ground has eroded quite badly, the following three routes all had new first bolts added for safety reasons. Please feel free to skip these bolts if you find this disturbing.

C. High Seas 7****

7 bolts. Vertical face. Lower off. ☞ Originally a very runout gear climb.

FA: Jay Smith, Bruce Pottenger, 6/1989, GU. Retrobolts: Marty Lewis.

D. Crowd Pleaser 9****

7 bolts. Sustained vertical face. Lower off.

FA: Gary Slate, Marty Lewis, 10/1990, GU.

E. Humbly, Mumbly, Jumbly 10b****

8 bolts. A bouldery start leads to a vertical face. Lower off.

FA: John Hartman, Merlin Fortner, Mike Thompson, 1990, GU.

F. Babushka 8*****

8 bolts. Varied vertical face. Lower off.

FA: Valerie Busch, Todd Graham, 1992, TD.

G. What Up? 10b**

6 bolts. Face to bulge. Lower off.

FA: Kelly Cordner, Jonathen Hartnett, Randy Jacobs, 4/1997, TD.

©2005 Maximus Press. *Marty Lewis Photo.*

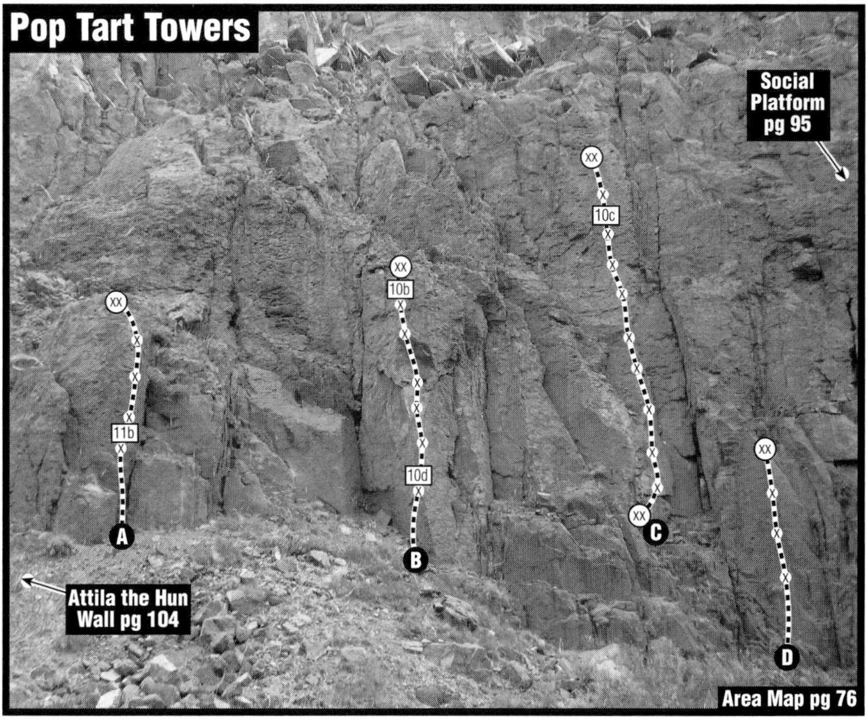

Scott Cole on the first ascent of **Kinder Gentler Arete** 10d**. ©*Marty Lewis Photo.*

Pop Tart Towers

Aretes and small pinnacle on the east side above a concrete sluice.

A. Pop Tart 11b**

4 bolts. Arete. Lower off.

FA: Tom Herbert, T.M. Herbert, Tony Puppo, Sondra Utterback, 11/1989, TD.

B. Kinder Gentler Arete 10d**

6 bolts. Arete. Lower off. ➤ Photo facing page.

FA: Scott Cole, Marty Lewis, 4/1990, GU.

C. That's a Cold Shut, Darlin' 10c***

9 bolts. Face. Lower off.

FA: Kelly Cordner, Urmas Franosch, 5/1997, TD.

D. 3.B.A. 11c*

3 bolts. Arete. Lower off.

FA: Jeff Schoen, Tom Kleinfelter, 1990, GU.

Sylvia Mireles on **Crybaby** 12c**** at the Faulty Tower. ©*Greg Epperson Photo.* **See Page 103**

Karine Croft on **From Chocolate to Morphine** 11d*****. ©*Greg Epperson Photo.* **See Page 103**

©2005 Maximus Press. *Marty Lewis Photo.*

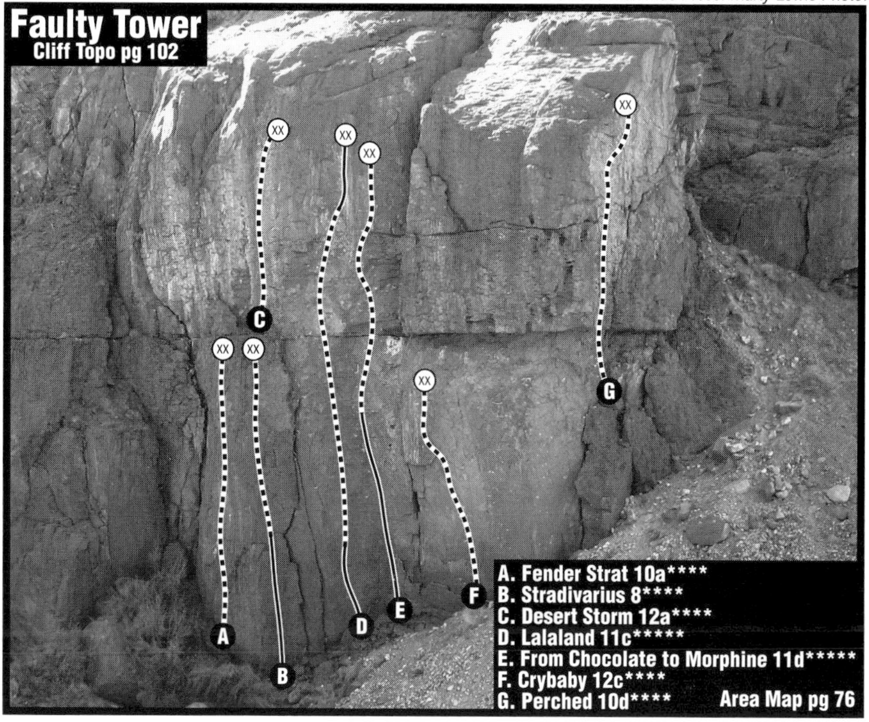

©2005 Maximus Press. *Marty Lewis Topo.*

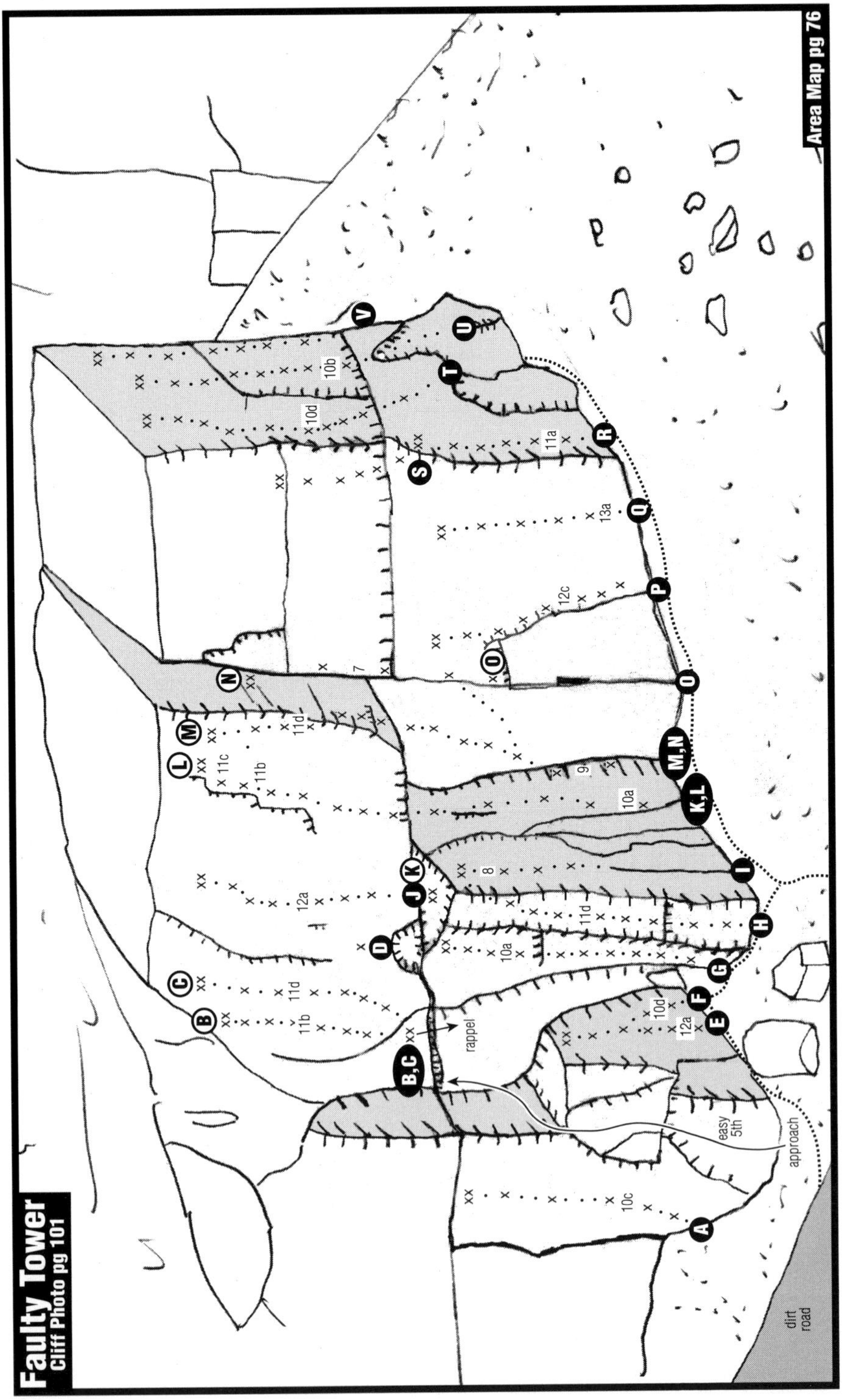

Faulty Tower

A large buttress on the west side.

A. Solito 10c**
5 bolts. Face. Lower off.
FA: Kelly Cordner, 5/1997, TD.

The following three routes are approached via an easy 5th class scramble to a ledge. Descend by a single rope rappel.

B. Baby Duck 11b***
6 bolts. Steep jugs to a technical face. Lower off.
FA: Tom Herbert, Sondra Utterback, 4/1991, TD.

C. Free Falling 11d***
6 bolts. Steep face. Lower off.
FA: Tom Herbert, Sondra Utterback, 4/1991, TD.

D. Open Project
1 bolt.
P: Tom Herbert.

E. Forkash and Riches 12a**
5 bolts. Face. Lower off.
FA: Mike Forkash, Kelly Cordner, Matt Ciancio, 10/2000, TD.

F. Finger Food 10d*
4 bolts. Face. Lower off.
FA: Kelly Cordner, Matt Ciancio, 5/1997, TD.

G. Fender Strat 10a****
9 bolts. Vertical face to bulge. Lower off.
FA: Kelly Cordner, 5/1997, TD.

H. Sly Little Fart Blaster 11d**
8 bolts. Vertical face, then go right across the arete to the *Stradivarius* anchor. Lower off.
FA: Wendy Borgerd, 5/1996, TD.

I. Stradivarius 8****
3 bolts, gear to 2.5". Hand crack to face. Lower off.
FA: Phil Green, Wendy Borgerd, 7/1989, GU. Retrobolts: Marty Lewis.

J. Desert Storm 12a****
Approach via *Fender Strat* or *Stradivarius.* 6 bolts. Gently overhanging sustained exposed face. Lower off.
FA: Tom Herbert, 4/1991, TD.

K. Slot Machine 10a*
2 bolts, gear to 2". Climb the finger crack then finish up a rotten chimney. 25m/80' rappel off ledge. ☞ To facilitate the sport climb *Lalaland* two bolts were added. Please feel free to skip them.
FA: Phil Green, Wendy Borgerd, 1989, GU.

L. Lalaland 11c*****
12 bolts. Start the crack, step right on to a slab, face climb, then attack the overhanging dihedral, sustained and strenuous. 35m/115' lower off.
FA: Peter Croft, Marty Lewis, Dayle Mazzarella, 9/1999, GU.

Variation: 11b*****. 10 bolts. Climb *Lalaland* but go right at the 10th bolt to a jug, then finish on *From Chocolate to Morphine*, the last bit is a little sporty. 35m/115' lower off.

M. From Chocolate to Morphine 11d*****
13 bolts. Start in a dihedral, then face climb up and right to a roof, pass this, continue up steep jugs, then move left around the arete to a beautiful gold headwall. 35m/115' lower off.
➤ Photo page 101.
FA: Fred Berman, Bruce Lella, 7/1991, GU.

N. From Chocolate to Chossman 9**
6 bolts, optional gear. Start *From Chocolate to Morphine*, but go right at the 3rd bolt to a dihedral. 30m/100' lower off.

O. Ballet Recital 10b•
Gear to 3.5". Loose wide crack through a bulge. Lower off a one bolt anchor. ☞ If you climb 35' then lower off one bolt, is it a route or a failed attempt?
FA: Mike Strassman, Dan McConnell, 1989, GU.

Variation: 10b*. 4 bolts, gear to 3.5". Start *Ballet Recital* but continue up the dihedral until reaching a proper anchor. 30m/100' lower off.

P. Crybaby 12c****
7 bolts. A reachy bouldery move leads to a strenuous lieback. Lower off. ➤ Photo page 100.
FA: Tom Herbert, Joe Rousek, 11/1989, TD.

Q. Desire 13a**
4 bolts, stick clip. Intense bouldering leads to a steep face. Lower off.
FA: Tom Herbert, 11/1989, TD.

R. Crash Landing 11a***
5 bolts. Bouldery start followed by cool edges up the arete. Lower off.
FA: Tom Herbert, Tony Puppo, 11/1989, TD.

S. Project
5 bolts. Future continuation of *Crash Landing*.
P: Mike Cann, Dennis Jensen.

T. Perched 10d****
9 bolts. Exposed face to arete, great position. Lower off.
FA: Greg Corliss, Charlie Johnson, Marty Lewis, Bruce Lella, 1992, GU.

U. What's its Face 10b***
7 bolts. Pass a roof then face climbing. Lower off.
FA: Mike Yost, Steve Case, 1992, GU.

V. Double Take 8*
6 bolts. Arete, a little sporty. Lower off.
FA: Charlie Johnson, Mike Yost, 1992, GU.

©2005 Maximus Press. *Marty Lewis Topo.*

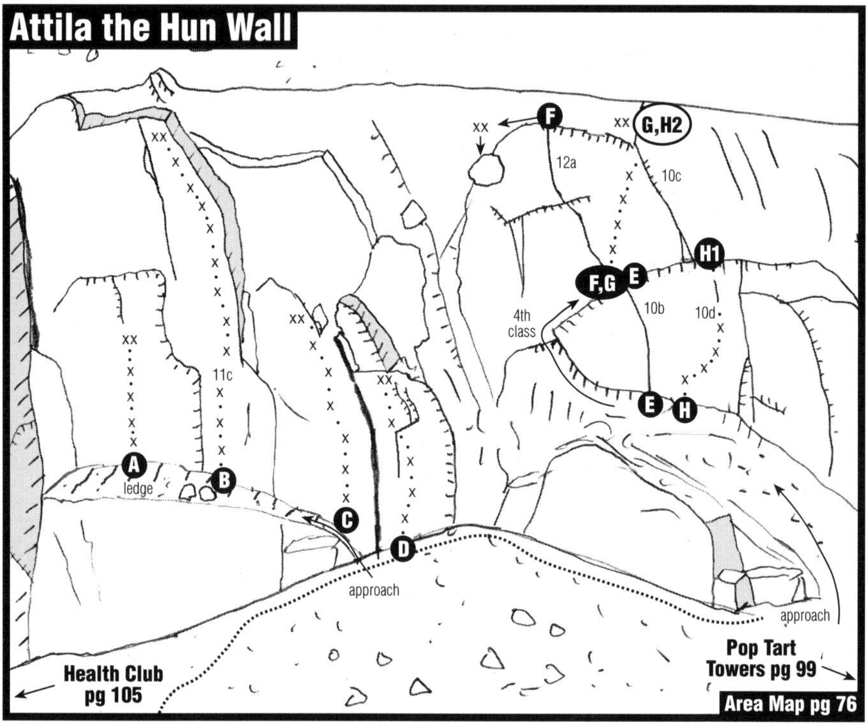

Attila the Hun Wall

Towers and parallel left-leaning cracks high on the east side. Cross the river just north of the Faulty Tower at some large boulders.

A. Sunstroke 9**

4 bolts. Face. Lower off.

FA: Tony Puppo, 1990, GU.

B. Pumpkin 11c****

11 bolts. Vertical face to a sustained arete. 27.5m/90' lower off.

FA: Kelly Cordner, Randy Jacobs, Jonathan Hartnett, Briant Phillips, 4/1997, TD.

C. Helga's Holiday 7**

6 bolts. Face. Lower off.

FA: Judy Rittenhouse, Dave German, 3/2002.

D. Hagar'n'hilti 9**

4 bolts, optional gear: 1.5" piece. Crack and face. Lower off.

FA: Dave German, Judy Rittenhouse, 3/2002.

E. Louisiana Liplock 10b*

Gear to 1.5". Short thin crack. Gear anchor, 4th class scramble off left.

FA: Todd Vogel, Fred Lifton, 1989, GU.

F. White Dwarf 12a***

Gear to 2". Excellent left-leaning finger crack. Gear anchor, traverse left to a belay station, rappel 25m/80'.

FA(Free): Tom Herbert, 1991. FA(Aid): Todd Vogel, Fred Lifton, 1989, GU.

G. Criss Cross 11d**

4 bolts, gear to 1.5". Start the crack then face climb up and right to the other crack. Lower off.

FA: Tom Herbert, 1991, TD.

F. Attila the Hun 10d**

Pitch 1: 10d*(r). 4 bolts, gear to 0.5". Face climbing leads to a hard to protect seam. Gear anchor, climb the 2nd pitch or do a 4th class scramble off left.

FA: Mark Blanchard, Phil Green, 1990, GU.

Pitch 2: 10c***. Gear to 2.5". The quality ever-widening left-leaning crack. Lower off.

FA: Phil Green, Wendy Borgerd, 7/1989, GU.

Can be done as one 25m/80' pitch.

©2005 Maximus Press. *Marty Lewis Topo.*

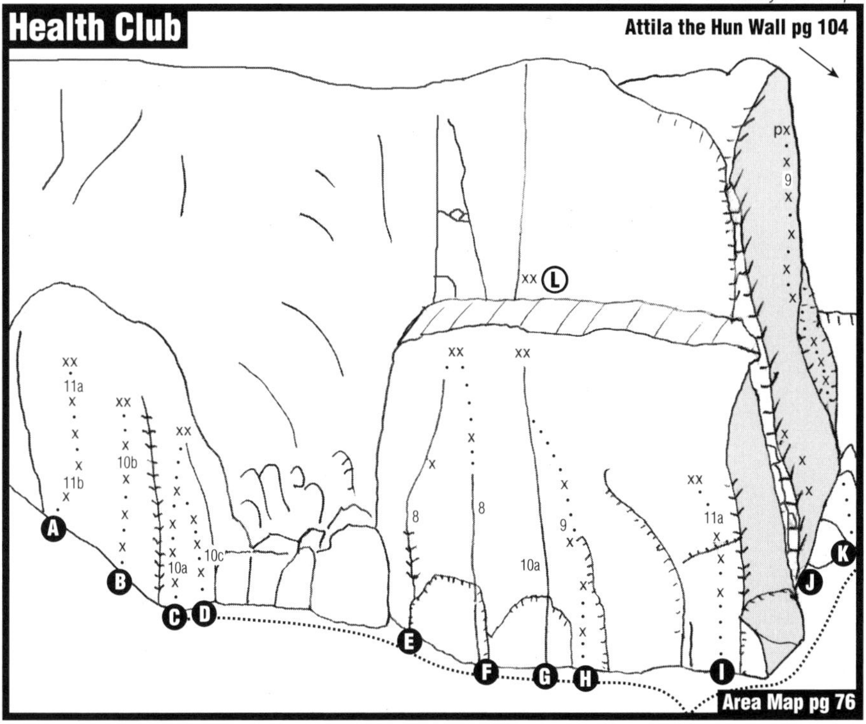

Health Club

Clean buttress on the east side. Cross the river just north of the Faulty Tower at some large boulders.

A. Flush Twice, L.A. Needs the Water 11b**

4 bolts. Face, bouldery start, exciting finish. Lower off.
FA: Scott Cole, Bill McChesney, 2/1990, GU.

B. Start Me Up 10b**

4 bolts. Vertical face. Lower off.
FA: Joe Rousek, Tony Puppo, 1989, TD.

C. Scrotal Hotpack 10a***

4 bolts. Nice face on awesome rock. Lower off.
FA: Todd Vogel, Fred Lifton, 1989, GU.

D. Scrotal Squeeze 10c*

4 bolts. Squeezed in face. Lower off.
FA: Todd Vogel, Dave Focardi, 1990, TD.

E. Health Club 8**

1 bolt, gear to 1.5". Seam. Lower off.
FA: Todd Vogel, Fred Lifton, 1989, GU.

F. Center Court 8*

1 bolt, gear to 1.5". Crack to face. Lower off.
FA: Dave Focardi, Grant Schumacher, Todd Vogel, 5/1990, GU.

G. Fashion Racket 10a***

Gear to 2". Nice thin crack. Lower off.
FA: Todd Vogel, Fred Lifton, 1989, GU.

H. Sneakaroma 9**

4 bolts, optional gear to 1". Dihedral to face. Lower off.
FA: Todd Vogel, Dave Focardi, Grant Schumacher, 5/1990, GU.

I. Bow Down to the Standard White Jesus 11a*

3 bolts. Face to small roof. Lower off.
FA: Todd Vogel, Dave Focardi, James Wilson, 5/1990, GU.

J. Open Project

3 bolts. Face.
P: Dave Focardi.

K. Flex Your Bazooka 9**

8 bolts. A sporty scramble leads to the 1st bolt, then exposed jug hauling to a technical crux. 30m/100' lower off.
FA: Mike Forkash, Kelly Cordner, 10/1999.

L. Project

2 bolts. Face.
P: Dusty Clark.

©2005 Maximus Press. *Marty Lewis Photo.*

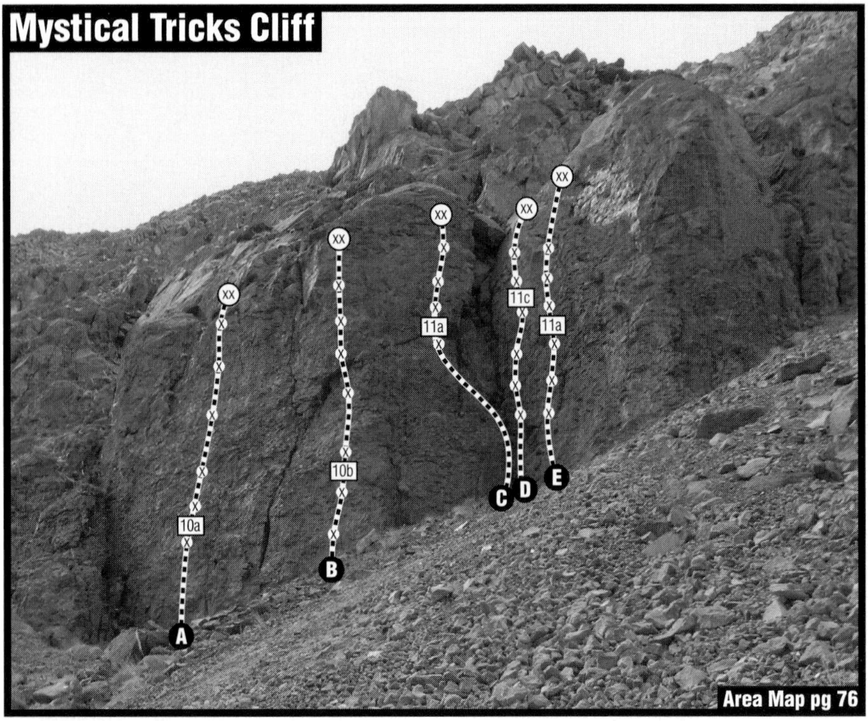

Mystical Tricks Cliff

Twin towers above talus on the west side.

A. Tricks in Motion 10a***

6 bolts. Nice face, a little sporty. Lower off

FA: Merlin Fortner, John Hartman, Mike Thompson, 1990, GU.

B. Done With Spare Change From Mikey's Pocket 10b**

7 bolts. Face to headwall. Lower off.

FA: John Hartman, Mike Thompson, Merlin Fortner, 3/1995, GU.

C. Baby Got Back 11a**

4 bolts. Scramble up to a ledge, then climb a steep face. Lower off.

FA: Mike Forkash, Jeff Neer, Urmas Franosch, 6/2005,TD.

D. Advocates of Babbling Thought 11c**

6 bolts. Stimulating face. Lower off.

FA: John Hartman, Bill Trethewey, 1991, GU.

E. Brian's Song 11a***

6 bolts. Face. Lower off.

FA: Mike Forkash, Jeff Neer, Brian Bennett, 6/2005, TD.

©2005 Maximus Press. *Marty Lewis Photo.*

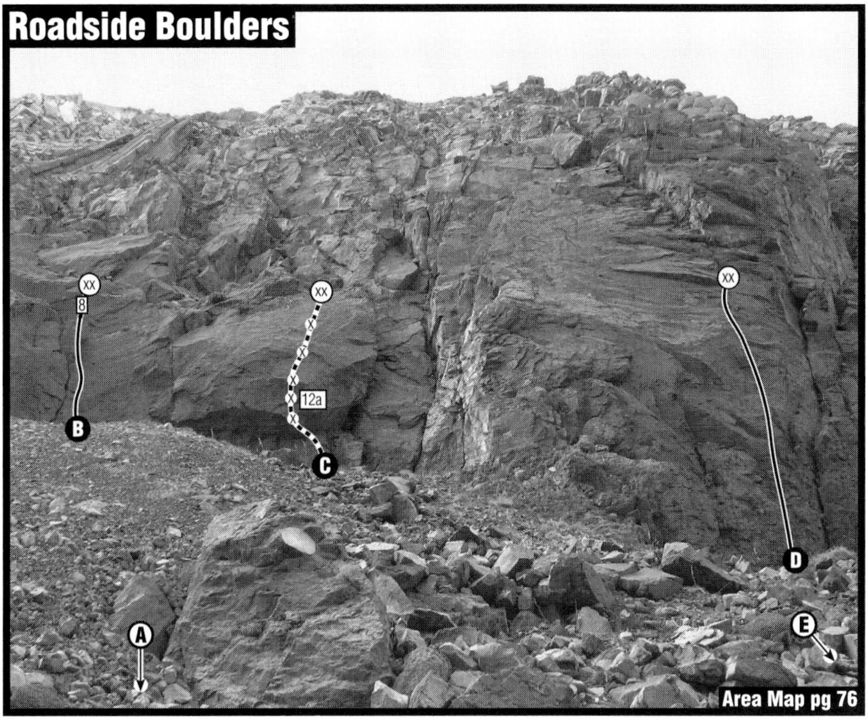

Roadside Boulders

The boulders on either side of the road and the cliff just above on the west side of the Gorge.

A. Rapid Fire 12d**

This northeast facing route is located on a boulder on the west side of the dirt road. 4 bolts, stick clip. Desperate face. Lower off a one bolt anchor.

FA: Tom Herbert, 1990, TD.

B. No Chapas 8**

Gear to 2". Dihedral to a crux mantle. Lower off.

FA: Eric Sorenson, 10/2003, GU.

C. Get Your War On 12a**

5 bolts. Difficult roof to a slab. Lower off.

FA: Dusty Clark, John Crumley, 2002, TD.

D. Narcolepsy 8****

Gear to 1.5". Clean hand crack. Lower off.

FA: Todd Vogel, Fred Lifton, Chris Iversen, 1989, GU.

E. Iceberg 12a*

This east facing route is located 100' north of *Rapid Fire* on the east side of the road. 4 bolts. Overhang to slab. Giant eye bolt anchor just off the dirt road.

FA: Tom Addison, Eirik Austlid, 1990, GU.

©2005 Maximus Press. *Marty Lewis Photo.*

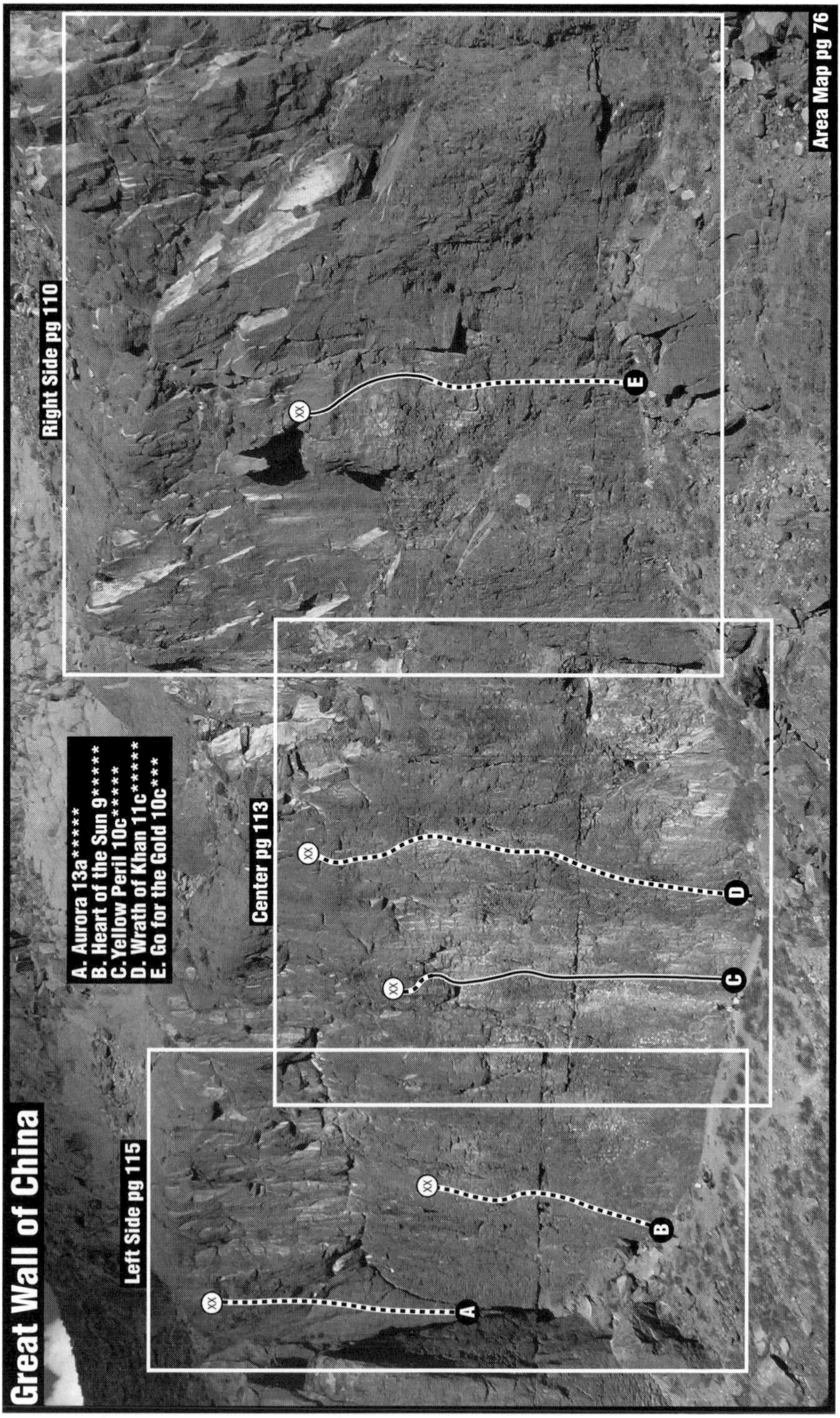

Great Wall of China - Overview

The long, tall, west facing wall on the east side. The most popular cliff in the Gorge. Of course there are great climbs here, but the main draw is a large number of consecutive routes all along a flat terrace. Please stay off of the slope below the trail; it is eroding badly. If you have to relieve yourself, follow the trail north past the Solarium, then cross a talus field, to a river crossing where there is a toilet.

Bouldering

There is an excellent long, moderate traverse along the base of the Great Wall of China.

Mike Melkonian on **Aurora** 13a*****. ©*Christian Pondella Photo.* **See Page 115**

©2005 Maximus Press. *Marty Lewis Photo.*

Great Wall of China - Right

A. Open Project
3 bolts. Face.
P: Mark Blanchard.

B. Go For the Gold 10c***
2 bolts, gear to 3". Face to ever widening steep crack. Lower off.
FA: Mark Blanchard, Bill McChesney, 2/1992, GU.

C. Marco Polo's Boys Go Dirty Dancing 8**
5 bolts. Face. Lower off.
FA: Bill Trethewey, Glenn Johnson, Kevin Bairey, 1992, GU.

Gary Slate and Marty Lewis on the first ascent of **Yellowstreak** 13a****. ©*Andy Selters Photo.* See Page 113

©2005 Maximus Press. *Marty Lewis Photo.*

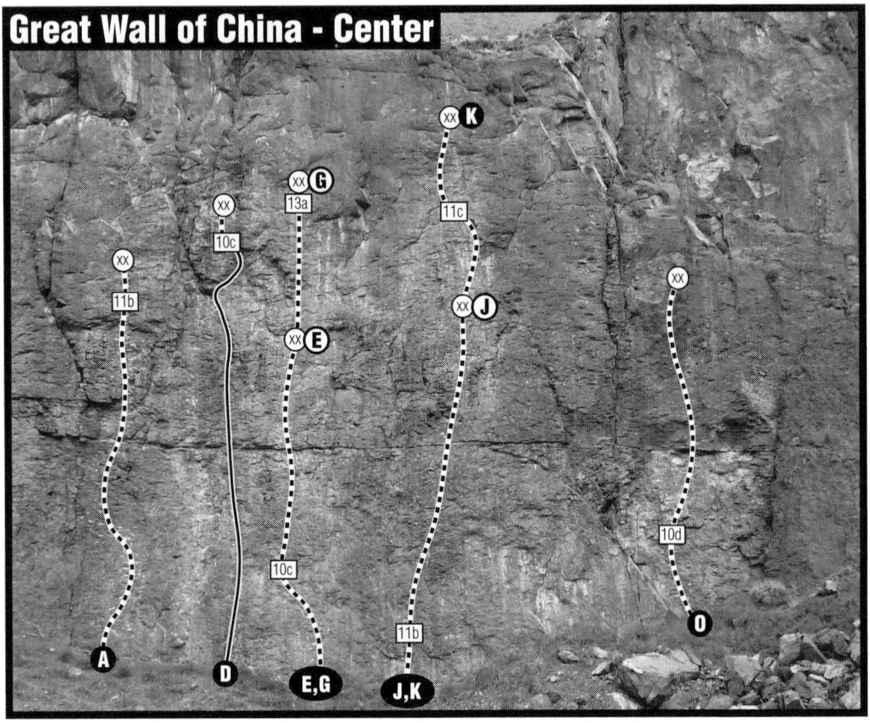

©2005 Maximus Press. *Marty Lewis Topo.*

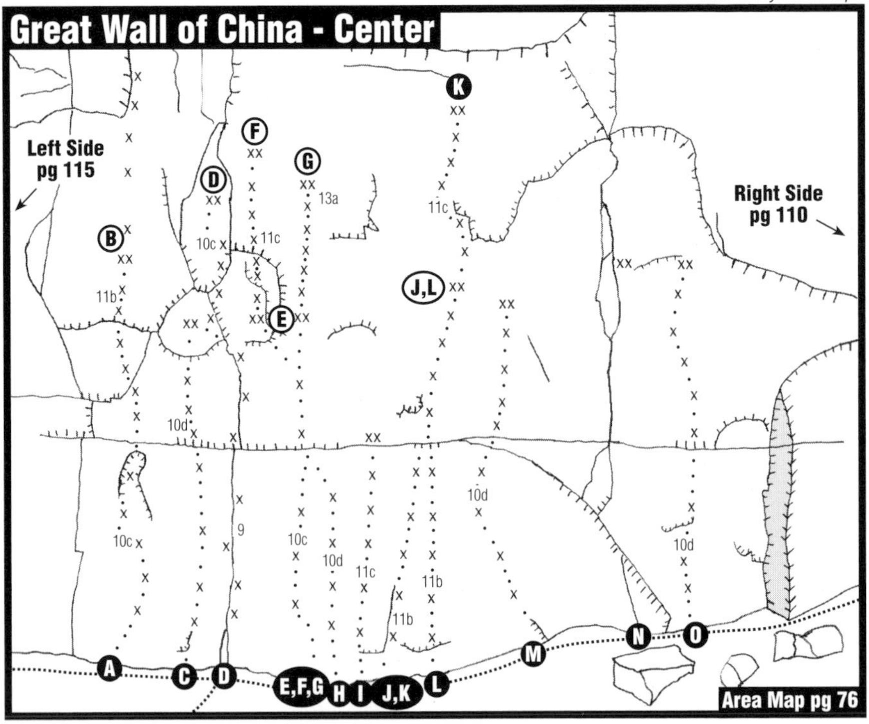

Great Wall of China - Center

A. Mandarin Orange 11b****
11 bolts. Vertical face to sustained gently overhanging headwall. 27.5m/90' lower off.
FA: Marty Lewis, Stan Vasily, 2/1994, TD.

B. Project
5 bolts. Slab to dihedral.
P: Todd Graham, Joe Rousek.

C. Peking Duck 10d***
7 bolts. Face to strenuous bulge. Lower off.
FA: Brian Huntsman, Joe Rousek, Robert Parker, 1/1994, GU.

Peking Peril Variation: 11 bolts. Climb *Peking Duck*, skip the anchors, move right and finish up *Yellow Peril*; really gets the blood flowing. 32.5m/105' lower off.

D. Yellow Peril 10c*****
11 bolts. Vertical crack to steep dihedral, then move left onto face. 32.5m/105' lower off.
FA: Peter Croft, Dayle Mazzarella, 11/1999, GU.

Yellow Belly Variation: 9****. 7 bolts. Climb *Yellow Peril*, then head left after the 7th bolt to the anchors of *Peking Duck*.

E. Tiananmen Square 10c***
5 bolts. Sporty face, well protected at crux. Lower off. ☞ Originally a 3 bolt route that ended at the major horizontal crack.
FA: Tom Herbert, Sondra Utterback, Sean Greer, 1990, TD. Route extension: Gary Slate, Marty Lewis.

F. Tsunami 11c****
12 bolts. Climb *Tiananmen Square*, then enter a steep dihedral, punch through and finish on a beautiful technical face. 35m/115' lower off. ➤ Photo this page.
FA: Kevin Calder, Marty Lewis, 5/1994, GU.

G. Yellowstreak 13a****
11 bolts. Climb *Tiananmen Square* then hit a steep desperate face. 35m/115' lower off. ☞ A key hold broke off this climb near the anchor making it much harder. ➤ Photo page 111.
FA: Gary Slate, Marty Lewis, 8/1991, GU.

H. Beijing 10d***
6 bolts. Face, a little sporty. Lower off.
FA: Phil Green, Wendy Borgerd, 8/1989, GU.

I. Geisha Girl 11c**
5 bolts. Technical face. Lower off.
FA: Louie Anderson, Pierre Daigle, 7/1994, GU.

J. Ghengis Khan 11b***
9 bolts. Slippery seam to fun jugs. 27.5m/90' lower off.
FA: Louie Anderson, Larry Kuechlin, 5/1993, GU.

K. Wrath of Khan 11c*****
15 bolts. Climb *Ghengis Khan* then climb a tricky dihedral to a face through a bulge. 40m/130' pitch, two single-rope rappels.
FA: Peter Croft, Marty Lewis, 11/1999, GU.

L. Kung Pao 11b***
9 bolts. Technical face to fun jugs. 27.5m/90' lower off.
FA: Louie Anderson, Larry Kuechlin, 5/1993, TD.

Kung Pao/Wrath of Khan Link-up: 11c*****. 15 bolts. Climb it in one pitch to avoid being a "Kung Pao Chicken". 40m/130' pitch, two single-rope rappels.

M. Shogun 10d**
8 bolts. Nebulous face. Lower off.
FA: Louie Anderson, Larry Kuechlin, Chris Murray, 6/1993, GU.

N. Project
Anchors. Crack.
P: John Hoffman.

O. Confusing Confucius 10d****
8 bolts. Technical sidepulls lead to overhanging face. Lower off.
FA: Bruce Lella, Todd Graham, Marty Lewis, 1992, GU.

Lonnie Kauk on **Tsunami** 11c****. ©*Andy Selters Photo.*

©2005 Maximus Press. *Marty Lewis Photo.*

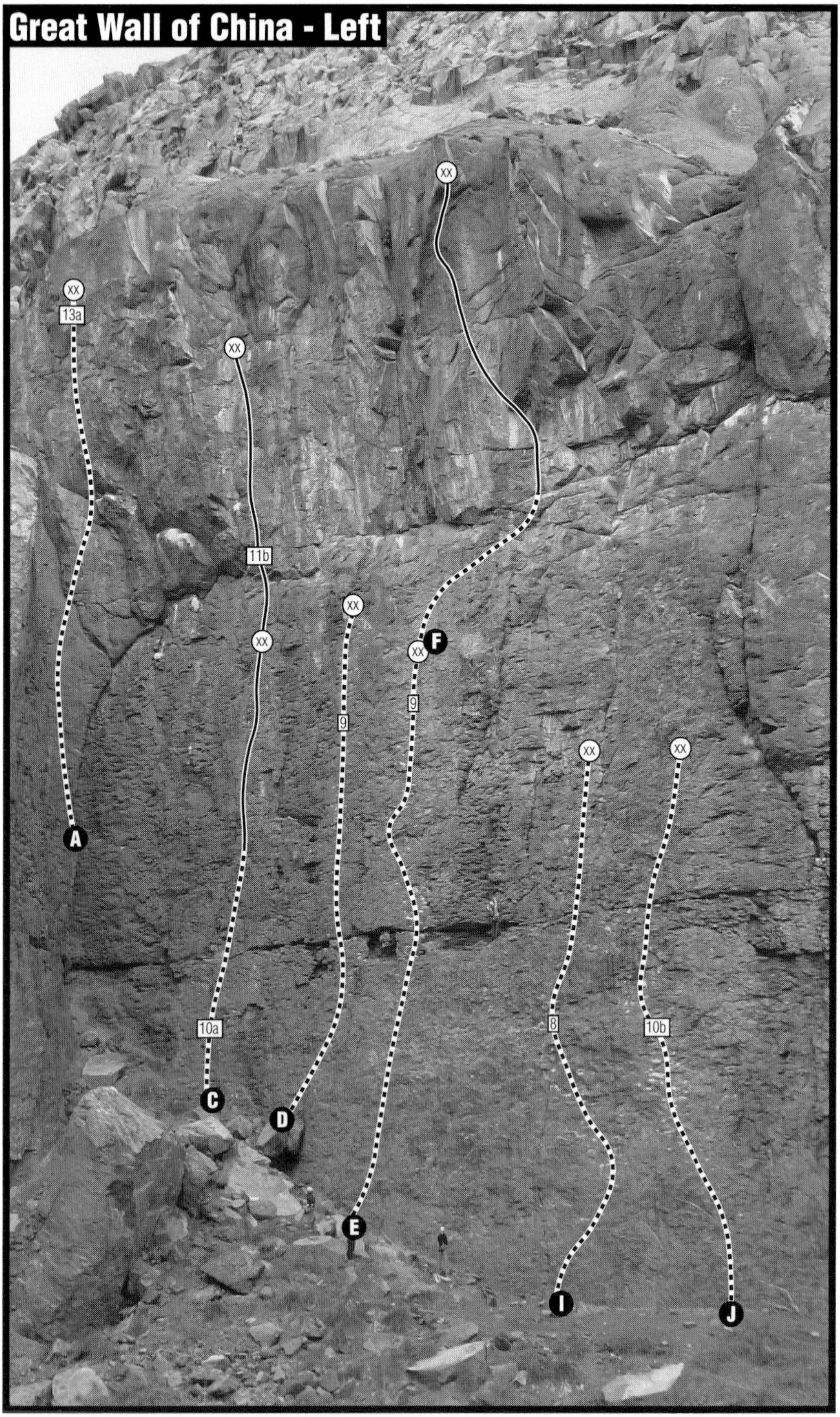

©2005 Maximus Press. *Marty Lewis Topo.*

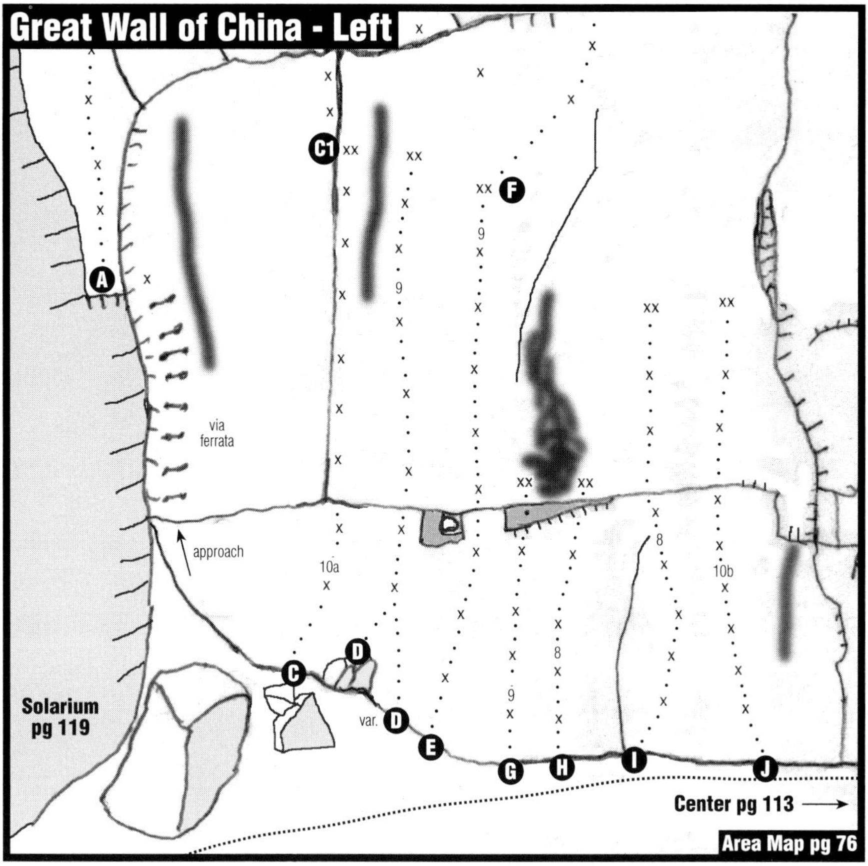

Great Wall of China - Left

A. Aurora 13a*****

Approach by climbing a via ferrata to a giant ledge. 13 bolts (mostly fixed draws). Awesome sustained pumpy line up a steep headwall. Lower off. ☞ Bruce Lella's brilliant coup de grace. He had it down to one hang, when he unfortunately suffered a severe climbing accident and graciously gave away the redpoint. ➤ Photo page 109.

FA: Mike Melkonian, Bruce Lella, 7/2001, TD.

B. Project

6 bolts. Parallels to the right of the top half of *Aurora.*

P: Todd Graham.

C. Cornercopia 11b***

Pitch 1: 10a*. 8 bolts. Bouldery decomposing face to crack. Climb 2nd pitch or lower off.

Pitch 2: 11b***. 8 bolts. Steep dihedral. Lower off.

Can be done as one pitch.

FA: Todd Graham, Marty Lewis, Bruce Lella, 5/1995, GU.

D. Child of Light 9****

7 bolts. Nice face, sporty to 1st bolt. 27.5m/90' lower off.

FA: Joe Rousek, Gary Slate, 3/1991, GU.

E. Heart of the Sun 9*****

8 bolts. Killer pumpy vertical face. Lower off.

➤ Photo page 116.

FA: Gary Slate, Sandy Redman, 3/1991, GU.

F. Hu Phlung Pu 8 A3***

3 bolts, aid gear to 1.5". Face to dihedral system. Double rope rappel to ground.

FA: Mike McGrale, 12/1994, GU.

G. Fortune Cookie 9**

4 bolts. Face. Lower off.

FA: Louie Anderson, Larry Kuechlin, 5/1993, GU.

H. Enter the Dragon 8**

4 bolts. Face. Lower off.

FA: Will Gove, Marty Lewis, Nancy Lust, 1992, GU.

I. China Doll 8****

7 bolts. Vertical face. Lower off.

FA: Todd Graham, Nancy Lust, 4/1991, GU.

J. Tsing Tao 10b****

8 bolts. Vertical face. Lower off.

FA: Marty Lewis, Kevin Calder, 5/1992, TD.

Howie Schwartz on **Heart of the Sun** 9***** at the Great Wall of China. ©*Patitucci Photo.* **See Page 115**

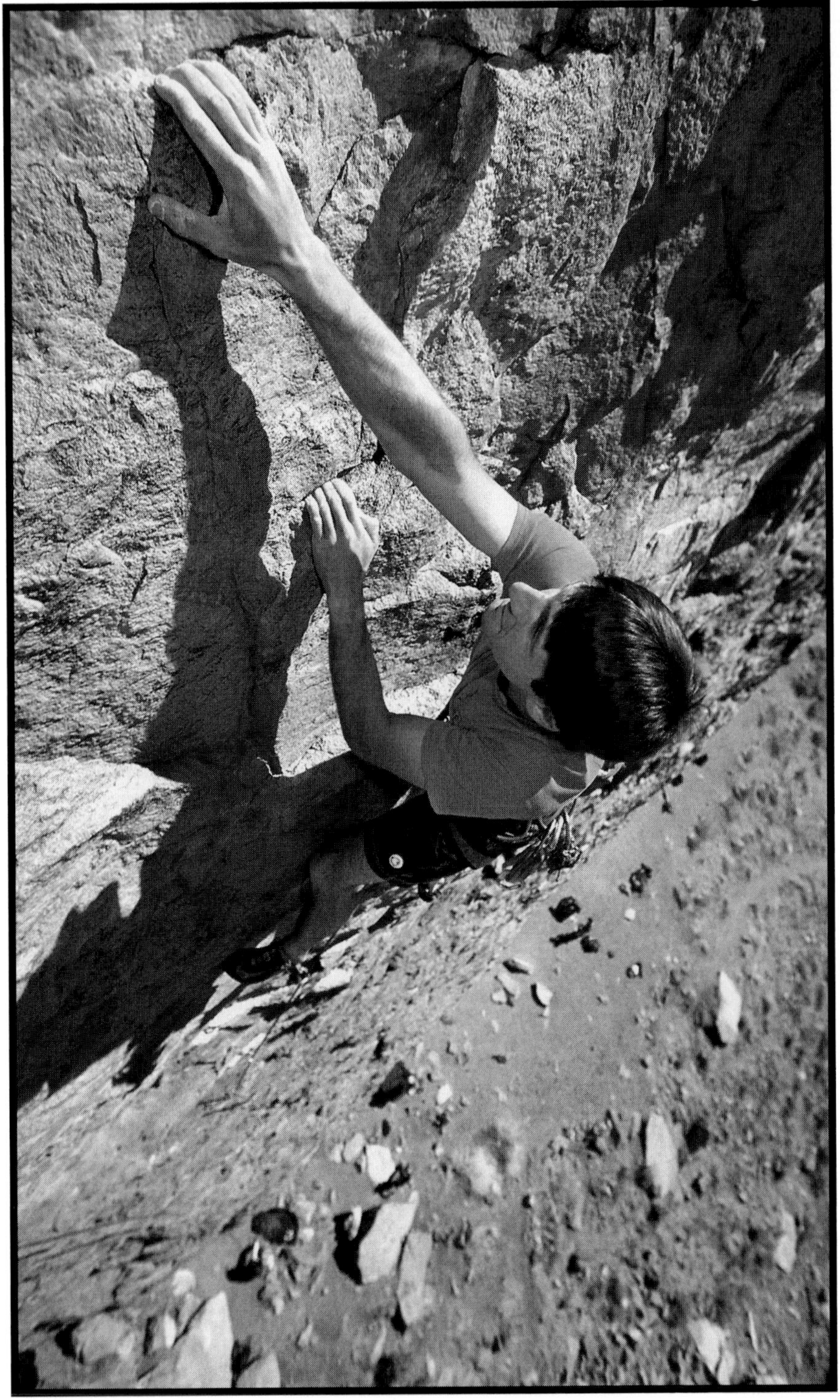

Doug Ingersoll on **Focus** 11b**** at the Solarium. ©*Andy Selters Photo.* **See Page 119**

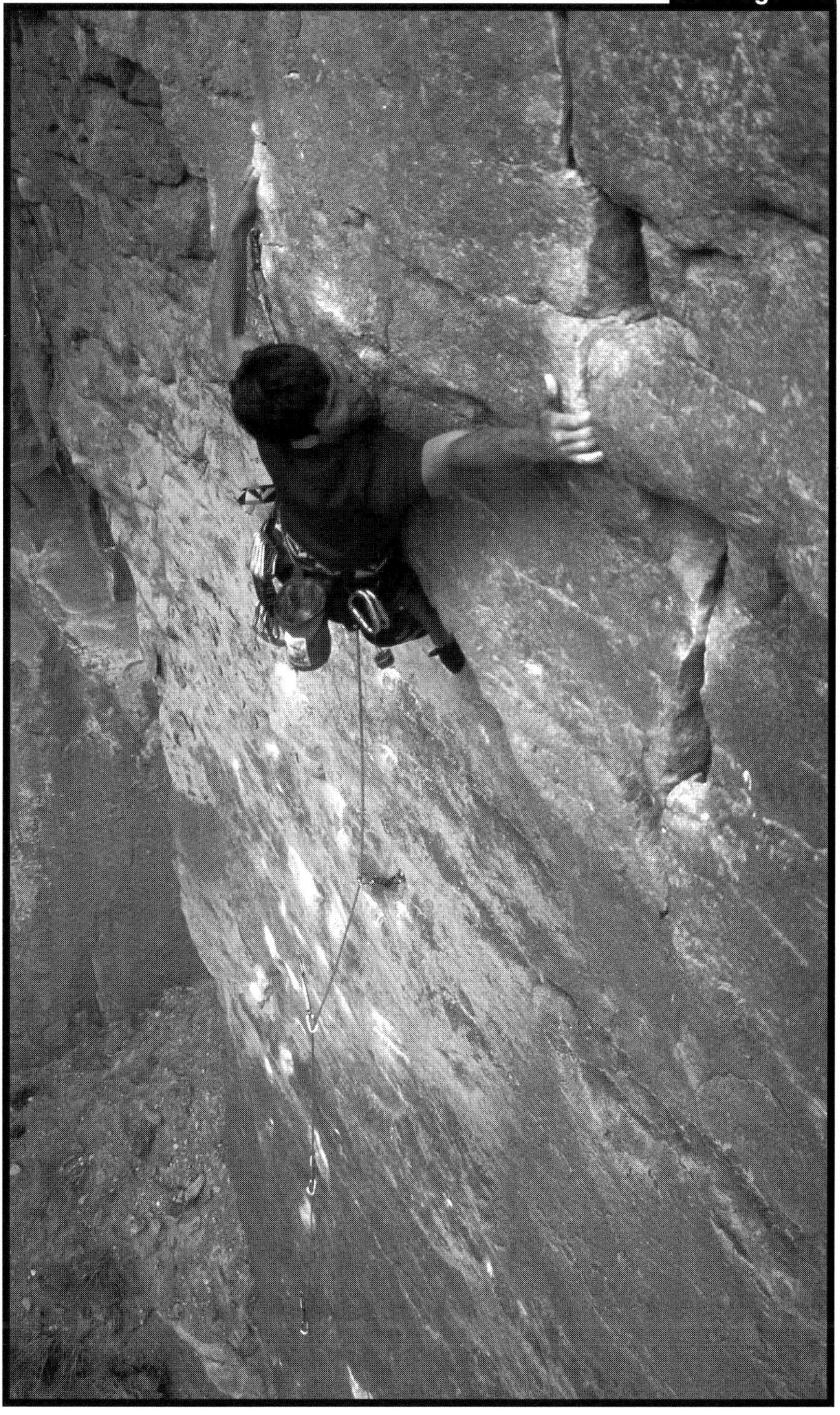

©2005 Maximus Press. *Marty Lewis Photo.*

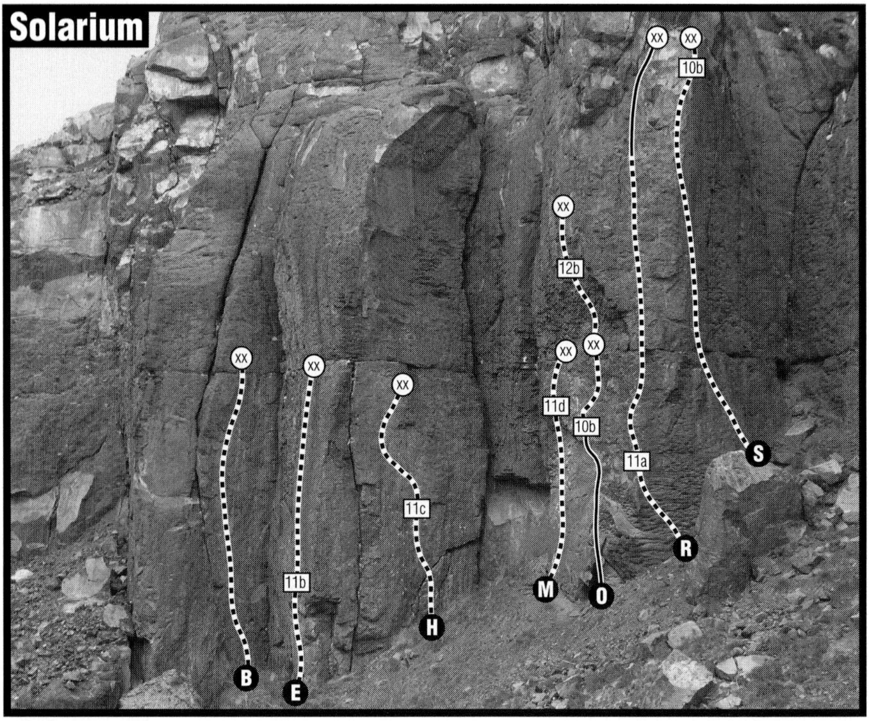

©2005 Maximus Press. *Marty Lewis Topo.*

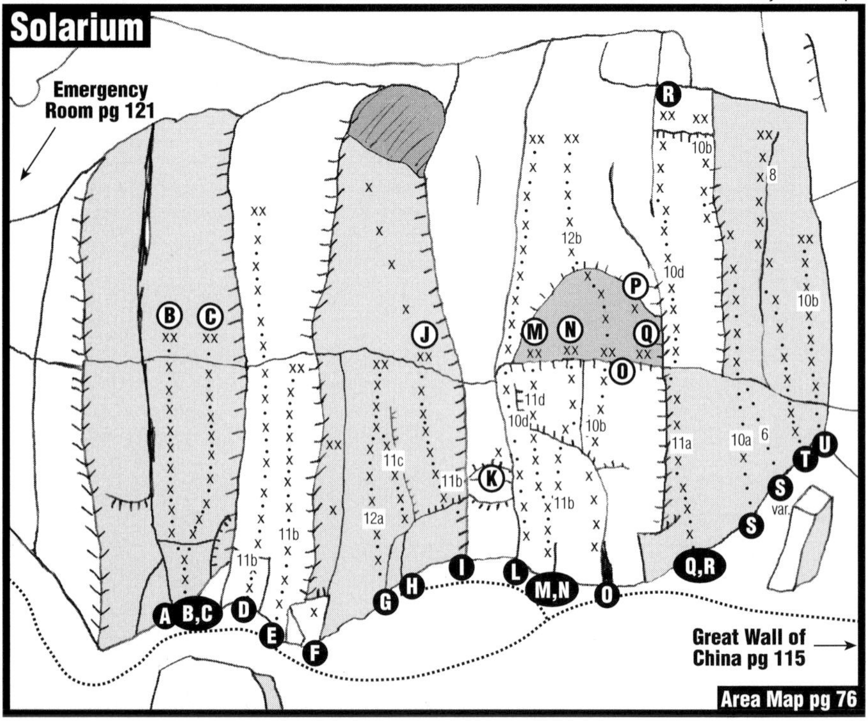

Solarium

Large south facing towers on the east side. From the south follow the trail under the Great Wall of China. From the north cross the river next to the toilet below the Staying Power Towers then scramble south.

A. Awful Offwidth 9•
Gear to 6". Heinous offwidth, then step right to the *Shocker* Belay. Lower off.
FA: Tom Herbert, Hidetaka Suzuki, 1990, GU.

B. Shocker 13b**
11 bolts. Steep face, boulder problem crux. Lower off.
FA: Tom Herbert, 1990, TD.

C. Hocus Pocus 13c**
11 bolts. Steep face, boulder problem crux. Lower off.
FA: Tom Herbert, 1992, TD.

D. Direchossimo 11b***
14 bolts, 35m/115'. Vertical face to bulge. Lower off.
FA: Tony Puppo, Joe Rousek, 4/1995, TD.

E. Psmead 11b***
9 bolts. Interesting face, a little sporty. 27.5m/90' lower off.
FA: Jay Decker, Bill McChesney, Steve Schneider, 3/1990, GU.

F. Project
2 bolts. Dihedral to face.
P. Tony Puppo.

G. Snake Eyes 12a**
8 bolts. Technical face that merges with *Venom,* a bit of a squeeze. Lower off.
FA: Tom Herbert, Tony Puppo, 1991, TD.

H. Venom 11c*****
7 bolts. Tricky crux followed by a strenuous face, sustained. Lower off.
FA: Tom Herbert, Gary Slate, Kevin Leary, 1990, TD.

I. Cobra 11b**
6 bolts. A reachy crux leads to a strenuous dihedral. Lower off.
FA: Joe Rousek, Tony Puppo, 1989, TD.

J. Project
4 bolts. Slab to headwall.
P: Joe Rousek, Tony Puppo.

K. Open Project
1 bolt. Arete.
P: Mark Blanchard.

L. Monkey See, Monkey Do 10b**
13 bolts. Long arete. 45m/150' pitch, single rope rappel to *Power.*
FA: Greg Corliss, Joe Rousek, 5/1996, GU.

M. Power 11d****
8 bolts. Start on *Focus*, then technical face leads to a powerful roof. Lower off.
FA: Marty Lewis, Mike Cann, 4/1995, TD.

N. Focus 11b****
8 bolts. A bouldery start leads to technical vertical face, then pass a roof to a steep crack. Lower off.
➤ Photo page 117.
FA: Tony Puppo, Joe Rousek, Gary Slate, 1/1991, GU.

O. Black Hole 12b*****
15 bolts, be mindful of rope drag. A crack leads to a steep face, rest on the ledge (if you belay here the upper headwall is more like 12a), then climb the brilliant, steep, pumpy exposed face. 35m/115' lower off.
FA: Tony Puppo, Joe Rousek, 1994, GU.

Variation: 10b***. 7 bolts. Climb *Black Hole* but stop on the rest/belay ledge, a bit sporty. Lower off.
FA: Tony Puppo, Grant Schumacher, 2/1995, TD.

Variation: 10d***. 7 bolts. Go left to *Focus* at the 5th bolt, making a nice crack climb. Lower off.

P. Project
1 bolt. Steep face.
P: Tony Puppo.

Q. Split Decision 11a***
6 bolts. Technical stimulating arete, then step left to the anchor. Lower off. ➤ Photo page 74, page 122.
FA: Tony Puppo, 1993, TD.

R. Morning Wood 11a****
16 bolts. Start the *Split Decision* arete then climb a vertical face to a crack finish. 45m/150' pitch, rappel 35m/115' down *Sendero Luminoso.*
FA: Brian Ketron, Marty Lewis, Sean Plunkett, Fred Berman, 1/1995, TD.

S. Sendero Luminoso 10b*****
9 bolts. Vertical pockets lead to a slabby crux, on an exposed arete. 35m/115' lower off. ➤ Photo page 79.
FA: Joe Rousek, Robert Parker, 1990, GU.

Variation: 10b*****. 8 bolts. Start to the right up an easy slabby face, skipping the 1st bolt, the main benefit being the belayer can stand further back in comfort. 35m/115' lower off.

T. Sabado Gigante 8***
12 bolts. Crunchy vertical face to a hand crack. 30m/100' lower off. ☞ First led on gear.
FA: Marty Lewis, Kevin Calder, Andrew Stevens, Peter Croft, Mike Forkash, Steve Calder, 11/2004, GU.

U. Menace II Society 10b**
6 bolts. Face. Lower off.
FA: Marty Lewis, Stan Vasily, 11/1993, GU.

Tracy Best on **Show Us Your Tits** 10c*****. ©*Greg Epperson Photo.*

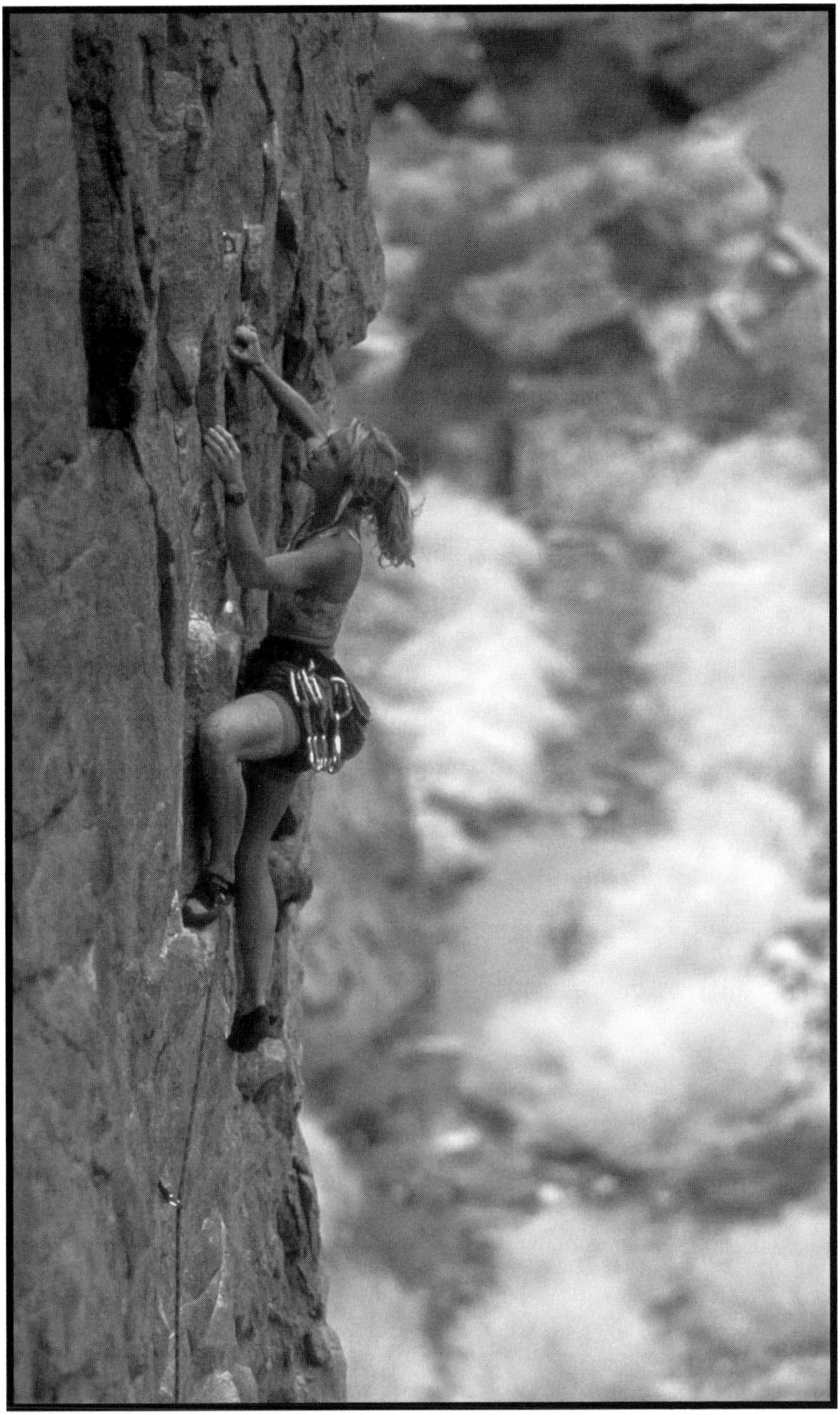

©2005 Maximus Press. *Marty Lewis Photo.*

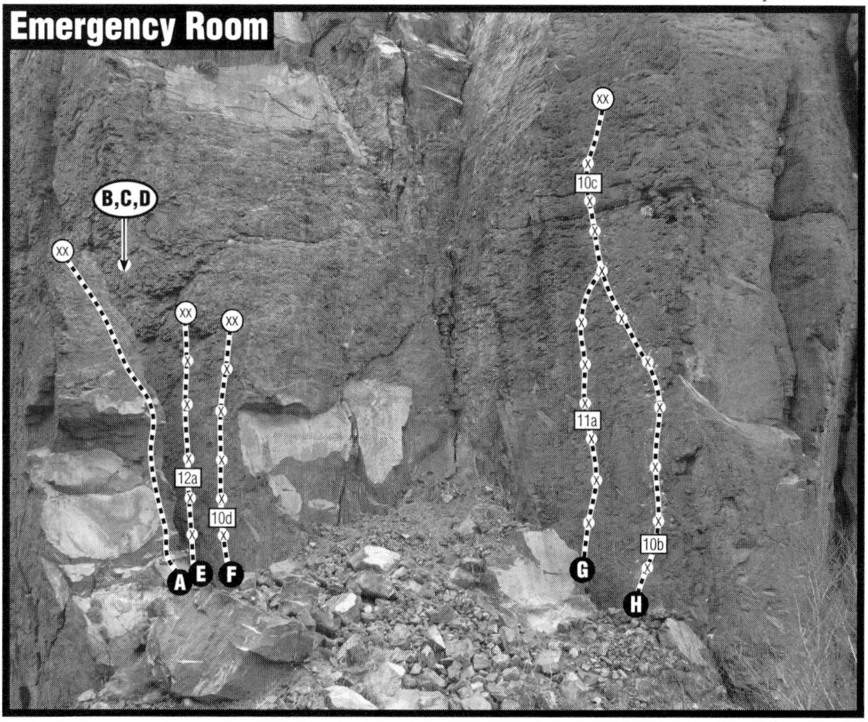

Emergency Room

Small wall and corridor above talus.

A. Unnatural Silence 9*

Gear. The south face of the tower. Rappel off the summit.
FA: Peter Fisher, James Wilson, 1989, GU.

B. Contagious 10b**

4 bolts, gear: 1.75" piece. Crack to face. On the back side of the tower opposite *Dead on Arrival*. Lower off.
FA: Todd Graham, 9/1991, TD.

C. Body Count 12a***

7 bolts. Vertical technical face. Lower off.
FA: Louie Anderson, Pierre Daigle, 7/1994, TD.

D. Dead on Arrival 11d**

5 bolts. Seam to face. Lower off.
FA: Louie Anderson, Larry Kuechlin, 4/1993, TD.

E. Vital Signs 12a**

5 bolts. Face. Lower off.
FA: Todd Graham, 1991, TD.

F. Dial 911 10d**

5 bolts. Face. Lower off.
FA: Todd Graham, 9/1991, GU.

G. Cabaret 11a***

10 bolts. Technical face. Lower off.
FA: Louie Anderson, Cory Zinngrabe, 10/1993, TD.

H. Show Us Your Tits 10c*****

10 bolts. Pumpy vertical face. Lower off.
➤ Photo facing page.
FA: Bruce Lella, Todd Graham, 6/1991, GU.

©2005 Maximus Press.

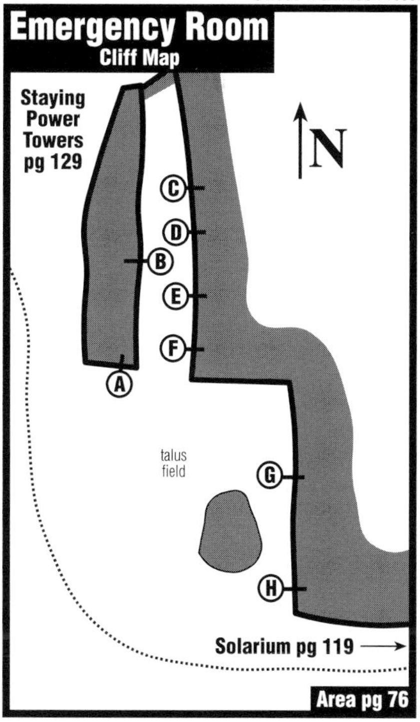

Tony Puppo on **Split Decision** 11a*** at the Solarium. ©*Andy Selters Photo.* **See Page 119**

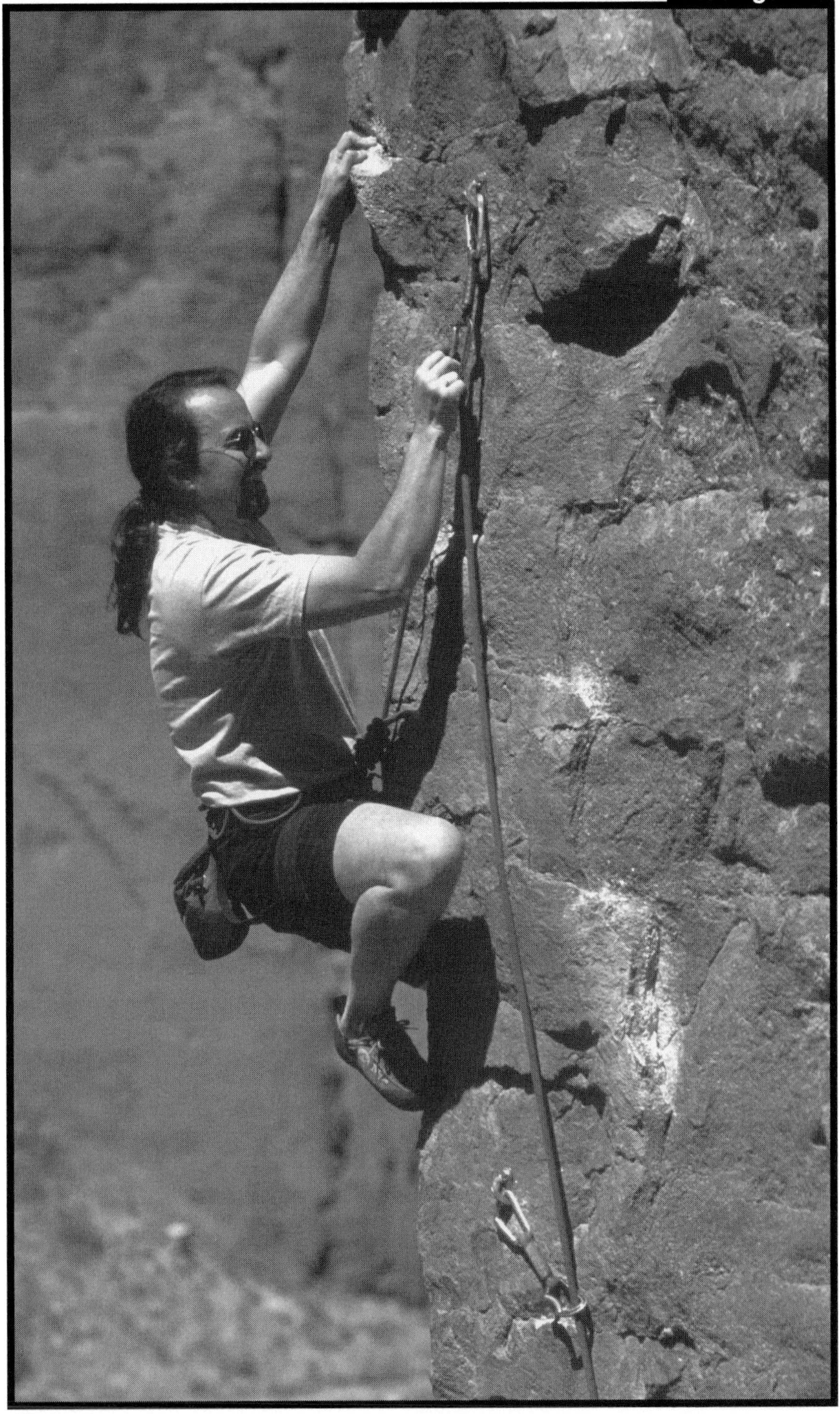

©2005 Maximus Press. *Marty Lewis Photo.*

Shaded Wall

This small cliff is adjacent to an old power plant ruin on the west side of the Gorge.

A. Guy With a Doberman 11c*
4 bolts. Face. Lower off.

B. Short But Steep 10c**
3 bolts. Steep arete. Lower off.
FA: Dennis Jensen, 1992, TD.

©2005 Maximus Press. *Marty Lewis Photo.*

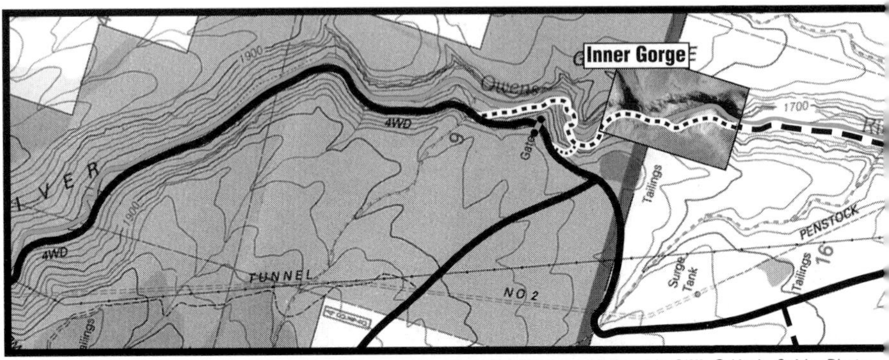

Tom Costa on **Piranha** 12b**** at the Mothership Cliff. ©*Kevin Calder Photo.*

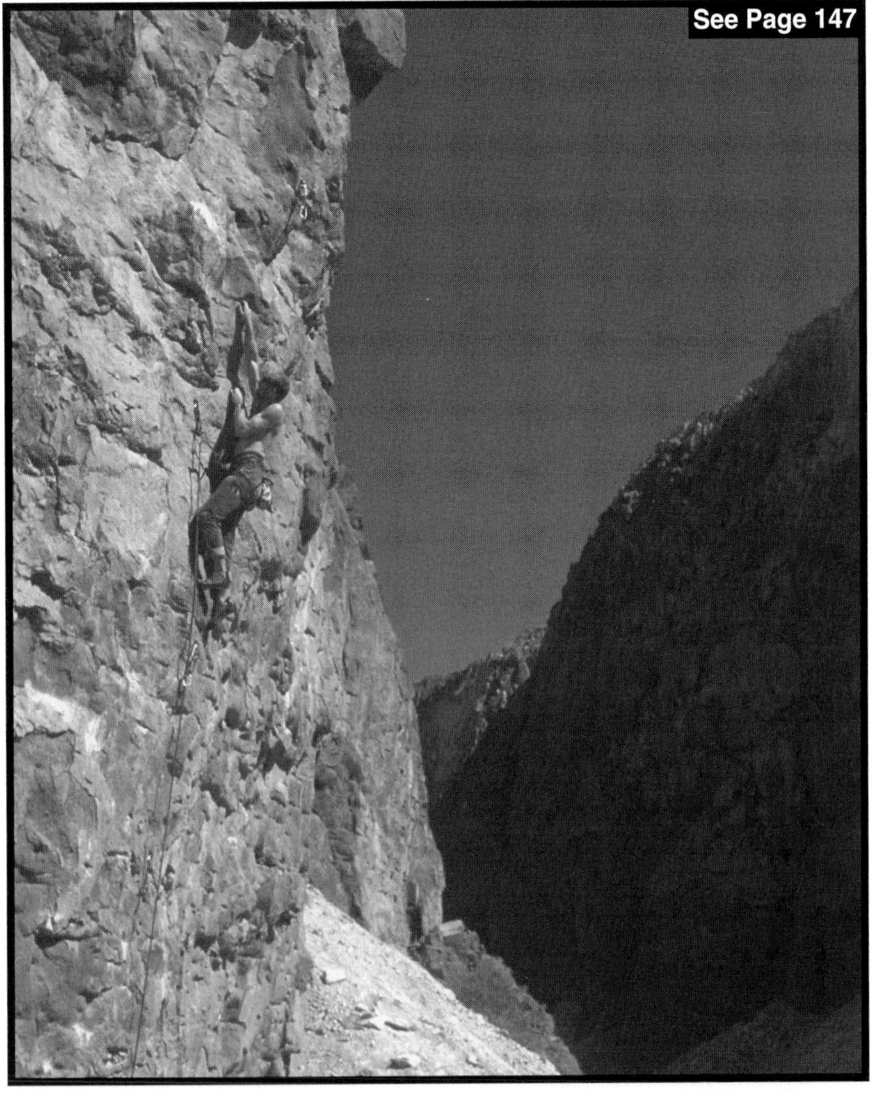

See Page 147

Adapted from the U.S.G.S. 1:24,000 Casa Diablo Mtn. and Rovana Quadrangles.

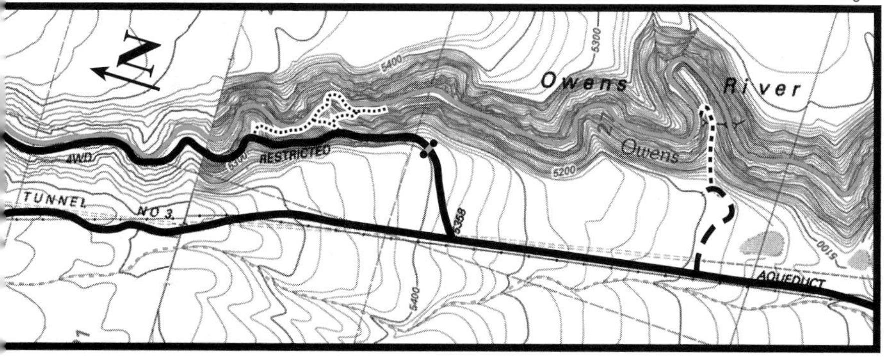

CHAPTER 5

Inner Gorge Basics.. pg 127
Staying Power Towers.. pg 129
Weird Corner.. pg 131
DMZ.. pg 133
Eldorado Roof - Overview.. pg 135
Eldorado Roof - Towering Inferno.. pg 137
Eldorado Roof - Right Side.. pg 139
Eldorado Roof - Left Side.. pg 143
Land of the Giants.. pg 145
Mothership Cliff.. pg 147
Fun House.. pg 149
Dilithium Crystal.. pg 153
Crystal Corridor.. pg 154
Rob's Rock.. pg 155
Megalithic.. pg 157
Local Trivia Tower.. pg 157
Narrows West.. pg 159
Narrows East.. pg 161
P.T. Barnum Wall.. pg 162
Monkey to Monk Cliff.. pg 163
Supreme Wizard Formation.. pg 165
McCracken Wall.. pg 166

INNER GORGE

©2005 Maximus Press.

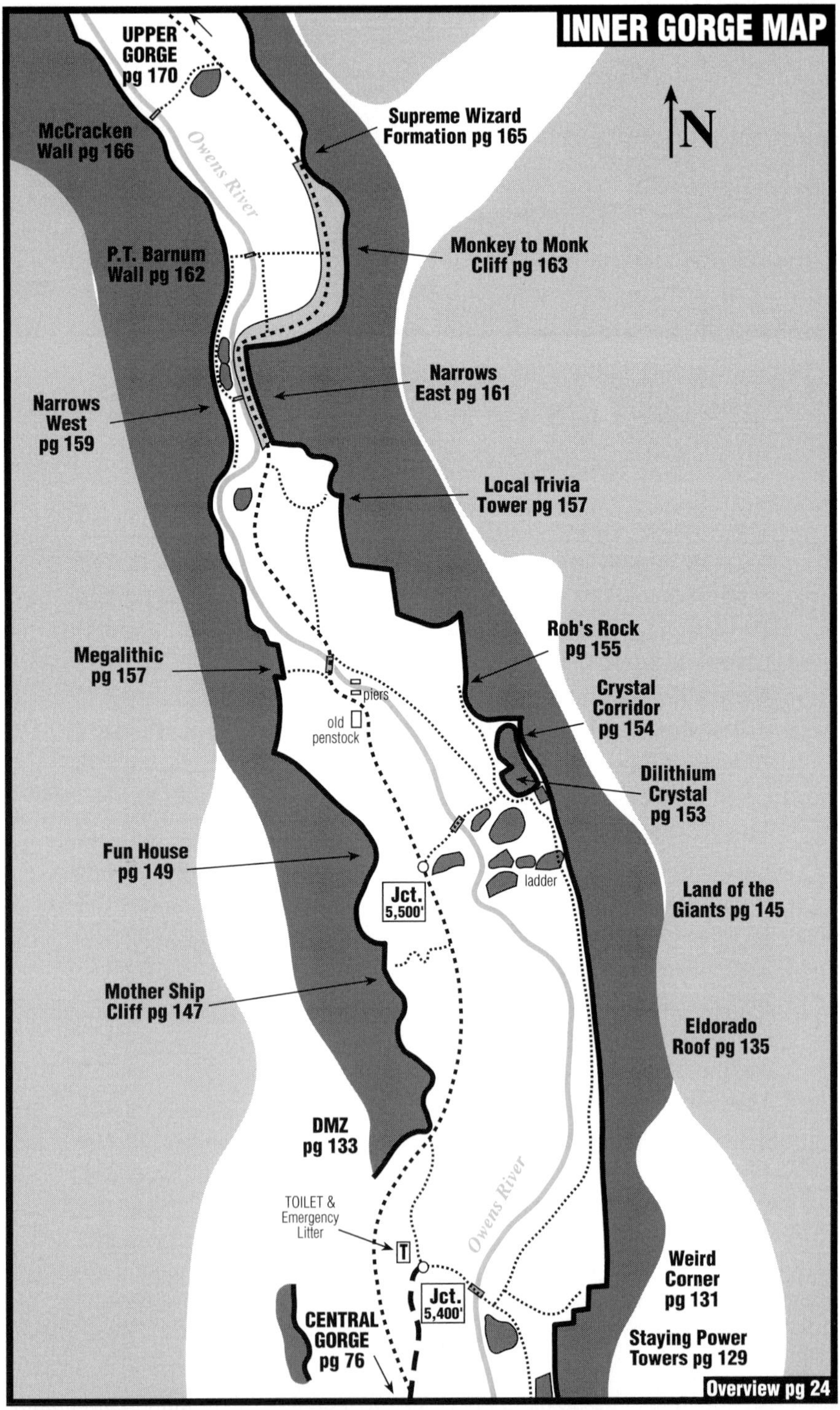
INNER GORGE MAP
N
UPPER GORGE pg 170
McCracken Wall pg 166
Supreme Wizard Formation pg 165
Owens River
P.T. Barnum Wall pg 162
Monkey to Monk Cliff pg 163
Narrows East pg 161
Narrows West pg 159
Local Trivia Tower pg 157
Rob's Rock pg 155
Megalithic pg 157
piers
old penstock
Crystal Corridor pg 154
Dilithium Crystal pg 153
Fun House pg 149
ladder
Jct. 5,500'
Land of the Giants pg 145
Mother Ship Cliff pg 147
Eldorado Roof pg 135
DMZ pg 133
Owens River
TOILET & Emergency Litter
T
Weird Corner pg 131
Jct. 5,400'
CENTRAL GORGE pg 76
Staying Power Towers pg 129
Overview pg 24

INNER GORGE BASICS

The Inner Gorge is demarcated in the south by an old power plant ruin and in the north by a large pink talus field.

The Inner Gorge contains outstanding climbing. Standouts include the popular Dilithium Crystal and the incredible Eldorado Roof. The roof is 300 feet wide and 30 feet deep and houses the highest concentration of steep hard climbing in the Gorge.

Inner Gorge Details

Elevation: 5,400 to 5,600 ft.
Sport Climbs: 138 routes, 5.7 to 13c.
Gear Climbs: 26 routes, 5.7 to 12d.
Approach: 20 minute hike with a 400 ft. descent.

The Approach: The Inner Gorge has no direct approach. This area can be approached from either the Central Gorge or the Upper Gorge just as easily.

From the Central Gorge: Park at the Central Parking Area and take the Central Gully Approach; then head north up the Gorge. Class 3; 20 minutes to the Staying Power Towers, 30 minutes to the Supreme Wizard Formation. See page 77.

From the Upper Gorge: Park at the North Parking Area and take the Upper Gorge Approach; then head south down the Gorge. Class 3; 25 minutes to the Supreme Wizard Formation, 35 minutes to the Staying Power Towers. See page 171.

©2005 Maximus Press. *Marty Lewis Photo.*

©2005 Maximus Press. *Marty Lewis Photo.*

©2005 Maximus Press. *Marty Lewis Topo.*

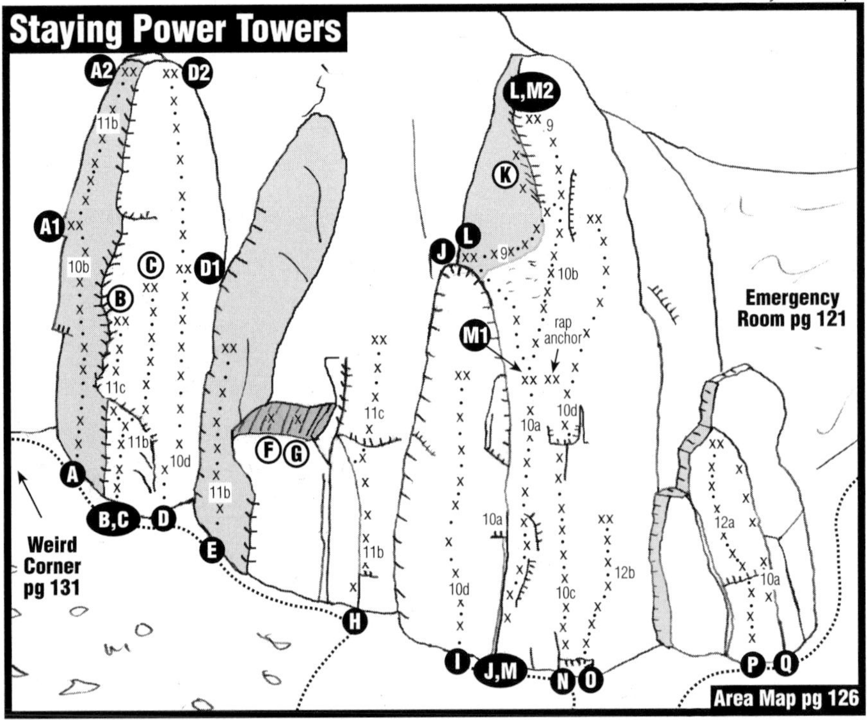

Staying Power Towers

Tall northwest facing towers on the east side of the Gorge.

A. Direct North Face 11b**

Pitch 1: 10b**. 7 bolts, optional gear: medium nut. Vertical face. Climb 2nd pitch or lower off 27.5m/90'.
Pitch 2: 11b**. 5 bolts. Technical face. Lower off.
FA: Mark Blanchard, 1992, GU.

B. Optimator 11c***

7 bolts. Climb past the first 4 bolts of *Bender* then go left to a steep arete. Lower off.
FA: Mike Cann, Marty Lewis, 4/1995, TD.

C. Bender 11b***

9 bolts. A technical vertical face leads to a traverse right along a roof, then climb more face. Lower off.
FA: Marty Lewis, Mike Cann, 4/1995, TD.

D. Members Only 10d*****

Pitch 1: 10d*****. 7 bolts. A technical bit leads to a continuous vertical face. 27.5m/90' lower off.
Pitch 2: 9**(r). 5 bolts. Face. 30m/100' lower off.
Can be done as one pitch if mindful of rope drag.
FA: Joe Rousek, Gary Slate, 1990, GU.

E. Destiny 11b*

5 bolts. Face, bolted sportily. Lower off.
FA: Louie Anderson, Ripley Casdorph, 10/1991, TD.

F. Open Project

1 bolt. Roof.
P: Tom Herbert.

G. Open Project

1 bolt. Roof.
P: Tom Herbert.

H. Ya Shoulda' Killed Me Last Year 11c***

9 bolts. Steep crack to a roof to face. Lower off.
FA: Marty Lewis, Fred Berman, 9/1991, TD.

I. Wired 10d***(r)

8 bolts. Sporty face, the crux is well protected. Lower off.
FA: Joe Rousek, Gary Slate, 5/1991, GU.

J. To Knee or Not to Knee 10a***

2 bolts, gear to 4". Wide crack in a corner. 40m/130' rappel, or a short rappel to the anchor of *Don't Look Up*.
FA: Greg Barnes, Barry Hutten, 10/2001, GU.

K. Project

2 bolts. Arete.
P: Greg Barnes, Barry Hutten.

L. Don't Look Down 9***

Approach by climbing the 1st pitch of *Don't Look Up*.
8 bolts. Wildly exposed overhanging jugs, then around a corner on a ledge system, finish on technical face climbing. Two 27.5m/90' rappels down *Don't Look Up*.
FA: Greg Barnes, Barry Hutten, 10/2001, GU.

M. Don't Look Up 10b****

Pitch 1: 10a****. 9 bolts. Climb a flaring chimney, then move right onto a flake and continue up a technical face. Climb 2nd pitch or lower off 27.5m/90' or pass the belay, and climb up and left to the belay on *Don't Look Down*, if you wish to climb that pitch.
Pitch 2: 10b****. 9 bolts. Amazing jug haul through roofs to technical face. 27.5m/90' lower off.
Can be done as one pitch if mindful of rope drag.
FA: Greg Barnes, Barry Hutten, 10/2001, TD.

N. Blood Sugar Sex Magik 10d*****

16 bolts. Long juggy vertical face, the fun never stops. 40m/130' pitch, 35m/115' lower off to the ledge at the base of the route or do a 27.5m/90' rappel to *Insane in the Membrane*. ➤ Photo page 130.
FA: Fred Berman, Marty Lewis, 12/1991, TD.

O. Insane in the Membrane 12b***

6 bolts. Crimpy technical vertical face. Lower off.
FA: Fred Berman, Marty Lewis, 2/1994, TD.

P. Thieves in the Temple 12a*****

9 bolts. Sustained gently overhanging face. Lower off.
☞ Thieves stole a rope off of this route when it was an unfinished project. ➤ Photo this page.
FA: Fred Berman, Marty Lewis, 6/1993, TD.

Q. Elephant Gun 10a**

5 bolts, optional gear to 1.5". Offwidth. Lower off.
FA: Dave Melkonian, Mike Melkonian, 11/1997, GU.

Keri Orton on **Thieves in the Temple** 12a*****.
©Ian Doleman Photo.

Dennis Phillips on **Blood Sugar Sex Magik** 10d***** at the Staying Power Towers. ©*Marty Lewis Photo.*

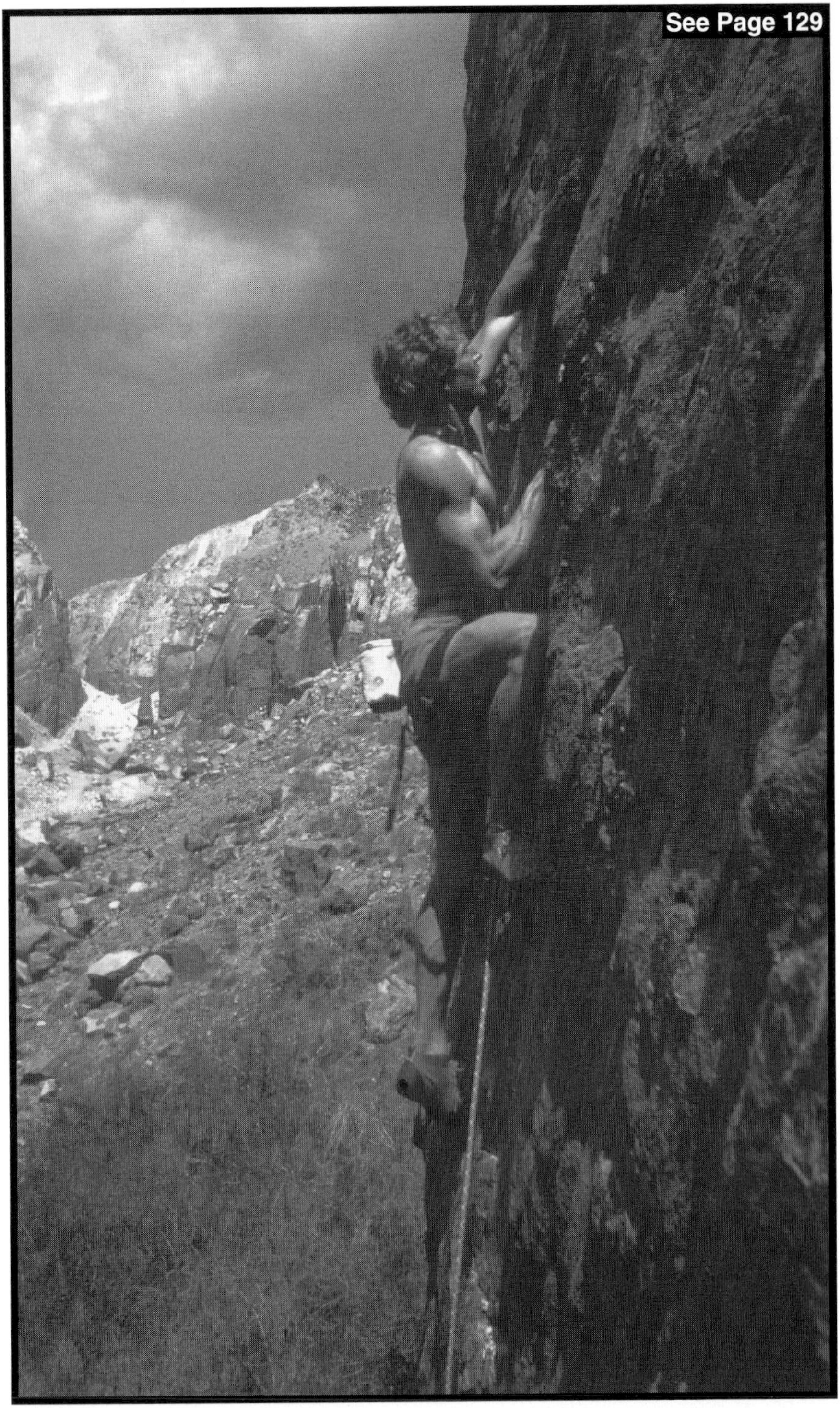

See Page 129

©2005 Maximus Press. *Marty Lewis Photo.*

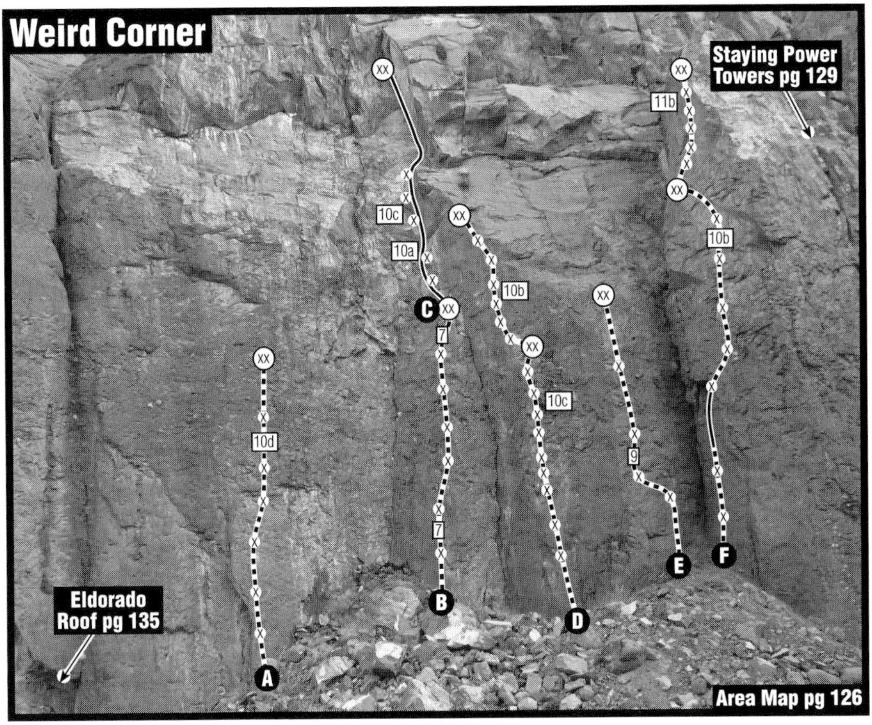

Weird Corner

Towers on the east side of the Gorge above a talus fan.

A. Chaos 10d**(r)

6 bolts. Sporty face. Lower off.

FA: Louie Anderson, Bart Groendycke, 5/1992, GU.

B. Weird Al 7***

6 bolts. Blunt arete. Lower off. ☞ First led on gear.

FA: Greg Barnes, Barry Hutten, 3/2002, GU.

C. Creaky Hollow Fracture Show 10c**

5 bolts, gear to 2". Dihedral past a difficult bulge to a hand crack. 30m/100' lower off.

FA: Greg Barnes, Barry Hutten, 3/2002, GU.

D. Hey Bubba, Watch This! 10c****

Pitch 1: 10c****. 9 bolts. Sustained overhung face. Climb 2nd pitch or lower off.

Pitch 2: 10b***. 6 bolts. Exposed technical face. 35m/115' to ground or rappel 15m/50' to *Weird Al*.

Can be done in one pitch if mindful of rope drag.

FA: Greg Barnes, Karin Wuhrmann, Barry Hutten, 5/2002, TD.

E. Don't Make Me Laugh 9**

4 bolts, optional gear to 1". Face. Lower off.

FA: Mark Blanchard, 1991, GU.

F. Direct North Face 11b**

Pitch 1: 10b**. 7 bolts, optional gear: medium nut. Vertical face. Climb 2nd pitch or lower off 27.5m/90'.

Pitch 2: 11b**. 5 bolts. Technical face. Lower off.

FA: Mark Blanchard, 1992, GU.

©2005 Maximus Press. *Marty Lewis Photo.*

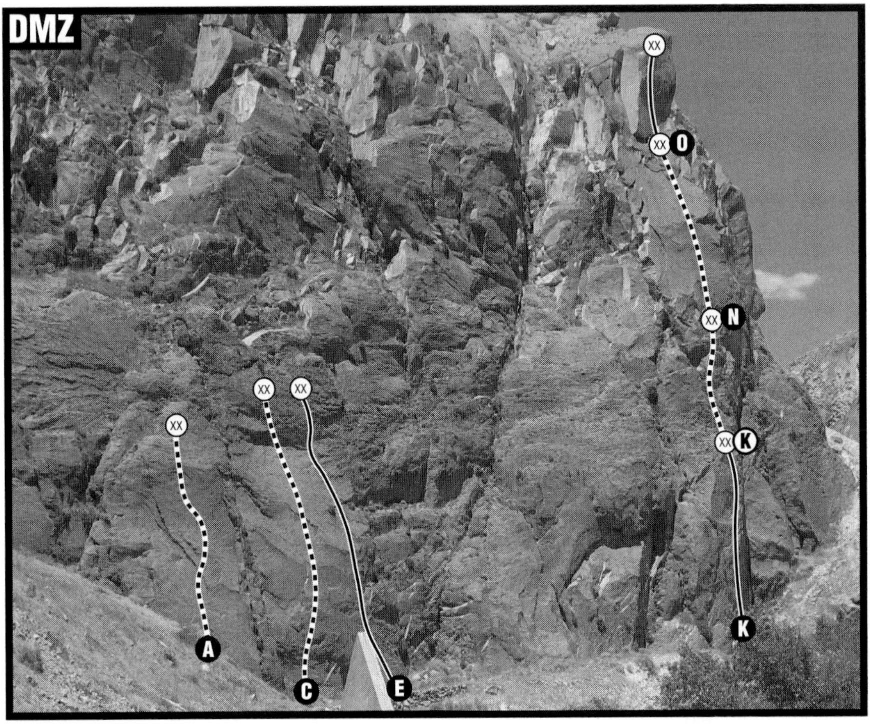

©2005 Maximus Press. *Marty Lewis Topo.*

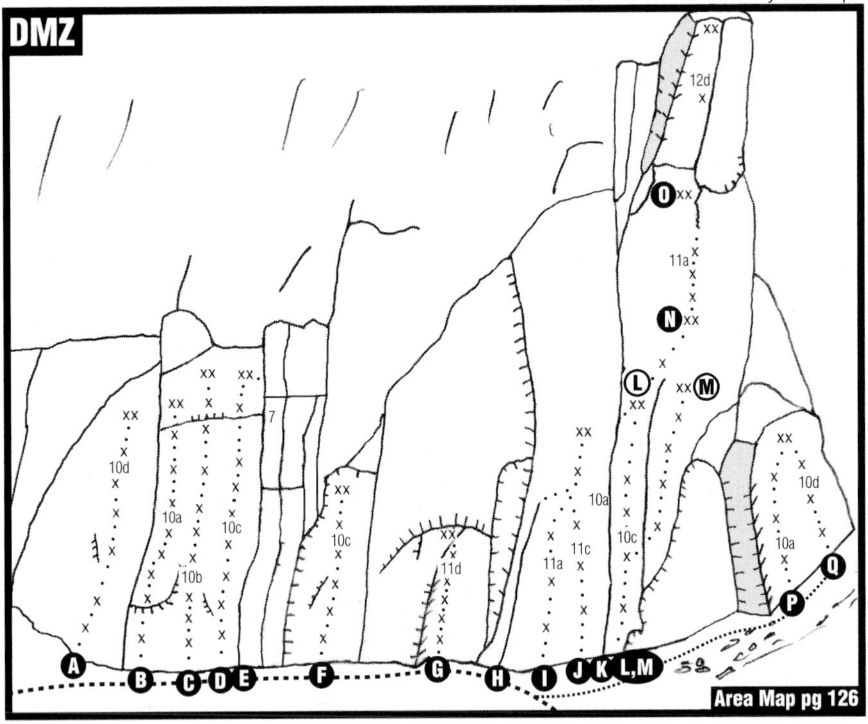

DMZ

Southeast facing slabs on the west side.

A. Berlin Wall 10d***

6 bolts. Slab. Lower off.

FA: Bruce Pottenger, Jeff Neer, 6/1989, TD.

B. Breaking the Law 10a***

8 bolts. Face to slab. Lower off.

FA: Marty Lewis, Mike Cann, 3/1995, TD.

C. Holocaust 10b****

9 bolts. Sustained slab. 27.5m/90' lower off.

FA: Louie Anderson, Bart Groendycke, 5/1992, TD.

D. Fingertip Ledge of Contentment 10c**

8 bolts. Slab. 27.5m/90' lower off. ☞ Originally this route required climbing up *Brandenburg Gate* then traversing left, the improved start was added later.

FA: Dave Focardi, Sean Greer, 1990, TD. Realignment: Brian Ketron, Sean Plunkett.

E. Brandenburg Gate 7***

Gear to 3". Crack. 27.5m/90' lower off.

FA: Dave Focardi, 1990, GU.

F. Doesn't Anybody Work Around Here? 10c**

5 bolts. Slab. Lower off. ☞ Hank Levine placed the 2nd bolt on this route back in the early 1980s.

FA: Dave Focardi, Todd Vogel, Hank Levine, 1990, GU.

G. No Fly Zone 11d*

5 bolts. Face. Lower off.

FA: Dan Spurlock, Pat Spurlock, 1994, TD.

H. People are Weird 9*

1 bolt, gear to 3". Crack to face. Lower off.

FA: Dave Focardi, Grant Schumacher, 1/1992, GU.

I. Come of Age 11a**

4 bolts. Face. Lower off.

FA: Sean Greer, Tom Herbert, 6/1990, TD.

J. Pump up the Trust Fund 11c**

4 bolts. Technical face. Lower off.

FA: Tom Kleinfelter, 1990, TD.

K. Cobbler's Delight 10a***

Gear to 2.5". Nice vertical finger crack. Lower off.

FA: Tom Kleinfelter, Tony Puppo, 1989, GU.

L. Transcendence 10c**

4 bolts. Face. Lower off.

FA: Joe Rousek, Kevin Leary, 1989, TD.

M. Fantasia 10c*

6 bolts. Clip the first 2 bolts of *Transcendence* then go right across a crack and up a face. Lower off.

FA: Louie Anderson, Todd Miller, 11/1991, GU.

N. Waterline 11a**(r)

Approach by climbing either *Cobbler's Delight* or *Transcendence*, pass the anchor and a bolt to a high belay on a ledge. 3 bolts, gear to 1". Runout slab. Lower off.

FA: Jeff Schoen, 1990, GU.

O. Blockbuster 12d***

1 bolt, gear to 1.5". Steep exposed crack. Lower off. ☞ The most difficult gear route in the Gorge.

FA: Tom Herbert, 1992, TD.

P. Easy Enough 10a**

3 bolts. Face. Lower off.

FA: T.M. Herbert, Tom Herbert, 1991, TD.

Q. Gecko 10d*

3 bolts. Face. Lower off.

FA: Louie Anderson, Todd Miller, 8/1991, GU.

Matt Ciancio on **Loony Binge** 12c*****. ©*Aaron Black Photo.* See Page 143

©2005 Maximus Press. *Marty Lewis Photo.*

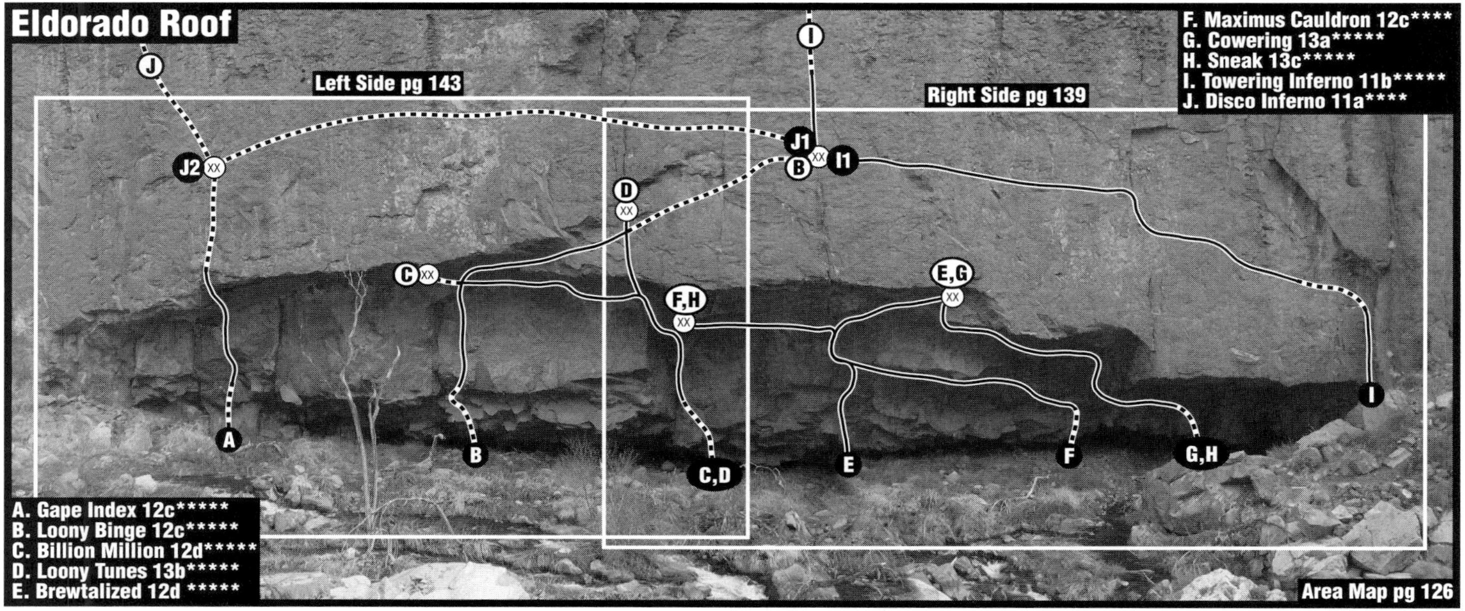

Eldorado Roof - Overview

The most massive wall in the Gorge sits on top of the tremendous Eldorado Roof. An awesome collection of steep and strenuous climbs are found here. Only a fraction of the routes are shown. Please check out the individual topos for more detail.

J. Disco Inferno 11a****

Pitch 1: 11a*****. 15 bolts. Climb the 1st pitch of the *Towering Inferno.*
Pitch 2: 10d**. 13 bolts. Huge face traverse left to the anchors of *Gape Index.*
Pitch 3: 10c***. 12 bolts. Climb up and left to the belay of the *Wiggly.* See page 145.
Descent: Two 30m/100' rappels.
FA: Peter Croft, Dayle Mazzarella, Marty Lewis, 11/2000, GU.

Marty Lewis on the 1st pitch of the **Towering Inferno** 11a*****. ©*Kevin Calder Photo.*

©2005 Maximus Press. *Marty Lewis Topo.*

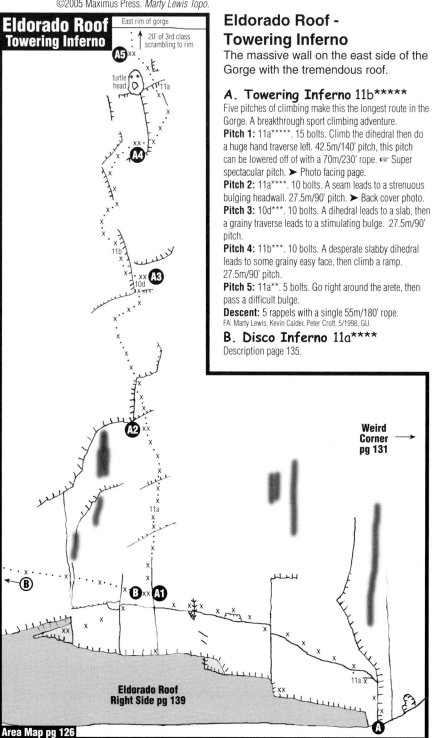

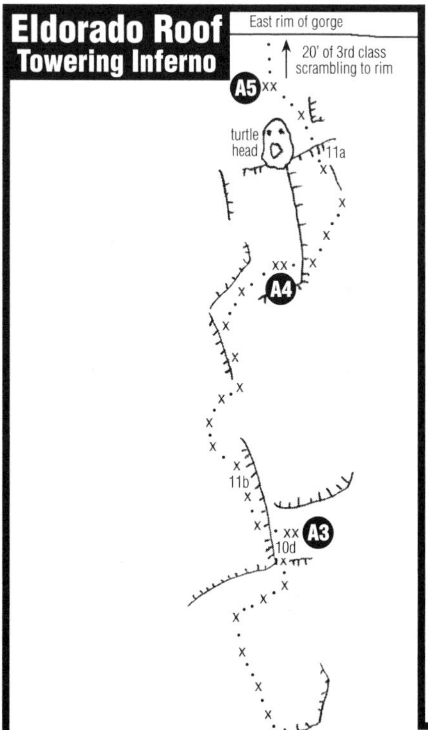

Eldorado Roof - Towering Inferno

The massive wall on the east side of the Gorge with the tremendous roof.

A. Towering Inferno 11b*****

Five pitches of climbing make this the longest route in the Gorge. A breakthrough sport climbing adventure.

Pitch 1: 11a*****. 15 bolts. Climb the dihedral then do a huge hand traverse left. 42.5m/140' pitch, this pitch can be lowered off of with a 70m/230' rope. ☞ Super spectacular pitch. ➤ Photo facing page.

Pitch 2: 11a****. 10 bolts. A seam leads to a strenuous bulging headwall. 27.5m/90' pitch. ➤ Back cover photo.

Pitch 3: 10d***. 10 bolts. A dihedral leads to a slab, then a grainy traverse leads to a stimulating bulge. 27.5m/90' pitch.

Pitch 4: 11b***. 10 bolts. A desperate slabby dihedral leads to some grainy easy face, then climb a ramp. 27.5m/90' pitch.

Pitch 5: 11a**. 5 bolts. Go right around the arete, then pass a difficult bulge.

Descent: 5 rappels with a single 55m/180' rope.

FA: Marty Lewis, Kevin Calder, Peter Croft, 5/1998, GU.

B. Disco Inferno 11a****

Description page 135.

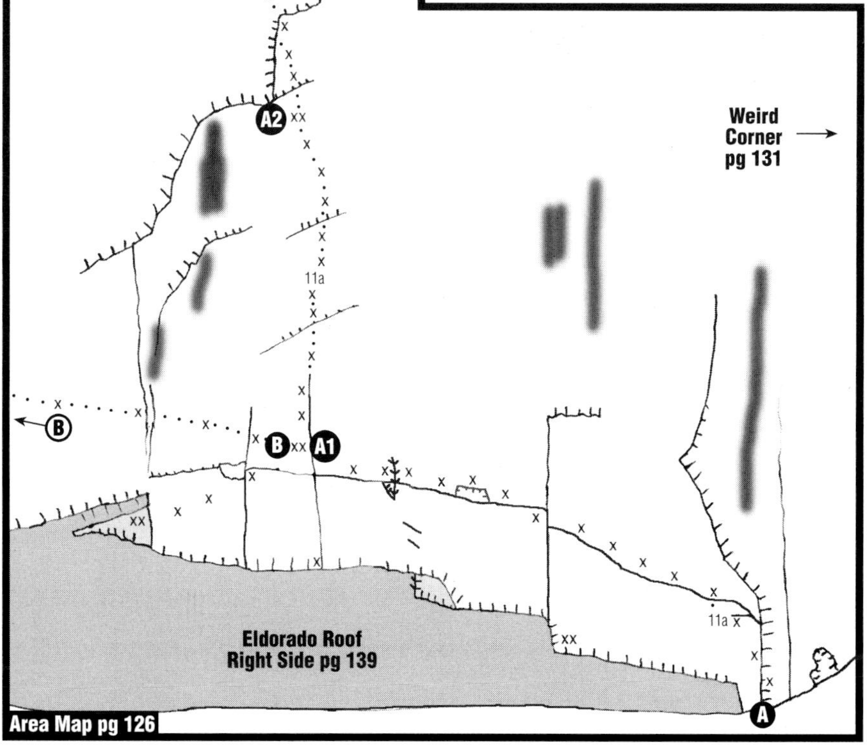

©2005 Maximus Press. *Marty Lewis Topo.*

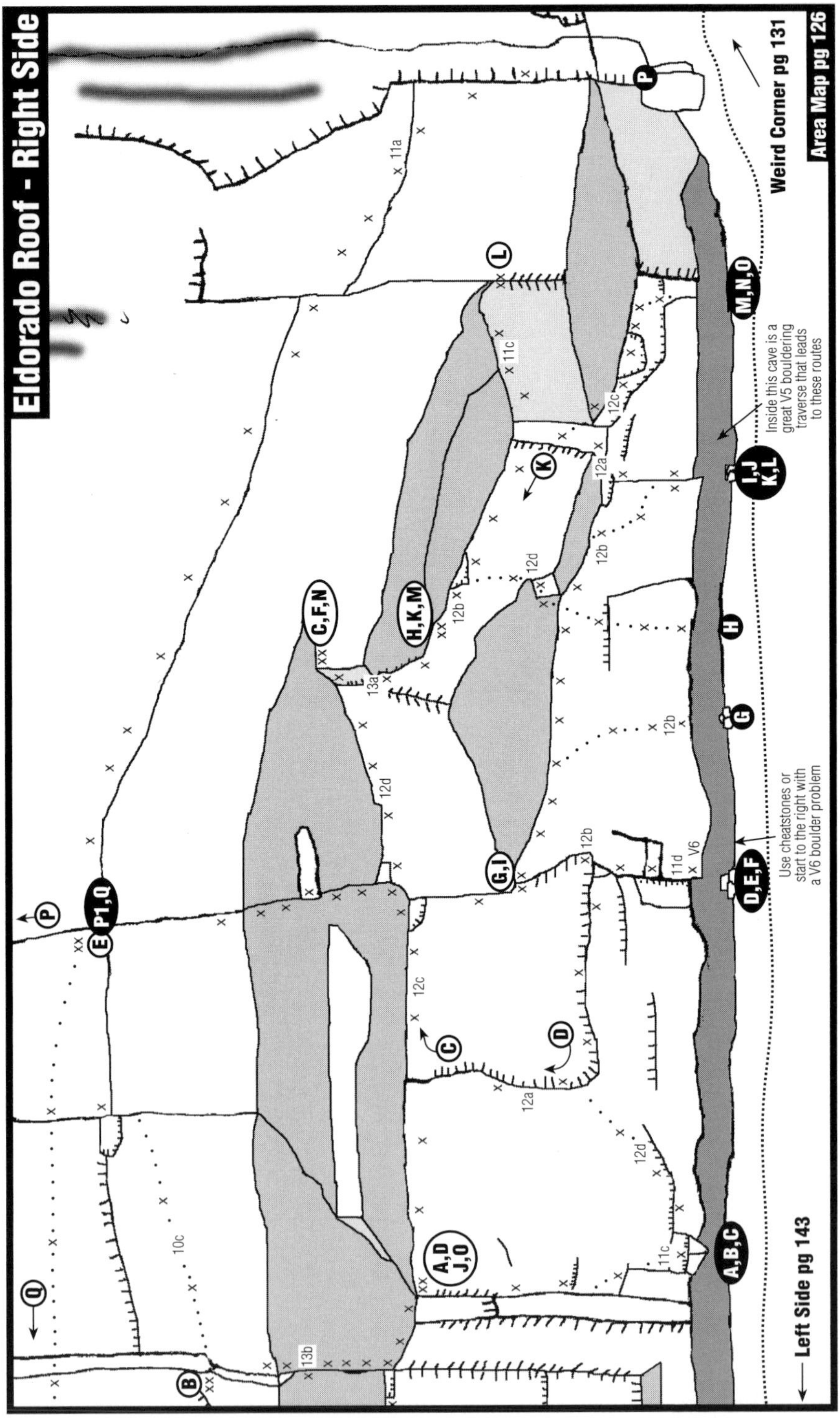

Eldorado Roof - Right Side

The massive wall on the east side of the Gorge with the tremendous roof. The Eldorado Roof is a crag within a crag. The climbing is a synthesis of Yosemite type features mixed with very steep rock and friendly Owens River Gorge style bolting. These climbs are strenuous gut wrenching endurance affairs that require judicious use of crack technique. The faint of heart need not apply. The roof is almost completely equipped with fixed draws. The ratings indicated on the topo indicate the difficulty of a section while on the go—if you are hangdogging you may find a crux to be only 5.11. Always dry.

A. Letter Bomb 11c**

4 bolts. Turn a steep block, then enter a chimney. Lower off. ☞ A good introduction to the roof.
FA: Eric Kohl, 11/1994, TD.

B. Loony Tunes 13b*****

13 bolts. Climb *Letter Bomb*, then undercling left to a striking horizontal roof crack. Lower off. ➤ Photo page 140.
FA: Peter Croft, Marty Lewis, Kevin Calder, 6/1998, GU.

C. Sniveling 13a****

15 bolts. Clip the first *Letter Bomb* bolt, then head right via thin technical climbing, go up a dihedral, and then climb a long strenuous undercling right. Lower off.
FA: Peter Croft, Kevin Calder, 5/1998, GU.

Variation: 12d***. 8 bolts. Start the *Sniveling*, but undercling left back to the anchors of *Letter Bomb*.

D. Slacker 12a****

10 bolts. A powerful overhang leads to a strenuous undercling left, then up a dihedral, then left again. Lower off.
➤ Photo page 141.
FA: Marty Lewis, Kevin Calder, Brian Ketron, 10/1994, GU.

Variation: 12c***. 11 bolts. Start *Slacker* but continue straight up past the initial undercling, then head left for the same finish. Lower off.

E. Project

13 bolts. Straight up, then straight out huge roof.
P: Peter Croft, Marty Lewis.

F. Brewtalized 12d*****

13 bolts. A powerful overhang followed by a steep dihedral, then a long brutal undercling right. Lower off.
➤ Photo page 145.
FA: Eric Kohl, 9/1994, GU.

G. What Me Worry 12b*

6 bolts. A boulder problem then an undercling left. Lower off.
FA: Tom Herbert, 1990, GU.

H. Downward Spiral 12d**

7 bolts. Steep face to a burly roof. Lower off. ☞ A giant drilled pocket makes this route the only chiseled route under the roof.
FA: Eric Kohl, 10/1994, GU.

I. Flakenstein 12b***

10 bolts. A bouldery face leads to a steep pumpy undercling left. Lower off.
FA: Kevin Calder, Marty Lewis, 7/1995, GU.

J. Maximus Cauldron 12c****

16 bolts. Climb *Flakenstein*, then continue up a dihedral, then do a powerful undercling left. Lower off.
FA: Peter Croft, Marty Lewis, Kevin Calder, 5/1998, GU.

K. Civilized 12b***

8 bolts. Climb the *Godzilla* overhang to a strenuous undercling left, followed by a boulderey finish. Lower off.
FA: Eric Kohl, Jeff Schoen, 9/1994, GU.

L. Godzilla Does the Dizzy Tango 12a***

7 bolts. Climb the overhang then do a tenuous traverse right. Lower off. ☞ The first route under the roof.
FA: Steve Schneider, 1990, GU.

M. Chongin' in the Hood 12c****

11 bolts. Undercling left to a horizontal roof crack, then finish out *Civilized*. Lower off.
FA: Scott Sederstrom, Brian Ketron, Marty Lewis, 5/1995, GU.

N. Cowering 13a*****

14 bolts. Climb *Chongin' in the Hood*, then continue left and up a wicked dihedral, then move right. Lower off.
FA: Peter Croft, Kevin Calder, Marty Lewis, 5/1998, GU.

O. Sneak 13c*****

23 bolts. Climb the *Cowering*, but then go left across *Brewtalized* past the corner and continue underclinging left all the way to the *Letter Bomb* anchor. A fantastic mega-endurance link-up. 50m/165' pitch, short rappel.
FA: Peter Croft, 2/1999, GU.

P. Towering Inferno 11a*****

15 bolts. Climb the dihedral then do a huge hand traverse left. 42.5m/140' pitch, this pitch can be lowered off of with a 70m/230' rope or do a 27.5m/90' rappel. ☞ One of the most spectacular pitches in the gorge.
FA: Marty Lewis, Peter Croft, 3/1998, GU.

This is the first pitch of a grand five pitch adventure, for a complete description see page 137.

Q. Disco Inferno 11a****

Description page 135.

Bouldering

Excellent bouldering is found all along the huge cave under the roof.

Peter Croft on **Loony Tunes** 13b***** at the Eldorado Roof. ©*Kevin Calder Photo.* See Page 143

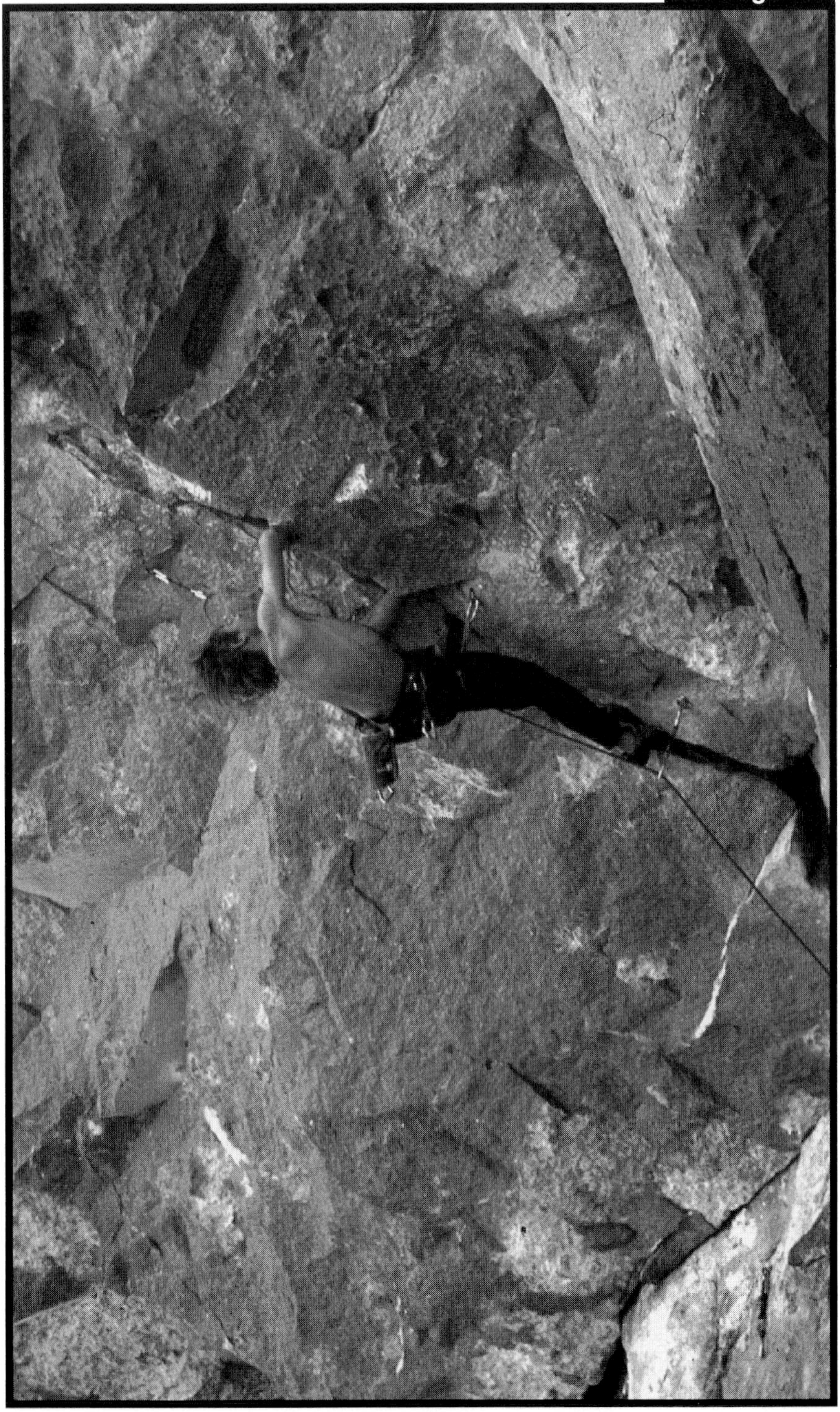

Josh Becker on **Slacker** 12a**** at the Eldorado Roof. ©*Shawn Reeder Photo.* **See Page 139**

©2005 Maximus Press. *Marty Lewis Topo.*

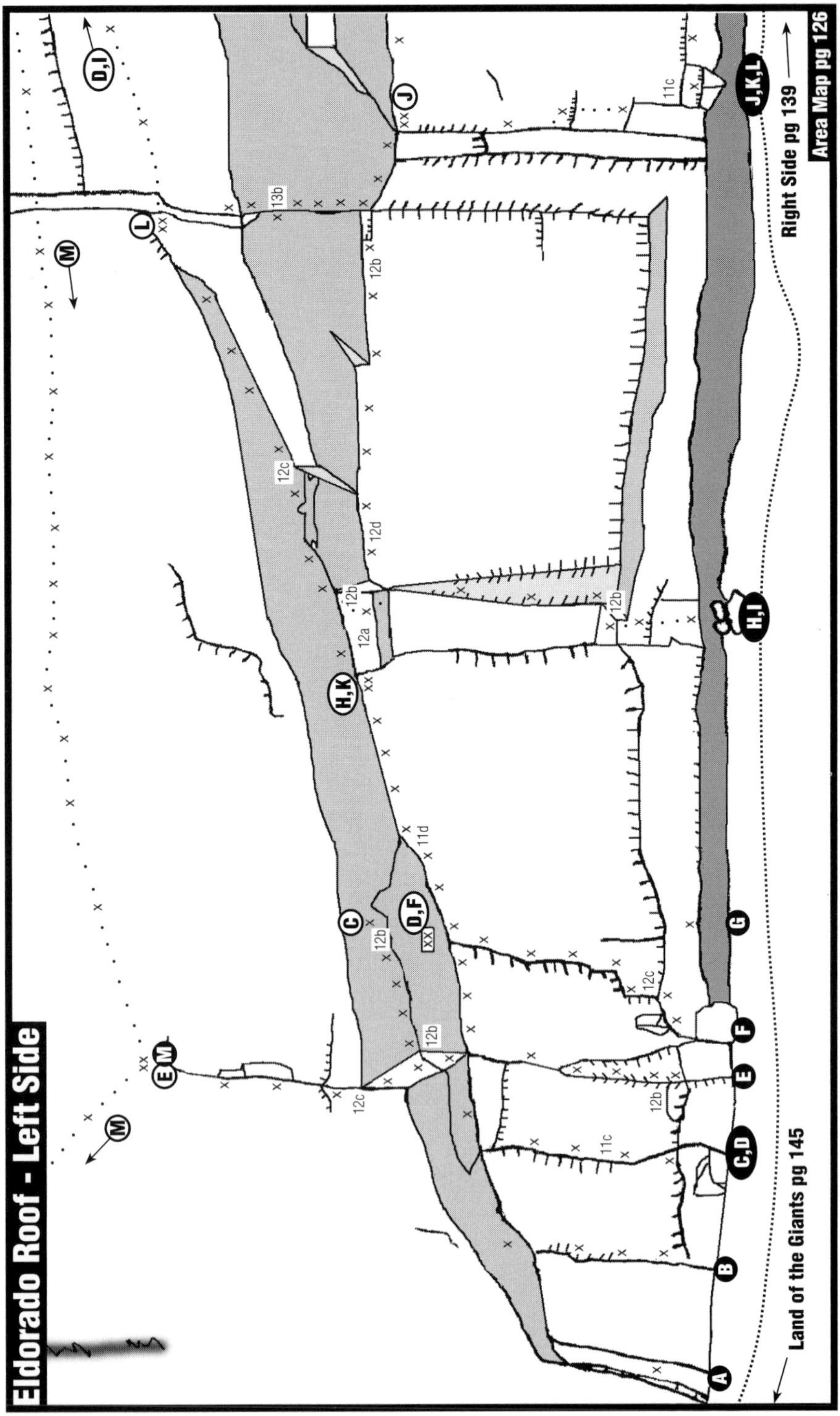

Eldorado Roof - Left Side

The massive wall on the east side of the Gorge with the tremendous roof. The Eldorado Roof is a crag within a crag. The climbing is a synthesis of Yosemite type features mixed with very steep rock and friendly Owens River Gorge style bolting. These climbs are strenuous gut wrenching endurance affairs that require judicious use of crack technique. The faint of heart need not apply. The roof is almost completely equipped with fixed draws. The ratings indicated on the topo indicate the difficulty of a section while on the go—if you are hangdogging you may find a crux to be only 5.11. Always dry.

A. Open Project
1 bolt.
P: Kevin Calder.

B. Open Project
4 bolts. Dihedral to a blank roof.
FA: Eric Kohl.

C. Independent Worm Saloon aka the Worm Rig 12b****
11 bolts. Climb the steep crack, then pull the *Gape Index* roof, then go right out a flake. Ends at a one bolt lower off.
FA: Eric Kohl, Janice Moore, 10/1994, GU.

D. Longest Yard 12c**
28 bolts. Climb the steep crack, then undercling right to the bombay chimney above *Proctology Exam*, exit the chimney via a difficult move, then continue underclinging right to the long strenuous horizontal flake of *Loony Binge*, pass this then traverse some interesting face to a belay on the *Towering Inferno*. 60m/200' pitch, 27.5m/90' rappel. ☞ This once proud testpiece is covered in bird crap from the 12th to the 14th bolt.
FA: Marty Lewis, Peter Croft, 1/2000, GU.

Variation: 11c***. 8 bolts. Climb the *Longest Yard*, but stop at the *Proctology Exam* belay. Lower off.

E. Gape Index 12c*****
11 bolts. A bouldery start leads to an awkward dihedral, then pull a roof to a strenuous undercling, turn the roof and climb some steep face. Lower off. ☞ This awesome route used to end at a knee bar at the lip of the roof.
FA: Tom Addison, Greg Jennings, 1991, GU. Route extension: Peter Croft, Marty Lewis.

F. Proctology Exam 12c**
7 bolts, bring 6 quickdraws. A powerful bouldery bulge leads to an awkward dihedral, then finish in a bombay chimney. This route can easily be cleaned when lowering off.
FA: Marty Lewis, Will Gove, Bruce Lella, Jeff Schoen, 7/1992, GU.

G. Open Project
1 bolt. Roof.
FA: Eric Kohl.

H. Loony Left 12b***
7 bolts. Climb *Loony Binge*, but head left at the apex of the roof. Lower off. ☞ A good introduction to the roof.
FA: Peter Croft, 12/1998, GU.

I. Loony Binge 12c*****
18 bolts. Pass a difficult bulge then climb a dihedral, pass another difficult bulge then head right on a long strenuous horizontal flake, then continue traversing right across an interesting face to a belay on the *Towering Inferno*. Use a 70m/230' rope to lower off. ☞ The ultra classic of the roof. ➤ Photo page 134.
FA: Alf, Marty Lewis, Jeff Schoen, Raleigh Collins, Huey Wilson, 10/1991, GU.

J. Letter Bomb 11c**
4 bolts. Turn a steep block, then enter a chimney. Lower off. ☞ A good introduction to the roof.
FA: Eric Kohl, 11/1994, TD.

K. Billion Million 12d*****
15 bolts. Climb *Letter Bomb* then undercling left across a strenuous then technical section, then cross the powerful bulge on *Loony Binge*. Lower off.
FA: Kevin Calder, Peter Croft, Marty Lewis, 6/1998, GU.

Billion Binge Variation: 13a*****. 28 bolts. Use double rope technique; climb the *Billion Million*, then drop the first rope and head right out the *Loony Binge* flake and continue right until reaching the *Towering Inferno* belay.
☞ Combines two of the best pitches under the roof.
FA: Peter Croft, 2/1999, GU.

L. Loony Tunes 13b*****
13 bolts. Climb *Letter Bomb*, then undercling left to a striking horizontal roof crack. Lower off. ➤ Photo page 140.
FA: Peter Croft, Marty Lewis, Kevin Calder, 6/1998, GU.

M. Disco Inferno 11a****
Description page 135.

Bouldering
Excellent bouldering is found all along the huge cave under the roof.

©2005 Maximus Press. *Marty Lewis Photo.*

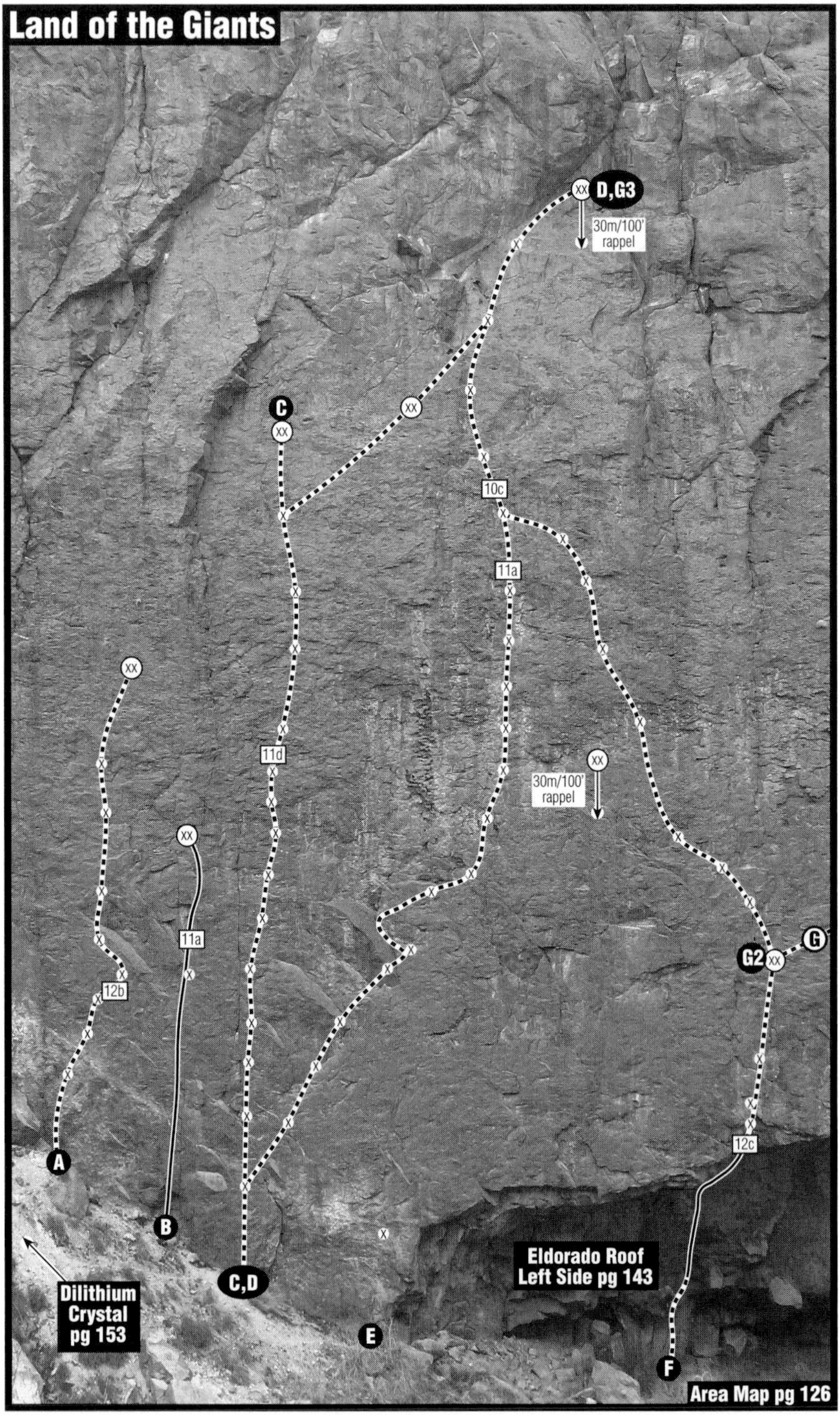

Land of the Giants

These routes are found on an eroding slope just left of the Eldorado Roof on the east side of the Gorge.

A. Drillin' Time Again 12b***

8 bolts. Tenuous technical face. Lower off. ☞ Holds must be breaking off of this one, making it way harder than the original 11b rating.

FA: Dan Haughelstine, 11/1992, GU.

B. Enraged Pixie 11a**

1 bolt, gear to 1". Thin crack. Lower off.

FA: Phil Green, Wendy Borgerd, 8/1989, GU.

C. Probation Violation 11d*****

14 bolts. Vertical crack to long technical face, the fun never stops. 42.5m/140' rappel or do a 30m/100' rappel to the top of *Enraged Pixie.*

FA: Fred Berman, Marty Lewis, 4/1993, TD.

Variation: 11d*****. 17 bolts. Climb *Probation Violation*, then angle up and right past 3 bolts. 60m/200' pitch, two 30m/100' rappels.

D. Wiggly 11a*****

19 bolts. Clip the 1st bolt of *Probation Violation* then climb up and right up a ramp system, from here attack a steep headwall, then up a slab. 60m/200' pitch, two 30m/100' rappels.

FA: Peter Croft, Dayle Mazzarella, 4/2001, GU.

E. Open Project

1 bolt. Blank face.

P: Marty Lewis.

F. Gape Index 12c*****

11 bolts. A bouldery start leads to an awkward dihedral, then pull a roof to a strenuous undercling, turn the roof and climb some steep face. Lower off. ☞ This awesome route used to end at a knee bar at the lip of the roof.

FA: Tom Addison, Greg Jennings, 1991, GU. Route extension: Peter Croft, Marty Lewis.

G. Disco Inferno 11a****

See page 135.

Pitch 1: 11a*****. 15 bolts. Climb the 1st pitch of the *Towering Inferno.*

Pitch 2: 10d**. 13 bolts. Huge face traverse left to the anchors of *Gape Index.*

Pitch 3: 10c***. 12 bolts. Climb up and left to the belay of the *Wiggly.*

Descent: Two 30m/100' rappels.

FA: Peter Croft, Dayle Mazzarella, Marty Lewis, 11/2000, GU.

Marty Lewis on **Brewtalized** 12d***** at the Eldorado Roof. ©*Kevin Calder Photo.* **See Page 139**

©2005 Maximus Press. *Marty Lewis Photo.*

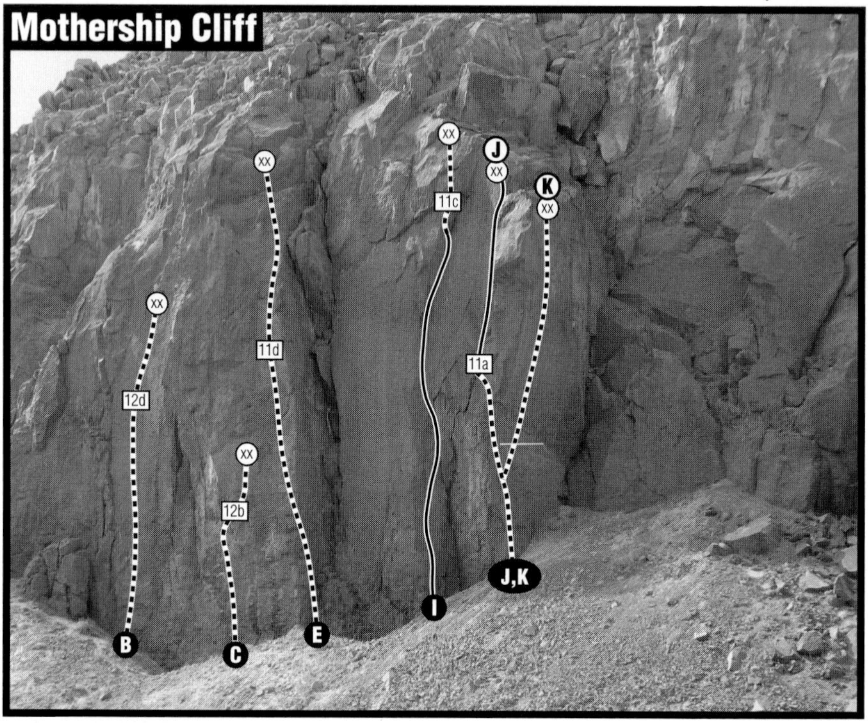

©2005 Maximus Press. *Marty Lewis Topo.*

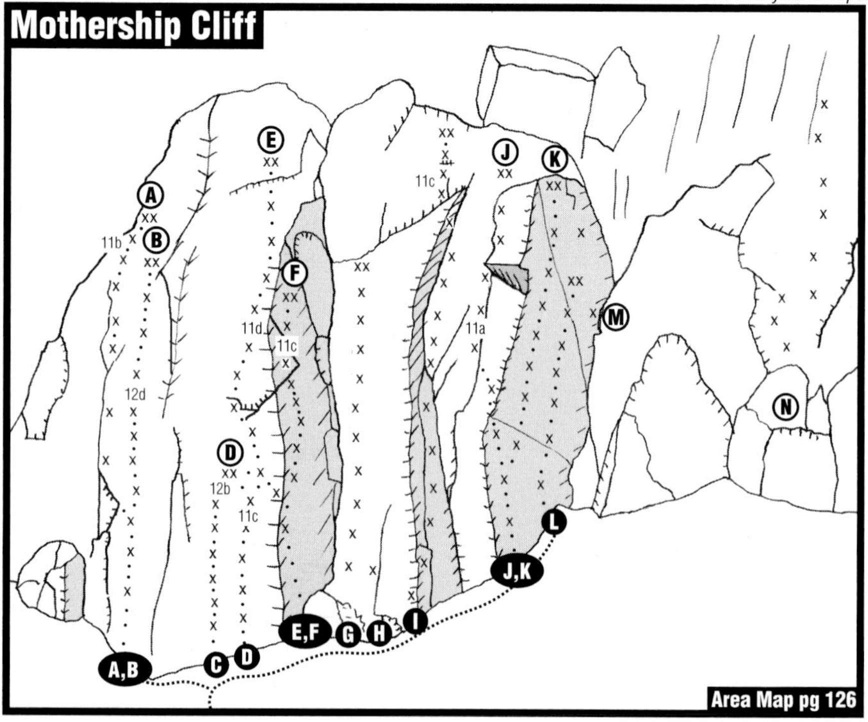

Mothership Cliff

The gray buttress above a pink talus fan on the west side.

A. Unknown 11b**

10 bolts, gear to 2". Clip the first 3 bolts of *Excelsior*, then move left to a crack, follow this to technical face climbing. 30m/100' lower off.
FA: Peter Croft, 10/2000, GU.

B. Excelsior 12d*****

10 bolts. Sustained vertical technical face. Lower off.
FA: Tom Herbert, 3/1990, TD.

C. Piranha 12b****

6 bolts. A steep pumpy face leads to a difficult boulder problem through a bulge. Lower off. ➤ Photo page 124.
FA: Gary Slate, Bill McChesney, Marty Lewis, 4/1991, GU.

D. Barracuda 11c**

5 bolts. Steep face. Lower off.
FA: Louie Anderson, Larry Kuechlin, 6/1994, TD.

E. Catch-n-Release 11d****

11 bolts. Clip 1st bolt of *Bird of Prey* then cross the arete and climb the face. 35m/115' lower off.
FA: Todd Graham, 2001, TD.

Variation: 11d****. 14 bolts. Start *Barracuda* then climb *Catch-n-Release*. 35m/115' lower off.

Variation: 7*. 3 bolts. Clip the first 3 bolts of *Catch-n-Release* then traverse left to anchors of *Piranha*. Lower off.

F. Bird of Prey 11c***

8 bolts. An off-vertical arete leads to a slick slabby seam. Lower off.
FA: Joe Rousek, Tony Puppo, 3/1990, GU.

G. Holey War 13a? (project)

10 bolts. Thin pocketed face.
P: Todd Graham.

H. Open Project

1 bolt. Crack to arete.
P: Joe Rousek.

I. Living Dead 11c*****

15 bolts. A crack leads to a strenuous dihedral, then move left around the arete and climb a series of technical moves through bulges. 30m/100' lower off.
FA: Kevin Leary, Joe Rousek, Bob Harrington, 11/1999, TD.

J. Northern Pike 11a****

9 bolts. Arete to killer dihedral. 27.5m/90' lower off.
FA: Perry Beckham, Becky Bates, 11/1995, TD.

K. Fight Club 13b*****

9 bolts. Big lockoffs between positive holds up a steep limestone like wall, finish on a sporty slab (11b). Lower off. ➤ Photo page 149.
FA: Robert Miller, Todd Graham, 3/2002, TD.

L. Blood Sport 13b***

6 bolts. Bouldery moves up a short steep wall, a bit crumbly. Lower off.
FA: Robert Miller, Todd Graham, 2/2003, TD.

M. Open Project

2 bolts.
P: Bill Russell.

N. Project

9 bolts. A steep slab leads to a dihedral.
P: Joe Rousek, Marty Lewis.

Kevin Calder on **Extreme Caffeine** 10b***** at the Dilithium Crystal. ©*Marty Lewis Photo.*

©2005 Maximus Press. *Marty Lewis Photo.*

©2005 Maximus Press. *Marty Lewis Topo.*

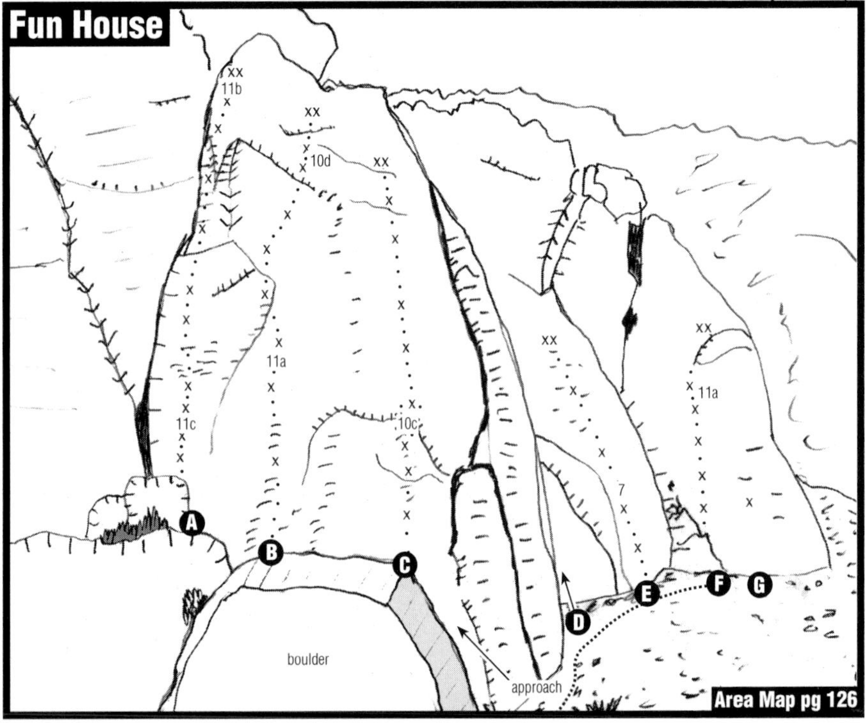

Robert Miller on **Fight Club** 13b***** at the Mothership Cliff. ©*Kevin Calder Photo.* **See Page 147**

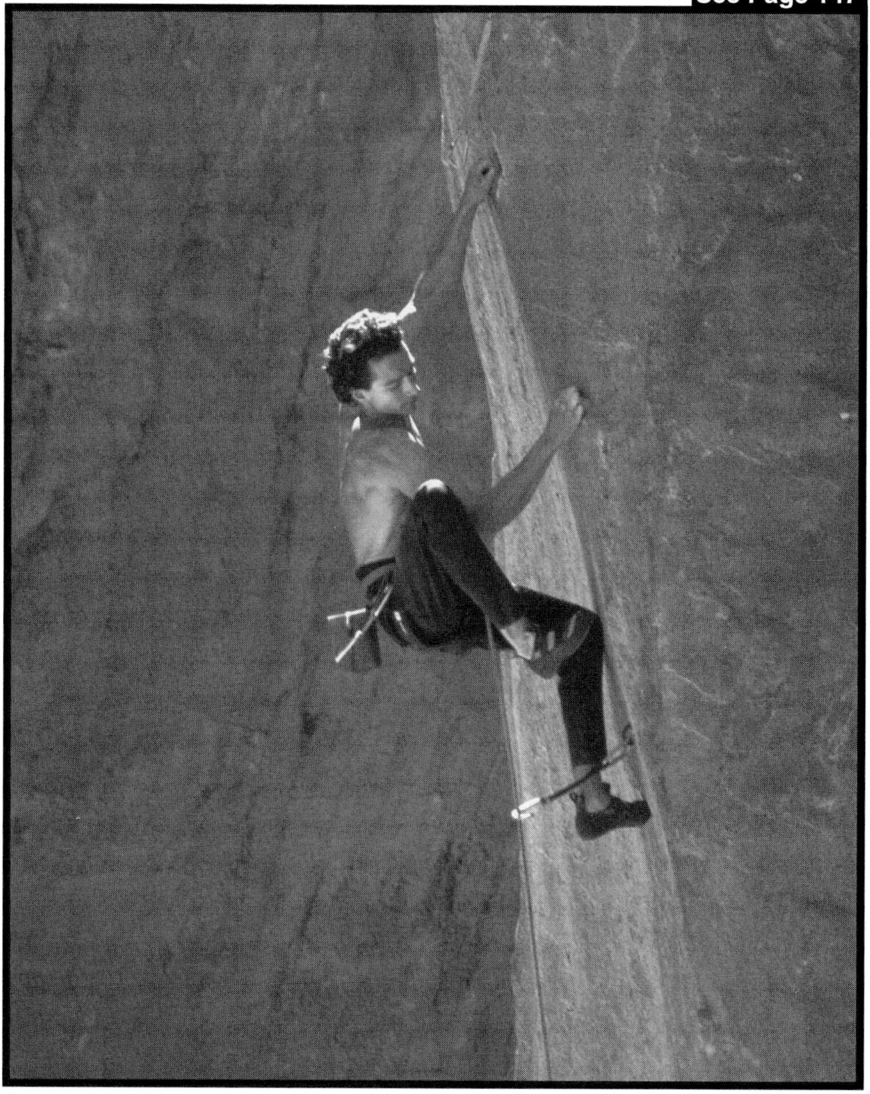

Fun House

Gray towers on the west side.

A. Thumbs Up 11c****

10 bolts. Steep face to slabby arete. 27.5m/90' lower off.
FA: Gary Slate, Joe Rousek, 1990, GU.

B. Escapade 11a*****

8 bolts. Vertical face to slab. 27.5m/90' lower off.
FA: Tom Herbert, 5/1990, TD.

C. Melts in Your Mouth 10c****

8 bolts. Pass a bulge on either side then climb amazing edges. Lower off.
FA: Tony Puppo, Dave Focardi, 1990, GU.

D. Unemployment Line 10a**

North facing. 5 bolts. Face. Lower off.
FA: Charlie Johnson, Greg Corliss, 1991, GU.

E. Expensive But Worth It 7**

4 bolts, gear: 1.25" piece. Slab. Lower off.
FA: Todd Vogel, Dave Focardi, Fred Lifton, 1992, GU.

F. Win, Lose or Claw 11a**

5 bolts. Technical face, then move right. Lower off.
FA: Tom Herbert, Tony Puppo, Sondra Utterback, 5/1990, TD.

G. Open Project

1 bolt. Face.

Gary Slate on **Klingon** 12a***** at the Dilithium Crystal. ©*Andy Selters Photo.* **See Page 153**

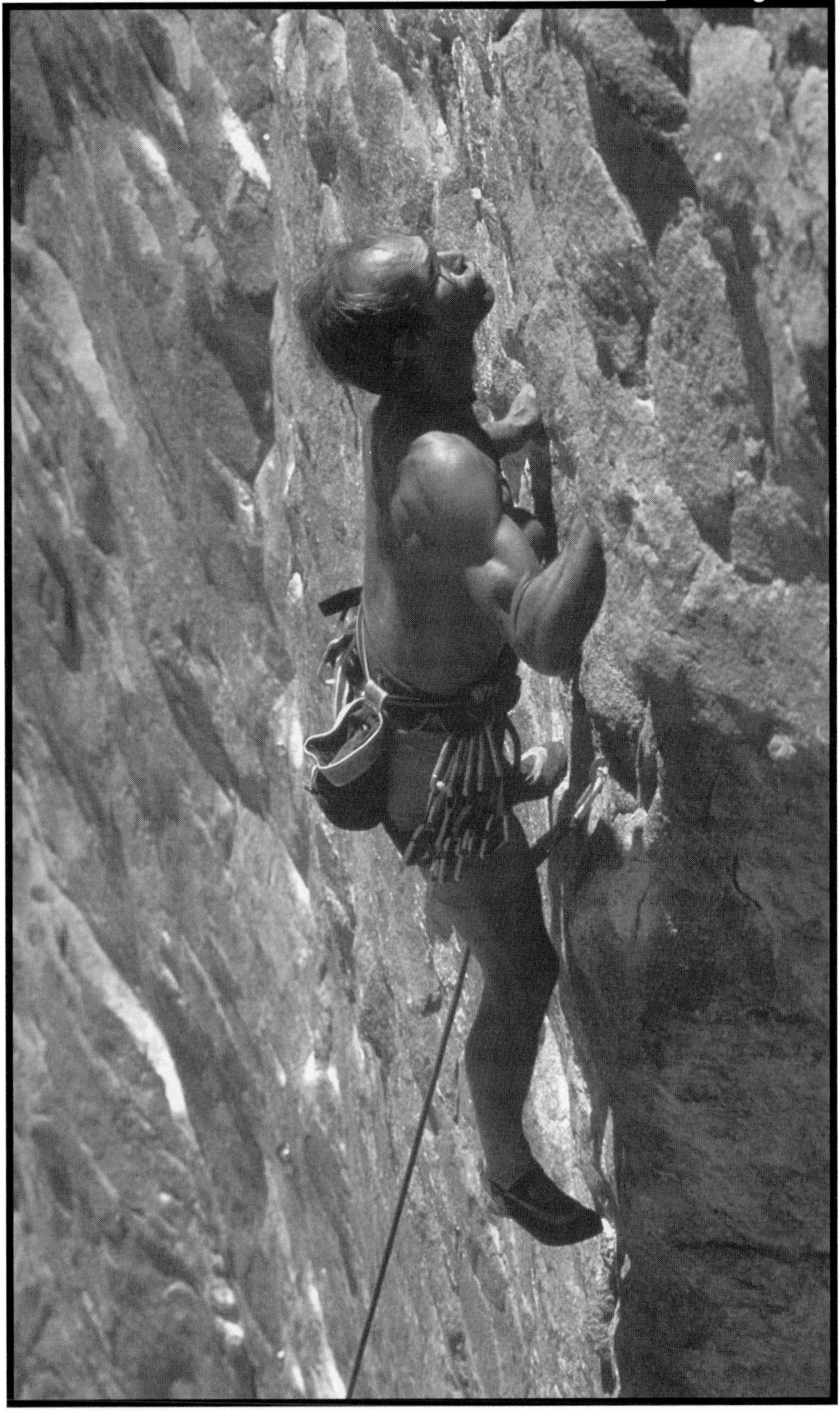

Kevin Leary on **Not for Sale** 12d**** at the Dilithium Crystal. ©*Andy Selters Photo.*

See Page 153

©2005 Maximus Press. *Marty Lewis Photo.*

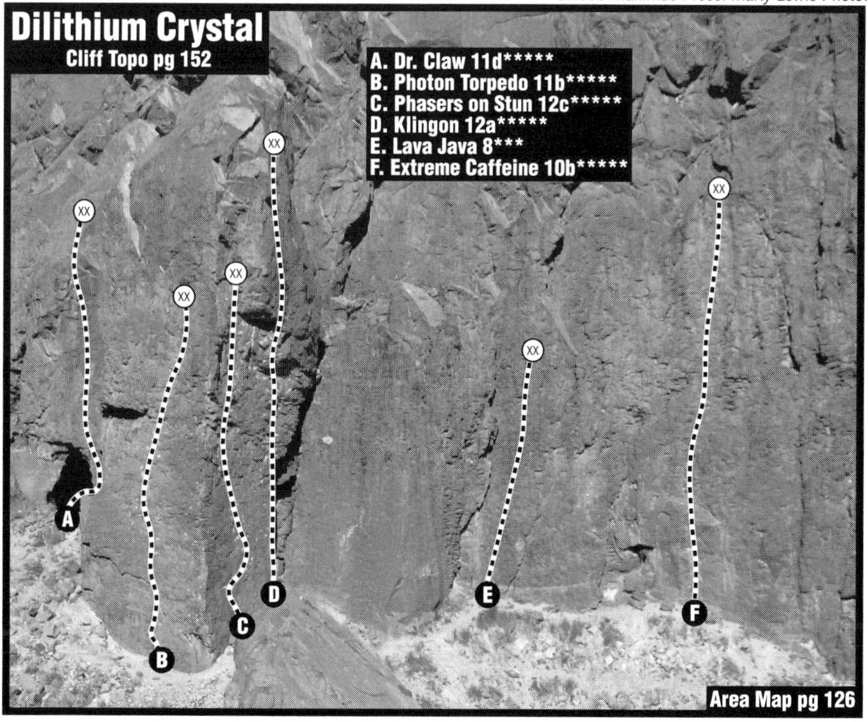

©2005 Maximus Press. *Marty Lewis Topo.*

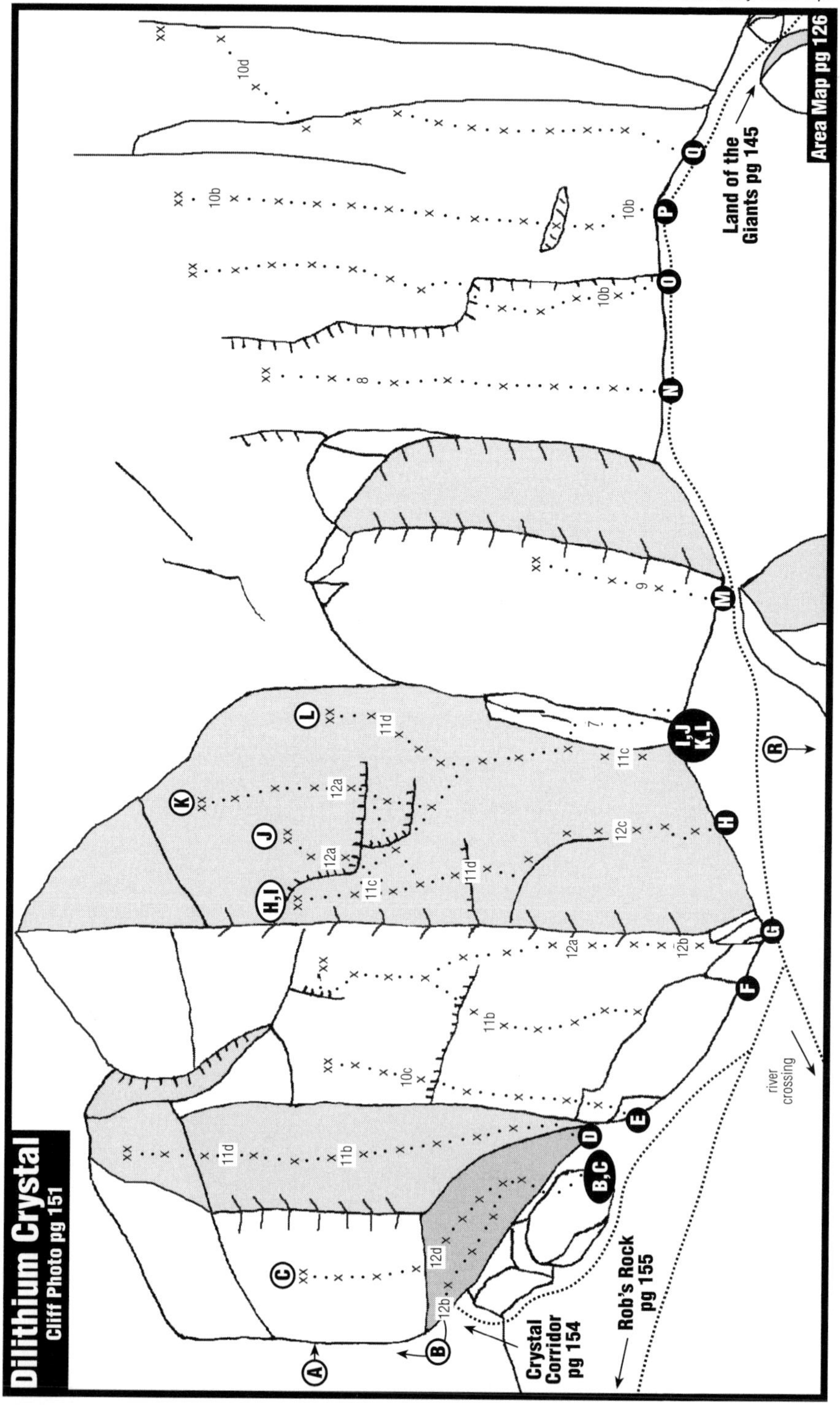

Dilithium Crystal

The free-standing tower on the east side. The most popular spot in the Inner Gorge. A wide range of difficulty on excellent rock.

A. Next *Generation* 11c*

5 bolts. Start on a block, then climb the face. Lower off.
FA: Tom Herbert, 10/1990, TD.

B. Enterprise 12b*****

10 bolts. Climb jugs through a roof with ever-thinning holds, then climb a slabby face. Lower off.
➤ Photo page 36.
FA: Tom Herbert, 1990, TD.

C. Not for Sale 12d****

8 bolts. Pull a big roof to a face. Lower off. ☞ Almost given a Star Trek name—but when the route was to be featured in a video, where it would be climbed, then a mountain bike was to be hauled to the summit and the climber was to ride off into the sunset—the route was deemed "Not for Sale."
➤ Photo page 151.
FA: Kevin Leary, Gary Slate, 1990, GU.

D. Dr. Claw 11d*****

10 bolts. A gently overhanging face leads to a tenuous slab. Lower off.
FA: Dan Haughelstine, Bob Hutchinson, 1990, GU.

E. Impulse Power aka the Trouble With Tribbles 10c***

7 bolts. An arete leads to a roof. Lower off. ☞ This route originally went left about 30' off the ground to a belay; the roof finish was added later.
FA(complete route): Dan Haughelstine, 8/1991, GU. FA(original version): Mike Strassman, Dana Drucker.

F. Photon Torpedo 11b*****

9 bolts. Sustained thin edges up a vertical face. Lower off. ☞ This classic seems to be getting harder and harder as time goes on.
FA: Joe Rousek, Tony Puppo, 4/1990, GU.

G. Mind Meld 12b****

10 bolts. A difficult bouldery start leads to a thin technical pocketed arete. Lower off.
FA: Gary Slate, Joe Rousek, Tony Puppo, Dennis Phillips, 1990, GU.

H. Phasers on Stun 12c*****

11 bolts. Sustained technical face leads to a pumpy endurance section. Lower off. ➤ Photo page 167.
FA: Scott Ayers, Marty Lewis, Eden Masters, Jay Ladin, 10/1990, GU.
Variation: 12d*****. 14 bolts. Go right at the 9th bolt to the *Klingon* finish for a huge pump. 30m/100' lower off.
Variation: 12d****. 12 bolts. Go right at the 10th bolt to the *Romulan Roof* for a big pump. Lower off.

I. Lieutenant Uhura 11c*****

8 bolts. Climb the *Romulan Roof*, but go left at the 7th bolt to *Phasers on Stun*. Lower off. ☞ Great jugs on this one.

J. Romulan Roof 12a****

9 bolts. Climb the chimney (or arete) to a steep face then head left to a very steep bulge. Lower off. ➤ Photo page 160.
FA: Todd Graham, Gary Slate, 2/1991, GU.

K. Klingon 12a*****

11 bolts. Climb the chimney (or arete) to a steep bulging face. 30m/100' lower off. ☞ The original start of this route is to chimney to the 3rd bolt, avoiding balancy technical arete moves.
➤ Photo page 150.
FA: Gary Slate, Bruce Lella, 1990, GU. Route Extension: Todd Graham.

L. Vulcan Variation 11d**

9 bolts. Climb the chimney (or arete) then head right. Lower off. ☞ A near pointless variation.
FA: Tom Herbert, 1991, TD.

M. Stardate 9*

2 bolts. Slabby arete. Lower off. ☞ Previously a solo warm up climb; this little route was then bolted as a gift to a girlfriend.
FA: John Bachar. Retrobolts: Mike Strassman, 1991, GU.

N. Lava Java 8***

6 bolts. Good climbing up an off-vertical face. Lower off.
FA: Dan Haughelstine, 1993, GU.

O. Coffee Achiever 10b***

10 bolts. Climb a tricky face then head right to a roof and a nice headwall. Lower off.
FA: Marty Lewis, Fred Berman, 12/1993, TD.

P. Extreme Caffeine 10b*****

10 bolts. A bouldery start leads to a beautiful pumpy gold headwall. 27.5m/90' lower off. ➤ Photo page 147.
FA: Fred Berman, Marty Lewis, 3/1993, GU.

Q. Liquid Fire 10d***

11 bolts. A vertical face leads to a crack then head right across an exciting face. 30m/100' lower off.
FA: Marty Lewis, Fred Berman, 11/1993, TD.

R. Shuttle Craft 11c**

On the north facing block below *Mind Meld*.
5 bolts. Steep face. Lower off.
FA: Tom Herbert, 1990, TD.

©2005 Maximus Press.

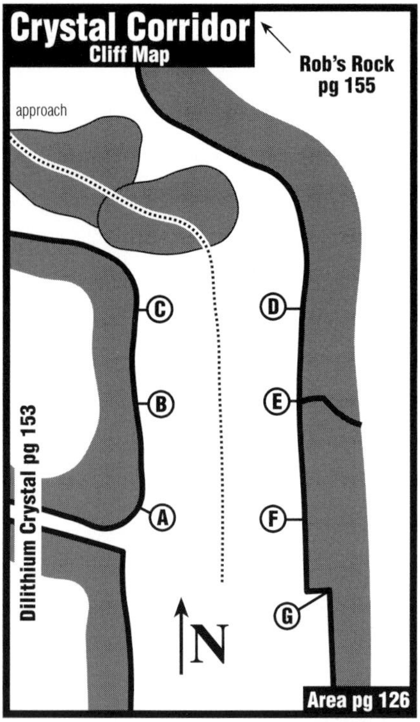

©2005 Maximus Press. *Mike McGrale Topo.*

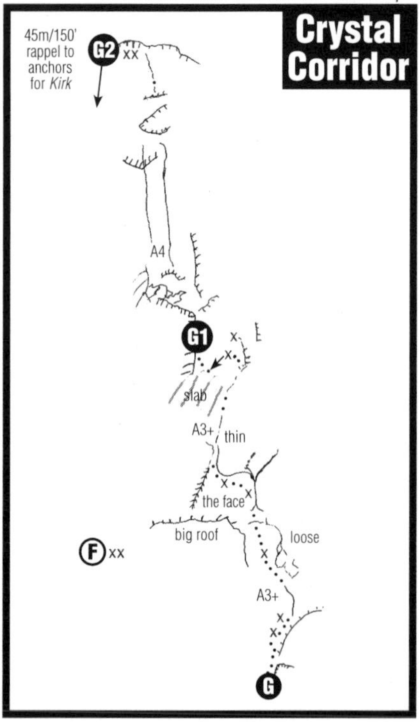

Crystal Corridor

A shaded narrow corridor behind the Dilithium Crystal. Approach by scrambling up a boulder in the notch between the Crystal and Rob's Rock.

A. Klingon Crabs 9**

3 bolts. Arete. Lower off.
FA: Dan Haughelstine, 1992, GU.

B. Romulan Roids 10b**

4 bolts. Face. Lower off.
FA: Dan Haughelstine, 1992, GU.

C. Vulcan Jock Itch 10a**

4 bolts. Face. Lower off. ☞ This was John's descent route when he would free solo *Klingon* and *Dr. Claw.*
FA: John Bachar, 1992, GU. Retrobolts: Dan Haughelstine.

D. Spock 10a**

3 bolts, optional gear to 1". Face to seam. Lower off.
FA: Dan Haughelstine, 1992, GU.

E. Bones 9*

Gear to 2.5". Flake. Lower off.
FA: Dan Haughelstine, 1992, GU.

F. Kirk 10b**

5 bolts. Face. Lower off.
FA: Dan Haughelstine, 1992, GU.

G. Off the Hook 6 A4***

Gear to 2.5", hooks, heads, rurps, beaks, pins, ants.
Pitch 1: 6 A3+***. Free climb up a wide crack to a ledge, from here hooking and nailing lead to a tension traverse left to a corner. Gear anchor.
Pitch 2: 6 A4***. Free moves to a ledge, then nail a thin seam, mantle a flake followed by another thin seam. Rappel 45m/150' left of the big roof to the top of *Kirk*.
FA: Mike McGrale, 1/2001, GU.

©2005 Maximus Press. *Marty Lewis Photo.*

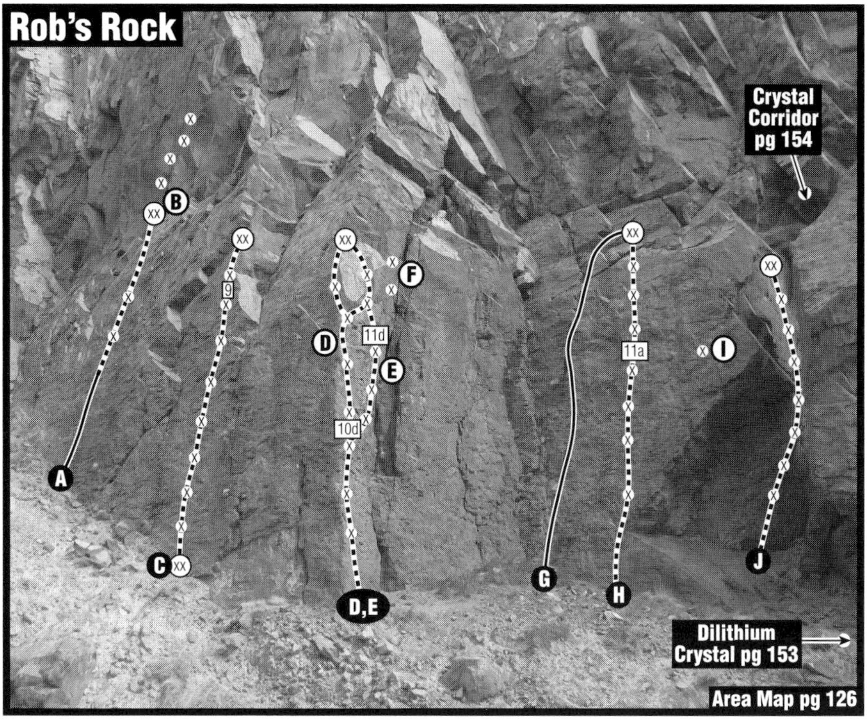

Rob's Rock

The west facing buttress on the east side, adjacent to the Dilithium Crystal.

A. Scalpel 8**(r)

2 bolts, gear to 1.5". Start the left crack of two cracks, finish up a pink slab. Lower off.

FA: Joe Rousek, 1991, GU.

B. Project

4 bolts. Attacks the headwall.

P: Joe Rousek.

C. Clip Jockeys 9****

8 bolts. Excellent off-vertical face. Lower off.

FA: Scott Ayers, Marty Lewis, 3/1991, GU.

D. Dellinger 10d***

7 bolts. Arete, goes way left near the top. Lower off.

☞ Named after Rob Dellinger who died tragically.

FA: Joe Rousek, Gary Slate, 1990, GU.

Variation: 10d***. 8 bolts. At the 6th bolt of *Dellinger* go up and right and finish on *Dust in the Wind*. Lower off.

E. Dust in the Wind 11d***

8 bolts. Clip the first 3 bolts of *Dellinger* then head right up a steep face. Lower off.

FA: Gary Slate, Joe Rousek, 1990, TD.

F. Project

2 bolts. Face.

P: Todd Graham.

G. Sulu 8***

Gear to 4". Sustained wide crack. Lower off.

FA: Scott Ayers, Eden Masters, 1990, GU.

H. Mr. Check-off 11a***

7 bolts. Technical face. Lower off.

FA: Scott Ayers, Eden Masters, 10/1990, GU.

I. Open Project

1 bolt. Steep rotten roof.

P: Marty Lewis.

J. Twister 11b**

7 bolts. Start a steep arete then twist up and right. Lower off.

FA: Dan Haughelstine, 1992, GU.

Hallie Lee on **Jesus Built My Tri-cam** 10a*****. ©*Aaron Black Photo.*

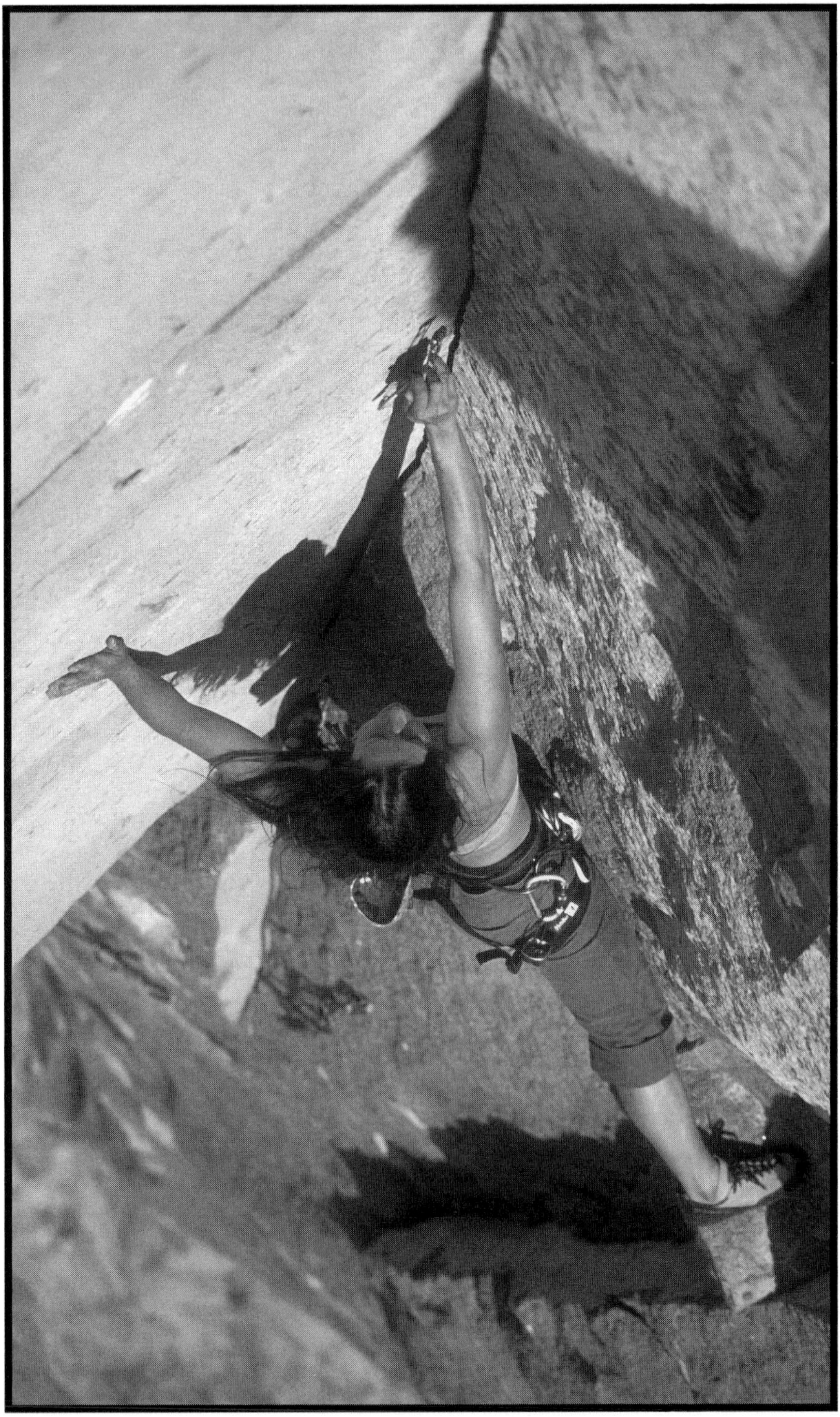

©2005 Maximus Press. Marty Lewis Photo.

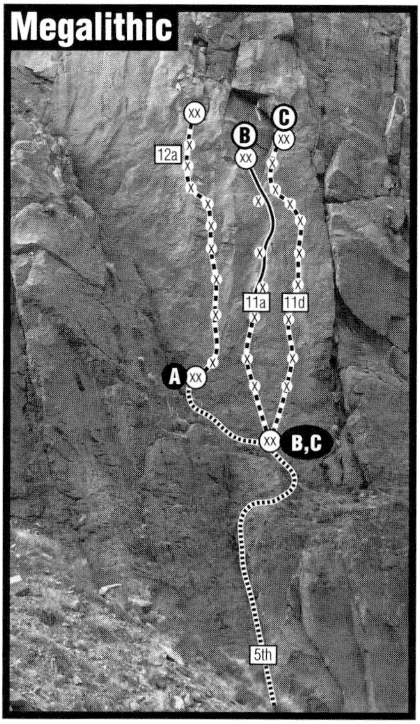

Megalithic

Southeast facing shield up above corners on the west side. Scramble up the left dihedral—the entry move is easy 5th class, then continue up 4th class ground. Descend via a single rope rappel. Technical climbing on near perfect rock.

A. Divine Sculptor 12a****

9 bolts. Porcelain face. Lower off.
FA: Gary Slate, Joe Rousek, 1991, TD.

B. Megalithic 11a***

6 bolts. Face to dihedral. Lower off.
FA: Gary Slate, Joe Rousek, 1990, GU.

C. Nectar 11d***

9 bolts. Off-vertical face. Lower off.
FA: Gary Slate, Joe Rousek, 1990, TD.

©2005 Maximus Press. Marty Lewis Photo.

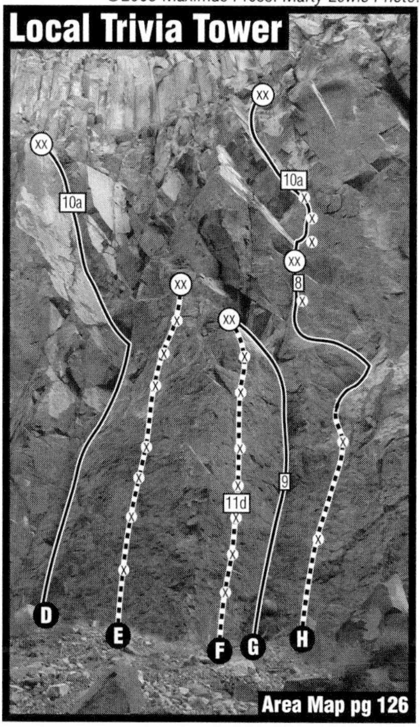

Local Trivia Tower

West facing pink tower on the east side above talus.

D. Focus Marty 10a**

Gear to 2". A broken corner leads to a beautiful hand crack in a dihedral. 45m/150' rappel.
FA: Mike McGrale, Chip White, 1997, GU.

E. Fobes 40 9***

7 bolts. Face. Lower off.
FA: Scott Ayers, Eden Masters, 1990, GU.

F. Another Day in Paradise 11d***

7 bolts. Vertical face with a long dyno crux. Lower off.
FA: Scott Ayers, Eden Masters, 1990, TD.

G. Another Day in Hell 9**

Gear to 4.5". Dihedral. Lower off.
FA: Greg Barnes, Barry Hutten, 11/1997, GU.

H. Jesus Built My Tri-cam 10a*****

Pitch 1: 8**. 3 bolts, gear to 3". Face to lieback to ramp to crack. Climb 2nd pitch or do a 27.5m/90' lower off.

Pitch 2: 10a*****. 3 bolts, gear to 3". Flake to an awesome splitter dihedral. Lower off. ➤ Photo facing page.

FA: Greg Barnes, Barry Hutten, 7/1998, GU.

Eric Kohl and Wendy Borgerd on the first ascent of **Coffin Lid** 11d***. ©*Andy Selters Photo.*

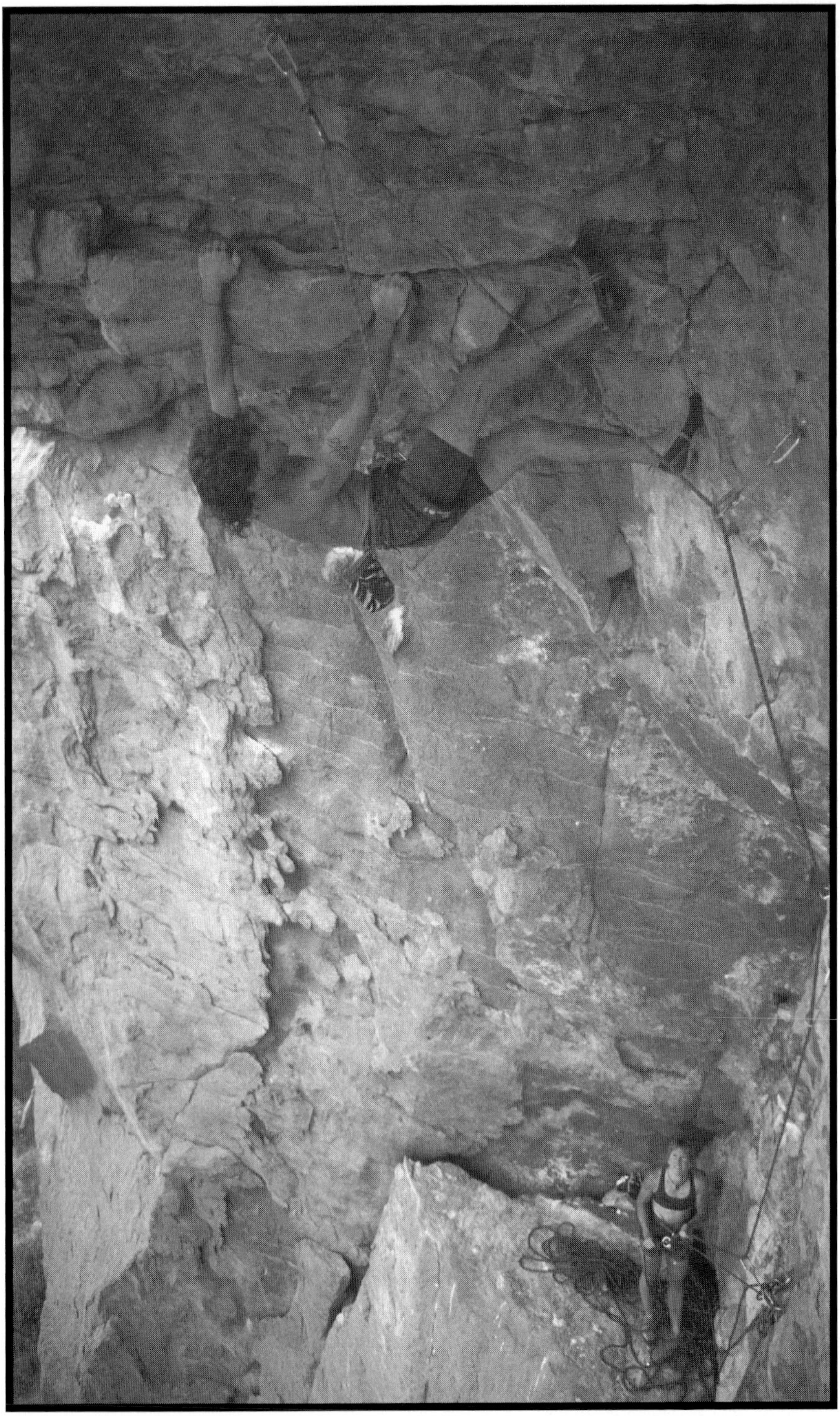

©2005 Maximus Press. *Marty Lewis Topo.*

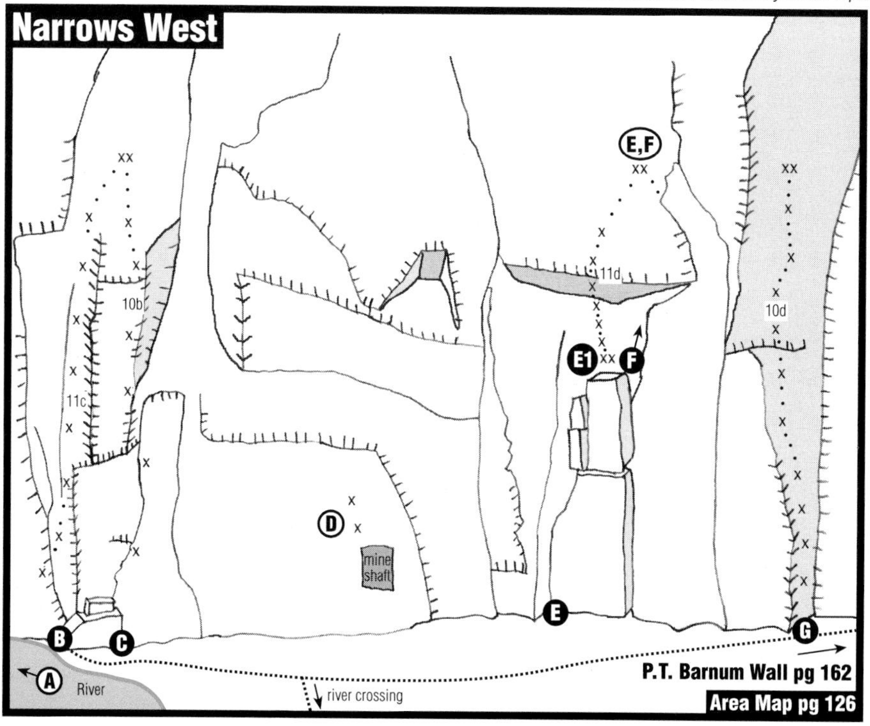

Narrows West

On the west side with a mine shaft splitting the cliff.

A. Nakin 10c**

This route is located 100' left of *Megalomanic.* You must wade across the river to access.

Pitch 1: 8•. Gear to 3". Climb a loose brushy crack then move right to a sling wad. Climb 2nd pitch or lower off.

Pitch 2: 10c***. 5 bolts, gear to 2". Face. Lower off.

Can be done as one pitch if mindful of rope drag.

FA: Mike Strassman, Scott Ayers, 1989, GU.

B. Megalomaniac 11c****

8 bolts. Steep arete. Lower off.

FA: Marty Lewis, Kevin Calder, Doug McDonald, 5/1996, TD.

C. Smokey the Beer 10b***

6 bolts. Crack to exposed arete. Lower off.

FA: Eric Kohl, 8/1994, GU.

D. Open Project

2 bolts. Starts out of a mine shaft.

P: Eric Kohl.

E. Coffin Lid 11d***

Pitch 1: 8*. Gear to 3". Wide crack. Climb 2nd pitch or lower off.

Pitch 2: 11d***. 6 bolts. Horizontal flake. Lower off.

➤ Photo facing page.

Can be done as one 30m/100' pitch.

FA: Eric Kohl, 7/1994.

F. D. Barbi-onslut A2*

Gear. Roof. Lower off.

FA: Eric Kohl, 7/1994, GU.

G. Supergroveler 10d***

10 bolts. Wide crack to a ramp, pass a roof, then finish on a vertical face. 27.5m/90' lower off.

FA: Marty Lewis, Kevin Calder, 3/1997, GU.

Todd Graham on the **Romulan Roof** 12a**** at the Dilithium Crystal. ©*Jim Stimson Photo.* **See Page 153**

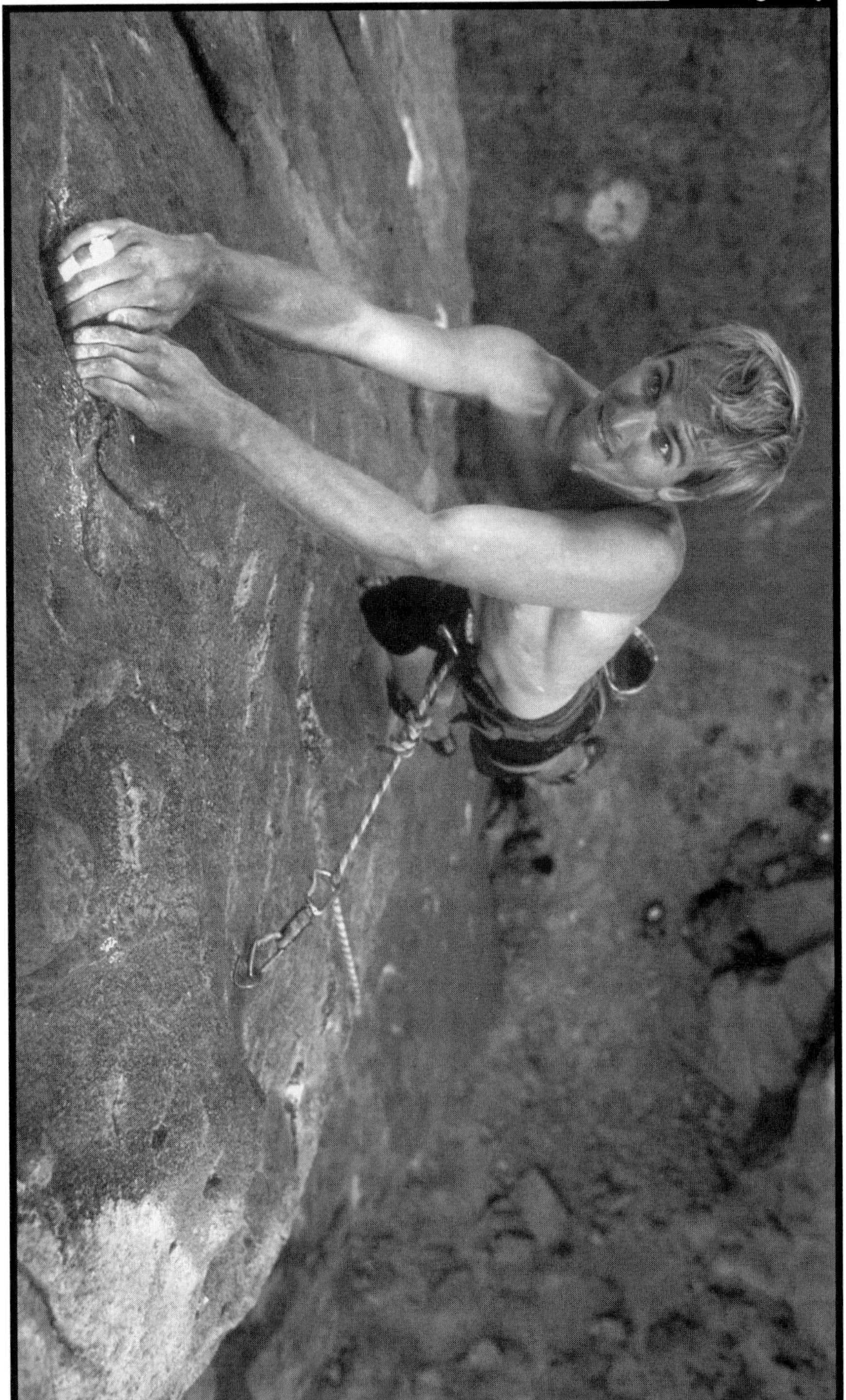

©2005 Maximus Press. *Marty Lewis Topo.*

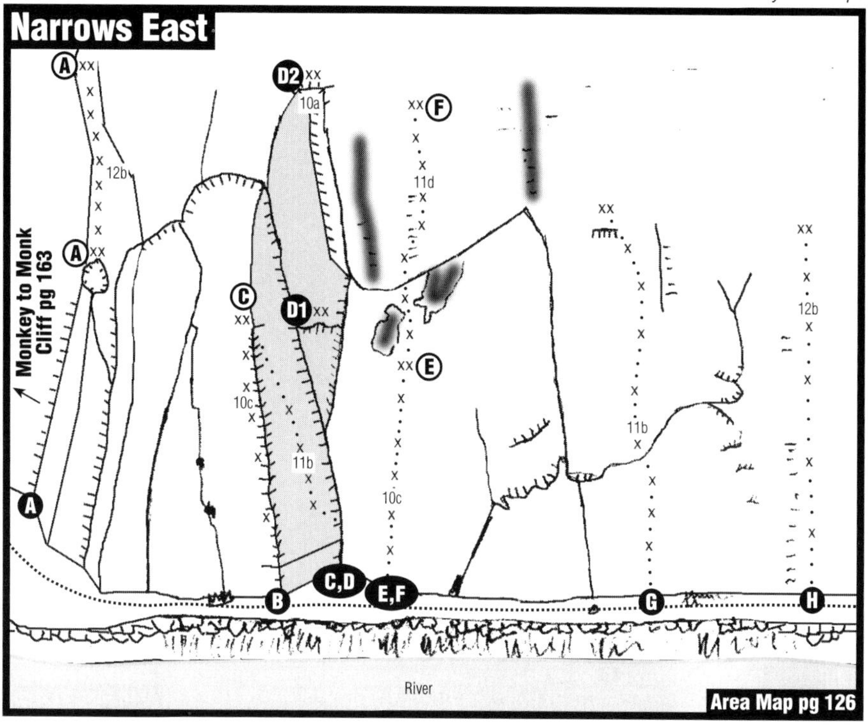

Narrows East

On the east side right above the trail.

A. Astroboy 12b***

Scramble up a 4th class dihedral to the base of this north facing arete. 7 bolts. Steep arete. 35m/115' lower off to ground.

FA: Todd Graham, Gary Slate, 4/1991, GU.

B. Mal a la Gorge 10c***

5 bolts. Arete, a little sporty to the 1st bolt. Lower off.

FA: Scott Ayers, Mike Strassman, 1989, GU.

C. No Known Cure 11b**

4 bolts. Slab to face. Lower off.

FA: Sean Greer, Dave Focardi, 1990, TD.

D. Sandbag 5.8 10a*

Pitch 1: 8*. Gear to 2". Dihedral to Ledge. Climb 2nd pitch or lower off.

Pitch 2: 10a*. Gear to 2". Crack to roof. Lower off.

FA: Bruce Lella, Fred Berman, 1991, GU.

E. Destination Oblivion 10c***

5 bolts. Slab. Lower off.

FA: Geoff Fullerton, John Martindale, 1989, GU.

F. Marty Party 11d****

13 bolts. Slab to steep face. 27.5m/90' lower off.

FA: Marty Lewis, Sean Plunkett, 5/1996, GU.

G. Missing Link 11b***

8 bolts. Sustained vertical face, the rock is a little friable towards the top. Lower off.

FA: Mark Blanchard, Phil Green, 1990, GU.

H. Malt Linker 12b**

5 bolts. Vertical face. Lower off.

FA: Eric Kohl, 7/1994, TD.

©2005 Maximus Press. *Marty Lewis Topo.*

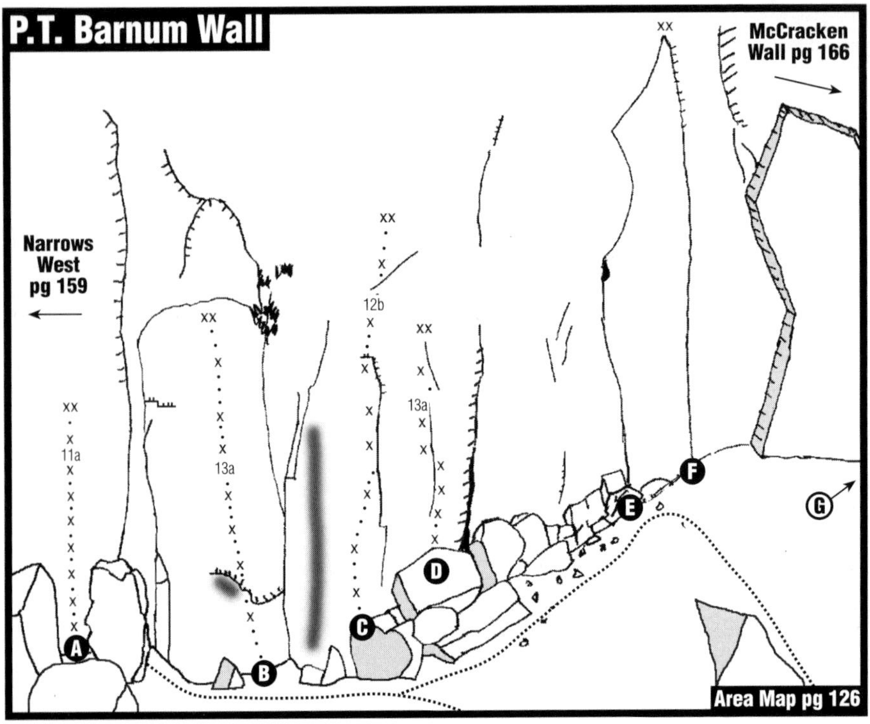

P.T. Barnum Wall

A massive east facing wall on the west side.

A. Out of the Pit 11a***

Starts in a cave. 8 bolts. Stemming to face. Lower off.

FA: Tony Puppo, Joe Rousek, 8/1995, GU.

B. Candy Colored Clown 13a***

7 bolts. Vertical face. Lower off.

FA: Erik Eriksson, Bill McChesney, 1990, GU.

C. Circo Gringo 12b****

8 bolts. Vertical seams. Lower off.

FA: Hassan Saab, Erik Eriksson, Bill McChesney, 1991, GU.

D. Pennywise 13a***

7 bolts. Seam to face. Lower off.

FA: Louie Anderson, Joe Rousek, Pierre Daigle, Aaron Nygren, 7/1995, TD.

E. Shafted 11c***

Gear to 3". Crack. 35m/115' lower off.

FA: Jay Smith, Joe Bentley, 6/1989, GU.

F. Oblique Slanting Dihedral of Death 10d**

Gear to 3". Crack. 35m/115' lower off.

FA: Bruce Lella, 1990, GU.

G. Party on Sean 8***

Approach from the left via a 4th class scramble.

6 bolts. Clean face. Lower off.

FA: Kevin Calder, Sean Plunkett, Shelly Mayfield, 5/1995, GU.

©2005 Maximus Press. *Marty Lewis Photo.*

Monkey to Monk Cliff

Small west facing wall on the east side. The main trail goes right under it.

A. Smell the Glove 12a**

6 bolts. Sporty vertical face. Lower off.

FA: Erik Eriksson, Gary Slate, Bill McChesney, 1992, GU.

B. Scorched Egos 11b**

7 bolts. Bouldery face to a seam to a hand traverse left. Lower off.

FA: Marty Lewis, Sean Plunkett, 4/1996, GU.

C. Stowaway 10c***

6 bolts. Sporty vertical face. Lower off.

FA: Louie Anderson, Steve Angelini, Cory Zinngrabe, 7/1992, GU.

D. Know the Drill 10c***

8 bolts. Continuous vertical face. Lower off.

FA: Kevin Calder, Marty Lewis, Shelly Mayfield, 6/1995, GU.

E. Have a Little Faith 10b**

4 bolts. Face. Lower off.

FA: Joe Rousek, John Aughinbaugh, 5/1993, TD.

©2005 Maximus Press. *Marty Lewis Photo.*

©2005 Maximus Press. *Marty Lewis Topo.*

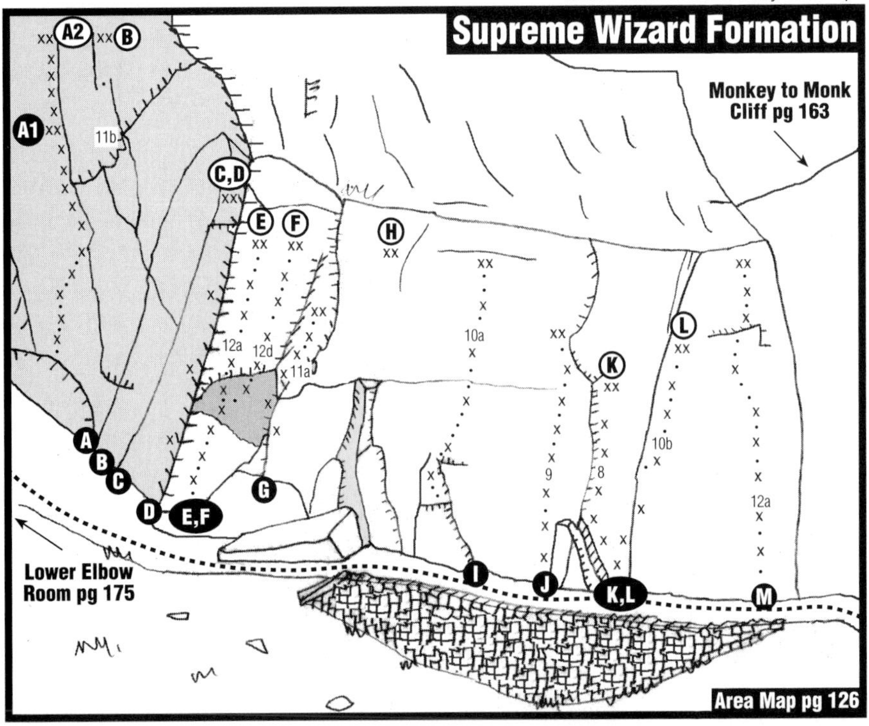

Supreme Wizard Formation

Southwest facing buttress on the east side.

A. And Now for Something Much Cleaner 10d***

Pitch 1: 9***. 10 bolts. Face to crack. Climb 2nd pitch or lower off.

Pitch 2: 10d**. 4 bolts. Dihedral. Lower off.

Can be done as one 35m/115' pitch.

FA: Kelly Cordner, Mike Forkash, 5/1999.

B. And Now for Something Completely Different 11b**

Gear to 3". Crack through roof. 35m/115' lower off.

FA: Bruce Lella, Fred Berman, Marty Lewis, 4/1994, GU.

C. Chipmunk Pancakes (With Batbrain Syrup) 10a**

Gear to 3". Crack. Lower off.

FA: Jay Ladin, Phil Green, 1989, GU.

D. Pretty in Pink 10b**(r)

3 bolts. Arete. Lower off.

FA: Eric Rhicard, Scott Ayers, 1989, GU.

E. Lat Machine 12a****

8 bolts. A steep juggy cave leads to a reachy technical headwall. Lower off.

Variation: 11d*** Step left at the 6th bolt to a rest ledge, then an awkward traverse leads back to the headwall. Lower off.

FA: Todd Graham, 1994, TD.

F. Gravitron 12d****

9 bolts. Climb the cave then go right and attack the steep headwall. Lower off.

FA: Todd Graham, 1994, TD.

G. Satori 11a•

5 bolts. Steep dihedral. Lower off.

FA: Alan Hirahara, Marshall Minobe, 5/1996, TD.

H. Project

Anchors. Face.

P: Joe Rousek.

I. Love of Jesus 10a***(r)

5 bolts. Gently overhanging face, poorly bolted. Lower off.

FA: Joe Rousek, 1990, GU.

J. His Spirit 9**

7 bolts. A block leads to fun face climbing. Lower off.

FA: Joe Rousek, Brian Huntsman, 1994, TD.

K. Drill Sergeant 8***

6 bolts. Hand crack in a dihedral. Lower off.

FA: Kevin Calder, Marty Lewis, Sean Plunkett, Brent Taylor, 3/1997, TD.

L. Corporal Clinger 10b**

6 bolts. Climb the seam then step right to a vertical face. Lower off.

FA: Marty Lewis, Kevin Calder, 3/1997, TD.

M. Hacking & Spitting 12a***

8 bolts. Off-vertical face, technical. Lower off.

FA: Scott Cole, Dave Caunt, Steve Schneider, 2/1990, GU.

©2005 Maximus Press. *Marty Lewis Topo.*

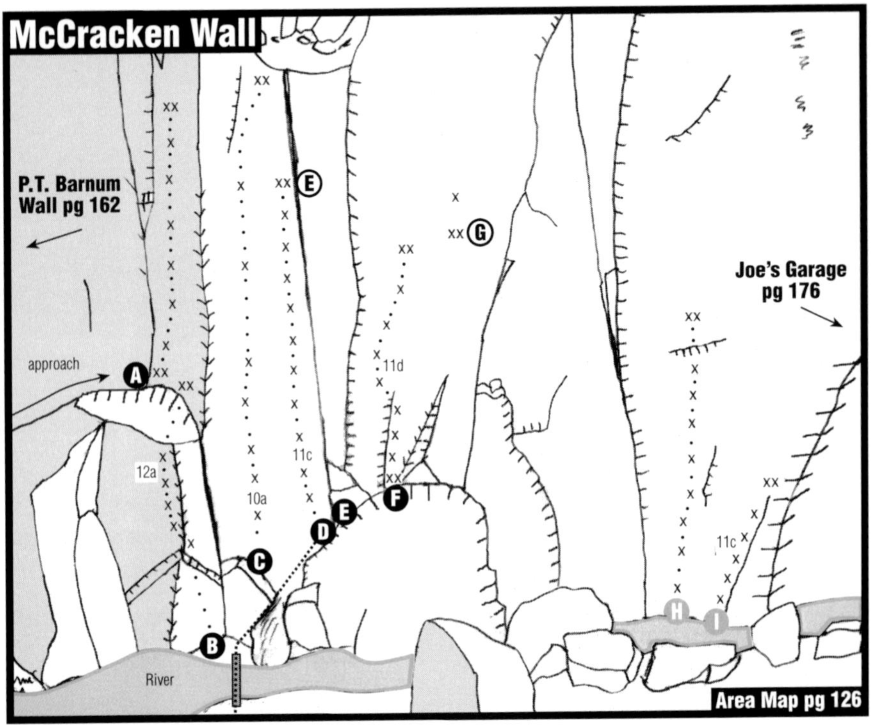

McCracken Wall

North facing wall on the west side.

A. Party on Sean 8***

Cross the river at the P.T. Barnum Wall then approach from the left via a 4th class scramble.

6 bolts. Clean face. Lower off.

FA: Kevin Calder, Sean Plunkett, Shelly Mayfield, 5/1995, GU.

B. Micro Pete 12a**

5 bolts. Arete. Lower off.

FA: Scott Ayers, Mike Strassman, Marty Lewis, 1990, TD.

C. Ego Unchained 10a****(r)

7 bolts. Off-vertical face, killer rock. 35m/115' lower off.

FA: Scott Ayers, Mike Strassman, 1989, GU.

D. Buddha Bless 11c**

10 bolts. Off-vertical face. Lower off.

FA: Mike Strassman, Scott Ayers, 1990, TD.

E. Squeezin' the Buddha's Titty 7•

Gear to 3". Brushy crack to chimney. 30m/100' lower off.

FA: Scott Ayers, 10/1990, GU.

F. Release the McCracken 11d***

7 bolts, optional gear: 0.5" piece. Lieback flakes lead to sporty face climbing. Lower off.

FA: Scott Ayers, Mike Strassman, 1990, GU.

G. Open Project

Anchors. Face.

P: Alan Hirahara, Joe Rousek.

H. End of an Era 12b***

Flooded. 8 bolts. Face. Lower off.

FA: Tom Herbert, 4/1992, TD.

I. Lone Star 11c*

Flooded. 5 bolts. Seam. Lower off.

FA: Scott Ayers, Jay Ladin, 11/1990, GU.

Gary Slate on **Phasers on Stun** 12c***** at the Dilithium Crystal. ©*Jim Stimson Photo.* **See Page 153**

©2005 Maximus Press. *Marty Lewis Photo.*

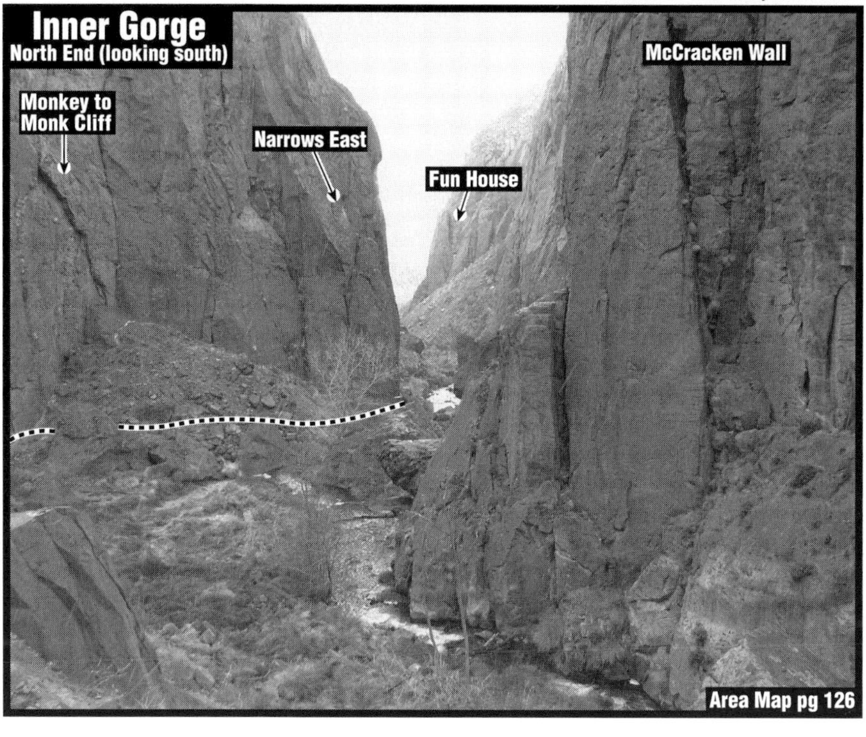

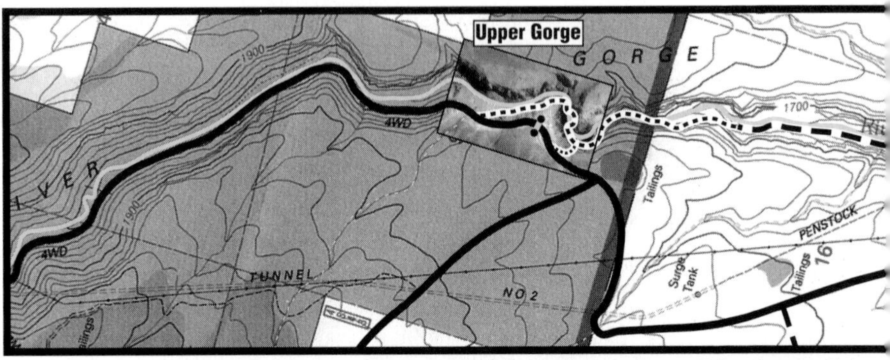

Schatzi Sovich on **Gorgeous** 10b***** at the Gorgeous Towers. ©*Greg Epperson Photo.*

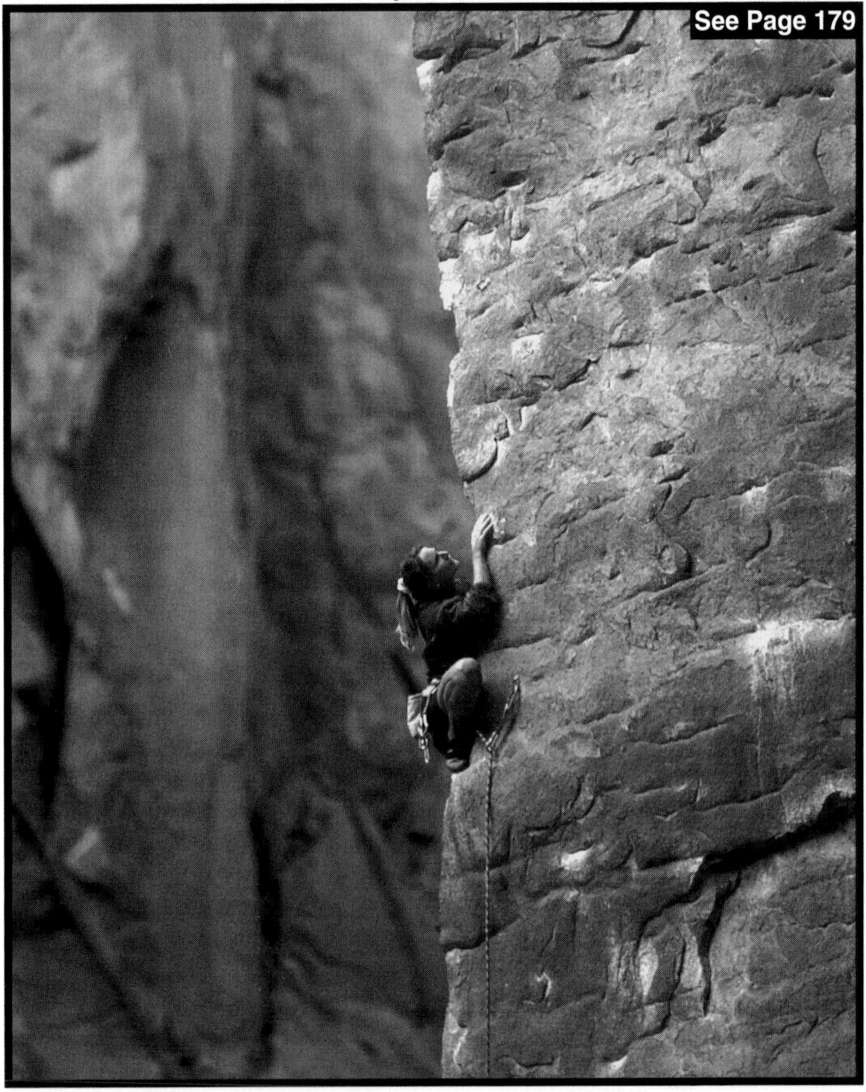
See Page 179

Adapted from the U.S.G.S. 1:24,000 Casa Diablo Mtn. and Rovana Quadrangles.

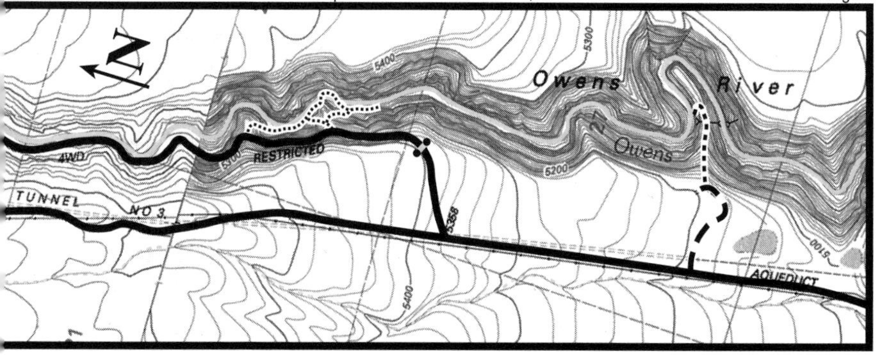

CHAPTER 6

Upper Gorge Basics .... pg 171
Lower Elbow Room .... pg 174
Joe's Garage .... pg 176
Gorgeous Towers .... pg 179
Triple Play Cliff .... pg 181
Holy Trinity Wall .... pg 183
Staging Tower .... pg 183
Flavin Haven .... pg 184
Middle Elbow Room .... pg 187
Upper Elbow Room .... pg 188
Warm Out Wall .... pg 189
Failsafe Wall .... pg 191
ICBM Tower .... pg 192
Trestle Wall .... pg 195
Underground Cliff .... pg 196
Junior Wall .... pg 197
Mini Buttress .... pg 197
All You Can Eat Cliff .... pg 199
Franklin's Tower .... pg 200
Gotham City .... pg 203
Cracked Towers .... pg 207
Dihedrals .... pg 211
Sanitarium .... pg 213

UPPER GORGE

©2005 Maximus Press.

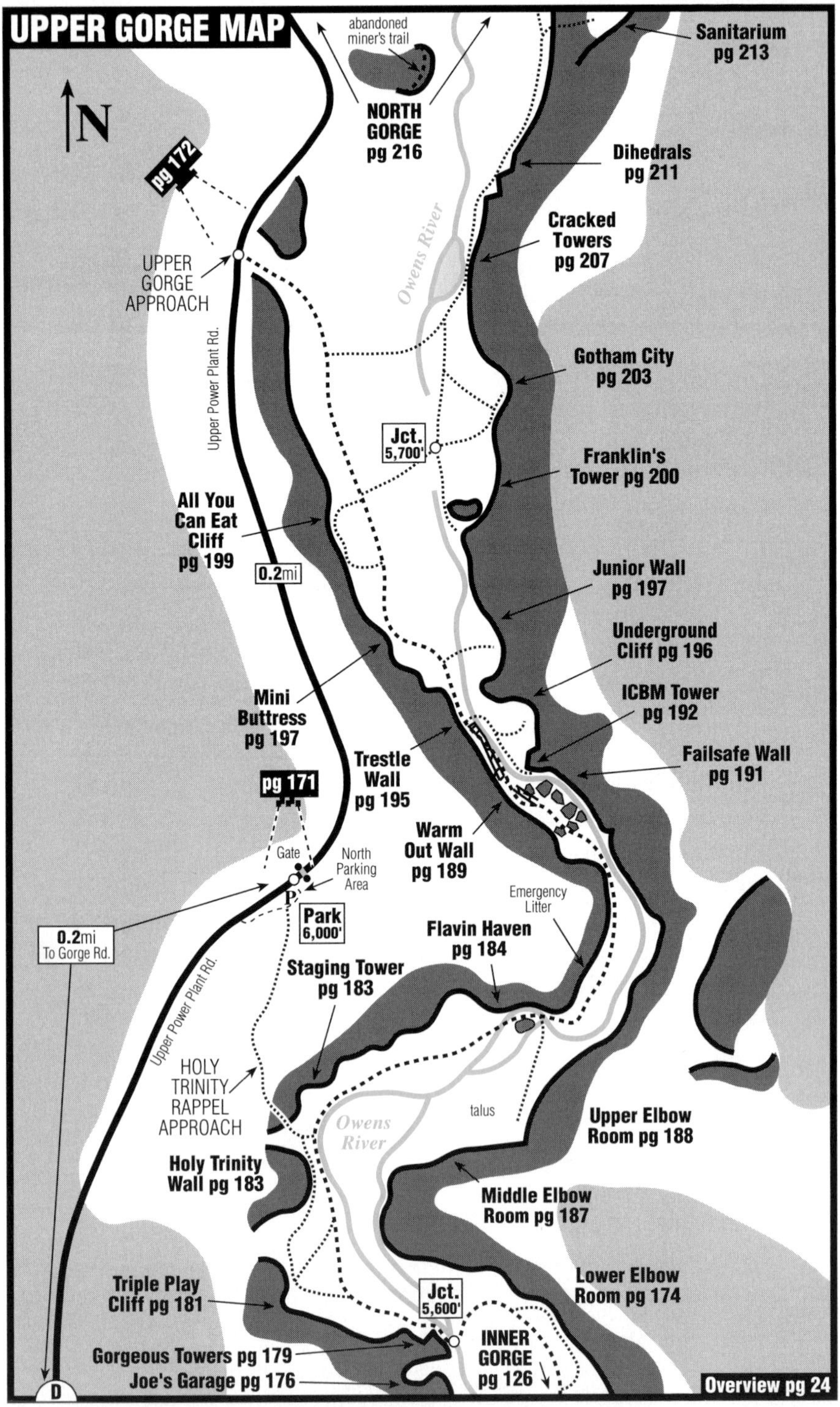
UPPER GORGE MAP
N
pg 172
abandoned miner's trail
NORTH GORGE pg 216
Sanitarium pg 213
Dihedrals pg 211
Cracked Towers pg 207
Owens River
UPPER GORGE APPROACH
Upper Power Plant Rd.
Gotham City pg 203
Jct. 5,700'
Franklin's Tower pg 200
All You Can Eat Cliff pg 199
0.2mi
Junior Wall pg 197
Underground Cliff pg 196
Mini Buttress pg 197
ICBM Tower pg 192
Trestle Wall pg 195
Failsafe Wall pg 191
pg 171
Warm Out Wall pg 189
Gate
North Parking Area
P
Park 6,000'
Emergency Litter
0.2mi To Gorge Rd.
Flavin Haven pg 184
Staging Tower pg 183
Upper Power Plant Rd.
HOLY TRINITY RAPPEL APPROACH
talus
Owens River
Upper Elbow Room pg 188
Holy Trinity Wall pg 183
Middle Elbow Room pg 187
Triple Play Cliff pg 181
Lower Elbow Room pg 174
Jct. 5,600'
Gorgeous Towers pg 179
INNER GORGE pg 126
Joe's Garage pg 176
D
Overview pg 24

UPPER GORGE BASICS

The Upper Gorge is wild and scenic with an easy approach. Many climbers have discovered the All You Can Eat Cliff and the Gorgeous Towers, while the rest of the cliffs see little traffic.

Upper Gorge Details

Elevation: 5,600 to 5,800 ft.
Sport Climbs: 164 routes, 5.6 to 13c.
Gear Climbs: 50 routes, 5.6 to 12a.
Approach: 10 minute talus gully to a good trail with a 300 ft. descent.

For those climbers who think routes in the Gorge tend to be generic edge pulls, I would highly recommend climbing at Gotham City or the Dihedrals. Near perfect rock will be found with monolithic aretes, dihedrals, flakes and faces. Lately, these two cliffs have been giving the Gorgeous Towers a run for their money in popularity.

The Upper Gorge also contains some great moderate climbing at the Lower Elbow Room and the Upper Elbow Room.

The Approach: From U.S. 395 take the Paradise / Swall Meadows Exit east. Drive up a steep hill for 0.7 miles until reaching the Gorge Rd. Turn left (north) on the Gorge Rd. and you will come to the North Parking Area after driving 6.4 miles up the Gorge Rd. Park on the southeast side before the gate.

©2005 Maximus Press. *Marty Lewis Photo.*

©2005 Maximus Press. *Marty Lewis Photo.*

Holy Trinity Rappel Approach: From the North Parking Area, traverse southwest down a loose slope (3rd class). Head into a notch and down climb a 4th class chimney until reaching a rappel station. Rappel 25m/80′ to the Gorge bottom. This point is between the Holy Trinity Wall and the Staging Tower in the Upper Gorge. Class 5; 10 minutes.

Upper Gorge Approach: From the North Parking Area follow the paved Upper Power Plant Road 0.2 miles (5 min.) beyond the gate. From here, drop down a steep eroding slope just a few feet until encountering a south-trending gully. Follow it (3rd class) to a good trail. Class 3; 10 minutes to the All You Can Eat Cliff, 20 minutes to the Gorgeous Towers, 15 minutes to the Dihedrals.

From the Central Gorge: You can also park at the Central Parking Area and take the Central Gully Approach; then head north up the Gorge. Class 3; 35 minutes to the Gorgeous Towers, 50 minutes to the Dihedrals. See page 77.

Kimberly Flores on **Machine Gun Jumblies** 10a***** at Gotham City. ©*Shawn Reeder Photo.*

©2005 Maximus Press. *Marty Lewis Photo.*

©2005 Maximus Press. *Marty Lewis Topo.*

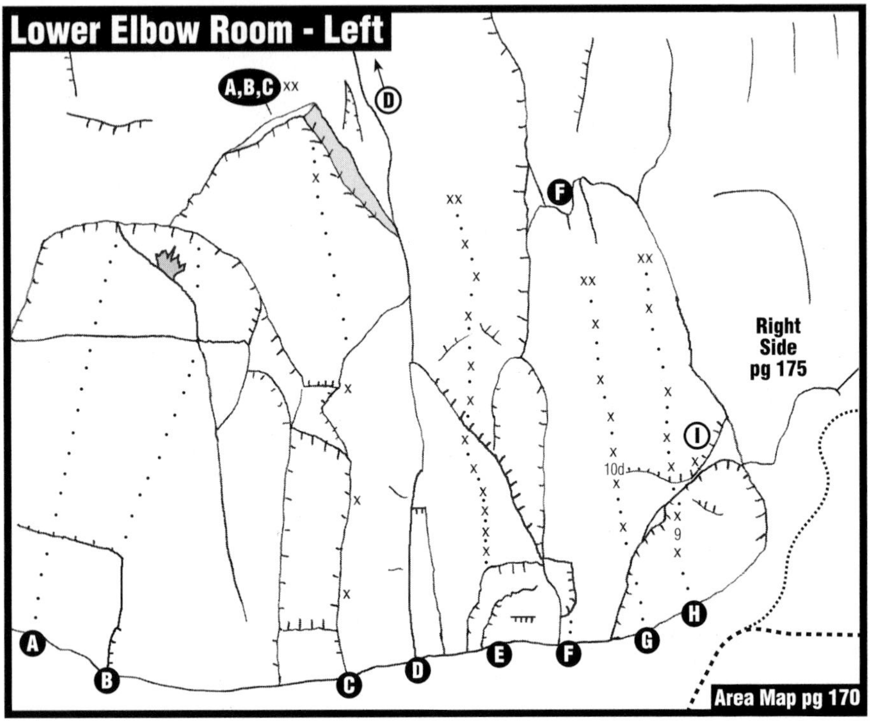

Lower Elbow Room - Left

South facing wall on the east side directly across from the Gorgeous Towers.

A. Gila Bender 10a•(x)

Gear. Pass an overlap, up a slab, then scramble up and right to the belay of *Elbow Macaroni.* 30m/100' lower off.
FA: Scott Ayers, GU, 1989.

B. 30 Miles to Water 8•(x)

Gear. A flake leads to pocketed rock, then scramble up and right to the belay of *Elbow Macaroni.* 30m/100' lower off.
FA: Scott Ayers, GU, 1989.

C. Elbow Macaroni 11b**

4 bolts, gear to 2". Start up a dihedral, then climb a pocketed face. 30m/100' lower off.
FA: Eric Rhicard, Scott Ayers, 1989.

D. A Life Shared is a Better Life 9***

Gear to 4.5". Climb a finger to fist crack, then continue up a dihedral. 50m/165' pitch, single-rope rappel to *Elbow Macaroni.*
FA: Barry Oswick, Jamie Stewart, Bob Bedore, 6/2005, GU.

E. Roller Coaster Ride 12a***

11 bolts. Slab to overhang to exposed face. Lower off.
FA: Barry Oswick, Eric Sorenson, Richard Castillo, 6/2005, TD.

F. Sweetie 6*

Gear to 3.5". Scramble up a decomposing mini-corner, then climb a dihedral. Rappel 30m/100' off a sling wad on a block.
FA: Mike Strassman, Moira Smith, 1990, GU.

G. You Don't Want None 10d**

6 bolts. Scramble to a ledge then up a slab. Lower off.
FA: Mike Strassman, Charlie Byrne, Mark McNally, 5/1997, TD.

H. Don't Kid, Minibike 9**

6 bolts. Slab. Lower off.
FA: Mike Strassman, Charlie Byrne, Mark McNally, Jackie Carrol, 5/1997, GU.

I. Open Project

1 bolt. Slab.

©2005 Maximus Press. *Marty Lewis Topo.*

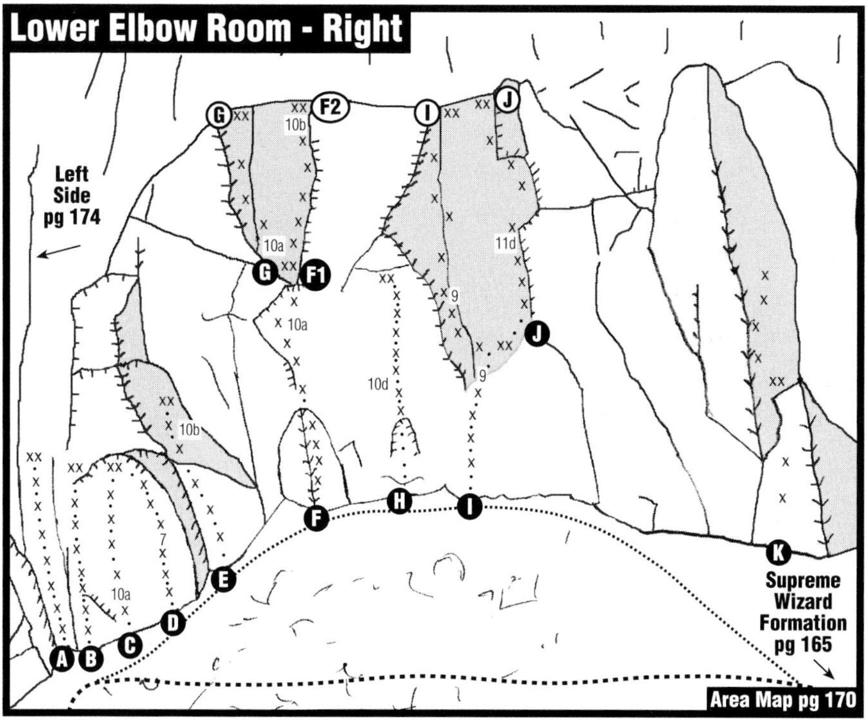

Lower Elbow Room - Right

South facing slabs above a talus fan on the east side.

A. Phoenix 7***

7 bolts. A blocky corner leads to face climbing. Lower off.
FA: Kelly Cordner, 12/1997, TD.

B. Iceberg II 9***

7 bolts. Crack to face. Lower off.
FA: Kelly Cordner, 12/1997, TD.

C. Pet Trackers 10a***

5 bolts. Face. Lower off. ☞ Originally this route had ground fall potential, 2 bolts were added making it a more reasonable climb.
FA: Scott Ayers, Richard Spencer, 1992, GU. Retrobolts: Marty Lewis.

D. P.D. Time 7***

6 bolts. Fun face. Lower off.
FA: Mike Strassman, Scott Ayers, 1992, TD.

E. Aunti Vigilante 10b**

5 bolts. Face to slab crux. Lower off.
FA: Barry Oswick, Kelly Cordner, 12/1997, TD.

F. Quail Trail 10b***

Pitch 1: 10a**. 9 bolts. Arete to leaning seam. Climb the 2nd pitch or lower off 27.5m/90'.
Pitch 2: 10b**. 5 bolts. Stemming dihedral. Lower off.
Can be done as one pitch.
FA: Kelly Cordner, Randy Jacobs, 11/1997, TD.

G. Quail Crack 10a**

4 bolts. A stimulating step left leads to a crack. Lower off.
FA: Kelly Cordner, 11/1997, TD.

H. Chuckers 10d***

7 bolts. Cool technical slab. Lower off.
FA: Kelly Cordner, 10/1997, TD.

I. Slip 'n Slide 9****

13 bolts. Face to slabby crack. 35m/115' lower off.
Can be broken into two pitches.
FA: Kelly Cordner, Barry Oswick, 10/1997, GU.

J. Palm Reader 11d**

8 bolts. A slabby dihedral leads to a roof crack. Lower off.
FA: Jay Goodwin, Kelly Cordner, 11/1999, TD.

K. Open Project

6 bolts and an anchor. Arete.
P: Mark Blanchard, Bill McChesney.

©2005 Maximus Press. *Marty Lewis Photo.*

Marty Lewis on **Bongo Fury** 12b****. ©*Francois Marsigny Photo.*

Joe's Garage

A north facing cliff on the west side with a mine shaft.

A. Open Project

1 bolt. Arete.
P: Marty Lewis.

B. You Are What You Is 11a**

2 bolts, gear to 2.5". Vertical crack to face. Lower off.
FA: Fred Berman, Marty Lewis, Bruce Lella, 3/1994, TD.

C. Bongo Fury aka Frank Zappa Memorial Buttress 12b****

8 bolts. Incredible vertical arete, technical and strenuous. Lower off. ➤ Photo this page.
FA: Fred Berman, Doug LaFarge, 2/1994, TD.

D. Good Thing 12d***

6 bolts. Gently overhanging face, dyno crux. Lower off.
FA: Tom Herbert, 1991, TD.

E. Bad Thing 12b***

7 bolts. Gently overhanging face, balancy crux. Lower off.
FA: Erik Eriksson, Bill McChesney, 1992, GU.

F. Soul Music 10b*(r)

2 bolts, gear to 2". Face. 1 bolt + gear anchor, scramble northwest to the top of the higher tower, single rope rappel to the top of *Gorge and Purge*.
FA: Gary Slate, John Aughinbaugh, 1987, GU.

©2005 Maximus Press. *Marty Lewis Photo.*

©2005 Maximus Press. *Marty Lewis Topo.*

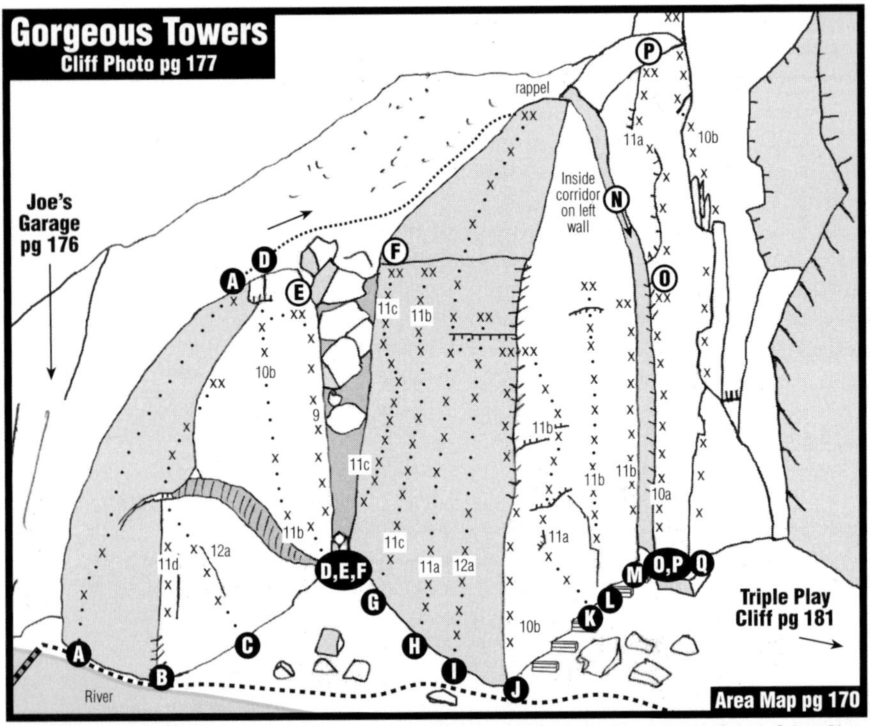

Matt Kerns on **C'mon Knucko** 11b****. ©*Andy Selters Photo.*

Gorgeous Towers

The beautiful north facing twin towers on the west side. The most popular crag in the Upper Gorge. Shady and cool.

A. Soul Music 10b*(r)

2 bolts, gear to 2". Face. 1 bolt + gear anchor, scramble northwest to the top of the higher tower, single rope rappel to the top of *Gorge and Purge*.
FA: Gary Slate, John Aughinbaugh, 1987, GU.

B. Engorged 11d***

5 bolts, optional gear 2" piece. Bear hug the arete to a ledge, then face climb. Lower off.
FA: Mike Strassman, Scott Ayers, Eric Rhicard, 1989, GU.

C. Enraged 12a**

5 bolts, optional gear 2" piece. Climb a technical seam to a ledge, then face climb. Lower off.
FA: Karl Rexer, Scott Ayers, 1990, TD.

D. Mumbles the Guzzler 11b•(r)

5 bolts, gear to 1.5". Head left up a traversing ramp to a lichen covered face, finish up a crack. Gear anchor, scramble northwest to the top of the higher tower, single rope rappel to the top of *Gorge and Purge*. ☞ The first ascensionist's rating of 10b made this sandbag a recipe for disaster.
FA: Mike Strassman, Scott Ayers, 1989, GU.

Variation: 11b*(r). 5 bolts, gear to 1". At the 5th bolt traverse right to the belay of *Pippy the Zenhead*, yielding a far better way to get down. Lower off.

E. Pippy the Zenhead 9**

7 bolts. Ledgy, blocky arete. Lower off.
FA: Elizabeth Gorin, Scott Ayers, 9/1990, GU.

F. Rap it Up 11c**

11 bolts. Uninspiring face. Lower off.
FA: Scott Ayers, Mike Strassman, 1992, TD.

G. You Have Been Nothing But Trouble Since the First Day I Laid Eyes on You; You're Like a Thorn in My Side; I Don't Know From One Day to the Next What Stupid Lame Brain Stunt You're Gonna Pull; Now Get Out of Here, Get Out of My Office, Get Out of My Life, Once and for all Get Out, Out, Out, Out! 11c***

9 bolts, 27.5m/90'. A technical slab leads to jugs then a reachy crux. Lower off. ☞ Current record holder for longest route name. A tirade that Sergeant Carter gave Gomer Pyle. Tho only known bolt failure (the 1st one) in the Gorge occurred on this route. I replaced it with a 1/2" bolt.
FA: Mike Strassman, Scott Ayers, 1989, GU.

H. 2 Feet to Hell 11a**

12 bolts. Climb a face past a tremendous ledge to a contrived slab. 45m/150' pitch, single-rope rappel to top of *Gorge and Purge*.
FA: Scott Ayers, Paul Linaweaver, 1989, GU.

Variation: 11a**. 7 bolts. Climb right at the 7th bolt to the belay of *Gorge and Purge* yielding a nice half-rope route. Lower off.

I. Gorge and Purge 12a***

7 bolts. Sustained crimpy off-vertical face. Lower off.
FA: Scott Ayers, Ron Farrell, 1990, GU.

J. Gorgeous 10b*****

8 bolts. Beautiful sustained, polished vertical arete. 27.5m/90' lower off. ➤ Photo page 168.
FA: Scott Ayers, Mike Strassman, Eric Rhicard, 1989, GU.

K. C'mon Knucko 11b****

8 bolts. A reachy technical move leads to a pumpy bulge. Lower off. ➤ Photo facing page.
FA: Scott Ayers, Ron Farrell, Jerry Smith, 6/1990, TD.

L. Knucko's Pride of the North 11b*****

9 bolts. Sustained technical vertical face, sporty to the 1st bolt. 27.5m/90' lower off.
FA: Mike Strassman, Scott Ayers, 1989, GU.

M. The-Aretical 11b****

8 bolts, the 1st one is in the corridor. Devious vertical arete. Lower off. ☞ Originally a bold 4 bolt mixed climb. Retrobolted by the first ascensionist.
➤ Photo page 180.
FA: Scott Ayers, Jay Ladin, 1989, GU.

N. Hidden 11a**

Inside the corridor on the left wall. 2 bolts, gear to 3.5". Face to crack. 30m/100' lower off.
FA: Jay Smith, Joe Bentley, 6/1989, GU.

O. Giveaway 10a****

8 bolts. A bouldery start leads to an arete. Lower off.
FA: Scott Ayers, John Hartman, 1992, GU.

P. Sea Cow 11a***

15 bolts. Climb *Giveaway* then continue up a technical flake. 35m/115' lower off.
FA: Kevin Calder, Marty Lewis, 4/2001, TD.

Q. Wacked Scenario 10b****

14 bolts. Hands and fists lead to an offwidth, up this to more strenuous crack climbing. 37.5m/125' pitch, single rope rappel to *Giveaway*. ☞ First led on gear. Feel free to emulate the challenge (bring a giant rack to 7").
FA: Marty Lewis, Kevin Calder, 11/2000, GU.

Sabrina Nioche on **The-Aretical** 11b**** at the Gorgeous Towers. ©*Mike Ayon Photo.* **See Page 179**

©2005 Maximus Press. *Marty Lewis Topo.*

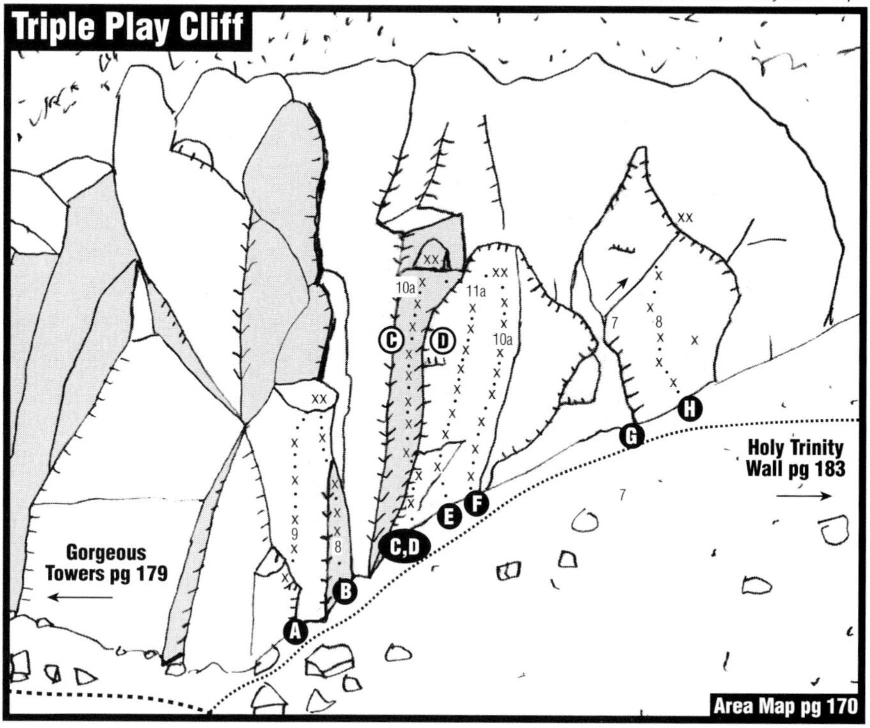

Triple Play Cliff

Northeast facing gray slabs on the west side.

A. Gorge Corner 9**

5 bolts. Dihedral to face. Lower off.
FA: John Martindale, 1990, GU.

B. Cat in the Hat 8**

4 bolts, gear: 1" piece. Arete. Lower off.
FA: Geoff Fullerton, 1990, GU.

C. Stonefly 10a*

10 bolts. The contrived left face of the dihedral. Lower off.
FA: Kelly Cordner, Bill MacBride, 4/1998, TD.

D. Bill's Black Book 8*

2 bolts, gear to 2". Pass 2 bolts, continue up the dihedral then at the top move left to the *Stonefly* anchor. Lower off.
FA: Kelly Cordner, Bill MacBride, 4/1998.

E. Jizz Soaked Action Pix 11a*

8 bolts. Slab to contrived face. Lower off.
FA: Mike Strassman, Scott Ayers, Eden Masters, 1991, TD.

F. Snapping Pussy Doll 10a****

8 bolts. Jugs and edges up an exposed arete. Lower off.
FA: Mike Strassman, Dana Drucker, 1991, TD.

G. Hey Amigo 7•

Gear to 3". A dihedral leads to a right leaning crack. Lower off.
FA: Brian Treanor, Bill MacBride, Andre Gharagozian, 1994, GU.

H. It's the Gaaazzz 8***

5 bolts. Wandering slab. Lower off.
FA: Jay Ladin, 1989, GU. Inadvertent retrobolts: Geoff Fullerton, John Martindale.

©2005 Maximus Press. *Marty Lewis Photo.*

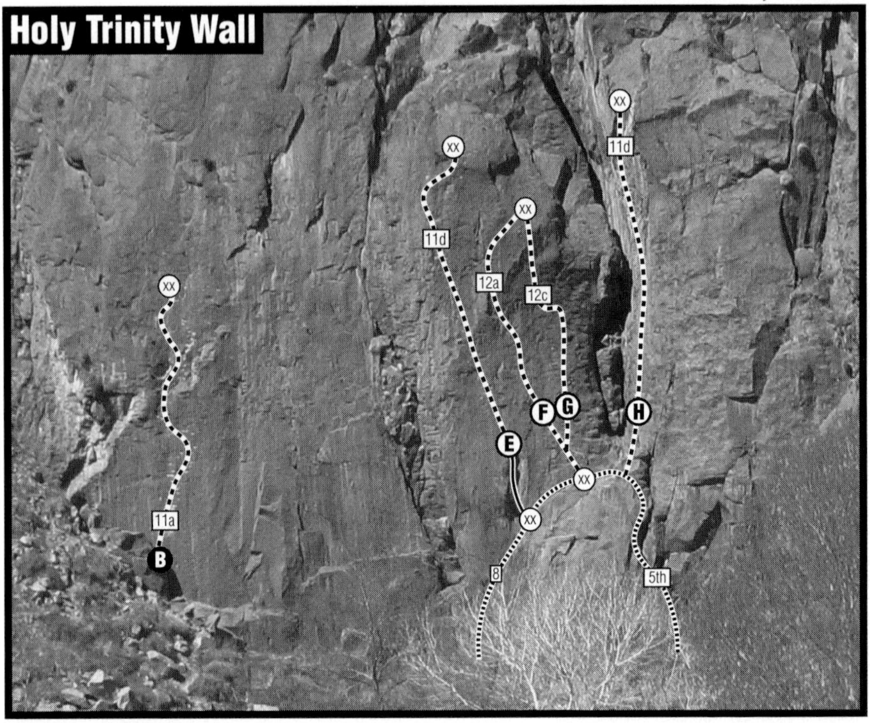

©2005 Maximus Press. *Marty Lewis Topo.*

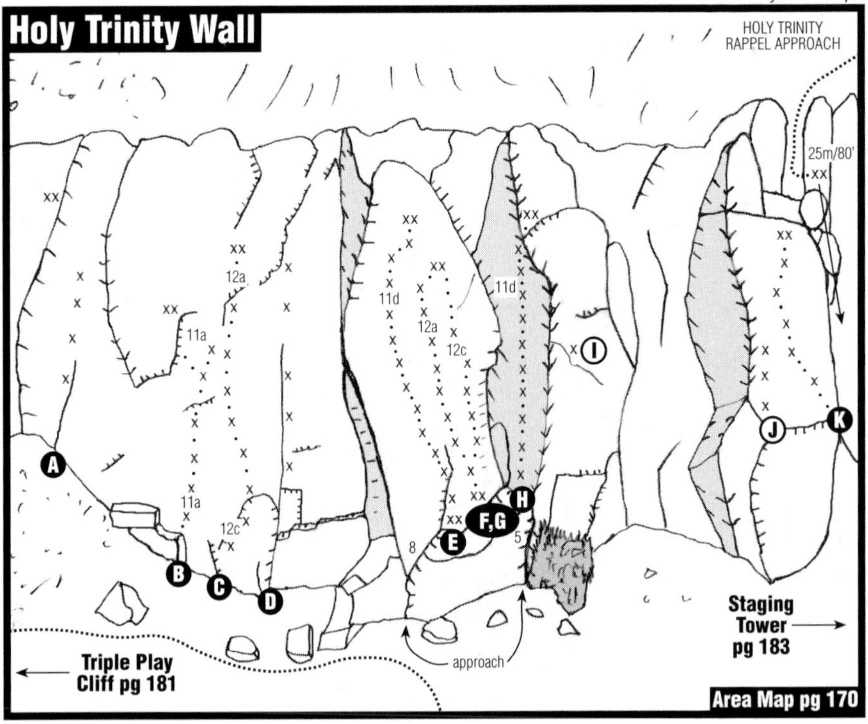

Holy Trinity Wall
East facing wall on the west side.

A. Open Project
4 bolts. Crack to face.
P: Kelly Cordner.

B. Pick Pocket 11a****
5 bolts. Clipping the 1st bolt can be reachy. A bouldery move leads to incredible pockets up a vertical face, finish with a sporty flake. Lower off. ☞ Visionary first bolted climb in the Gorge.
FA: John Bachar, Rick Cashner, 1988, GU.

Variation: 11a***. 6 bolts. From the 5th bolt go up and right, clip a bolt, then traverse back left to the anchor. Lower off.

C. Please Baby, Baby, Baby, Please 12c**
10 bolts. A bouldery shallow dihedral leads to a pocketed face. Lower off. ➤ Photo page 36.
FA: Steve Schneider, Marty Lewis, 1989, GU.

D. Open Project
5 bolts. Seam to face.
P: Jay Smith.

The next four routes start on a terrace that is best approached by an easy 5th class scramble up the right side or by a 5.8 corner/ramp on the left side.

E. Sex 11d*****
12 bolts. A short crack leads to a long sustained exposed face. 27.5m/90' to the ledge or 35m/115' to the ground. ☞ Originally named *Biochemically Compacted Sexual Affection.* This route along with *Sex Packets, Doowutchyalike, Freaks of the Industry, Be Prepared to G* and *Gimme the Helmet, I'll Be the Stunt Man* are all songs or phrases featured on the influential 1990 Digital Underground album "Sex Packets."
FA: Scott Ayers, Jeff Schoen, Eden Masters, 1990, TD.

F. Sex Packets 12a*****
8 bolts. Great technical moves up a vertical face. 22.5m/75' to the ledge or 30m/100' to the ground.
FA: Scott Ayers, Mike Strassman, Eden Masters, Jay Ladin, 1990, GU.

G. Faith No More 12c***
6 bolts. Gently overhanging pocketed face. 22.5m/75' to the ledge or 30m/100' to the ground.
FA: Joe Hedge, 1992, TD.

H. Doowutchyalike 11d***
10 bolts. Crusier face to bouldery bulge. 25m/80' to the ledge or 35m/115' to the ground.
FA: Scott Ayers, Fred Berman, Paul Linaweaver, 1992, GU.

I. Open Project
1 bolt. Face.
P: Gary Slate, Phil Green.

©2005 Maximus Press. *Marty Lewis Photo.*

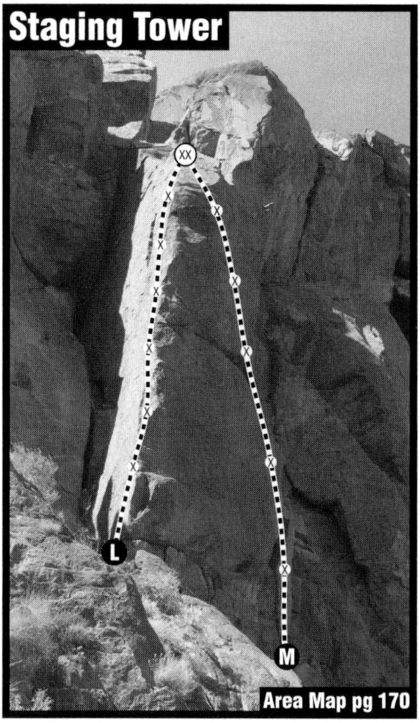

J. Open Project
3 bolts. Face.
P: Paul Linaweaver.

K. Broski/Linaweaver 10b**
5 bolts. Face. Lower off. ☞ Use to reverse the Holy Trinity Rappel Approach.
FA: Paul Linaweaver, Mike Broski, 1991, GU.

Staging Tower
A quick 4th class slidey scramble leads up to this south facing tower.

L. Enslaved by the Belle 10a***
6 bolts. Nice arete. Lower off.
FA: Eric Kohl, 6/1994.

M. Dummy Up 11a*
5 bolts. Weird face. Lower off.
FA: Eric Kohl, 6/1994.

©2005 Maximus Press. *Marty Lewis Photo.*

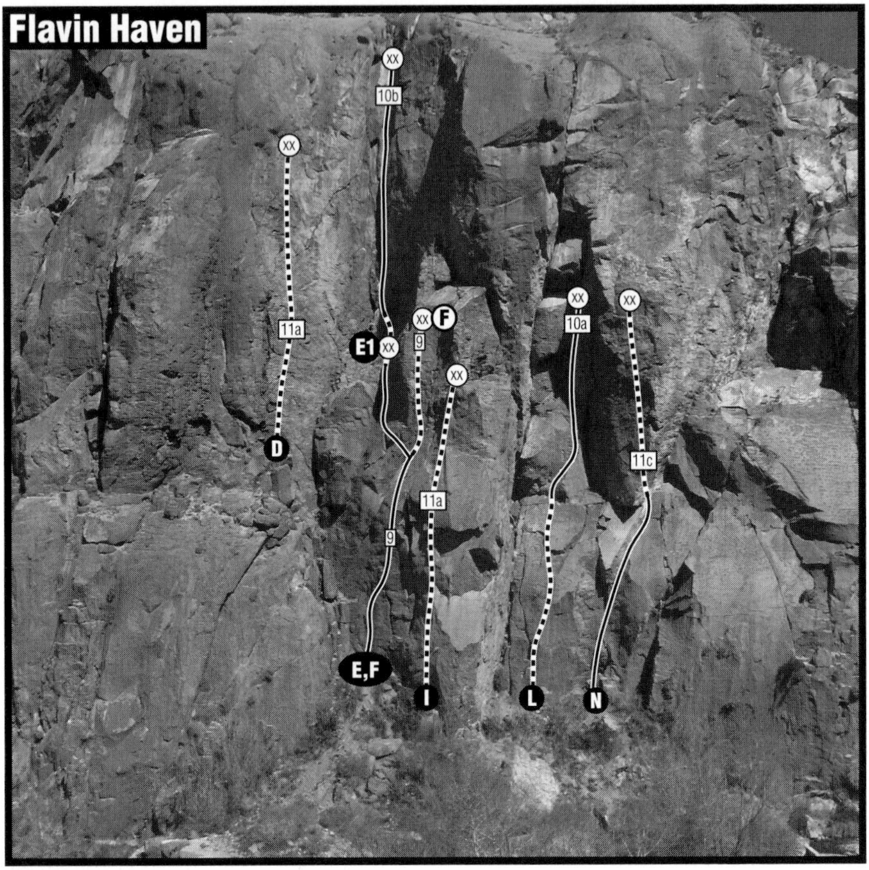

Flavin Haven

South facing dihedrals and towers on the west side.

Routes A-D all start on a terrace that is approached by a short 4th class gully.

A. Gunned Down by Goofy 10a**

7 bolts. Exposed arete. Lower off.

FA: Scott Ayers, Mark Hathaway, Eden Masters, 1992, TD.

B. Schneider/Clay 12c**

7 bolts. Steep face. Lower off.

FA: Steve Schneider, Lionel Clay, Scott Ayers, 1992, TD.

C. Open Project

2 bolts. Steep face.

D. Tore Down 11a***

10 bolts. Varied vertical face. 27.5m/90' lower off.

FA: Tony Puppo, Joe Rousek, 8/1994, GU.

E. Jaws of Life 10b****

Pitch 1: 9**. 6 bolts. Start *Nice Jugs*, but at the 4th bolt head left up a dihedral to a belay. Climb the 2nd pitch or lower off.

Pitch 2: 10b****. 11 bolts. Climb a long sustained overhanging dihedral, hands to offwidth. 30m/100' lower off. ☞ First led on gear. Please feel free to emulate the challenge (bring gear to 7").

Can be done in one pitch if mindful of rope drag.

FA: Kevin Calder, Marty Lewis 12/2000, GU.

F. Nice Jugs 9***

10 bolts. Crack to face. 27.5m/90' lower off.

FA: Kelly Cordner, Urmas Franosch, 6/1997, TD.

G. Project

2 bolts. Face.

P: Kevin Calder, Marty Lewis.

H. Hole in the Wall 9*

Gear to 3". Wide crack/chimney. Lower off.

FA: Kelly Cordner, John DiAnnibale, Randy Jacobs, 6/1997, TD.

©2005 Maximus Press. *Marty Lewis Topo.*

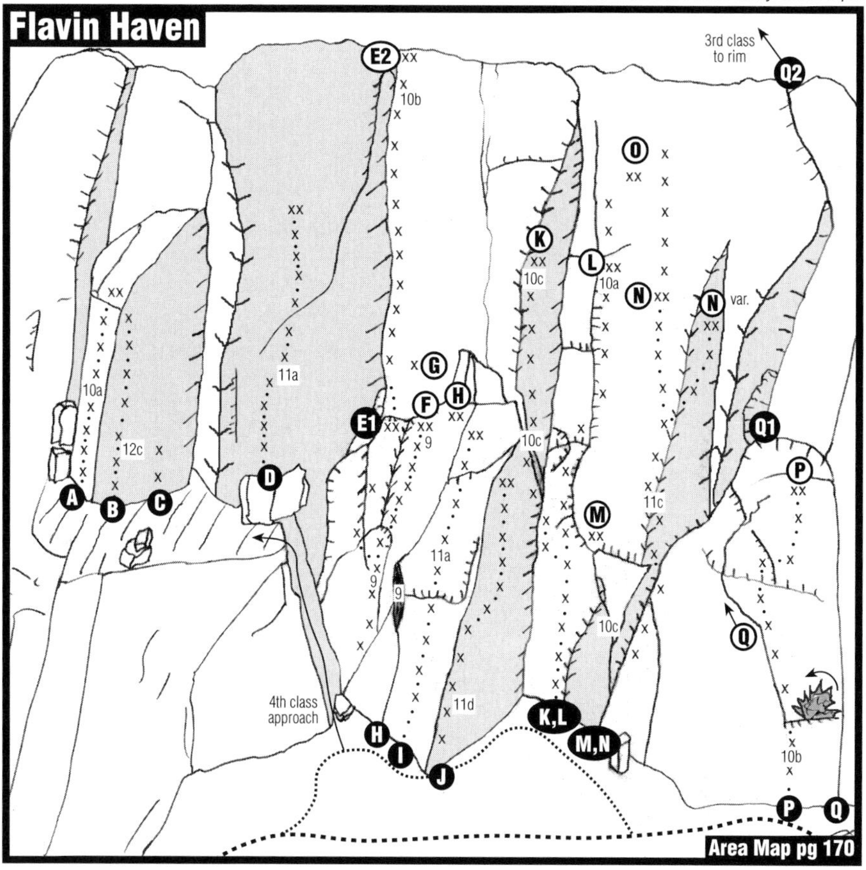

I. C-4 Yourself 11a***
8 bolts. A slab leads to a roof then more slab climbing. Lower off.
FA: Kelly Cordner, Urmas Franosch, John DiAnnibale, 6/1997, TD.

J. Pyroclasm 11d***
10 bolts. Climb the arete then head right onto a vertical face, sustained. Lower off.
FA: Mike Forkash, Kelly Cordner, 8/1997, TD.

K. Air Walk aka See What Happens When You Force It! 10c**
14 bolts. Clip the first 5 bolts of *Lava Haul* then go left, then go right across a chimney, then climb an arete, contrived. 30m/100' lower off. ☞ The name says it all!
FA: Kelly Cordner, 7/1997, TD.

L. Lava Haul 10a****
13 bolts. Face to dihedral, varied climbing. 27.5m/90' lower off.
FA: Kelly Cordner, 7/1997, TD.

M. Kicking Ash 10c**
Gear to 3". Short crack. Lower off
FA: Mike Forkash, Kelly Cordner, 6/1997, TD.

N. Caldera 11c****
11 bolts. A hand crack leads to exposed arete climbing. Lower off. ➤ Photo page 186.
FA: Mike Forkash, Kelly Cordner, 8/1997, TD.

Variation: 11c**. 10 bolts. Climb *Caldera* then go right at the 8th bolt. ☞ A pointless variation.

O. Open Projects
Bolts, anchor. Lots of curious activity.
P: Kelly Cordner.

P. Tephra Sampler 10b*
9 bolts, 27.5m/90'. Face climb to the *Exit Stage Left* crack, but at the 5th bolt go up to a contrived slab. Lower off.
FA: Kelly Cordner, Matt Ciancio, 5/1997, TD.

Q. Exit Stage Left 9•
Pitch 1: 9•. 3 bolts, gear to 3". Climb a short dihedral, move left at a bush, continue up a clean left leaning crack and pass a bulge. Gear anchor. ☞ To facilitate the sport climb *Tephra Sampler* three bolts were added, please feel free to skip them.

Pitch 2: 9•. Gear to 3". Climb loose cracks to the rim. Gear anchor, scramble to the North Parking Area!
FA: Steve Grossman, Paul Linaweaver, Mike Strassman, 1989, GU.

Tiffany Campbell on **Caldera** 11c**** at the Flavin Haven. ©*Kevin Calder Photo.* See Page 185

©2005 Maximus Press. *Marty Lewis Photo.*

Middle Elbow Room

North facing on the east side. The routes start on an unstable scree slope.

A. In Your Red Truck 9*

3 bolts. Pocketed mini-face. Lower off.
FA: Kelly Cordner, Bill MacBride, 7/1998, GU.

B. Pumice Facial 10c**

4 bolts. Climb a pocketed face, then clip a lone coldshut and traverse right to the belay of *Monkey Bean*. Lower off.
FA: Kelly Cordner, Bill MacBride, Grant Schumacher, 10/1998.

C. Monkey Bean 10b**

5 bolts. Pocketed face to a seam. Lower off.
FA: Kelly Cordner, Bill MacBride, 10/1998, TD.

D. Spivey for Breakfast 11a***

4 bolts, gear to 2". Crack to seam. Lower off.
FA: Scott Ayers, Eric Rhicard, 1989, GU.

E. Init 10a***

Gear to 5". Offwidth crack. Lower off.
FA: Scott Ayers, Doug Jaffe, 1989, GU.

F. Loony Bar 10a**

8 bolts. Crack to face. Lower off.
FA: Kelly Cordner, Bill MacBride. 11/1998, TD.

The following routes are found around the toe of the buttress. The base is overgrown with brush.

G. Buddha's Bivy Buddy's Biddy's Booty 9•

2 bolts, gear to 1.5". Face to crack. Lower off.
FA: Scott Ayers, 1991, GU.

H. Original Gorgeous 9*

Gear to 2.5". Hand crack in a corner. Lower off. ☞ The first route named *Gorgeous* in the Gorge; the name however seemed to stick better on the five star arete climb at the Gorgeous Towers.
FA: John Aughinbaugh, Gary Slate, Bill Russell, 1988, GU.

I. Neanderthal 12a**

Approach by climbing *Original Gorgeous* then go up and right. 7 bolts. Arete. Lower off.
FA: Jim Gregg, 1992.

©2005 Maximus Press. *Marty Lewis Topo.*

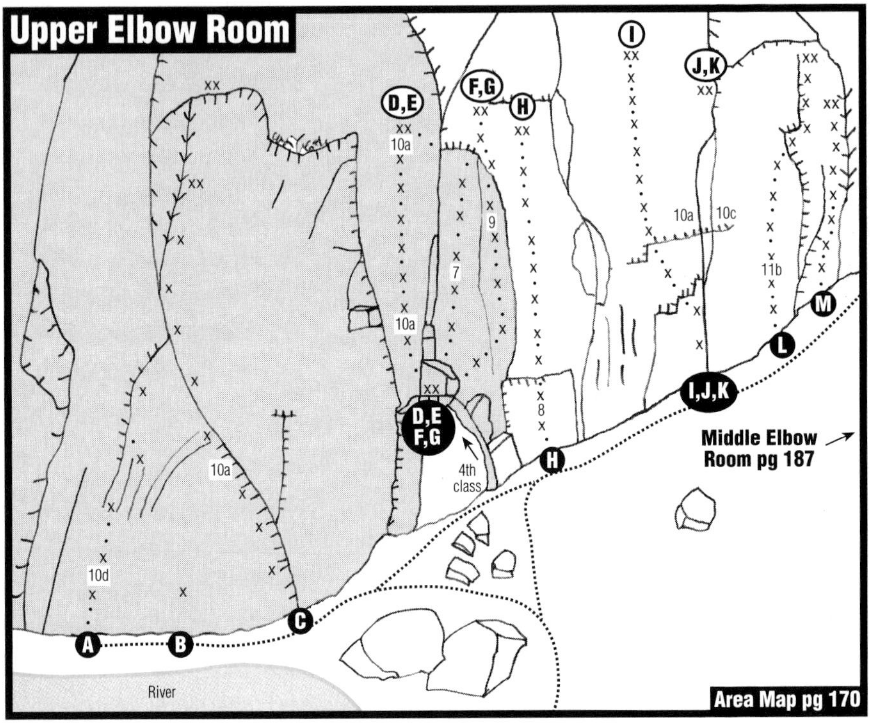

Upper Elbow Room

North and west facing cliffs above and left of a big talus fan on the east side.

A. Induced Labor 10d****

8 bolts. Technical face to a flake. Lower off.
FA: Tony Puppo, Joe Rousek, 1994, TD.

B. Pitocin (open project)

1 bolt. Thin face.
P: Tony Puppo, Joe Rousek.

C. Post Partum 10a****

8 bolts. A balancy ramp leads to a face. Lower off.
FA: Joe Rousek, Tony Puppo, 1994, GU.

The following four routes start on a terrace with a belay. Alternately you can start from the ground and lower off 30m/100' back to the ground.

D. Sparky the Drillhead 10a**

7 bolts. Face. Lower off.
FA: Eden Masters, Scott Ayers, 1991, GU.

E. Sunset Sam 6*

Gear to 3". Climb a crack, then go left to the anchor on *Sparky the Drillhead*. Lower off.
FA: Scott Ayers, 1991, GU.

F. For Patricia 7***

6 bolts. Face. Lower off.
FA: Scott Ayers, Eden Masters, 1990, GU.

G. Frank 9***

7 bolts. Blunt arete. Lower off.
FA: Mike Strassman, Dana Drucker, 1990, TD.

H. Stella 8***

9 bolts. Face to slab. Lower off.
FA: Dana Drucker, Mike Strassman, L. Drucker, T. Drucker, 1990, GU.

I. Cajun Barbecue 10b***

10 bolts. Start cracks then head left up a technical face. Lower off.
FA: Kelly Cordner, Bill MacBride, 7/1998, TD.

J. Stella's Fella 10a**

2 bolts, gear to 2". Crack. Lower off.
FA: Kelly Cordner, Randy Jacobs, 9/1996, GU.

K. Kelly's Heroes 10c**

2 bolts, gear. Thin crack. Lower off.
FA: Urmas Franosch, Kelly Cordner, 9/1996, GU.

L. Walk the Yellow Line 11b****

11 bolts. Climb a technical vertical face to a bulge then step right to an interesting dihedral. Lower off.
FA: Urmas Franosch, Kelly Cordner, 9/1996, TD.

M. Serial Driller 12c***

7 bolts. Technical arete. Lower off.
FA: Eric Kohl, 6/1994, GU.

©2005 Maximus Press. *Marty Lewis Photo.*

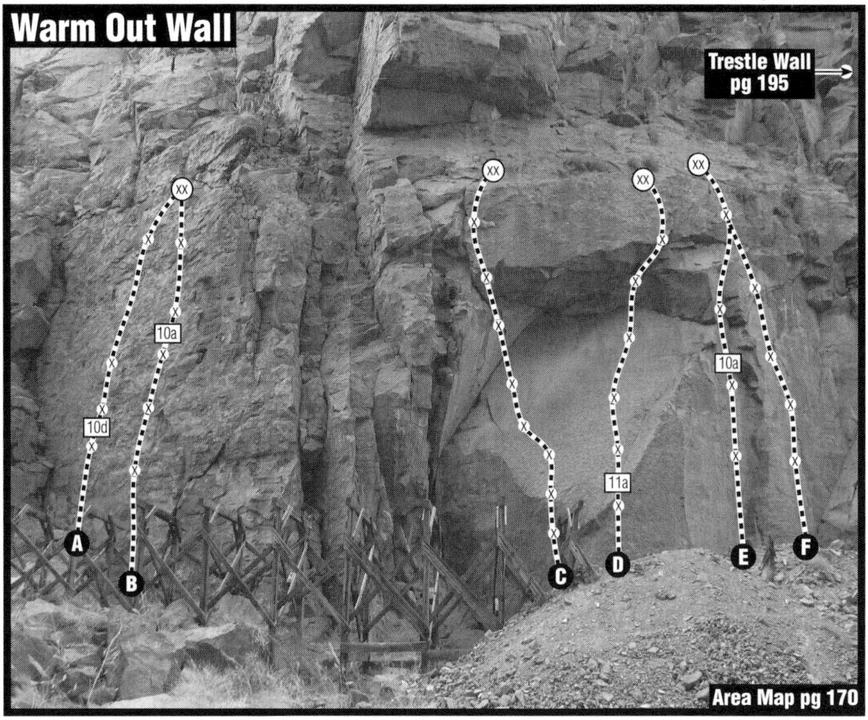

Warm Out Wall

Small east facing cliff where the main trail goes behind a trestle.

A. Home Skillet 10d*
4 bolts. Face. Lower off.
FA: Marty Lewis, Kevin Calder, 5/1994, TD.

B. Chicken Belly 10a**
5 bolts. Face. Lower off.
FA: Kevin Calder, Marty Lewis, 5/1994, GU.

C. Herniated Bone 10c***
8 bolts. Slab to a roof. Lower off.
FA: Dusty Clark, Nate Greenberg, 6/2005, TD.

D. Meringueutan Arch 11a**
6 bolts. Slab to roof. Lower off.
FA: Urmas Franosch, Kelly Cordner, 5/1996, TD.

E. Ace Cashier 10a**
4 bolts. Vertical dihedral. Lower off.
FA: Kelly Cordner, Urmas Franosch, 5/1996, TD.

F. Mini Me 11d**
5 bolts. Face. Lower off.
FA: Kelly Cordner, 2001, TD.

Josh Huckaby rope soloing the 1st pitch of **Flailsafe** 9**. ©*Kevin Calder Photo.*

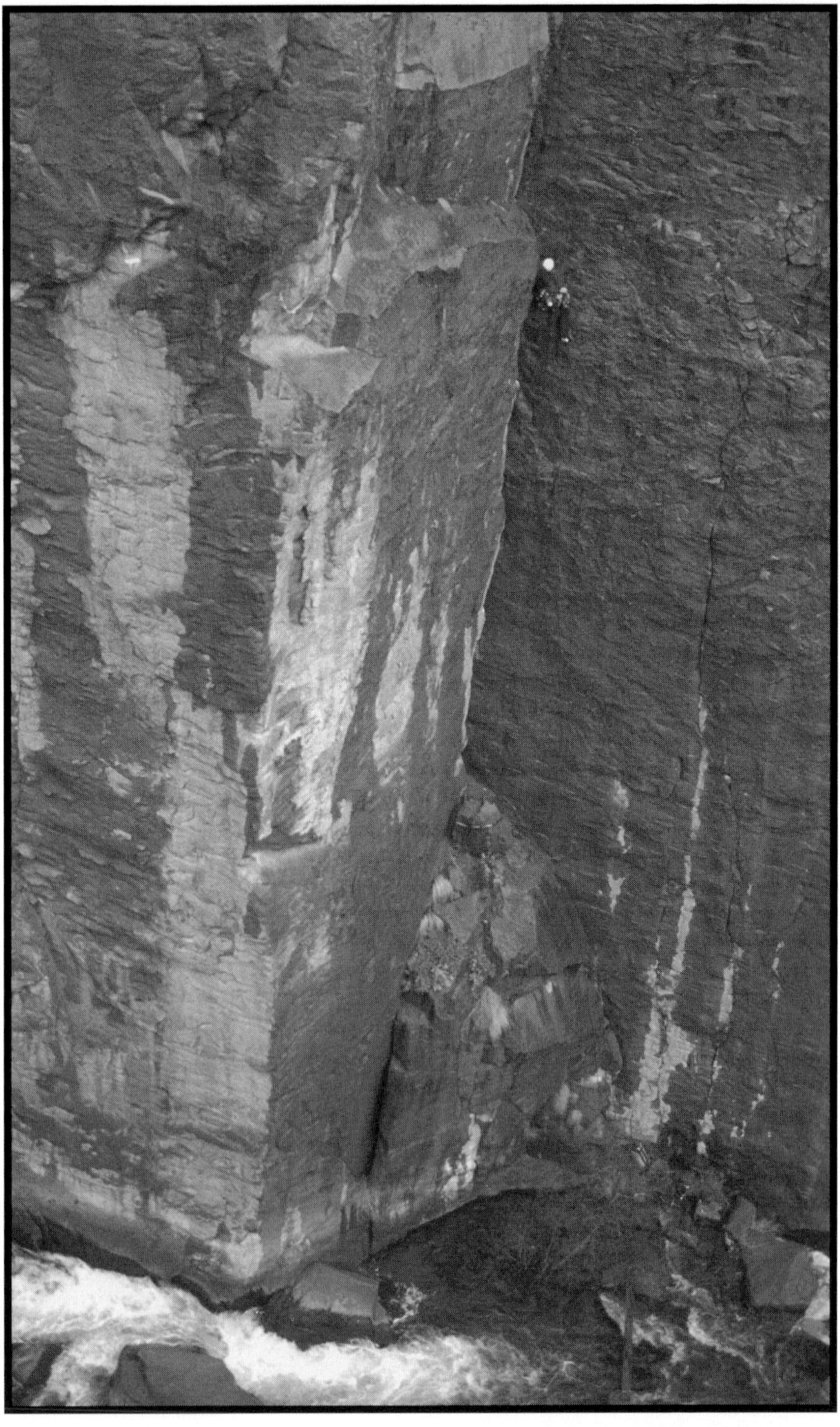

©2005 Maximus Press. *Marty Lewis Topo.*

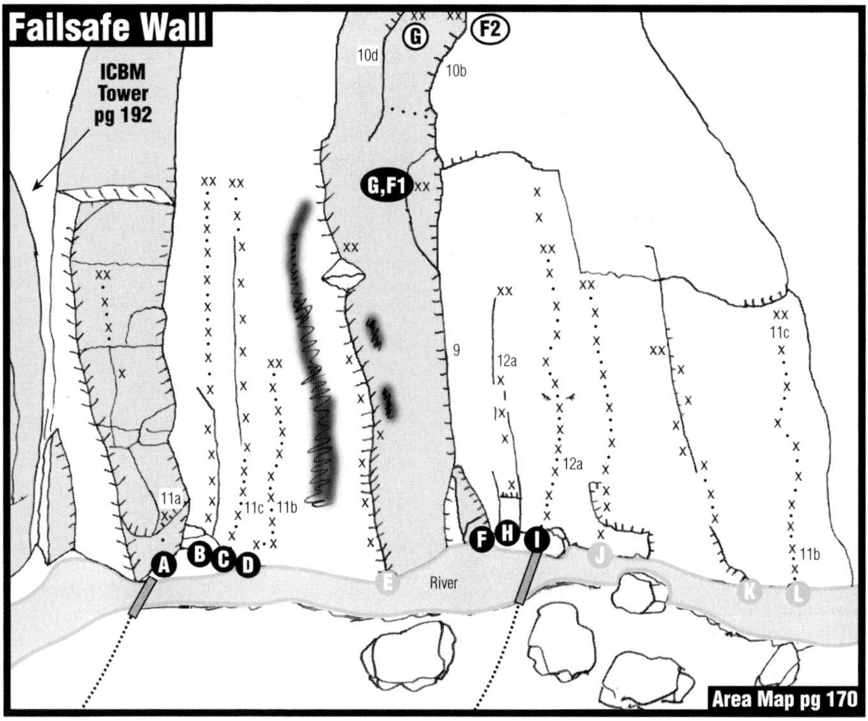

Failsafe Wall

The west facing wall right on the river on the east side. The right side of this wall has succumbed to flooding.

A. Malteese Flamoingo 11a**
4 bolts, gear to 1.5". Pass the roof then slabby cracks lead to a face. Lower off.
FA: Jay Ladin, Scott Ayers, 1989, GU.

B. Thrill Pig 11d****
13 bolts. Seam to sustained face. 30m/100' lower off.
FA: Nils Davis, Keri Orton, 6/2005, TD.

C. Drill Rig 11c****
12 bolts. A technical face to a gently overhanging seam, classic. 30m/100' lower off.
FA: Eric Kohl, Tony Puppo, Joe Rousek, 8/1994, GU.

D. Crumb Donut 11b***
9 bolts. Head right over the river, then go straight up the vertical face. Lower off.
FA: Tony Puppo, Joe Rousek, 1990, GU.

E. Captain Crunch 12a*
Flooded. Bolts. Crumbly arete. 30m/100' lower off.

F. Flailsafe 10c**
Pitch 1: 9**. Gear to 5". A wide crack in a dihedral. Climb the 2nd pitch or do a 40m/130' rappel.
➤ Photo facing page.
Pitch 2: 10b***. Gear to 4". A right-trending dihedral. 35m/115' lower off or climb the bogus 3rd pitch.
Pitch 3: 10c•. Gear to 4". Move left from the belay to a crack system and climb it. Gear anchor, walk off right (south) to a gully, descend this (5th class) to the Gorge bottom.
FA: Scott Ayers, Richard Spencer, 1989, GU.

G. Controversial Insert 10d***
Gear to 4.5". The beautiful crack on the left face of a huge dihedral. 35m/115' lower off.
FA: Jay Ladin, Scott Ayers, 1989, GU.

H. Failsafe 12a****
4 bolts, gear to 2". A strenuous vertical discontinuous crack. Lower off. ☞ An old aid climb free'd.
FA(Aid): Dean Hobbs, 1980s, GU. FA(Free): Scott Ayers, Jay Ladin, 1989.

I. Chompin' at the Bit 12a***
11 bolts, 27.5m/90'. Vertical face.
FA: Steve Schneider, Phil Green, 1990, GU.

J. Crotch Pasta 11c***
Flooded. 9 bolts. Dihedral to face.
FA: Jay Ladin, Scott Ayers, Mike Strassman, Steve Grossman, 4/1992, GU.

K. My Name's Not Harold 12b**
Flooded. 7 bolts. Shallow dihedral. Lower off.
FA: Steve Schneider, 1990, GU.

L. Fever 11c****
Flooded. 9 bolts. Vertical face. Lower off.
FA: Gary Slate, Joe Rousek, 1989, GU.

©2005 Maximus Press. *Marty Lewis Photo.*

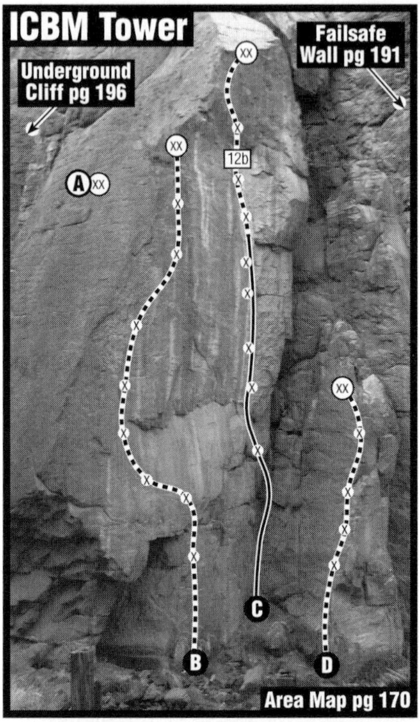

ICBM Tower

The south facing tower just left of the Failsafe Wall. Cross the river at the Trestle Wall.

A. Open Project

Anchor. Arete.
P: Alan Hirahara.

B. My Mom Can Crank 12a***

8 bolts. Vertical arcing face. Lower off.
FA: Mike Forkash, Kelly Cordner, Jody Liedecker, Randy Jacobs, 5/1998, TD.

C. Child's Play 12b*****

8 bolts. Technical crack climbing leads to a tenuous seam, then finish on a steep headwall. Lower off. ☞ The bold Jay Smith was attempting this route ground up with natural gear. Tom Herbert felt it was "child's play" to rap bolt and free this line.
FA: Tom Herbert, 1990, TD.

D. Size Doesn't Matter 10b*

4 bolts. Slabby little arete. Lower off. ☞ Well, actually size does matter.
FA: Bill MacBride, Kelly Cordner, 10/1998, TD.

Ernie Colflesh on **Bazooka Country** 12a**** at the Trestle Wall. ©*Kevin Calder Photo.* See Page 195

Lonnie Kauk on **Redemption** 12c*** at the Trestle Wall. ©*Mike Ayon Photo.* **See Page 195**

Lonnie Kauk on **Ascension** 13b****. ©*Mike Ayon Photo.*

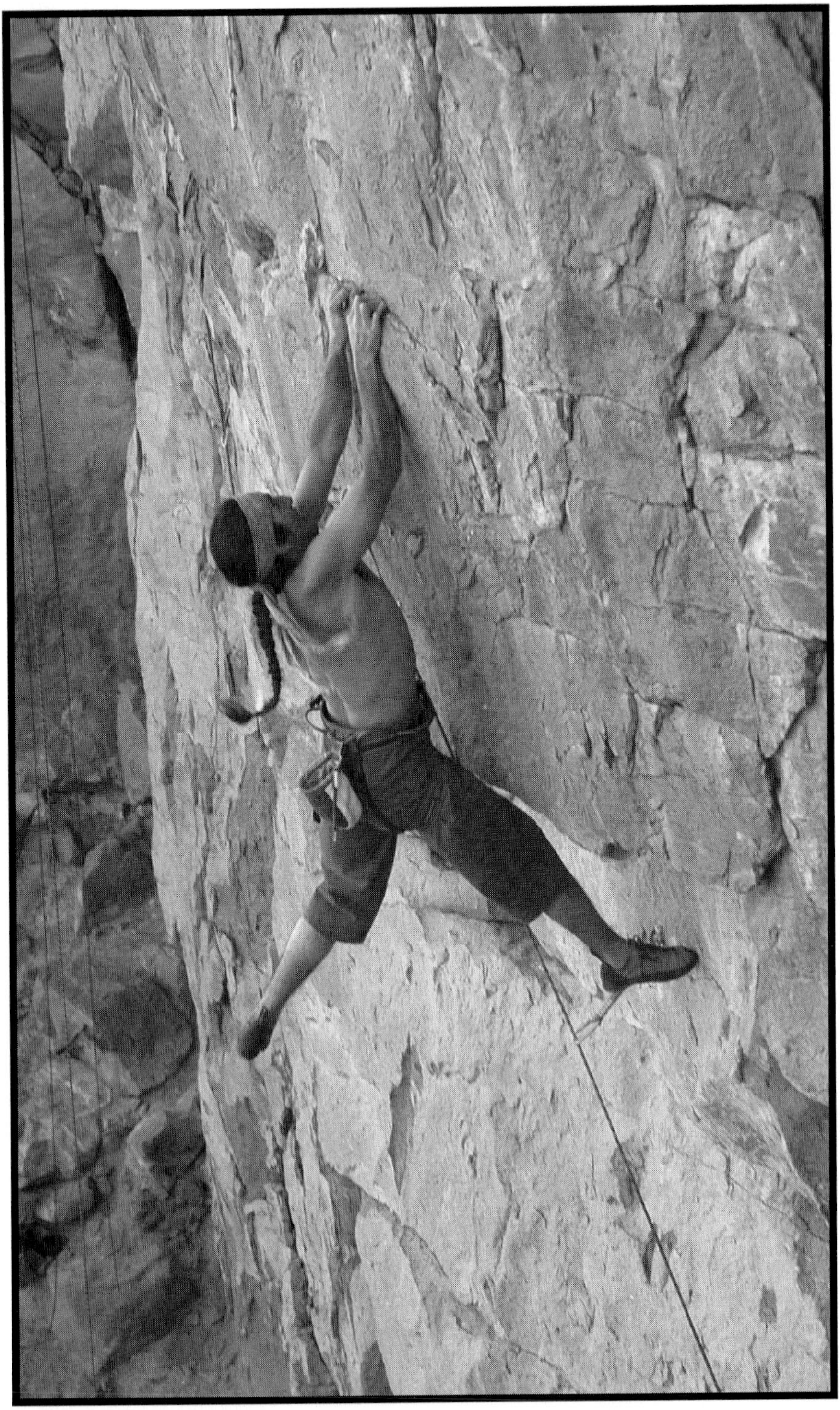

©2005 Maximus Press. Marty Lewis Topo.

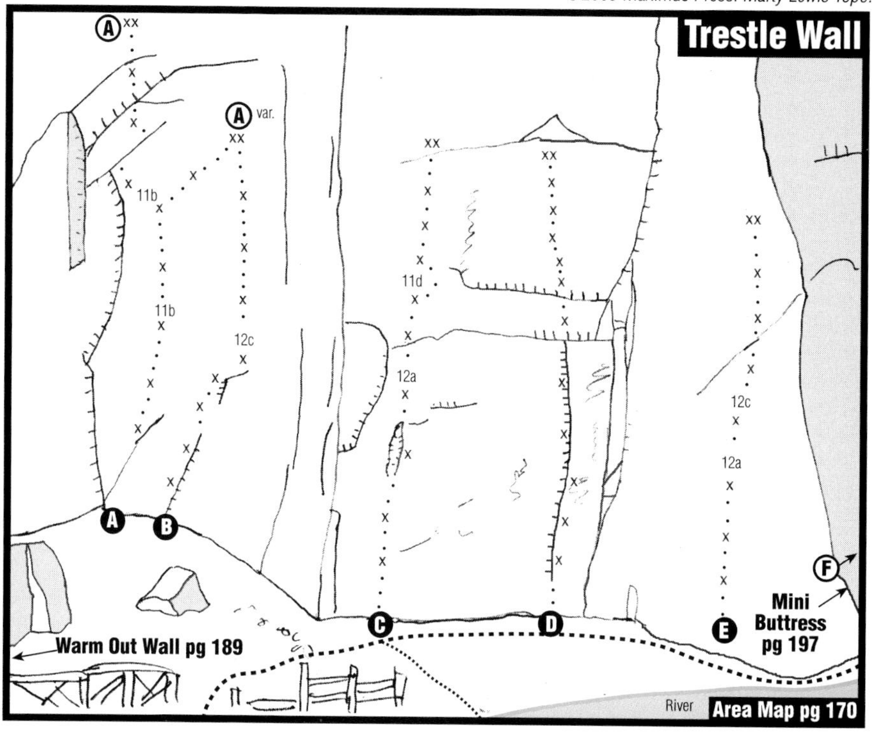

Trestle Wall

Orange wall on the west side above an abandoned trestle.

A. Pop Goes the Weasel 11b****

8 bolts. Gently overhanging seams lead to an exciting roof finish. Lower off. ☞ Used to end before turning the lip of the roof.

FA: Scott Ayers, Eden Masters, Mike Strassman, 1990, GU. Route extension: Marty Lewis, Kevin Calder.

Variation: 11b***. 6 bolts. Go right at the 5th bolt following a weakness, avoids the final roof. Lower off.

B. White Zombie 12c***

8 bolts. An awkward ramp leads to a bouldery crux. Lower off.

FA: Louie Anderson, Bob Beall, 9/1992, TD.

C. Bazooka Country 12a****

9 bolts. A balancy crux is followed by a long strenuous gently overhanging face. Lower off. ☞ At the 6th bolt you have to go way right because a major hold broke off.

➤ Photo page 192.

FA: Marty Lewis, Kevin Calder, Gregg Davis, 10/1992, TD.

D. Ascension 13b****

11 bolts (5 chain draws). A dihedral leads to double roofs then a steep difficult face. Lower off.

➤ Photo facing page.

FA: Lonnie Kauk, 6/2205, TD.

E. Redemption 12c***

7 bolts. Vertical technical face. Lower off.

➤ Photo page 193.

FA: Louie Anderson, Larry Kuechlin, Mark Reber, 5/1993, TD.

F. Main Vein 12a***

Southeast facing streaked wall located 50 ft. right of *Redemption*. 9 bolts. Crack to face. Lower off.

FA: Lonnie Kauk, Trevor Benson, Sabrina Nioche, 6/2005, TD.

G. Open Project

North facing, located 50' right of *Main Vein*. 3 bolts. A very old mystery project.

©2005 Maximus Press. *Marty Lewis Photo.*

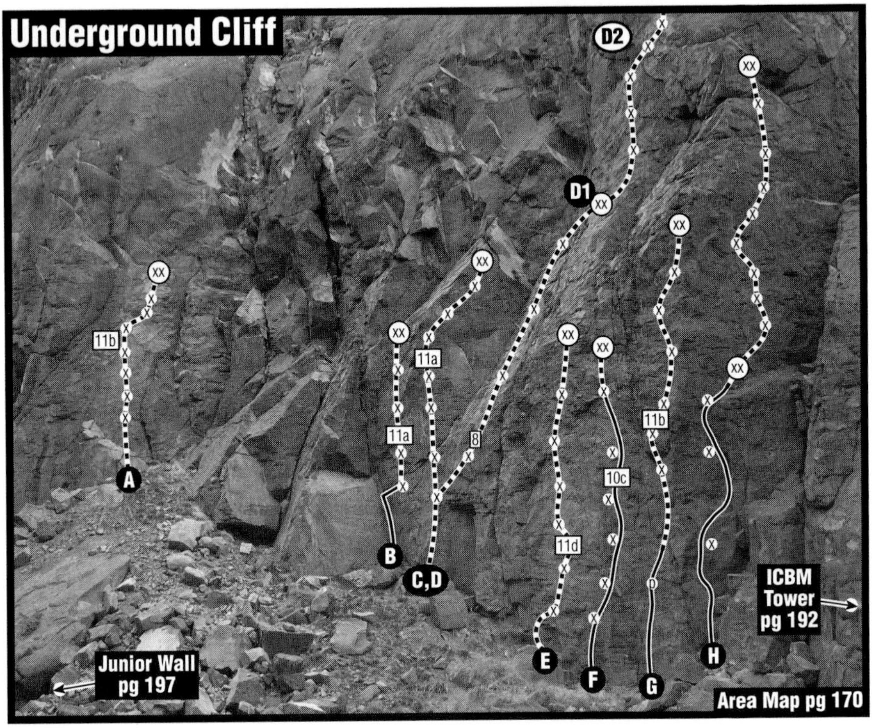

Underground Cliff

Orange buttress on the east side.

A. Seam's Difficult 11b***

7 bolts. Technical edging up a seam. Lower off.
FA: Kelly Cordner, Klaus Auer, 3/1998, GU.

B. Whiteout 11a**

4 bolts. Vertical face. Lower off.
FA: Klaus Auer, Kelly Cordner, 2/1998, TD.

C. King Spud 11a*

7 bolts. A technical face leads to a contrived traverse right. Lower off. ☞ Not to be confused with the classic at Clark Canyon with the same name.
FA: Kelly Cordner, 12/1997, GU.

D. You Like it Sideways? 10b**

Pitch 1: 8*. 5 bolts. One move leads to a 4th class slab. Climb 2nd pitch or lower off.
Pitch 2: 10b**. 6 bolts. Face climb up and right. Lower off or do a single-rope rappel to *Freaks of the Industry*.
FA: Kelly Cordner, 1/1998, GU.

E. Freaks of the Industry 11d****

6 bolts. Crimpy sustained vertical face. Lower off.
FA: Scott Ayers, Marty Lewis, 1990, GU.

F. Get Over It 10c****

6 bolts. Tricky cerebral crack. Lower off.
FA: Kelly Cordner, Klaus Auer, 2/1998, TD.

G. Be Prepared to G 11b**

6 bolts, 1 piton. Crack to committing arete. Lower off.
FA: Mike Strassman, Scott Ayers, 1991, GU.

H. La Pavoni 11d***

Pitch 1: 8*. 3 bolts. Dihedral. Climb 2nd pitch or lower off.
Pitch 2: 11d***. 8 bolts. Vertical face. Lower off.
Can be done in one pitch if mindful of rope drag.
FA: Klaus Auer, Kelly Cordner, 2/1998, TD.

©2005 Maximus Press. Marty Lewis Photo.

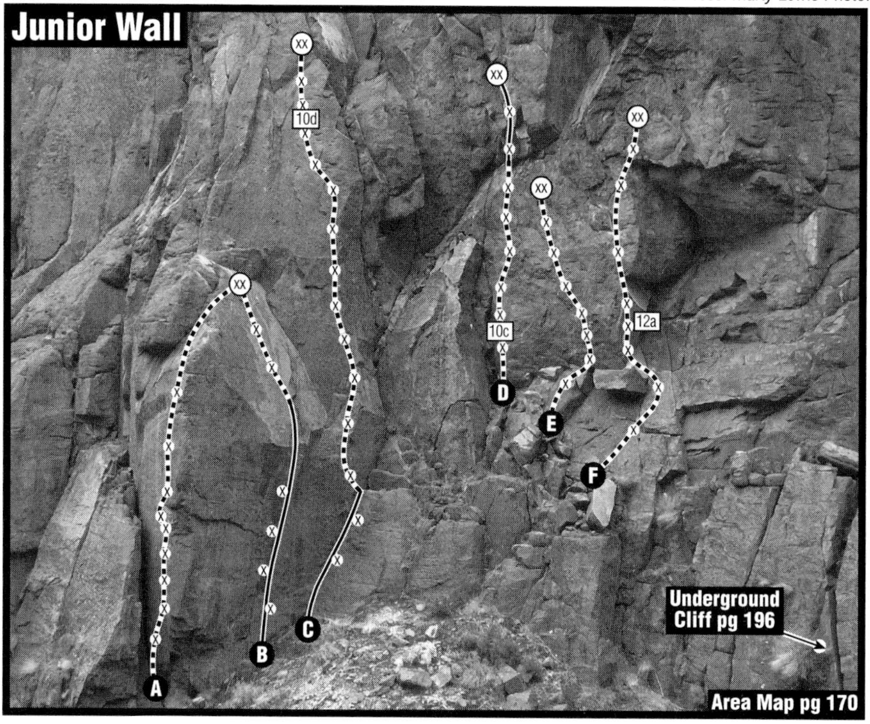

Junior Wall
Towers on the east side.

A. Sport Trac 12a*
9 bolts. Chimney to arete. Lower off.
FA: Tiffany Campbell, Jason Campbell, Jim Campbell, 3/2000, TD.

B. Junior Achievement 11d****
6 bolts, gear to 2". An awkward seam in a dihedral leads to a thin slab. Lower off.
FA: Scott Ayers, Jay Ladin, Mike Strassman, 1989, GU.

C. Dimples 10d***
14 bolts. A slabby corner leads to an awesome arete, then climb a slab right of the bolt line—the bolts follow a strength between two weaknesses—at some point you must cross from the right side of the bolts to the left side, making the clips difficult. 35m/115' lower off.
FA: Kelly Cordner, Briant Phillips, 10/1997, TD.

D. Jump Start 10c***
8 bolts. Clipping the 1st bolt can be reachy. A long opening move leads to a gently overhanging face, then climb a steep crack. Lower off.
FA: Kelly Cordner, Barry Oswick, 10/1997, TD.

E. Pre-erosive Force 12a***
7 bolts. Short sustained face. Lower off.
FA: John Heizer, Kelly Cordner, 4/1998, TD.

F. Hook 12a**
8 bolts. Arete to face to roof. Lower off.
FA: Todd Snyder, Kelly Cordner, Mike Forkash, 5/1998, TD.

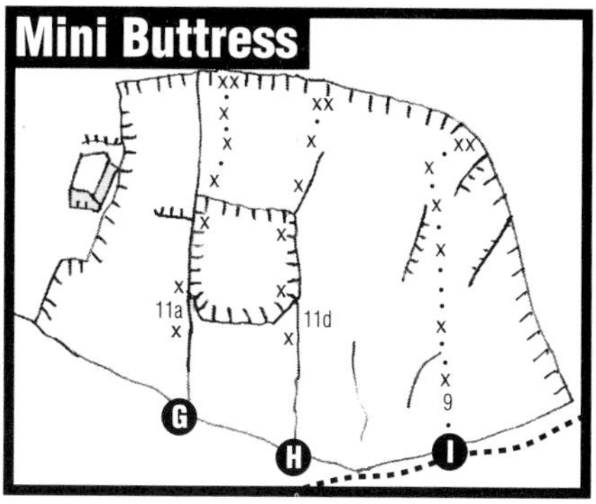

Mini Buttress
Small formation right on the trail on the west side of the Gorge.

G. Nose Ring 11a**
6 bolts. Dihedral to face, sustained. Lower off.
FA: Urmas Franosch, Kelly Cordner, 5/1996, TD.

H. Family Man 11d**
5 bolts. Dihedral to face. Lower off.
FA: Kevin Leary, Joe Rousek, 5/1997, TD.

I. Who Knows? 9**
5 bolts. Face. Lower off.

©2005 Maximus Press. *Marty Lewis Photo.*

©2005 Maximus Press. *Marty Lewis Topo.*

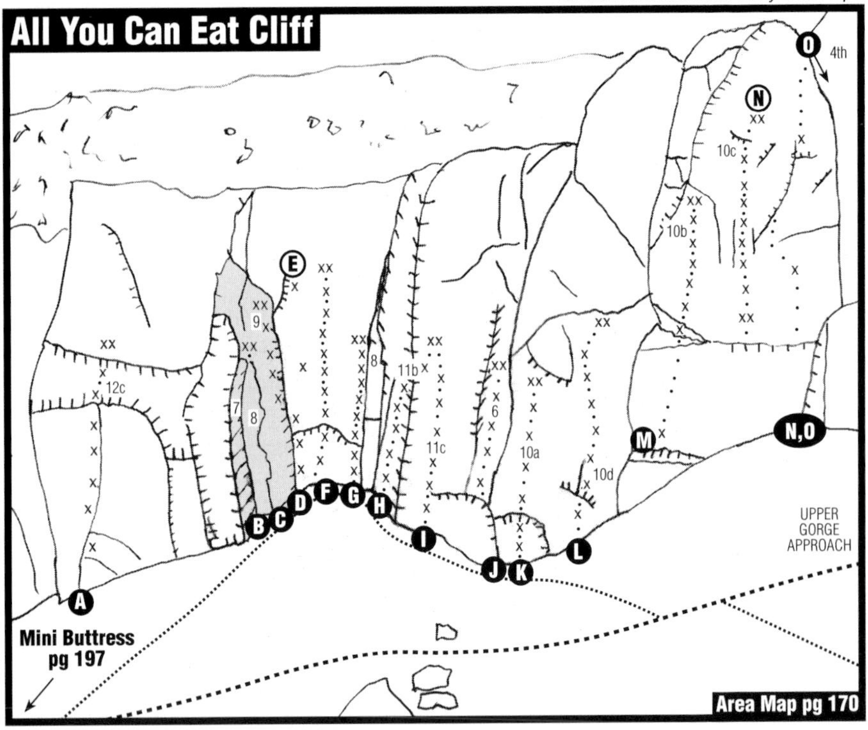

All You Can Eat Cliff

The gray towers on the west side. The first cliff reached when hiking the main trail during the Upper Gorge Approach.

A. Sting of the Honeybee 12c***

8 bolts. Seam to desperate roof. Lower off.
FA: Wendy Borgerd, Eric Kohl, 11/1995, TD.

B. Fine Dining 7**

Gear to 4". Wide crack in a dihedral. Lower off.
FA: Kelly Cordner, Craig Tufeld, 8/1997, TD.

C. Alfred Hitchcrack 8**

Gear to 3". Hand crack. Lower off.
FA: Wendy Borgerd, 6/1995, GU.

D. Cinderella 9****

7 bolts. A beautiful stemming corner. Lower off.
FA: Kelly Cordner, Mike Forkash, 8/1997, TD.

E. Project

2 bolts. Face.

F. Trundle of Joy 12b**

9 bolts. Easy face to a difficult reachy move. Lower off.
FA: Chris Miller, Kelly Cordner, Mike Forkash, 5/1998, TD.

G. Step Right Up 8**

8 bolts. Face to arete/hand crack, heavily bolted. Lower off. ☞ The combination of the grade, the bolts and the location make this route the most popular 2 star climb in the Gorge.
FA: Kelly Cordner, Mike Forkash, 8/1997, TD.

H. Posers on the Rig 11b**

6 bolts. Climb the seam, then step right around the arete at the 5th bolt, finish on tenuous face climbing. Lower off.
FA: Hank Means, Scott Ayers, Mike Strassman, 1992, TD.

I. O Henry! 11c***

6 bolts. A boulder problem is followed by a difficult bulge, finish on a tricky off-vertical face. Lower off.
➤ Photo this page.
FA: Scott Ayers, Hank Means, Mike Strassman, 1992, GU.

J. Crotalulsley Challenged 6**

4 bolts. Face. Lower off.
FA: Kelly Cordner, Briant Phillips, 9/1997, TD.

K. Carnubiator 10a**

6 bolts. A contrived start leads to a slab. Lower off.
FA: Kelly Cordner, Briant Phillips, Craig Tufeld, 9/1997, TD.

L. Elephant's Butt 10d**

7 bolts. An awkward bulge to a vegetated slab. Lower off.
FA: Kelly Cordner, Briant Phillips, 9/1997, TD.

M. Stay Hungry 10b**

Approach via a 4th class ledge to a one bolt anchor.
6 bolts. Slab, sporty to the 1st bolt. 27.5m/90' lower off.
FA: Paul Linaweaver, Mike Strassman, 1991, GU.

N. Szechwan Bambi 10c***

8 bolts. Scramble up a dihedral, traverse left on a ledge, pass a false belay, now climb the slab. 30m/100' lower off.
FA: Mike Strassman, Paul Linaweaver, 1991, GU.

O. All You Can Eat 10c•

2 bolts, gear to 3.5". Scramble up a dihedral, traverse left on a ledge, then up a slab past a bolt, enter a right-leaning right-facing dihedral up this, then face climb. Gear anchor, 4th class scramble off right.
FA: Steve Grossman, Paul Linaweaver, 1989, GU.

Marek Hajek on **O Henry!** 11c***. ©*Kevin Calder Photo.*

©2005 Maximus Press. *Marty Lewis Photo.*

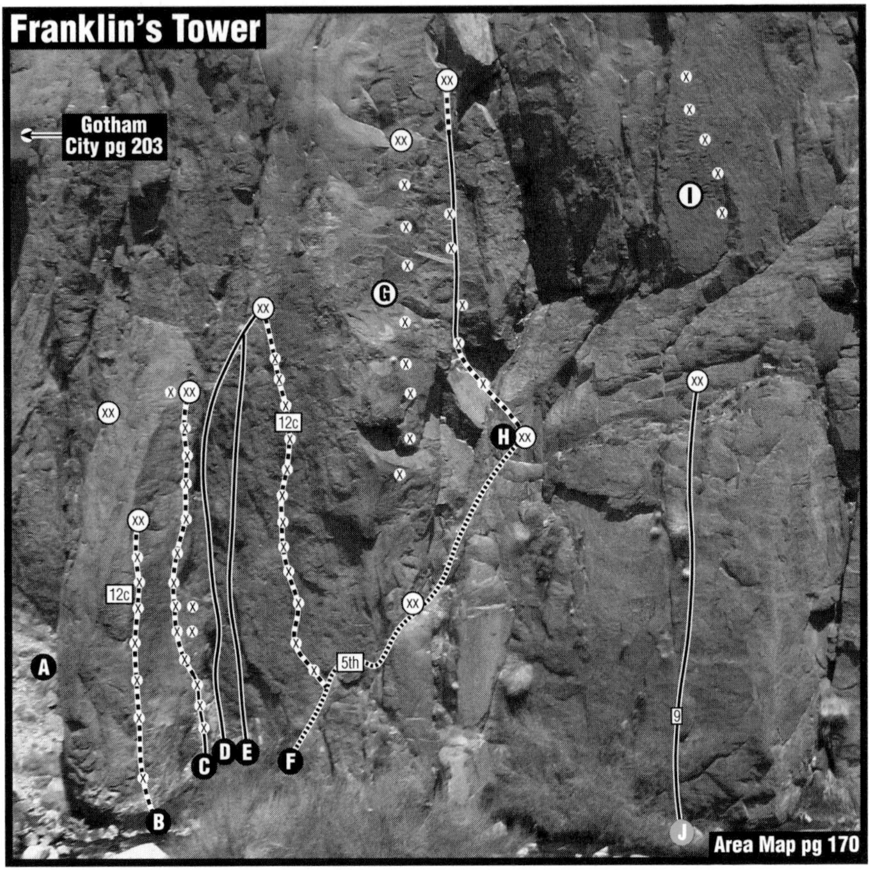

Franklin's Tower

A detached pinnacle and the adjoining wall to its right on the east side. From Gotham City you can just squeeze between the tower and the river to access these climbs.

A. Franklin's Frosty Funeral 10b**
6 bolts. Climb a face to a ledge then step right and climb more face. Lower off.
FA: Mike Strassman, 1991, GU.

B. Help on the Way 12c***
7 bolts. Vertical arete. Lower off.
FA: Steve Schneider, Scott Ayers, Mike Strassman, Steve Grossman, 1990, GU.

C. Tower Line 12a***
12 bolts. Seam to vertical face. Lower off. ☞ A mysterious set of bolts parallels this route part way up.
FA: Chris Miller, Kelly Cordner, 5/1998, GU.

D. Slipknot 8•
Gear to 4". Chimney. Lower off.
FA: Scott Ayers, 11/1990, GU.

E. Gimme the Helmet, I'll Be the Stunt Man 10a*
Gear to 3". Broken crack. Lower off.
FA: Mike Strassman, Dana Drucker, 1990, GU.

F. Steel Monkey 12c*****
12 bolts. Vertical face, thin and sustained. Lower off.
FA: Mike Strassman, Scott Ayers, Dana Drucker, 1992, TD.

The next three routes are approached by a 5th class scramble to a ledge.

G. Project
8 bolts. Steep face.
P: Lonnie Kauk.

H. Cruella 10c***
9 bolts. Dihedral to arete. Lower off.
FA: Kelly Cordner, Bill MacBride, 1998, GU.

I. Open Project
5 bolts. Slab climb off a ledge.
P: Joe Rousek.

J. Roberto Clemente 9*
Flooded. Gear to 2". Brushy crack. Lower off.
FA: Bill MacBride, Kelly Cordner, 10/1998.

Tiffany Campbell on **Flex Your Head** 11c***** at Gotham City. ©*Kevin Calder Photo.* **See Page 203**

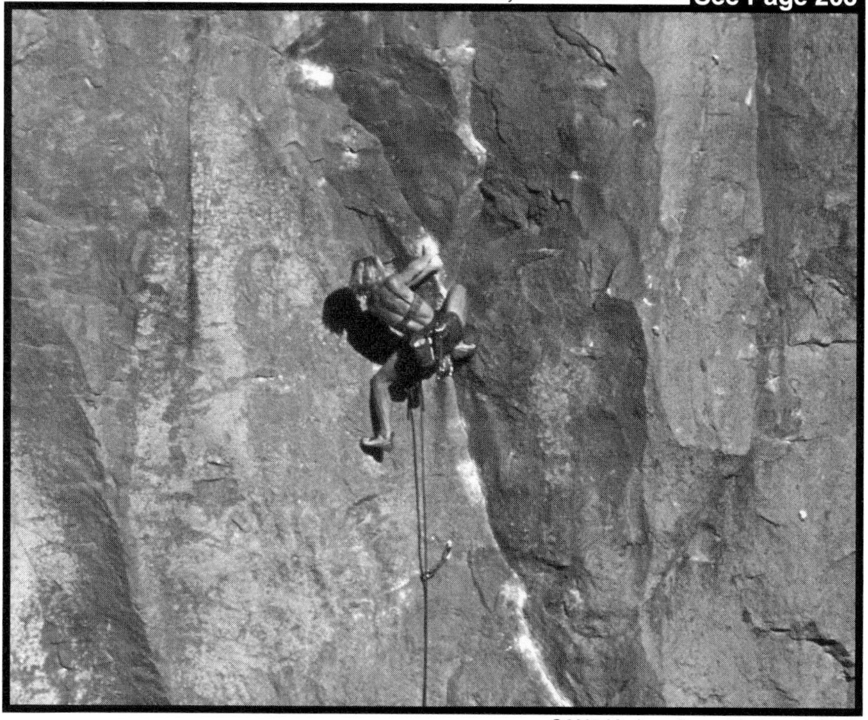

©2005 Maximus Press. *Marty Lewis Photo.*

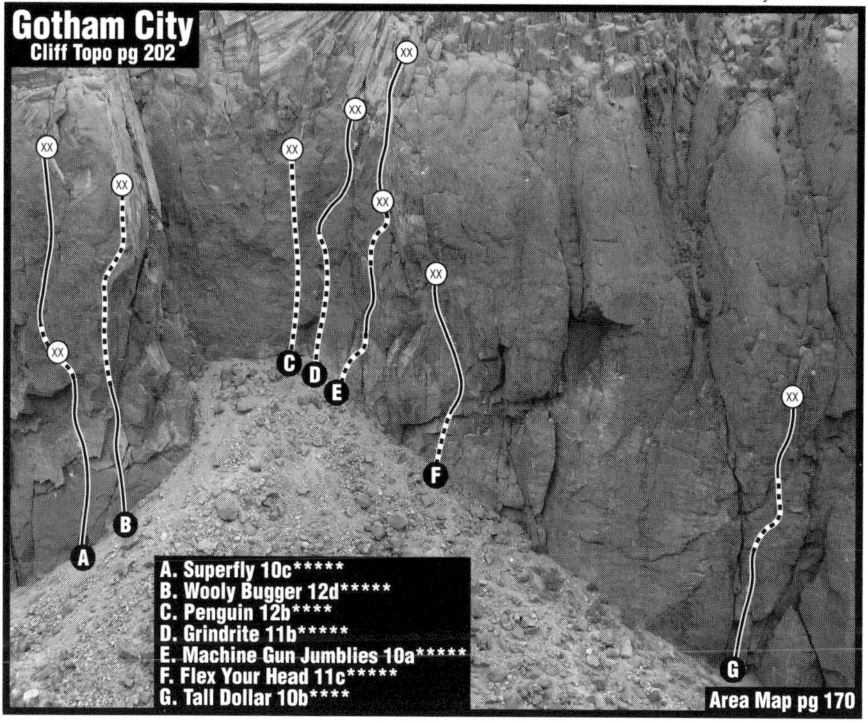

©2005 Maximus Press. *Marty Lewis Topo.*

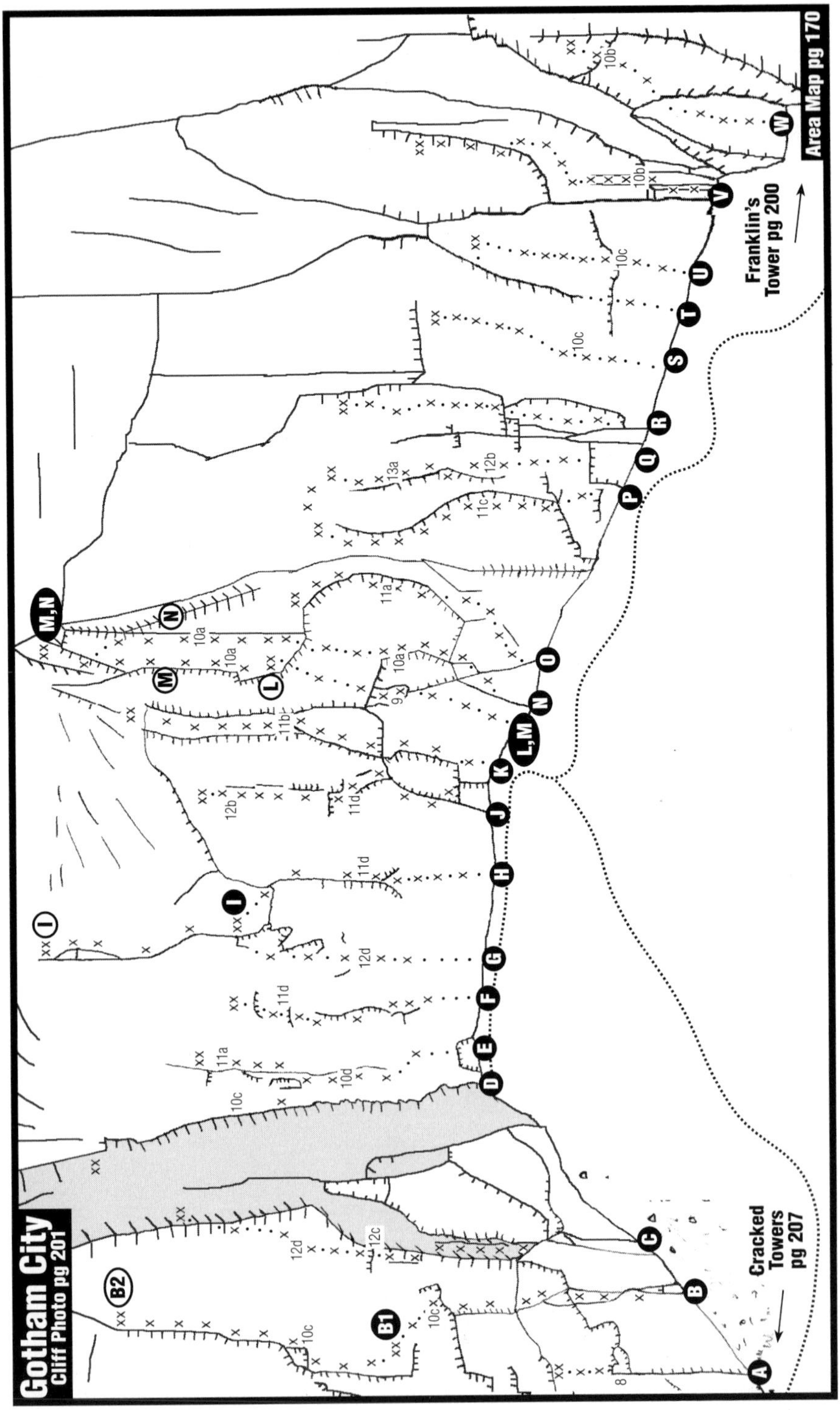

Gotham City

Starts with a recessed wall above a talus fan and continues down the slope to the right until reaching a tower, on the east side.

A. Silence of the Poodles 8****
2 bolts, gear to 2". Excellent crack climbing leads to a seam. Lower off.
FA: Geoff Fullerton, Jeff Pulice, 1992, GU.

B. Superfly 10c*****
Pitch 1: 10c****. 9 bolts. Climb slabby cracks to a steep dihedral, then tackle an exciting roof. Climb the 2nd pitch or lower off 30m/100'. ➤ Photo page 205.
Pitch 2: 10c*****. 9 bolts. An overhanging lieback flake to a slabby dihedral, very exposed. Lower off.
Can be done in one pitch if mindful of rope drag.
FA: Marty Lewis, Kevin Calder, 5/1997, GU.

C. Wooly Bugger 12d*****
12 bolts, use a long runner on the 1st and 5th bolt. Scramble up a crack to a dihedral, then move left to a spectacular overhanging arete. 35m/115' lower off.
➤ Front cover photo.
FA: Peter Croft, Andrew Stevens, 6/2004, TD.

D. In the Pink 10c**
1 bolt, gear to 2". Grovel up a gully then climb a clean pink dihedral. 35m/115' lower off to ground.
FA: Steve Grossman, Scott Ayers, Paul Linaweaver, 1989, GU.

E. Boy Wonder 11a***
8 bolts. Slippery seams and face. Lower off.
FA: Mike Strassman, Scott Ayers, 1990, GU.

F. Bat Angel 11d***
7 bolts. Fun face to a reachy, bouldery crux. Lower off
FA: Mike Strassman, Paul Linaweaver, Scott Ayers, 1991, GU.

G. Joker's Acid Bath 12d**
5 bolts. Blank face. Lower off.
FA: Doug Englekirk, Steve Schneider, 1990, TD.

H. Riddler 11d***
8 bolts. Face climb to a tenuous vertical seam. Lower off.
FA: Scott Ayers, Mike Strassman, Ron Farrell, 1990, GU.

I. Mr. Freeze 11c***
4 bolts, gear to 1.5". Seam. Lower off.
FA: Scott Ayers, Bill McChesney, Steve Schneider, 1990, GU.
Can be done as one pitch.

J. Penguin 12b****
11 bolts. Sustained crimpy vertical seam. Lower off.
FA: Scott Ayers, Mike Strassman, 1990, GU.

K. Grindrite 11b*****
12 bolts. A slabby ramp leads to a beautiful Yosemite like dihedral. 30m/100' lower off. ➤ Photo page 204.
FA: Kevin Calder, Marty Lewis, 5/1997, GU.

L. Double Flipper 9***
7 bolts. Face climb to a crack, finish on a slab. Lower off.
FA: Kevin Calder, Marty Lewis, 6/1999, TD.

M. Machine Gun Jumblies 10a*****
14 bolts. Climb *Double Flipper*, then continue up a strenuous flake in a corner. 37.5m/125' pitch, two single-rope rappels.
➤ Photo page 173.
FA: Kevin Calder, Marty Lewis, 6/1999, GU.

N. Dr. Evil 10a*****
16 bolts. Climb a beautiful dihedral, continue up a slab, then step right and climb the vertical straight-in crack. 37.5m/125' pitch, two single-rope rappels.
FA: Marty Lewis, Kevin Calder, 6/1999, TD.
Variation: 10a****. 8 bolts. Climb *Dr. Evil* but step left at the top of the slab to the *Double Flipper* Anchor. Lower off.
Variation: 10a*****. 15 bolts. Climb *Dr. Evil* but step left at the top of the slab and finish up *Machine Gun Jumblies*. 37.5m/125' pitch, two single-rope rappels.

O. She's a Man, Man 11a***
9 bolts. Face climb up and right, then climb a steep dihedral. Lower off.
FA: Marty Lewis, Kevin Calder, 10/1999, TD.

P. Flex Your Head 11c*****
10 bolts. Strenuous gently overhanging dihedral, continuous and varied. Lower off. ➤ Photo page 201.
FA: Marty Lewis, Fred Berman, 6/1993, GU.
Flex Your Anaconda Variation: 12d***. 10 bolts. Start *Flex Your Head*, but go right at the 5th bolt and finish on *Anaconda*. Lower off.

Q. Anaconda 13a***
9 bolts. Steep dihedral. Lower off.
FA: Louie Anderson, Cory Zinngrabe, Larry Kuechlin, Bob Beall, 12/1993, TD.

R. Kingsnake 11c***
9 bolts. A slab leads to a break, then crank out the overhanging face. 30m/100' lower off.
FA: Brian Ketron, Mike Melkonian, 2002.

S. You're Soaking in it 10c*(r)
7 bolts. Slab. Lower off.
FA: Mike Strassman, Dana Drucker, 1991, TD.

T. Stronger than Dirt 9•
1 bolt, gear to 3". Slab to crumbly dihedral. Lower off.
FA: Mike Strassman, Dana Drucker, 1990, GU.

U. More than Just Mild 10c*
7 bolts. Slab. Lower off.
FA: Mike Strassman, Dana Drucker, 1990, TD.

V. Tall Dollar 10b****
13 bolts. A dihedral lead to a roof, follow double cracks, then face climb right to a dihedral. 30m/100' lower off.
FA: Kevin Calder, Marty Lewis, 5/2001, GU.

W. Franklin's Frosty Funeral 10b**
6 bolts. Climb a face to a ledge then step right and climb more face and pass a bulge. Lower off.
FA: Mike Strassman, 1991, GU.

Lisa Coleman on **Grindrite** 11b***** at Gotham City. ©*Shawn Reeder Photo.* See Page 203

Kevin Calder and Marty Lewis on the 1st pitch of **Superfly** 10c****. ©*Mike Bonnie Photo.* **See Page 203**

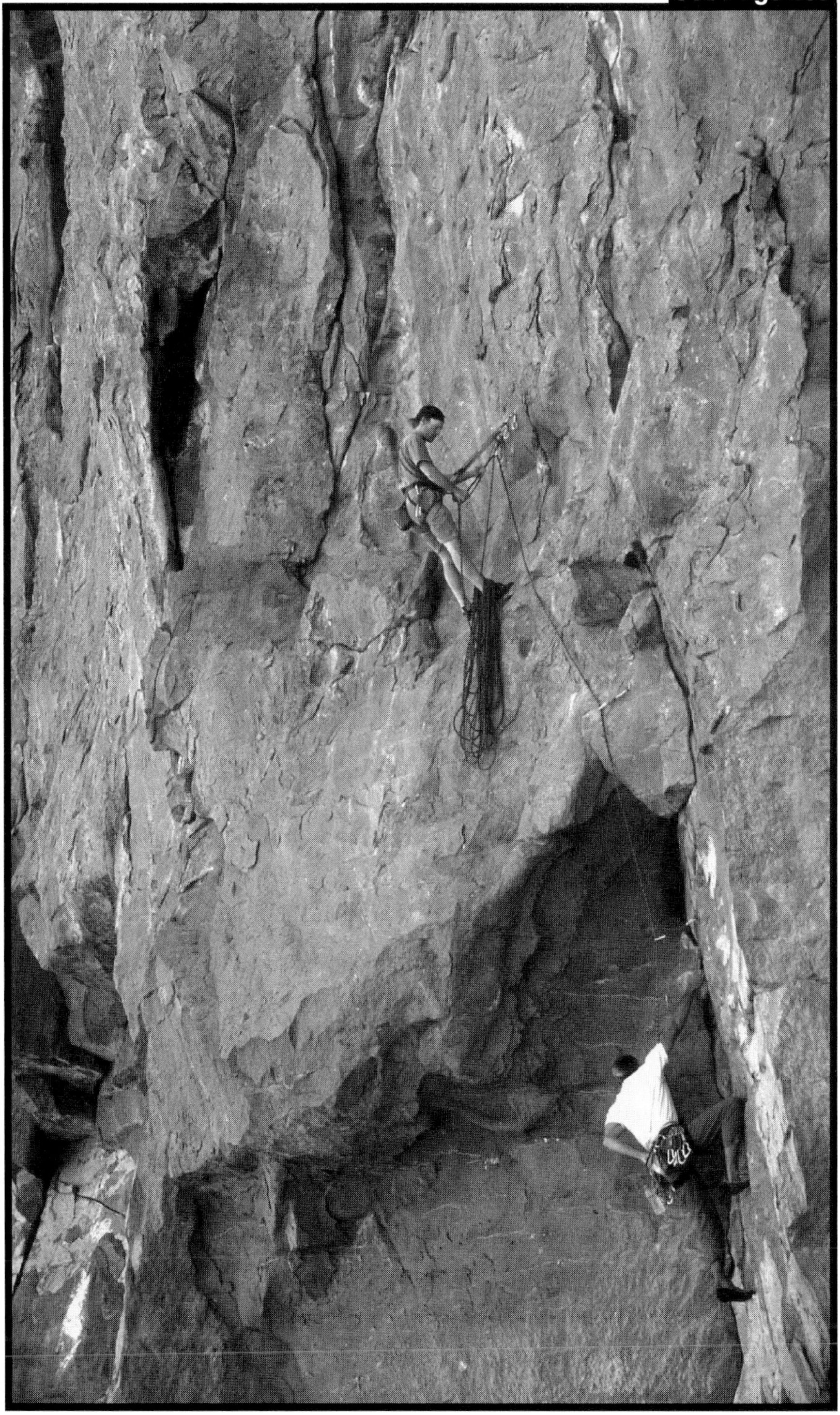

©2005 Maximus Press. *Marty Lewis Photo.*

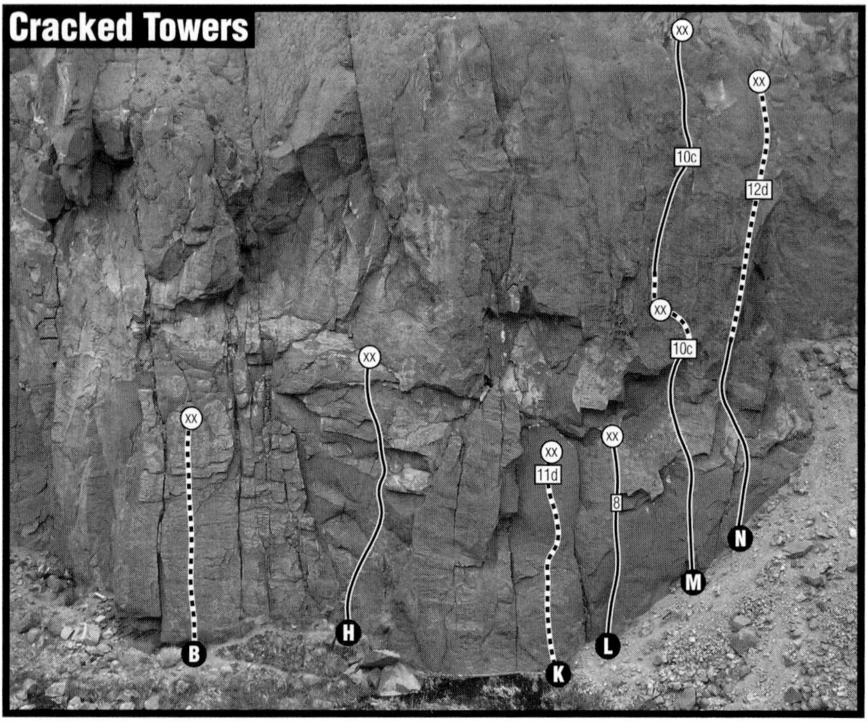

©2005 Maximus Press. *Marty Lewis Topo.*

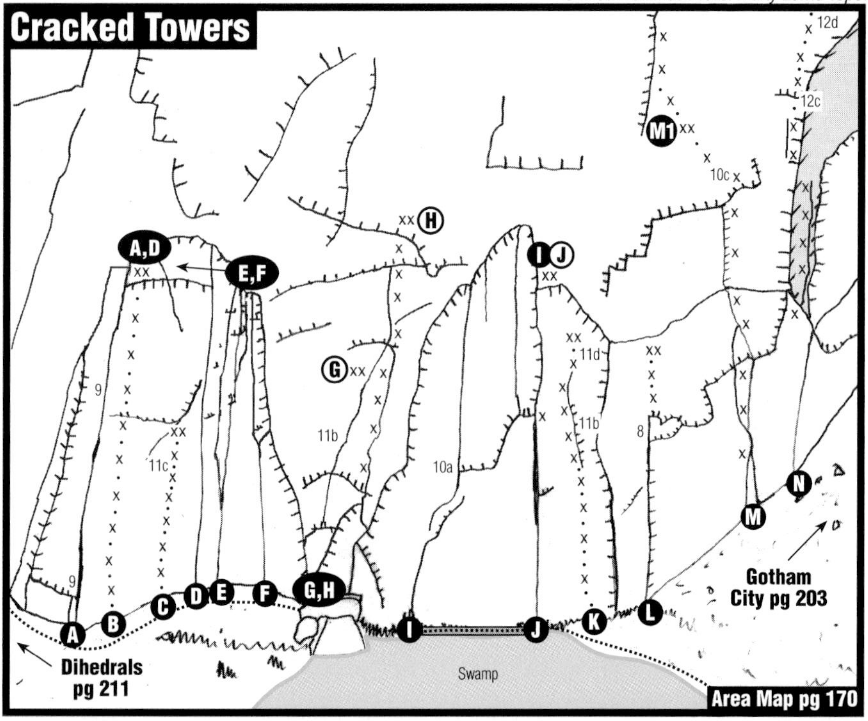

Cracked Towers

A pair of towers on the east side above a swampy area.

A. M.O. 9**

Gear to 4". Wide crack. Rappel *Scalded by Spivey.*
FA: Mike Strassman, Moira Smith, 1989, GU.

B. Scalded by Spivey 12a***

9 bolts. Super-sustained slab. Lower off.
FA: Mike Strassman, Scott Ayers, 1990, TD.

C. Flying Tigers 11c**

6 bolts. Slab. Lower off.
FA: Geoff Fullerton, Bill Herzog, 11/1989, GU.

D. No Mo' M.O. 7•

Gear to 3.5". Wide crack. Rappel *Scalded by Spivey.*
FA: Mike Strassman, Eden Masters, 11/1990, GU.

E. Left Barley Crack 10b*

Gear. Crack. Gear anchor, then traverse left and rappel *Scalded by Spivey.*
FA: Robin Barley, Judy Komori, 10/2000.

F. Right Barley Crack 10b*

Gear. Crack. Gear anchor, then traverse left and rappel *Scalded by Spivey.*
FA: Robin Barley, Judy Komori, 10/2000.

G. Urrr! 11b*

Gear to 2.5". Thin crack. Lower off.
FA: Urmas Franosch, Kelly Cordner, 5/1996, GU.

H. My Favorite Animal is a Liger 10b**

8 bolts. Scramble up a dihedral to a flake, then follow a crack through roofs. Lower off.
FA: Kevin Calder, Josh Huckaby, 2001, GU.

I. La Chappeau 10a•(r)

Gear to 3.5". Crack. Traverse right behind tower to the poor rappel station on *Swamp Thing.*
FA: Mike Strassman, John Masters, 11/1990, GU.

J. Swamp Thing 9*

1 bolt, gear to 3.5". Right facing dihedral. Lower off a poor anchor. ☞ Possibly the first route in the entire Gorge.
FA: Bob Harrington, Rick Wheeler, Will Crljenko,1978, GU.

K. And Monkeys Might Fly Out of My Butt 11d***

9 bolts. A slab leads to a technical dihedral. Lower off.
FA: Geoff Fullerton, John Martindale, 1992, GU.

L. Silence of the Poodles 8****

2 bolts, gear to 2". Excellent crack climbing leads to a seam. Lower off.
FA: Geoff Fullerton, Jeff Pulice, 1992, GU.

M. Superfly 10c*****

Pitch 1: 10c****. 9 bolts. Climb slabby cracks to a steep dihedral, then tackle an exciting roof. Climb the 2nd pitch or lower off 30m/100'. ➤ Photo page 205.
Pitch 2: 10c*****. 9 bolts. An overhanging lieback flake to a slabby dihedral, very exposed. Lower off.
Can be done in one pitch if mindful of rope drag.
FA: Marty Lewis, Kevin Calder, 5/1997, GU.

N. Wooly Bugger 12d*****

12 bolts, use a long runner on the 1st and 5th bolt. Scramble up a crack to a dihedral, then move left to a spectacular overhanging arete. 35m/115' lower off.
➤ Front cover photo.
FA: Peter Croft, Andrew Stevens, 6/2004, TD.

Fred Berman on **Chossman of the Desert** 10d****.
©Marty Lewis Photo.

See Page 211

Doug Ingersoll on **Pumping the Slots** 9**** at the Dihedrals. ©*Kevin Calder Photo.* See Page 211

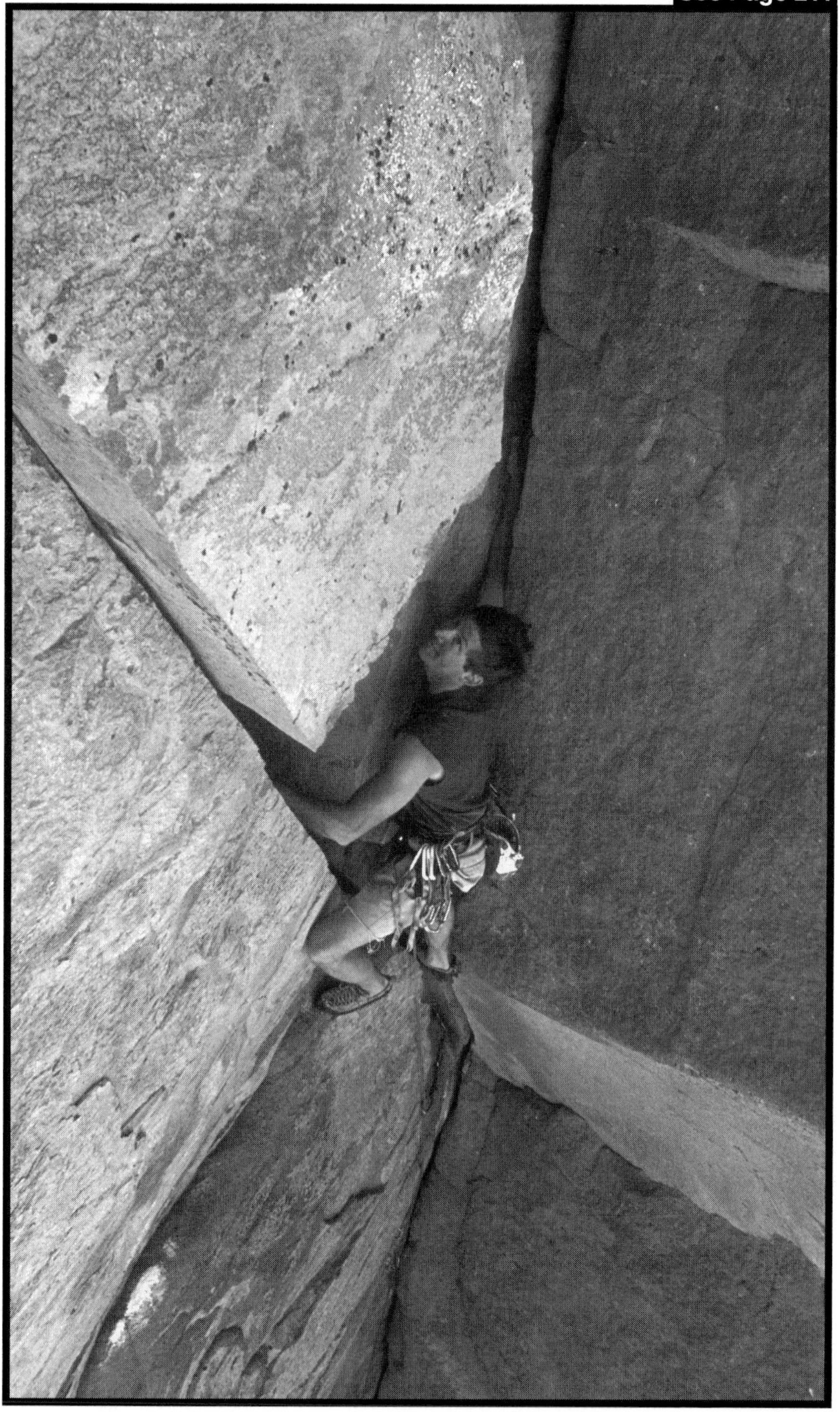

Peter Croft on **Bushfire** 13a*** at the Dihedrals. ©*Kevin Calder Photo.* **See Page 211**

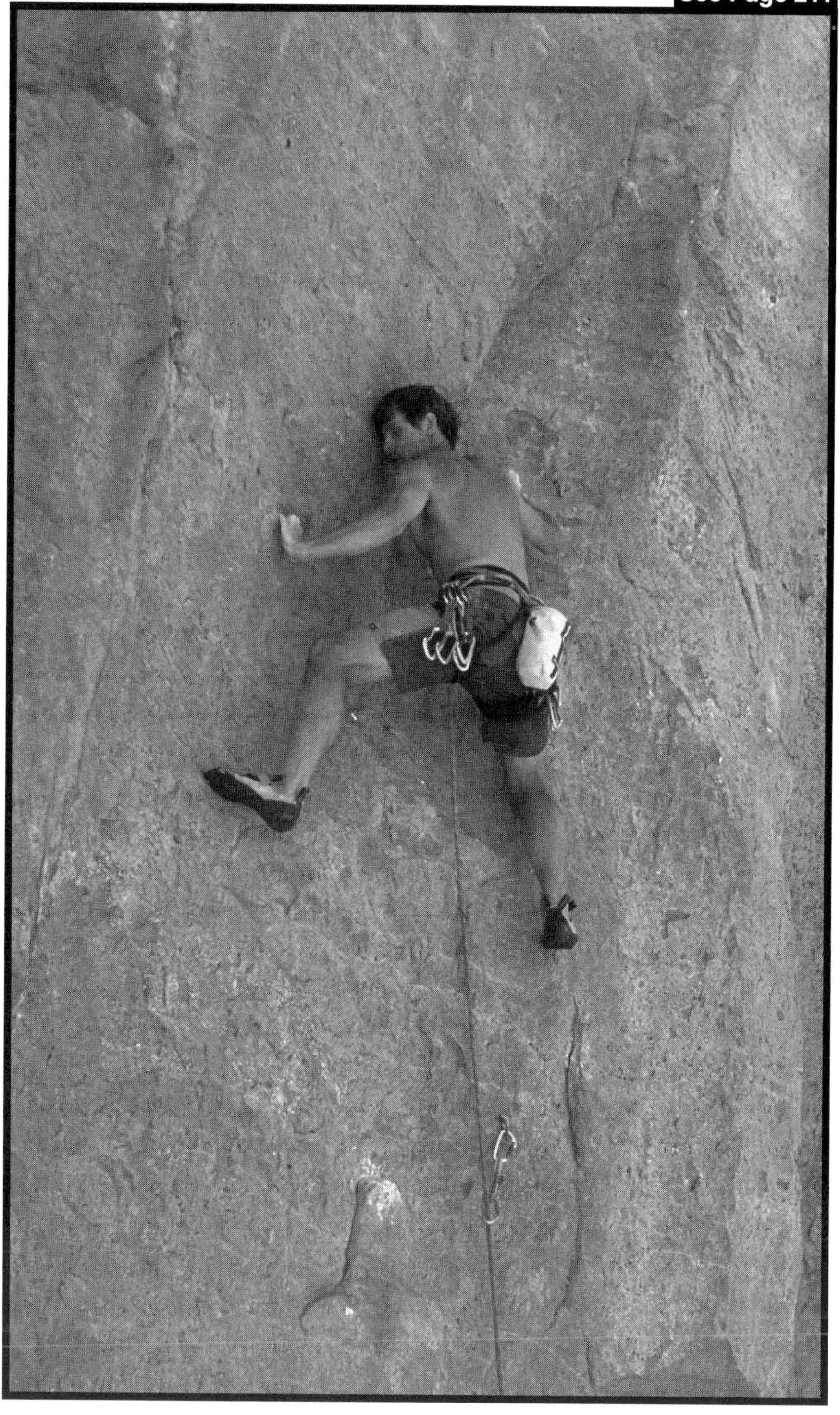

©2005 Maximus Press. *Marty Lewis Photo.*

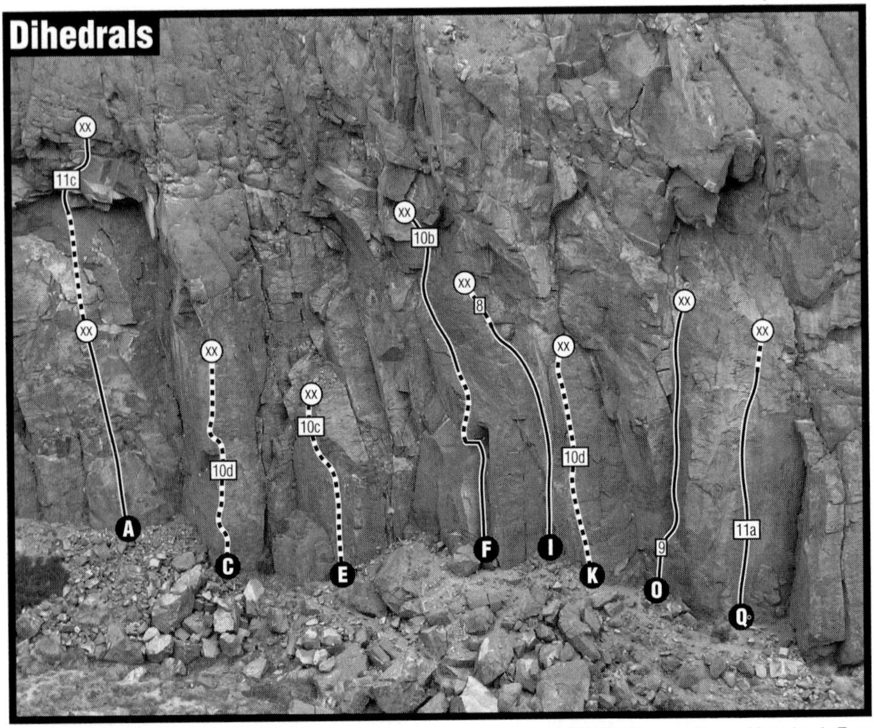

©2005 Maximus Press. *Marty Lewis Topo.*

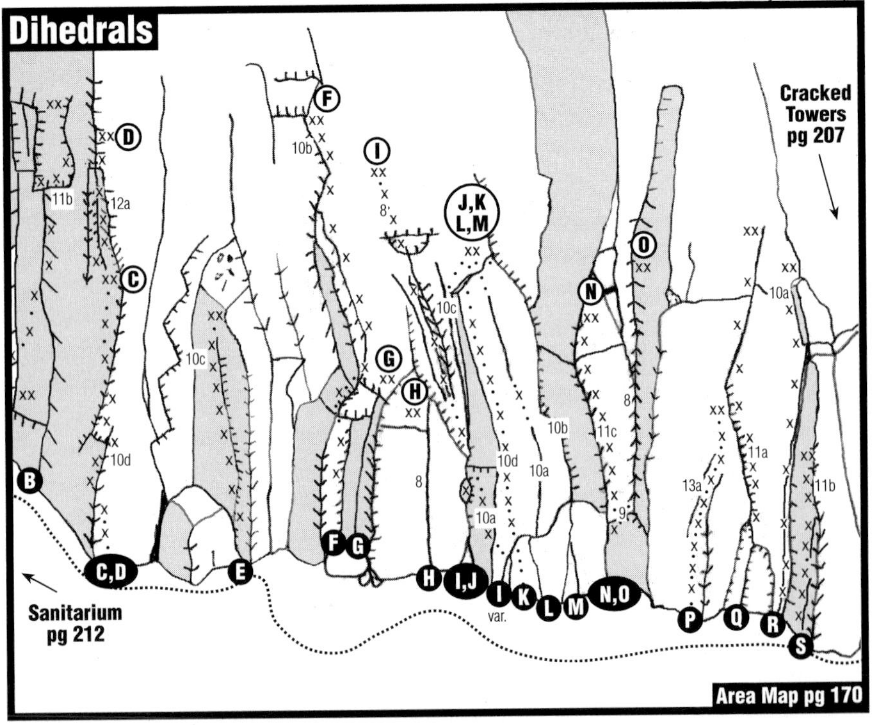

Dihedrals

A series of monolithic dihedrals on the east side with amazing rock quality. One of the best collections of clean cracks in the Gorge.

A. Bombay on the Rocks 11c****

Scramble up to a fixed belay (easy 5th class) to approach this route. 9 bolts. Face climb to an intimidating right leaning crack/chimney, very exposed. Lower off to belay.

FA: Eric Kohl, Luke Miller, 9/1994, GU.

B. Mini Jones 11b**

8 bolts. Climb a broken dihedral, then move right via a strenuous undercling. 35m/115' lower off to ground or 30m/100' lower off to anchor on ledge.

FA: Brian Ketron, 2001, GU.

C. Chossman of the Desert 10d****

9 bolts. Varied off-vertical arete, ends abruptly at a balancy clip. Lower off. ➤ Photo page 207.

FA: Mike Strassman, Scott Ayers, Scott Loomis, 1990, GU.

D. Chossman's Dessert 12a**

15 bolts. Climb *Chossman of the Desert*, then step left and climb a steep corner to a roof. 30m/100' lower off.

FA: Peter Croft, Andrew Stevens, 4/2005, GU.

E. Good Friday 10c***

8 bolts. Varied dihedral, climbs better than it looks. Lower off.

FA: Marty Lewis, Paul Nordquist, 4/1992, TD.

F. Delicate Mechanism 10b***

11 bolts. Start in a dihedral, turn an awkward roof to the left, climb a short arete to a ramp, then finish up a steep dihedral. 35m/115' lower off.

FA: Kevin Calder, Marty Lewis, 5/2002, GU.

G. Too Proud to Ignore 10b**

Gear to 4". Hand/fist crack. Lower off.

FA: Urmas Franosch, Kelly Cordner, 5/1996, GU.

H. Not Proud Enough to Name 8**

Gear to 2.5". Slabby crack. Lower off. ➤ Photo page 34.

FA: Kevin Calder, Marty Lewis, 1985, GU.

I. Gangsta Lean 8****

8 bolts, optional gear to 2". Start *Mildew Encrusted Shower Stall*, then head left up a long left leaning rampy dihedral. 30m/100' lower off. ➤ Photo page 213.

FA: Marty Lewis, Kevin Calder, 5/2002, GU.

Variation: 10a**. 9 bolts. Start just right of the toe of the buttress, face climb up and left and cross *Mildew Encrusted Shower Stall*. 30m/100' lower off.

J. Mildew Encrusted Shower Stall 10c**

2 bolts, gear to 5". A broken dihedral leads to a steep ever-widening crack. ☞ To facilitate the sport climb *Gangsta Lean* two bolts were added, please feel free to skip them.

FA: Todd Vogel, Dave Focardi, 1991, GU.

K. Towel Rack 10d***

8 bolts. Technical off-vertical arete. Lower off.

FA: Geoff Fullerton, Bill Herzog, 11/1989, GU.

L. Life During Wartime 10a***

1 bolt, gear to 2". Crack to seam. Lower off.

FA: Geoff Fullerton, John Martindale, 1989, GU.

M. One Armed Bandit 10b***

Gear to 3". Lieback dihedral. Lower off.

FA: Steve Grossman, Paul Linaweaver, 1989, GU.

N. Bonfire of the Panties 11c***

8 bolts. Vertical arete. Lower off.

FA: Scott Ayers, Paul Linaweaver, 1992, GU.

O. Pumping the Slots 9****

1 bolt, gear to 4". Mantle a ledge then climb a hand crack in a dihedral. 27.5m/90' lower off. ➤ Photo page 208.

FA: Steve Grossman, Paul Linaweaver, 1989, GU.

P. Bushfire 13a***

8 bolts. Sustained technical face to a squeezed and contrived finish. Lower off. ➤ Photo page 209.

FA: Scott Ayers, Jay Ladin, Mike Strassman, Paul Linaweaver, 1992, TD.

Q. O.R.G. asm 11a*****

8 bolts, optional gear to 1". A beautiful steep dihedral to a slabby seam. 27.5m/90' lower off. ☞ Originally a 2 bolt (the 2nd and 3rd) mixed route, little by little bolts have been added, now it's a sporty sport climb.

FA: Scott Ayers, Doug Jaffe, 1989, GU.

R. Slackjaw 10a***

8 bolts. Double cracks in a dihedral lead to a strenuous left leaning block. Lower off.

FA: Scott Ayers, Doug Jaffe, 1989, GU. Inadvertent retrobolts: Kelly Cordner, Bill MacBride, Randy Jacobs.

S. Super Fine Booty 11b***

7 bolts. Discontinuous vertical flake, short but sweet. Lower off.

FA: Paul Linaweaver, Scott Ayers, Hank Means, Mike Strassman, 1992, TD.

©2005 Maximus Press. *Marty Lewis Photo.*

Sanitarium

Northwest facing columns in a hanging valley high on the east side. Scramble up ledges to a right facing corner, climb this (easy 5th) about 25 ft. to a ledge. Traverse right here, then continue up a 4th class drainage. Descend via two single-rope rappels.

A. Amnesia 12b**
4 bolts. Face. Lower off.
FA: Louie Anderson, Ripley Casdorph, 1992, TD.

B. Schitzo 11a**
4 bolts. Face/arete. Lower off.
FA: Louie Anderson, Bart Groendycke, 1992, TD.

C. Psycho 13c**
4 bolts. Brutal stemming. Lower off.
FA: Louie Anderson, Bart Groendycke, 1992, TD.

D. Neurotic Waltz 11d****
7 bolts. Face. Lower off.
FA: Louie Anderson, Bart Groendycke, 1992, TD.

E. Paranoia 11d***
8 bolts. Dihedral. Lower off.
FA: Louie Anderson, Tom Kidwell, 1992, TD.

F. Basket Case 12b****
9 bolts. Arete. Lower off.
FA: Louie Anderson, Cory Zinngrabe, Daniel Guerrero, 1992, TD.

G. Shock Treatment 11a****
9 bolts. Dihedral. 27.5m/90' lower off.
FA: Louie Anderson, Tom Kidwell, 1992, TD.

H. Insanity 11d***
8 bolts. Seam to face. 27.5m/90' lower off.
FA: Louie Anderson, Tom Kidwell, 1992, TD.

©2005 Maximus Press. *Louie Anderson Topo.*

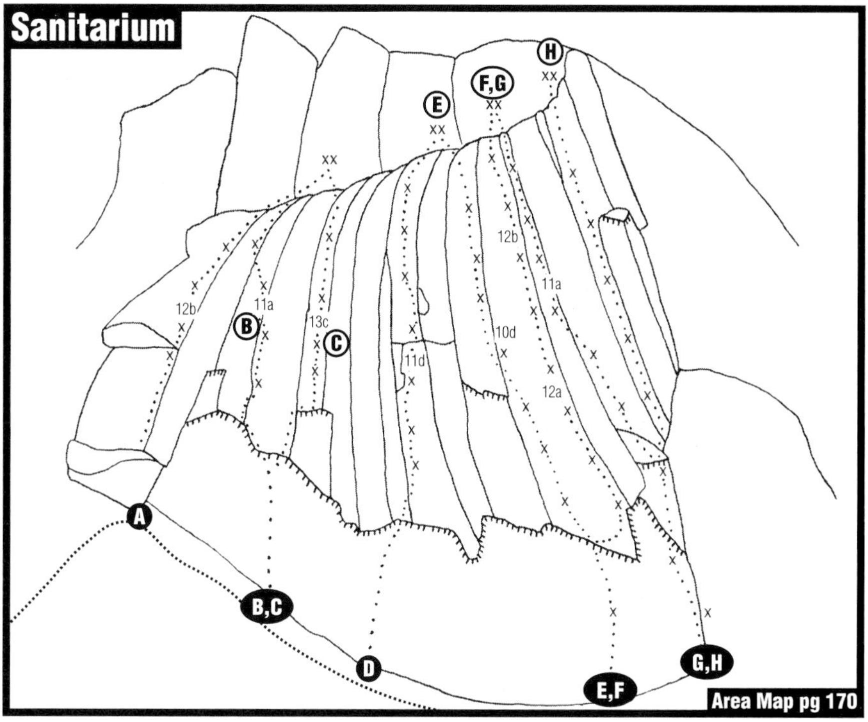

John Dyer on **Gangsta Lean** 8**** at the Dihedrals. ©*Kevin Calder Photo.*

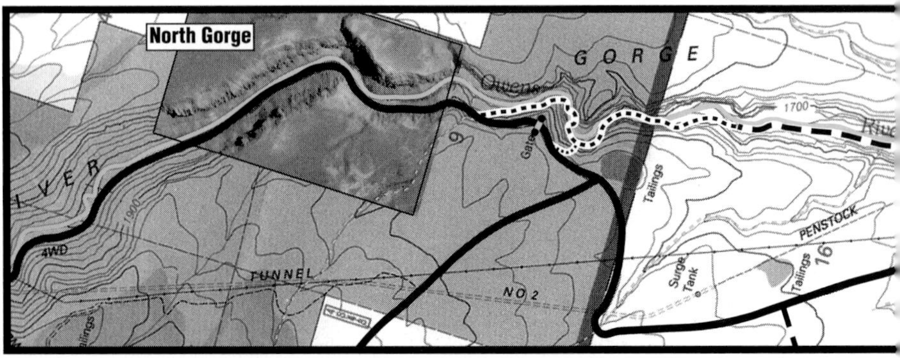

Becky Calder on **Wounded Knee** 10a* at the Chuckwalla Wall. ©*Kevin Calder Photo.*

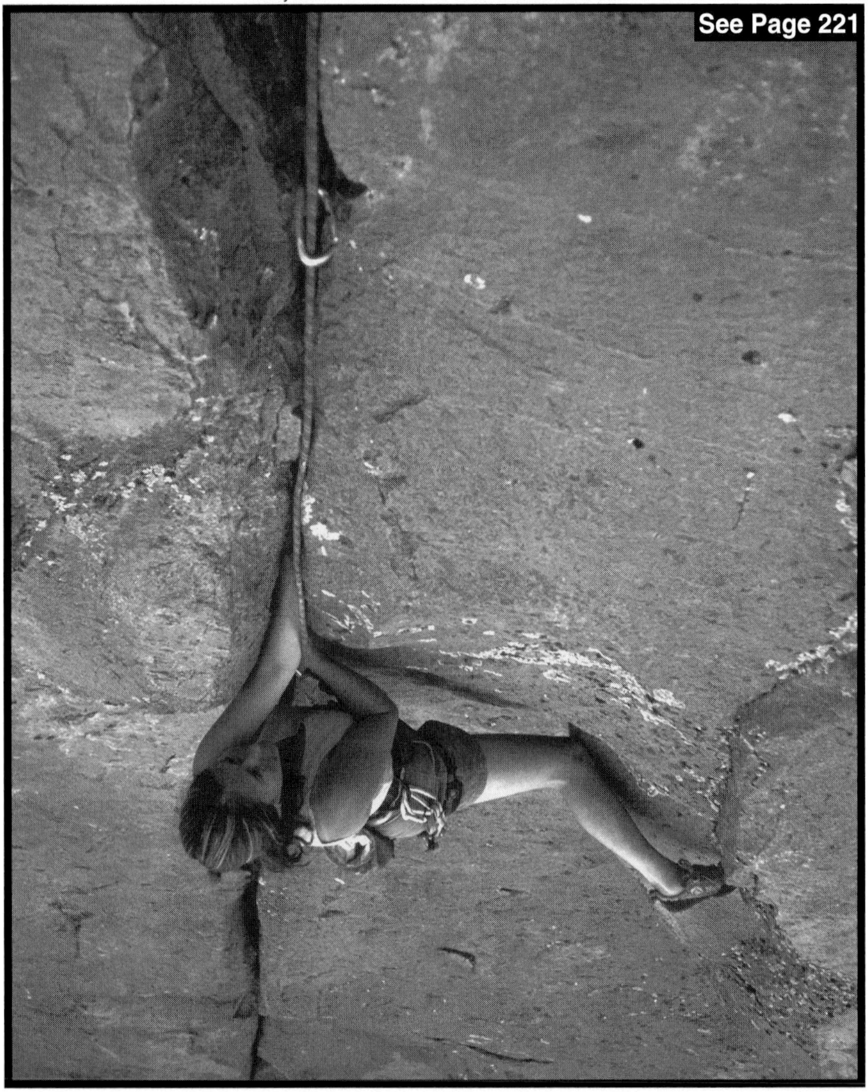

Adapted from the U.S.G.S. 1:24,000 Casa Diablo Mtn. and Rovana Quadrangles.

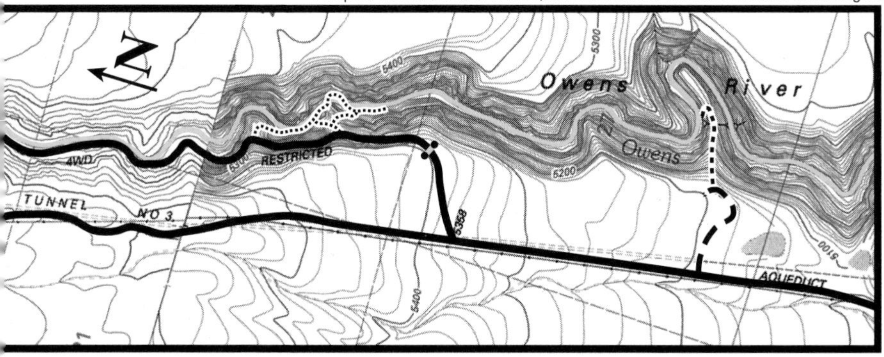

CHAPTER 7

North Gorge Basics .... pg 217
Savage Garden .... pg 218
Organ Pipes .... pg 218
El Pollo Grande .... pg 219
Chuckwalla Wall .... pg 221
Last Frontier .... pg 221

NORTH GORGE

©2005 Maximus Press.

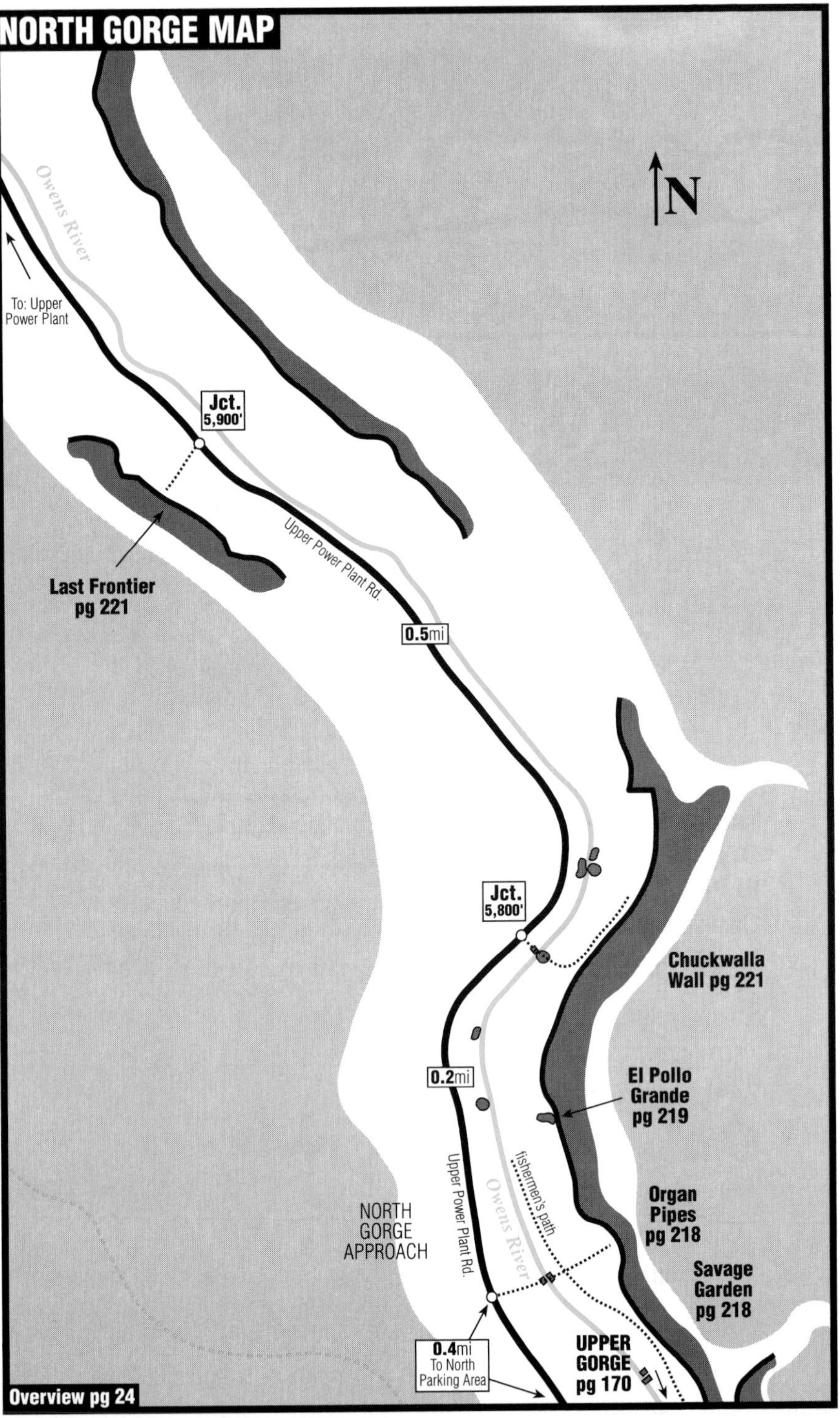
NORTH GORGE MAP
N
Owens River
To: Upper Power Plant
Jct. 5,900'
Last Frontier pg 221
Upper Power Plant Rd.
0.5mi
Jct. 5,800'
Chuckwalla Wall pg 221
0.2mi
El Pollo Grande pg 219
fishermen's path
Owens River
Upper Power Plant Rd.
NORTH GORGE APPROACH
Organ Pipes pg 218
Savage Garden pg 218
0.4mi To North Parking Area
UPPER GORGE pg 170
Overview pg 24

NORTH GORGE BASICS

A rarely visited part of the Gorge, with a quick approach on a paved road. Once down there you usually scramble down scree and talus, then cross the river and go back up the other side.

Fishermen usually outnumber climbers in this beautiful, fun to explore section of the Gorge. Slab masters should check out the fine climbs at the Chuckwalla Wall.

North Gorge Details

Elevation: 5,800 to 5,900 ft.
Sport Climbs: 7 routes, 5.9 to 12a.
Gear Climbs: 4 routes, 10a to 12b.
Approach: 20 minute walk with a 200 ft. descent.

The Approach: From U.S. 395, take the Paradise/Swall Meadows Exit east. Drive up a steep hill for 0.7 miles until reaching the Gorge Rd. Turn left (north) on the Gorge Rd. and you will come to the North Parking Area after driving 6.4 miles up the Gorge Rd. Park on the southeast side before the gate.

North Gorge Approach: From the North Parking Area follow the paved Upper Power Plant Road 0.4 miles beyond the gate. This point is directly across from the Organ Pipes in the North Gorge. Class 1; 15 minutes to the Savage Garden, 25 minutes to the Last Frontier. Bicycles can be used for this approach. Yield to D.W.P. vehicles.

©2005 Maximus Press. *Marty Lewis Photo.*

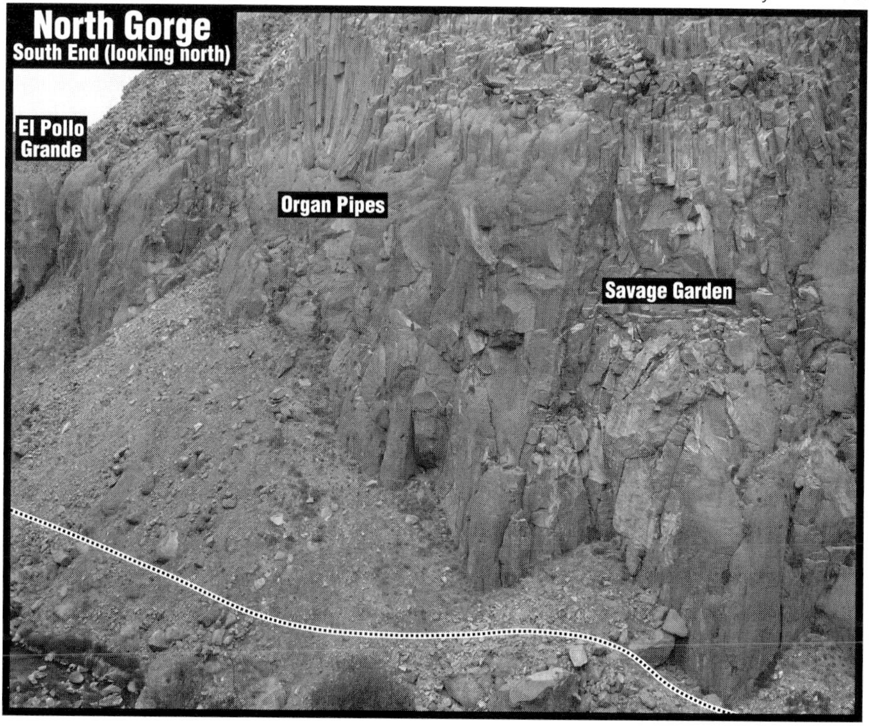

©2005 Maximus Press. *Marty Lewis Photo.*

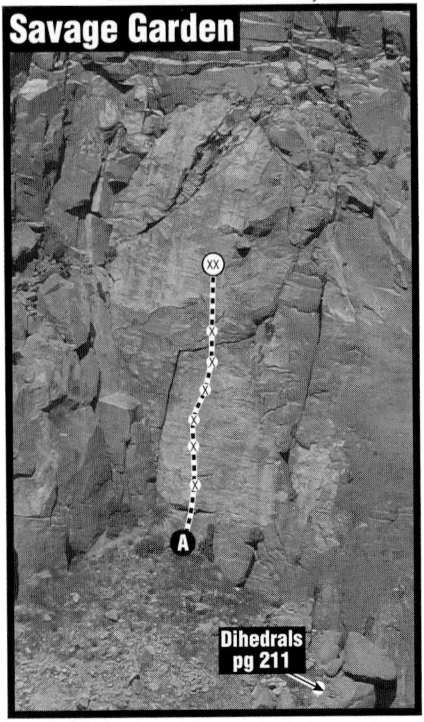

Savage Garden

A pink slab scattered amongst towers on the east side. Located right above giant boulders in the river.

A. Savage Garden 11b**

6 bolts. Slab climb past a horizontal. Lower off.
FA: Mike Strassman, Scott Ayers, 1992, TD.

Organ Pipes

Nice looking columns high on the east side. The closer you get the shorter it looks. Large boulders make for an easy river crossing

B. Shadow Catcher 9*

3 bolts. Slab. Lower off.
FA: Phil Green, Cindy Phares, 1990, GU.

C. Super Pipe 12b*

Pitch 1: 10a•. 2 bolts, 1 piton, gear to 3.5". Climb an easy decpmposing slab past bolts that guard a move to the anchor. Climb the 2nd pitch or lower off.
Pitch 2: 12b**. 3 bolts, 1 piton, gear to 1.5". Climb between columns, then move left and turn a roof. Lower off.
☞ This mysterious climb has been around for as long as anyone can remember.

©2005 Maximus Press. *Marty Lewis Photo.*

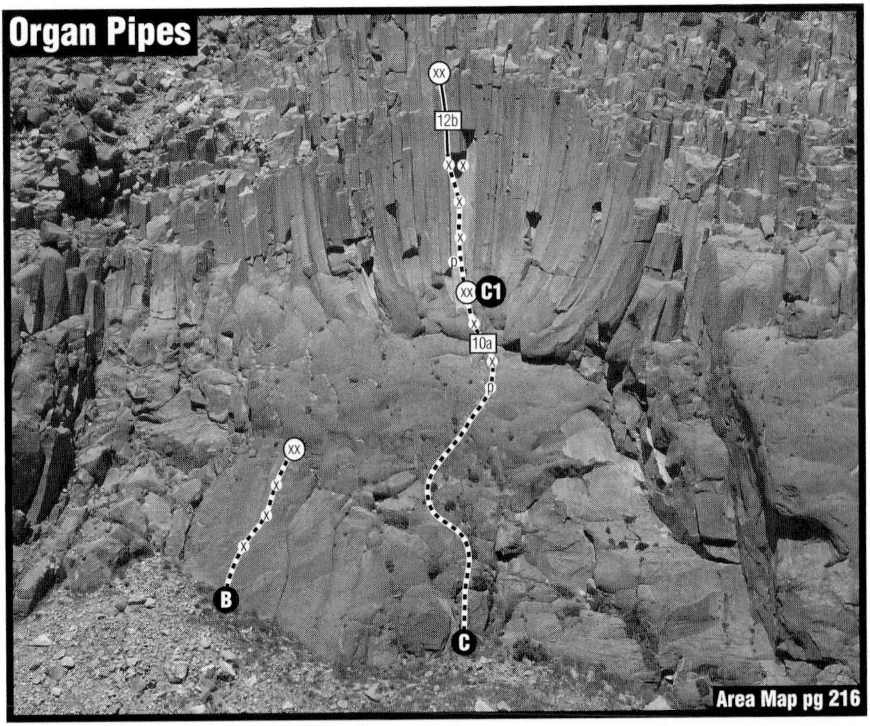

Marty Lewis on **Chuckwalla Wall** 11a** at the Chuckwalla Wall. ©*Kevin Calder Photo.* **See Page 221**

©2005 Maximus Press. *Marty Lewis Photo.*

El Pollo Grande

Free standing tower on the east side.

A. Project

100' left of *Light Rangers.* Anchors on a tower.

B. Unknown ?

2 bolts, gear: wide. Offwidth to face. Lower off.

C. Light Rangers 12a***

8 bolts. Off-vertical arete to a dihedral. Lower off.

FA: Mike Strassman, Scott Ayers, Tony Puppo, 1990, GU.

©2005 Maximus Press. *Marty Lewis Photo.*

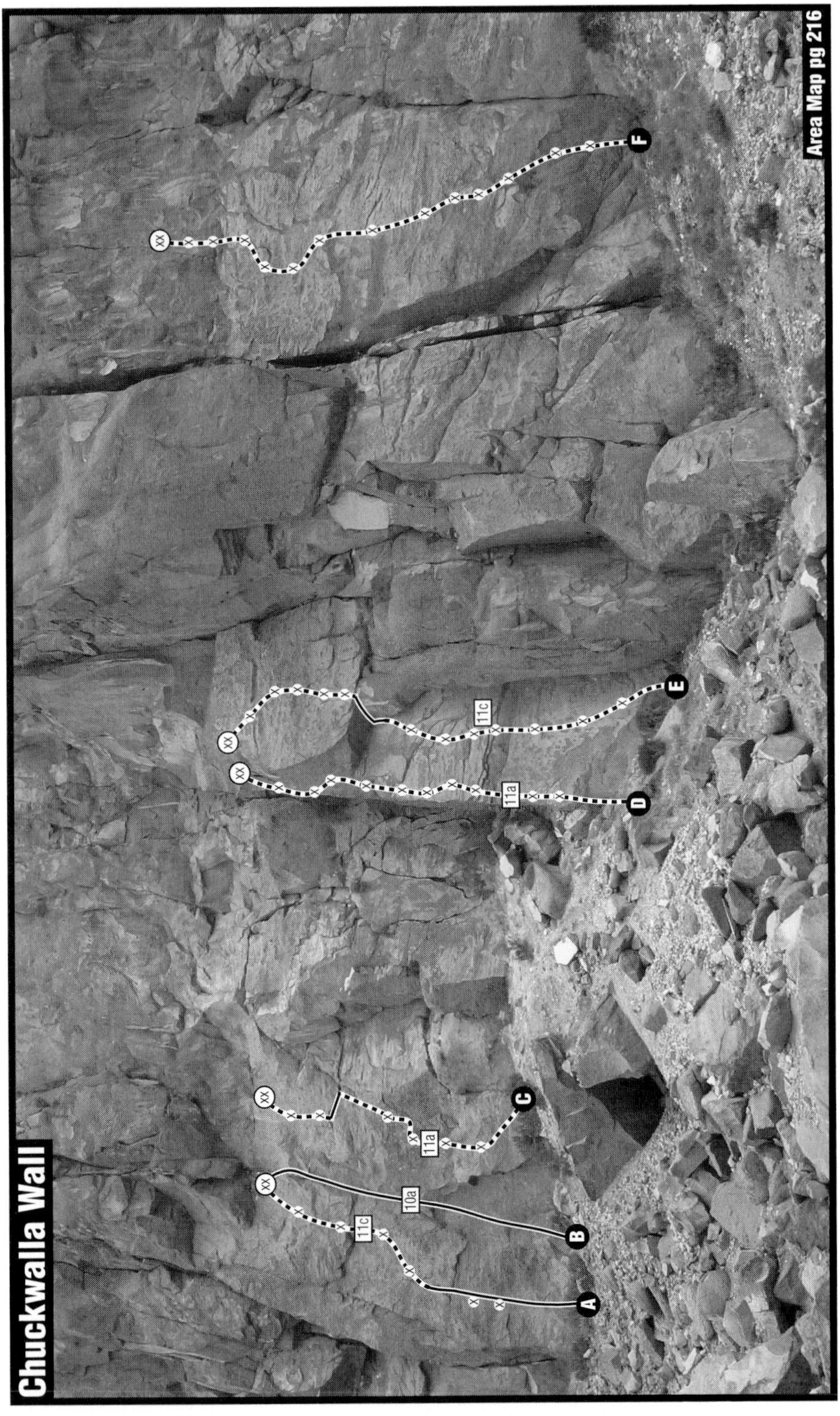

©2005 Maximus Press. *Marty Lewis Photo.*

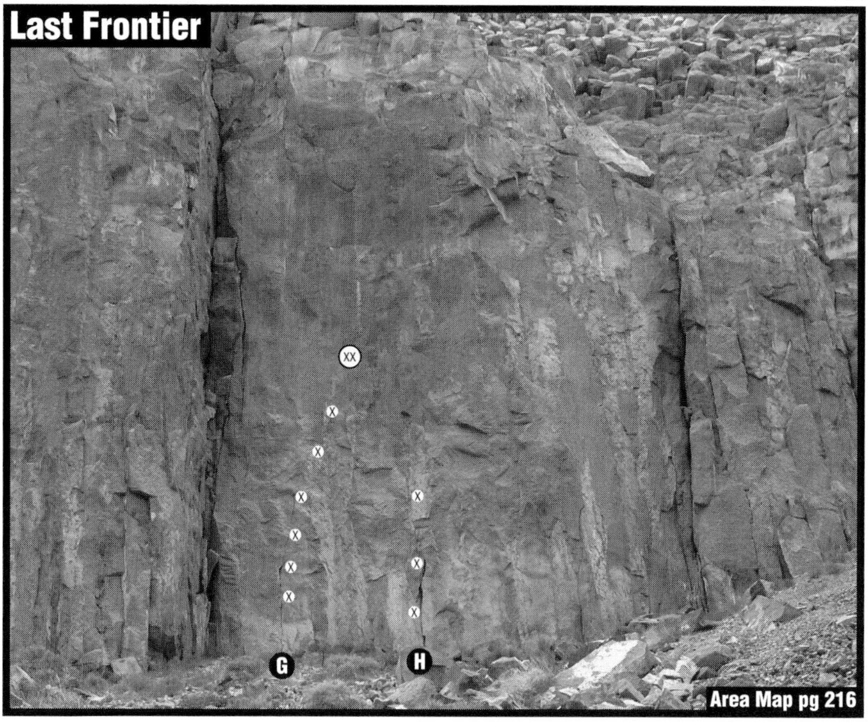

Last Frontier

A Long east facing wall on the west side above a talus field. These two projects are located in the middle of the wall. Approach via a decomposing slab that almost touches the road.

G. Project
6 bolts. Seam to face.

H. Project
3 bolts. Crack/seam.

Chuckwalla Wall

Northwest facing on the east side, just past where the road levels out. Cross the river before the cliff utilizing a giant decomposing boulder in the river. A 4th class mantle gets you across.

A. Trigger Finger 11c***
6 bolts, gear to 1". Seam to slab. Lower off.
FA: Phil Green, Doug McDonald, 1989, GU.

B. Wounded Knee 10a*
Gear to 4". Varied crack, a little loose. Lower off.
➤ Photo page 214.
FA: Phil Green, James Wilson, 1989, GU.

C. Chuckwalla Wall 11a**
6 bolts. Wander up the slab. Lower off. ➤ Photo page 219.
FA: Phil Green, Marlowe Fenne, 1989, GU.

D. Adventure of Gladys Stokepamphlet 11a***
10 bolts. Slabby arete. Lower off.
FA: Geoff Fullerton, 1992, GU.

E. Wafer Thin Mint 11c***
12 bolts. Slab climbing through some overlaps, then turn a roof to the right to a slab finish. Lower off.
FA: Geoff Fullerton, 1992, TD.

F. Hanging Garden 11b***
13 bolts. Slab. 27.5m/90' lower off.
FA: Geoff Fullerton, John Martindale, 1992, GU.

The Owens River Gorge from above.

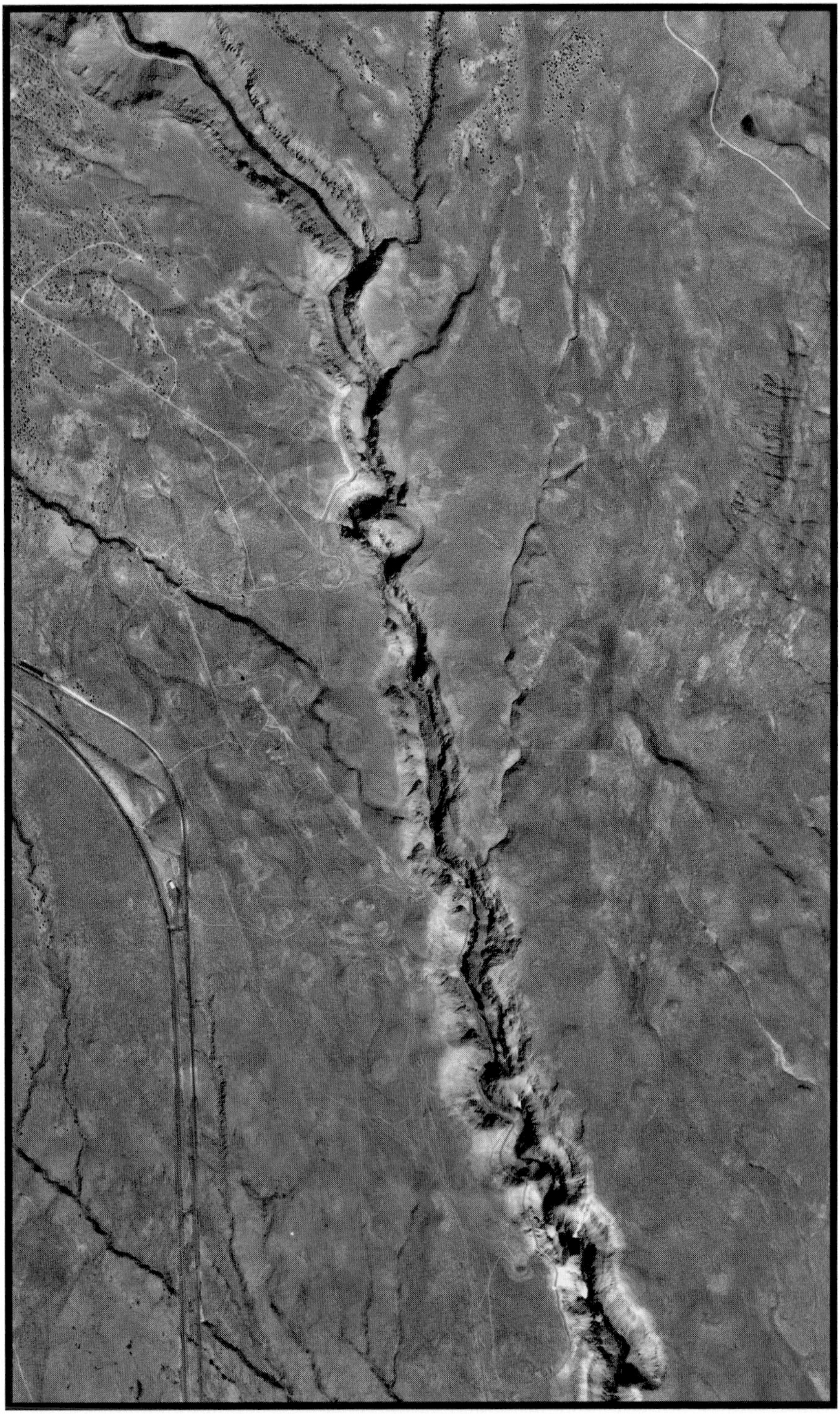

Ernie Colflesh and Marty Lewis discussing ethics after a giant day in the Gorge. *Kevin Calder Photo.*

CHAPTER 8

Hot Springs - North .... pg 224
Hot Springs - South.................... pg 226
Players.................... pg 227
Routes by Rating.................... pg 228
Further Reading.................... pg 236
Guide Services.................... pg 236
Advertisements.................... pg 237
Index.................... pg 242
About the Author .... pg 251
About Maximus Press.................... pg 252

APPENDIX

©2005 Maximus Press.

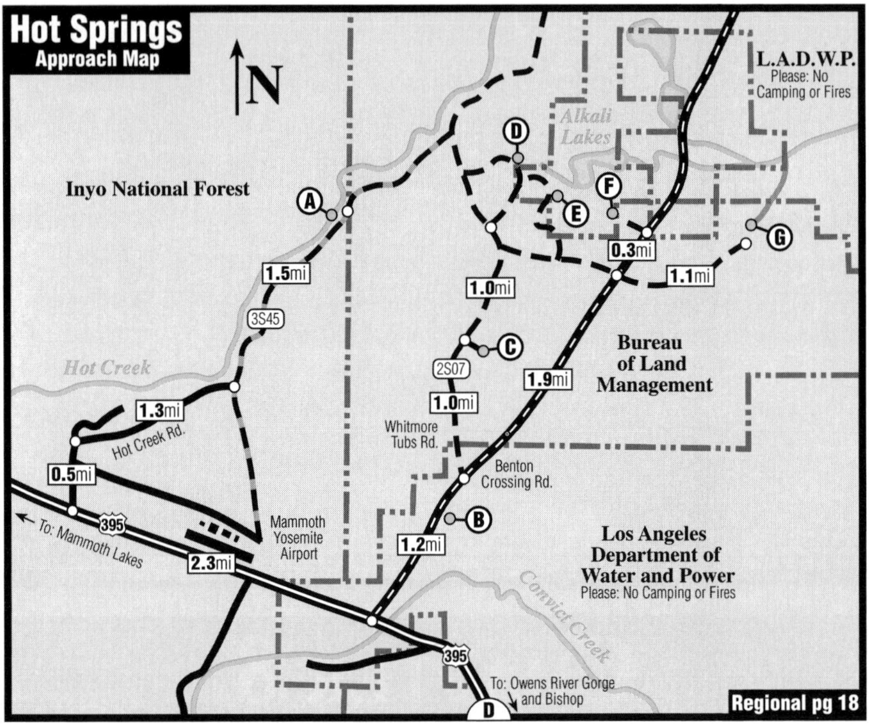

Hot Springs - North

Hot Springs are located 25 minutes north of the Gorge. This activity is included in this book because soaking in them seems to be one of the most popular post climbing activities.

The Eastern Sierra is a hotbed of geologic activity. The area surrounding Crowley Lake is located in a humongous crater formed by a giant volcanic eruption 760,000 years ago, and is now known as the Long Valley Caldera. There is still a pool of magma two miles down that keeps the bedrock in the area hot. When groundwater passes through these areas it is heated and forced to the surface creating hot springs. Enterprising individuals have built natural hot tubs out of rock and concrete that take advantage of these heated waters.

Access Information

Most of the Hot Springs are on public land administered by the Bureau of Land Management. The rest are on private property (with public access) that is owned by the Los Angeles Dept. of Water and Power. Hot Creek is a recreation site in the Inyo National Forest.

- ☞ Be courteous to Land Managers.
- ☞ Do not camp in the parking areas for the Hot Springs.
- ☞ Never use soap in the tubs.
- ☞ Clean up trash, even if it's not yours.
- ☞ Maintain a low profile.

Etiquette

These are busy places with a limited amount of space, so you will often have to stay back, be polite and wait your turn.

You will encounter nudity at the Hot Springs, but it is also perfectly acceptable to wear bathing suits.

Safety Concerns

- ☞ Always test the temperature of the water before entering.
- ☞ Kids and dogs should be watched closely.
- ☞ Alcohol and hot water can be a dangerous mix.
- ☞ When possible, drain the tubs and refill them before entering.

A. Hot Creek

An official Forest Service Recreation Site that is open from sunrise to sunset. Restrooms are available. A cold river crosses over some hot vents in a wild gorge. From the U.S. 395/Gorge Rd. junction drive north 23.3 miles and turn right onto the Airport Rd. From here drive 0.5 miles and turn right on Hot Creek Rd. Follow this 2.8 miles to a paved parking area on the left. A paved trail heads down into the gorge.

The following locations are all accessed off of Benton Crossing Rd. From the U.S. 395/Gorge Rd. junction drive north on U.S. 395 for 21 miles and turn right.

B. Whitmore Hot Springs

Swimming pool, jacuzzi and restrooms. This is a public facility and there is a fee. Drive north on Benton Crossing Rd. for 1.2 miles and turn right.

C. Rock Tub

A small concrete tub. Drive north on Benton Crossing Rd. 1.2 miles. Turn left at Whitmore Tubs Rd. and drive 1.0 miles. Turn right here and park, the tub is just a short walk ahead.

D. Shepherd's Hot Spring

A concrete tub. Drive north on Benton Crossing Rd. 1.2 miles. Turn left at Whitmore Tubs Rd. and drive 2.0 miles and turn right just before a lone pine tree. Follow this for 0.5 miles, when the road forks take the left branch to a pond. The tub is in front of the pond.

E. Crab Cooker

A nice concrete tub. Drive north on Benton Crossing Rd. for 3.1 miles and turn left at a cattle guard. Follow this dirt road 0.5 miles, then turn right. Drive 0.5 miles to the tub.

F. Hilltop Hot Spring

A nice concrete pool with great views. Drive 3.4 miles north on Benton Crossing Rd. Turn left on a dirt road and drive 0.2 miles, then park. Follow a path east up a hill, and cross a stream.

G. Wild Willy's Hot Spring

A large concrete pool and a smaller tub, with awesome views. Drive 3.1 miles north on Benton Crossing Rd. Turn right at a cattle guard onto a dirt rd. Follow this for 1.1 miles to its end at a parking area. From here a short walk on a boardwalk leads to the tubs.

Warning—Frequenting hot springs is an inherently dangerous activity and the user of this book accepts a number of unavoidable risks. Hazards include: scalding water, sharp rocks, sudden volcanic activity, broken glass, arsenic, bacteria and crazed perverts.

The authors, editors, publishers, distributors and land owners accept no liability for any injuries incurred from using this book.

Hot Springs - South

Hot Springs are also located 25 minutes south of the Gorge. To get there drive south on U.S. 395 for 7 miles, turn right on to Keough Hot Springs Rd. 0.6 miles down this road on the right under some power lines are a series of pools along a creek known as Hot Ditch. This site is located on private property (with public access) that is owned by the L.A.D.W.P. If you continue 0.2 miles beyond this point you come to a fantastic commercial site: Keough's Hot Springs Resort.

Keough's Hot Springs Resort

Features the largest natural hot springs pool in the Eastern Sierra. There is a snack bar, picnic area, rock garden and gift shop. Camping and lodging facilities are available. ☎ 872-4670. www.keougshotsprings.com.

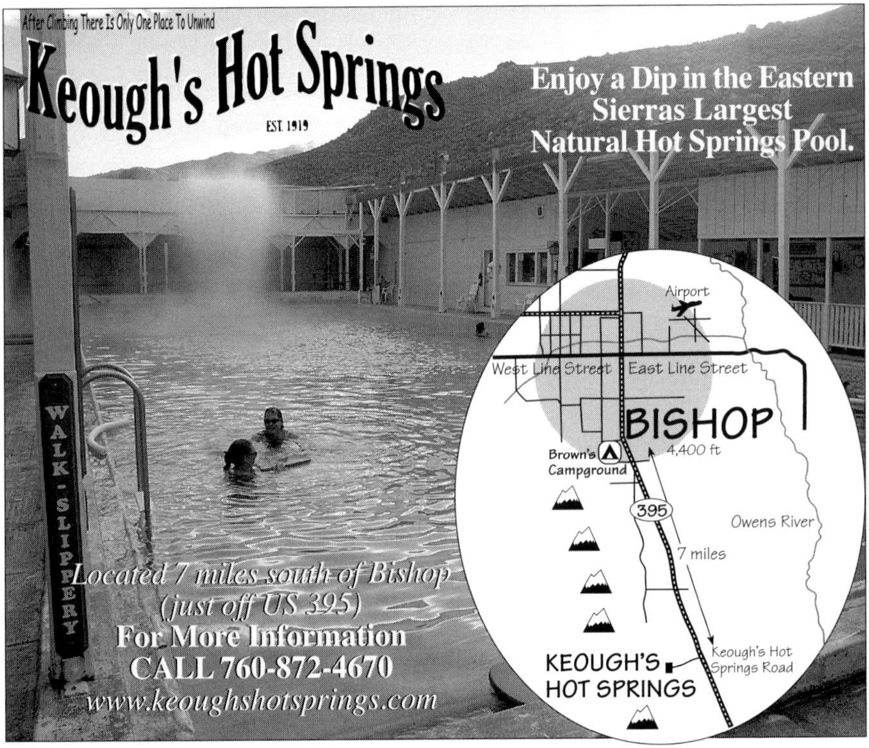

After Climbing There Is Only One Place To Unwind
Keough's Hot Springs
EST. 1919
Enjoy a Dip in the Eastern Sierras Largest Natural Hot Springs Pool.
WALK - SLIPPERY
Located 7 miles south of Bishop
(just off US 395)
For More Information
CALL 760-872-4670
www.keoughshotsprings.com
Airport
West Line Street
East Line Street
BISHOP
4,400 ft
Brown's Campground
395
Owens River
7 miles
Keough's Hot Springs Road
KEOUGH'S HOT SPRINGS

Players

This list represents the main contributors in the development of the Owens River Gorge. These are the passionate climbers that spent their time, sweat and money creating this remarkable climbing area. In an effort to form an unbiased list a point system was devised. The quality rating for each pitch determines the number of points given; one star equals one point. For each route 2/3 of the points went to the person who first redpointed the route, 1/3 of the points were divided among other route contributors.

Lewis, Marty
143.3
Ayers, Scott
110.7
Cordner, Kelly
103.7
Herbert, Tom
93.3
Rousek, Joe
85.0
Strassman, Mike
81.7
Calder, Kevin
64.7
Puppo, Tony
61.0
Slate, Gary
53.3
Anderson, Louie
50.0
Croft, Peter
48.7
Kohl, Eric
45.0
Graham, Todd
42.0
Schneider, Steve
39.3
Berman, Fred
34.0
Barnes, Greg
30.7
Lella, Bruce
30.0
Focardi, Dave
27.0
Vogel, Todd
26.7
Blanchard, Mark
24.3
Haughelstine, Dan
24.3
Hartman, John
22.7
Fullerton, Geoff
22.3
Leary, Kevin
18.7
Pottenger, Bruce
18.7
Forkash, Mike
18.3

Placing one of the 5,000 bolts found in the Gorge.

Routes by Rating

4*

- ❑ Leave No Trace 63

5*

- ❑ Little Crack 62

5***

- ❑ Anonymous Bolter 62

6*

- ❑ Sunset Sam 188
- ❑ Sweetie 174

6**

- ❑ Crotalulsley Challenged 199
- ❑ Natural Lite 63

6***

- ❑ Imprisoned Behind Lies 97

6****

- ❑ Clip Jr. 98

7*

- ❑ Sparky Does Power Tower (1st pitch) 85

7**

- ❑ Bonus Features 62
- ❑ Expensive But Worth It 149
- ❑ Fine Dining 199
- ❑ Helga's Holiday 104
- ❑ Not Too Stout 87
- ❑ Rapscallion 63

7***

- ❑ Brandenburg Gate 133
- ❑ For Patricia 188
- ❑ P.D. Time 175
- ❑ Phoenix 175
- ❑ Weird Al 131

7****

- ❑ High Seas 98
- ❑ Northern Lite 83

8*

- ❑ Bill's Black Book 181
- ❑ Center Court 105
- ❑ Coffin Lid (1st pitch) 159
- ❑ Dirt Pile 65
- ❑ Double Take 103
- ❑ La Pavoni (1st pitch) 196
- ❑ Sandbag 5.8 (1st pitch) 161
- ❑ You Like it Sideways? (1st pitch) 196

8**

- ❑ Alfred Hitchcrack 199
- ❑ Blocky Top 66
- ❑ Cat in the Hat 181
- ❑ Electric Launderland 81
- ❑ Enter the Dragon 115
- ❑ Health Club 105
- ❑ Jesus Built My Tri-Cam (1st pitch) 157
- ❑ Marco Polo's Boys Go Dirty Dancing 110
- ❑ No Chapas 107
- ❑ Not Proud Enough to Name 211
- ❑ Oompa Loompa 69
- ❑ Scalpel 155
- ❑ Step Right Up 199

8***

- ❑ Butterknife 95
- ❑ Coming Attractions 62
- ❑ Drill Sergeant 165
- ❑ It's the Gaaazzz 181
- ❑ Lava Java 153
- ❑ Mile High Crack 63
- ❑ Party on Sean 166
- ❑ Sabado Gigante 119
- ❑ Stella 188
- ❑ Sulu 155
- ❑ Warning: Laser Beam 69
- ❑ Watch for Rocks 69

8****

- ❑ China Doll 115
- ❑ Gangsta Lean 211
- ❑ Narcolepsy 107
- ❑ Silence of the Poodles 207
- ❑ Stradivarius 103

8*****

- ❑ Babushka 98

9*

- ❑ Bones 154
- ❑ Book of Bones 95
- ❑ Botswana Baby 97
- ❑ Hole In the Wall 184
- ❑ In Your Red Truck 187
- ❑ L.A. is Burning 71
- ❑ Original Gorgeous 187
- ❑ People are Weird 133
- ❑ Shadow Catcher 218
- ❑ Sneak Preview 62

❑ Stardate 153
❑ Swamp Thing 207
❑ Unnatural Silence 121

9**

❑ Another Day in Hell 157
❑ Don't Kid, Minibike 174
❑ Don't Make Me Laugh 131
❑ Flailsafe (1st pitch) 191
❑ Flex Your Bazooka 105
❑ Fortune Cookie 115
❑ From Chocolate to Chossman 103
❑ Gorge Corner 181
❑ Hagar'n'hilti 104
❑ His Spirit 165
❑ I'm Like This Because I Live in My Van 57
❑ Jaws of Life (1st pitch) 184
❑ Klingon Crabs 154
❑ M.O. 207
❑ Members Only (2nd pitch) 129
❑ Pippy the Zenhead 179
❑ Sharptooth 69
❑ Sidewinder 97
❑ Sneakaroma 105
❑ Sunstroke 104
❑ 20/20 56
❑ Who Knows? 197

9***

❑ A Life Shared is a Better Life 174
❑ And Now For Something Much... (1st pitch) 165
❑ Don't Look Down 129
❑ Double Flipper 203
❑ Electric Kachina 85
❑ Fobes 40 157
❑ Frank 188
❑ Humjob 81
❑ Iceberg II 175
❑ Low Octane 70
❑ Nice Jugs 184
❑ PG13 69
❑ Positive Approach 81
❑ Scorpion (2nd pitch) 85
❑ Welcome to the Gorge 97

9****

❑ Abitafun 87
❑ Child of Light 115
❑ Cinderella 199
❑ Clip Jockeys 155
❑ Crowd Pleaser 98
❑ Paradise 83
❑ Pumping the Slots 211
❑ Slip 'n Slide 175

9*****

❑ Heart of the Sun 115

10a*

❑ Brief Intermission 62
❑ Butt Wipe 83
❑ Cornercopia (1st pitch) 115
❑ Gimme the Helmet, I'll be the Stunt Man 200
❑ Hireaeth 66
❑ Ratso (2nd pitch) 91
❑ Sandbag 5.8 (2nd pitch) 161
❑ Slot Machine 103
❑ Stonefly 181
❑ Surgeon General 69
❑ Tempest (2nd pitch) 87
❑ Time Will Tell 69
❑ Wounded Knee 221

10a**

❑ Ace Cashier 189
❑ Bob & Eric Crack 65
❑ Carnubiator 199
❑ Chicken Belly 189
❑ Chipmunk Pancakes (With Batbrain Syrup) 165
❑ Easy Enough 133
❑ Elephant Gun 129
❑ Exit Stage Left II 62
❑ Focus Marty 157
❑ Gunned Down by Goofy 184
❑ Hotcake Flake 95
❑ Humdinger 81
❑ Just Under the Wire 85
❑ Land Before Time 69
❑ Late for Work 70
❑ Loony Bar 187
❑ Quail Crack 175
❑ Quail Trail (1st Pitch) 175
❑ Ratso (1st pitch) 91
❑ Sparky the Drillhead 188
❑ Spock 154
❑ Stella's Fella 188
❑ Sweet & Sour 97
❑ Uncontrollable Urge 65
❑ Unemployment Line 149
❑ Vulcan Jock Itch 154
❑ Wonka 69
❑ Zig Zag 65

10a***

❑ Black Chicks in Heat 85
❑ Boating Prohibited 69
❑ Breaking the Law 133
❑ Cobbler's Delight 133
❑ Enslaved by the Belle 183
❑ Fashion Racket 105

❑ Fear of a Black Planet 97
❑ Grey Scale 64
❑ Init 187
❑ Life During Wartime 211
❑ Love of Jesus 165
❑ Nirvana 95
❑ Pet Trackers 175
❑ Scratch 'n Sniff 56
❑ Scrotal Hotpack 105
❑ Slackjaw 211
❑ Three Stooges 56
❑ To Knee or Not to Knee 129
❑ Tricks in Motion 106
❑ Wowie Zowie 63

10a****

❑ Abitarot 87
❑ Don't Look Up (1st pitch) 129
❑ Ego Unchained 166
❑ Fender Strat 103
❑ Giveaway 179
❑ Lava Haul 185
❑ Post Partum 188
❑ Snapping Pussy Doll 181
❑ Valley 5.8 71
❑ Z Dong 97

10a*****

❑ Dr. Evil 203
❑ Jesus Built My Tri-Cam (2nd pitch) 157
❑ Machine Gun Jumblies 203

10b*

❑ Left Barley Crack 207
❑ Louisiana Liplock 104
❑ Right Barley Crack 207
❑ Shell of a Man 63
❑ Size Doesn't Matter 192
❑ Slander Session 57
❑ Soul Music 179
❑ Tephra Sampler 185

10b**

❑ Approach Pitch 81
❑ Aunti Vigilante 175
❑ Big Screen 62
❑ Broski/Linaweaver 183
❑ Contagious 121
❑ Corporal Clinger 165
❑ Direct North Face (1st pitch) 129
❑ Done With Spare Change From Mikey's Pocket 106
❑ Franklin's Frosty Funeral 203
❑ Gunnin' For a Heart Attack 64
❑ Hatchett Job 85
❑ Have a Little Faith 163
❑ Kirk 154
❑ Mad Cat 65
❑ Menace II Society 119
❑ Monkey Bean 187
❑ Monkey See, Monkey Do 119
❑ My Favorite Animal is a Liger 207
❑ Old & in the Way 91
❑ Power Surge 69
❑ Pretty in Pink 165
❑ Quail Trail (2nd Pitch) 175
❑ R.P. #4 69
❑ Romulan Roids 154
❑ Scorpion (1st pitch) 85
❑ Start Me Up 105
❑ Stay Hungry 199
❑ Tempest (1st pitch) 87
❑ Too Crazy to Be Gripped 57
❑ Too Proud to Ignore 211
❑ What Up? 98
❑ You Like it Sideways? (2nd pitch) 196

10b***

❑ Cajun Barbecue 188
❑ Coffee Achiever 153
❑ Delicate Mechanism 211
❑ Dollar Three Ninety Eight 81
❑ Flailsafe (2nd pitch) 191
❑ Gary Gray 87
❑ Hey Bubba, Watch This! (2nd pitch) 131
❑ Nicely Displayed But Wrappers Weren't... 54
❑ One Armed Bandit 211
❑ Praying Mantle 56
❑ Results May Vary 69
❑ Smokey the Beer 159
❑ Sparky Does Power Tower (2nd pitch) 85
❑ Upwardly Mobile 81
❑ Wedge-O 83
❑ What's its Face 103

10b****

❑ Ambassadors of Funk 97
❑ Don't Look Up (2nd pitch) 129
❑ George Bush 91
❑ Holocaust 133
❑ Humbly, Mumbly, Jumbly 98
❑ Jaws of Life (2nd pitch) 184
❑ Life in Electric Larvae Land 54
❑ One Holer 95
❑ Tall Dollar 203
❑ Tsing Tao 115
❑ Wacked Scenario 179

10b*****

❑ Extreme Caffeine 153
❑ Gorgeous 179
❑ Sendero Luminoso 119

10c*

- ❑ Batting Cage 69
- ❑ Double Insulated 85
- ❑ Fantasia 133
- ❑ Fixings for a Sandwich 56
- ❑ Global Warming 66
- ❑ More Than Just Mild 203
- ❑ Mouth T. Dung 97
- ❑ Naked Gun 63
- ❑ Quest 83
- ❑ Scrotal Squeeze 105
- ❑ Somerot 87
- ❑ You're Soaking in it 203

10c**

- ❑ Air Walk aka See What See What Happens... 185
- ❑ Creaky Hollow Fracture Show 131
- ❑ Doesn't Anybody Work Around Here? 133
- ❑ Fingertip Ledge of Contentment 133
- ❑ Fork it Over 95
- ❑ Headbanger 55
- ❑ In the Pink 203
- ❑ Incorncentric 54
- ❑ Kelly's Heroes 188
- ❑ Kicking Ash 185
- ❑ Michelin Man 56
- ❑ Mildew Encrusted Shower Stall 211
- ❑ Pulp Friction 97
- ❑ Pumice Facial 187
- ❑ Range of Light 83
- ❑ Red Circle With a Slash 69
- ❑ Safety in Numbers 54
- ❑ Short But Steep 123
- ❑ Solito 103
- ❑ Transcendence 133

10c***

- ❑ Attila the Hun (2nd pitch) 104
- ❑ Black Ice 97
- ❑ C.L.O.T. 85
- ❑ Cadillac Desert 81
- ❑ Cruella 200
- ❑ Destination Oblivion 161
- ❑ Disco Inferno (3rd pitch) 135
- ❑ Go for the Gold 110
- ❑ Good Friday 211
- ❑ Held Over 62
- ❑ Herniated Bone 189
- ❑ Impulse Power aka the Trouble With Tribbles 153
- ❑ Jump Start 197
- ❑ Know the Drill 163
- ❑ Mal a la Gorge 161
- ❑ Nakin (2nd pitch) 159
- ❑ Right for Life 54
- ❑ Set Free 87
- ❑ Stowaway 163
- ❑ Szechwan Bambi 199
- ❑ That's a Cold Shut, Darlin' 99
- ❑ Tiananmen Square 113

10c****

- ❑ Environmental Terrorist 83
- ❑ Get Over It 196
- ❑ Hey Bubba, Watch This! (1st pitch) 131
- ❑ Melts in Your Mouth 149
- ❑ Orange Peel 95
- ❑ Superfly (1st pitch) 203

10c*****

- ❑ Buried Treasure 54
- ❑ Hardly Wallbanger 87
- ❑ Light Within 87
- ❑ Show Us Your Tits 121
- ❑ Superfly (2nd pitch) 203
- ❑ Yellow Peril 113

10d*

- ❑ Attila the Hun (1st pitch) 104
- ❑ Finger Food 103
- ❑ Gecko 133
- ❑ Home Skillet 189
- ❑ Penstock Slab 73
- ❑ Subdivisions 66

10d**

- ❑ And Now For Something Much... (2nd pitch) 165
- ❑ Chaos 131
- ❑ Dial 911 121
- ❑ Disco Inferno (2nd pitch) 135
- ❑ Elephant's Butt 199
- ❑ High Octane 70
- ❑ Kinder Gentler Arete 99
- ❑ No Lifeguard on Duty 69
- ❑ Oblique Slanting Dihedral of Death 162
- ❑ Shogun 113
- ❑ Slab Metrical Illusions 55
- ❑ Wonderbar 87
- ❑ You Don't Want None 174

10d***

- ❑ Beijing 113
- ❑ Berlin Wall 133
- ❑ Chuckers 175
- ❑ Controversial Insert 191
- ❑ Dellinger 155
- ❑ Dimples 197
- ❑ Enter at Your Own Risk 69
- ❑ Liquid Fire 153
- ❑ Offramp 95
- ❑ Peking Duck 113
- ❑ Spare Change 81
- ❑ Supergroveler 159

❑ Towel Rack 211
❑ Towering Inferno (3rd pitch) 137
❑ Wired 129

10d****
❑ Bone Up 95
❑ Brothers in Arms 85
❑ Chossman of the Desert 211
❑ Confusing Confucius 113
❑ Feudal Beerlords 95
❑ Induced Labor 188
❑ Perched 103
❑ Timeless 69

10d*****
❑ Blood Sugar Sex Magik 129
❑ Members Only (1st pitch) 129
❑ Tumbling Dice 95
❑ Warning Signs 69

11a*
❑ Bow Down to the Standard White Jesus 105
❑ Dummy Up 183
❑ Jizz Soaked Action Pix 181
❑ King Spud 196
❑ Stress Puppet 73

11a**
❑ Baby Got Back 106
❑ Chuckwalla Wall 221
❑ Come of Age 133
❑ Daughters of a Coral Dawn 65
❑ Enraged Pixie 145
❑ Hidden 179
❑ Look Out Below 65
❑ Malteese Flamoingo 191
❑ Meringueutan Arch 189
❑ Noble Mouse 91
❑ Nose Ring 197
❑ Schitzo 212
❑ Towering Inferno (5th pitch) 137
❑ 2 Feet to Hell 179
❑ Waterline 133
❑ Whiteout 196
❑ Win, Lose or Claw 149
❑ You Are What You Is 176

11a***
❑ Adventure of Gladys Stokepamphlet 221
❑ Boy Wonder 203
❑ Brian's Song 106
❑ C-4 Yourself 185
❑ Cabaret 121
❑ Crash Landing 103
❑ If I Told You I'd Have to Kill You 71
❑ Malibu 91
❑ Megalithic 157
❑ Membership Has Its Privileges 66
❑ Mr. Check-off 155
❑ Out of the Pit 162
❑ Rim Job (1st pitch) 83
❑ Sea Cow 179
❑ She's a Man, Man 203
❑ Spinal Fracture 95
❑ Spivey for Breakfast 187
❑ Split Decision 119
❑ Tore Down 184

11a****
❑ Hip Pockets 83
❑ Morning Wood 119
❑ Northern Pike 147
❑ Pick Pocket 183
❑ Shock Treatment 212
❑ Towering Inferno (2nd pitch) 137

11a*****
❑ Escapade 149
❑ Love Stinks 83
❑ O.R.G. asm 211
❑ Towering Inferno (1st pitch) 137
❑ Wiggly 145

11b*
❑ Destiny 129
❑ Don't Nuke Nevada 54
❑ Urrr! 207

11b**
❑ And Now for Something Completely Different 165
❑ Be Prepared to G 196
❑ Cobra 119
❑ Direct North Face (2nd pitch) 129
❑ Elbow Macaroni 174
❑ Flashing With Jeckyl Juice 56
❑ Flush Twice, L.A. Needs the Water 105
❑ Mickey Mantle 65
❑ Mini Jones 211
❑ Monsters of Rock 83
❑ No Known Cure 161
❑ Pop Tart 99
❑ Posers on the Rig 199
❑ Savage Garden 218
❑ Scorched Egos 163
❑ Twister 155

11b***
❑ Baby Duck 103
❑ Bender 129
❑ Cornercopia (2nd pitch) 115
❑ Crumb Donut 191
❑ Direchossimo 119

❑ Funky Cole Patina 73
❑ Ghengis Khan 113
❑ Hanging Garden 221
❑ Homebrew 87
❑ King Rat 91
❑ Kung Pao 113
❑ Love Over Gold 83
❑ Missing Link 161
❑ Psmead 119
❑ Seam's Difficult 196
❑ Super Fine Booty 211
❑ Towering Inferno (4th pitch) 137

11b****

❑ C'mon Knucko 179
❑ Focus 119
❑ Hammered 87
❑ James Brown 97
❑ Left for Dead 54
❑ Mandarin Orange 113
❑ Pop Goes the Weasel 195
❑ The-Aretical 179
❑ Walk the Yellow Line 188

11b*****

❑ Expressway 95
❑ Grindrite 203
❑ Hungover 87
❑ Knucko's Pride of the North 179
❑ Photon Torpedo 153

11c*

❑ Fresh Squeezed 95
❑ Guy With a Doberman 123
❑ Next Generation 153
❑ 3.B.A. 99

11c**

❑ Advocates of Babbling Thought 106
❑ Barracuda 147
❑ Buddha Bless 166
❑ Flying Tigers 207
❑ Geisha Girl 113
❑ Letter Bomb 139
❑ Pump up the Trust Fund 133
❑ Rap it Up 179
❑ Shuttle Craft 153
❑ Some Kind of Wonderful 71

11c***

❑ Bird of Prey 147
❑ Bonfire of the Panties 211
❑ Chillin' at the Grill 95
❑ Kingsnake 203
❑ Mr. Freeze 203
❑ O Henry! 199
❑ Optimator 129
❑ Scrutinized 95
❑ Shafted 162
❑ Trigger Finger 221
❑ Wafer Thin Mint 221
❑ Ya Shoulda' Killed Me Last Year 129
❑ You Have Been Nothing But Trouble Since the... 179

11c****

❑ Bombay on the Rocks 211
❑ Caldera 185
❑ Drill Rig 191
❑ Megalomaniac 159
❑ Menace to Sobriety 87
❑ Pumpkin 104
❑ Santana 95
❑ Skeletons in the Closet 95
❑ Thumbs Up 149
❑ Tsunami 113

11c*****

❑ Abraxas Finish 95
❑ D.W.P. 73
❑ Flex Your Head 203
❑ Lalaland 103
❑ Lieutenant Uhura 153
❑ Living Dead 147
❑ Venom 119
❑ Wrath of Khan 113

11d*

❑ Dynamite Face 81
❑ Guns & Poses 62
❑ Mandela 97
❑ No Fly Zone 133
❑ Shout Around 81

11d**

❑ Broken Battery 97
❑ Chocolate City 97
❑ Criss Cross 104
❑ Dead on Arrival 121
❑ Family Man 197
❑ Mini Me 189
❑ Palm Reader 175
❑ Short Cake 66
❑ Sly Little Fart Blaster 103
❑ Unrepentant Sinner 95
❑ Vulcan Variation 153

11d***

❑ And Monkeys Might Fly Out of My Butt 207
❑ Another Day in Paradise 157
❑ Bat Angel 203
❑ Bloody Pawprints 83
❑ Coffin Lid (2nd Pitch) 159

❑ Doowutchyalike 183
❑ Dust in the Wind 155
❑ Engorged 179
❑ Free Falling 103
❑ Insanity 212
❑ La Pavoni (2nd pitch) 196
❑ Nectar 157
❑ Oceanside 91
❑ Paranoia 212
❑ Pick a Finger 56
❑ Pyroclasm 185
❑ Release the McCracken 166
❑ Riddler 203

11d****

❑ Catch-n-Release 147
❑ Freaks of the Industry 196
❑ High Ball 87
❑ Junior Achievement 197
❑ Marty Party 161
❑ Ned Guy's Proud Pearl Necklace 95
❑ Neurotic Waltz 212
❑ Power 119
❑ Splashdown 55
❑ Thrill Pig 191

11d*****

❑ Dr. Claw 153
❑ From Chocolate to Morphine 103
❑ Probation Violation 145
❑ Sex 183

12a*

❑ Iceberg 107
❑ Idol Maker 81
❑ Sport Trac 197
❑ Z Crack 97

12a**

❑ Bust a Move 62
❑ Chossman's Desert 211
❑ Enraged 179
❑ Forkash and Riches 103
❑ Get Your War On 107
❑ Go Back Where You Came From 81
❑ Going Back to Cali 91
❑ Hook 197
❑ Micro Pete 166
❑ Neanderthal 187
❑ Pitstop 70
❑ Return to Forever 95
❑ Smell the Glove 163
❑ Snake Eyes 119
❑ Vital Signs 121

12a***

❑ Body Count 121
❑ Chompin' at the Bit 191
❑ Embrace This 91
❑ Godzilla Does the Dizzy Tango 139
❑ Gorge and Purge 179
❑ Hacking & Spitting 165
❑ Hard Copy 91
❑ Light Rangers 219
❑ Main Vein 195
❑ Me So Horny 91
❑ My Mom Can Crank 192
❑ Pre-erosive Force 197
❑ Roller Coaster Ride 174
❑ Scalded by Spivey 207
❑ Tower Line 200
❑ White Dwarf 104

12a****

❑ Bazooka Country 195
❑ Desert Storm 103
❑ Divine Sculptor 157
❑ Failsafe 191
❑ Lat Machine 165
❑ Romulan Roof 153
❑ Slacker 139

12a*****

❑ Klingon 153
❑ Pumping Groundwater 73
❑ Sex Packets 183
❑ Thieves in the Temple 129

12b*

❑ What Me Worry 139

12b**

❑ Amnesia 212
❑ Cement Overshoes 73
❑ Malt Linker 161
❑ Super Pipe (2nd pitch) 218
❑ Trundle of Joy 199

12b***

❑ Astroboy 161
❑ Bad Thing 176
❑ Civilized 139
❑ Drillin' Time Again 145
❑ Flakenstein 139
❑ Insane in the Membrane 129
❑ Loony Left 143
❑ Malcolm X 97

12b****

- ❑ Basket Case 212
- ❑ Bongo Fury aka Frank Zappa Memorial Buttress 176
- ❑ Circo Gringo 162
- ❑ Independent Worm Saloon 143
- ❑ Mind Meld 153
- ❑ Penguin 203
- ❑ Piranha 147

12b*****

- ❑ Black Hole 119
- ❑ Child's Play 192
- ❑ Darshan aka Ripoff 95
- ❑ Enterprise 153
- ❑ Flashflood 73

12c*

- ❑ Custom Made 81

12c**

- ❑ Electric Vex 71
- ❑ Longest Yard 143
- ❑ Please Baby, Baby, Baby, Please 183
- ❑ Proctology Exam 143
- ❑ Schneider/Clay 184
- ❑ Smoothie 97

12c***

- ❑ Faith No More 183
- ❑ Help on the Way 200
- ❑ Redemption 195
- ❑ Serial Driller 188
- ❑ Skin Tight 91
- ❑ Sting of the Honeybee 199
- ❑ White Zombie 195

12c****

- ❑ Chongin' in the Hood 139
- ❑ Crybaby 103
- ❑ Maximus Cauldron 139

12c*****

- ❑ Gape Index 143
- ❑ Loony Binge 143
- ❑ Phasers on Stun 153
- ❑ Steel Monkey 200

12d**

- ❑ Downward Spiral 139
- ❑ Joker's Acid Bath 203
- ❑ Rapid Fire 107
- ❑ Thing That Wouldn't Leave 71

12d***

- ❑ Blockbuster 133
- ❑ Good Thing 176

12d****

- ❑ Gravitron 165
- ❑ Not For Sale 153

12d*****

- ❑ Billion Million 143
- ❑ Brewtalized 139
- ❑ Excelsior 147
- ❑ Wooly Bugger 203

13a**

- ❑ Desire 103
- ❑ Gringuita 87
- ❑ Roadkill 95

13a***

- ❑ Anaconda 203
- ❑ Bushfire 211
- ❑ Candy Colored Clown 162
- ❑ Pennywise 162

13a****

- ❑ Sniveling 139
- ❑ Yellowstreak 113

13a*****

- ❑ Aurora 115
- ❑ Cowering 139

13b**

- ❑ Shocker 119

13b***

- ❑ Blood Sport 147
- ❑ Conquistadors Without Swords 91

13b****

- ❑ Ascension 195

13b*****

- ❑ Fight Club 147
- ❑ Loony Tunes 143

13c**

- ❑ Hocus Pocus 119
- ❑ Psycho 212

13c*****

- ❑ Sneak 139

Further Reading

Rock & Ice #34

November/December 1989—page 43

Owen's River Gorge, Bishop, California

MIKE STRASSMAN, SCOTT AYERS

The Rock & Ice Guide.

Climbing #129

December 1991/January 1992—page 82

Gorge Yourself

TODD GRAHAM

Already the most popular sport-climbing destination in California, the Owens River Gorge offers year-round entertainment on steep, solid volcanic tuff.

Rock & Ice #69

September/October 1995—page 42

Take Me to the River

WILLS YOUNG

Sun-drenched days, hot springs at night, and lots of little edges in between—the Owens River Gorge is California cragging at its finest.

Guide Services

Peter Croft

☎ 760-872-9309
595 South Barlow Lane
Bishop, CA 93514
petercroft@verizon.net

Sierra Mountain Center

☎ 760-873-8526
174 West Line St.
Bishop, CA 93514
sierramountaincenter.com

Sierra Mountain Guides

☎ 760-648-1122
P.O. Box 446
June Lake, CA 93529
www.themountainguide.com

Sierra Mountaineering International

☎ 760-872-4929
236 North Main St.
Bishop, CA 93515-1011
www.sierramountaineering.com

Sierra Rock Climbing School

☎ 877-686-7625
242 N. Tumbleweed Rd.
Bishop, CA 93514
SierraRockClimbingSchool.com

MAMMOTH MOUNTAINEERING SUPPLY

Guide Referrals, Information, Books, Maps

760-934-4191

www.MammothGear.com

Climbing
alpine, free, bouldering, aid, winter

Skiing
telemark, alpine touring, split boards

Backpacking
ultralight, PCT, boots, mountaineering

Rentals
telemark, AT, split boards, backpacking

3189 Main St., Next to Wave Rave
in Mammoth Lakes

CRATER

The strongest, most durable, longest lasting climbing holds on the planet.

Double replacement, lifetime guarantee against breakage!

visit craterholds.com or call 989.779.1792

Wilson's Eastside Sports
224 North Main Street, Bishop
(760) 873-7520
www.eastsidesports.com

Guidebooks, Local Maps
Approach Shoes
Climbing Gear
Ropes
Rock Shoes
Bouldering Pads
Rental Rock Shoes

Open 7 days a week
The Eastern Sierra Climbing HQ

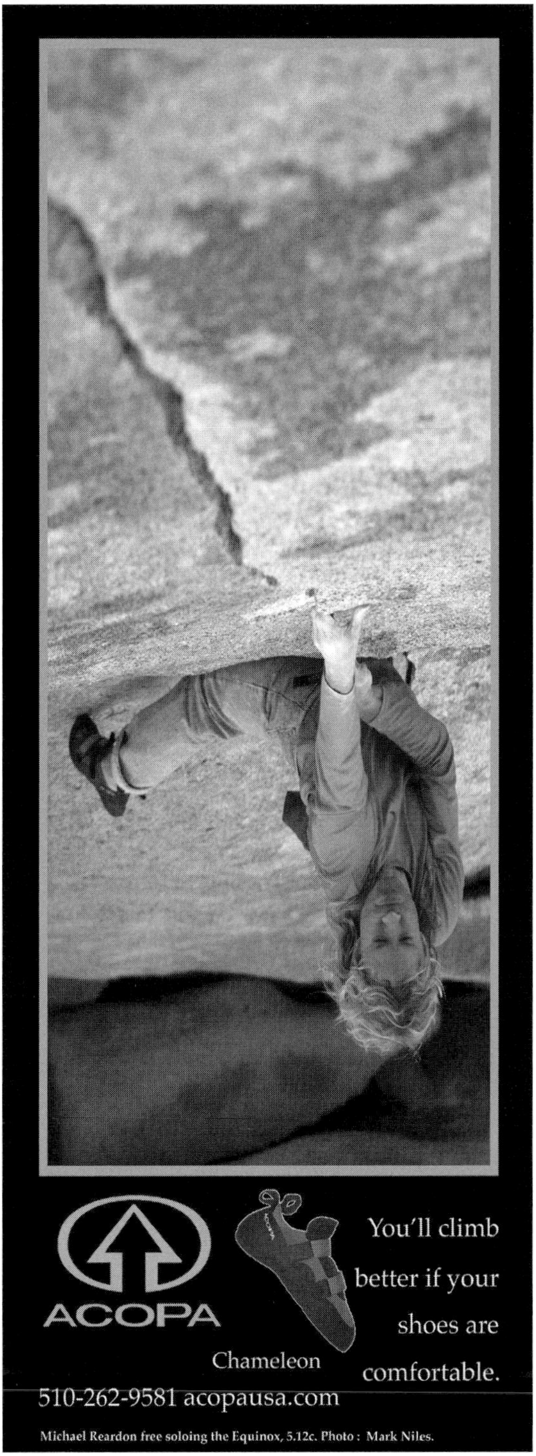
ACOPA
Chameleon
You'll climb
better if your
shoes are
comfortable.
510-262-9581 acopausa.com
Michael Reardon free soloing the Equinox, 5.12c. Photo : Mark Niles.

Mick Ryan Photo.

"discipline...training...integrity"

Killer Resoles

t-shirts & stickers

www.**rubberroomresoles**.com

1-888-395-ROCK

175-B North Main

Bishop, CA 93514

FISH
Portaledges
Haul Bags
Duffel Bags
Copperheads
Daisy Chains
Aiders
Bolts & Drills
Chalk Bags
Gee, all that gym climbing is finally going to pay off... I think I'm gonna' score!
...maybe the Zodiac this spring. Better dump this loser quick!
Wall Bags
Poop Tubes
Atom Smashers
Harnesses
Butt Bags
Repairs
Wall Bags
Rivet Hangers
Alpine Aiders
Doubloons
Fish Hooks
Gear Slings
Grain Tamers
T-Shirts
Crag Packs
Maxi Pads
and More
www.FishProducts.com

Index

A

A Life Shared is a Better Life 9*** 174
Abitafun 9**** 87
Abitarot 10a**** 87
Abraxas Finish 11c***** 95
Access Information *31*
Ace Cashier 10a** 189
Acopa *239*
Adventure of Gladys Stokepamphlet 11a*** 221
Advertisements *237*
Advocates of Babbling Thought 11c** 106
Air Walk aka See What Happens When You... 10c** 185
Alfred Hitchcrack 8** 199
All You Can Eat Cliff **199**
All You Can Eat 10c• 199
Alotarot 11a• 87
Ambassadors of Funk 10b**** 97
Amenities - Bishop *27*
Amenities - Mammoth Lakes *29*
Amnesia 12b** 212
Anaconda 13a*** 203
Anchors *43*
And Monkeys Might Fly Out of My Butt 11d*** 207
And Now for Something Completely... 11b** 165
And Now for Something Much Cleaner 10d*** 165
Anonymous Bolter 5*** 62
Another Day in Hell 9** 157
Another Day in Paradise 11d*** 157
Appendix *223*
Approach Pitch 10b** 81
Approach Instructions *46*
Approaches *25*
Ascension 13b**** 195
Astroboy 12b*** 161
Attila the Hun Wall **104**
Attila the Hun 10d** 104
Aunti Vigilante 10b** 175
Aurora 13a***** 115
Awful Offwidth 9• 119

B

Babushka 8***** 98
Baby Got Back 11a** 106
Baby Duck 11b*** 103
Bad Light 7• 64
Bad Thing 12b*** 176
Ballet Recital 10b• 103
Banana Belt **83**
Barbara Bush 8* 91
Barracuda 11c** 147
Basket Case 12b**** 212
Bat Angel 11d*** 203
Batting Cage 10c* 69
Bazooka Country 12a**** 195
Be Prepared to G 11b** 196
Beijing 10d*** 113
Bender 11b*** 129
Berlin Wall 10d*** 133
Big Screen 10b** 62
Big Tower **62**
Billion Million 12d***** 143
Bill's Black Book 8* 181
Bird of Prey 11c*** 147
Black Chicks in Heat 10a*** 85
Black Hole 12b***** 119
Black Ice 10c*** 97
Blockbuster 12d*** 133
Blocky Top Wall **66**
Blocky Top 8** 66
Blood Sport 13b*** 147
Blood Sugar Sex Magik 10d***** 129
Bloody Pawprints 11d*** 83
Boating Prohibited 10a*** 69
Bob & Eric Crack 10a** 65
Body Count 12a*** 121
Bombay on the Rocks 11c**** 211
Bone Up 10d**** 95
Bones 9* 154
Bonfire of the Panties 11c*** 211
Bongo Fury aka Frank Zappa Memorial... 12b**** 176
Bonus Features 7** 62
Book of Bones 9* 95
Bot's Folly 11a• 64
Botswana Baby 9* 97
Bow Down to the Standard White Jesus 11a* 105
Boy Wonder 11a*** 203
Brandenburg Gate 7*** 133
Breaking the Law 10a*** 133
Brewtalized 12d***** 139
Brian's Song 11a*** 106
Brief History *32*
Brief Intermission 10a* 62
Broken Battery 11d** 97
Broski/Linaweaver 10b** 183
Brothers in Arms 10d**** 85
Buddha Bless 11c** 166
Buddha's Bivy Buddy's Biddy's Booty 9• 187
Buried Treasure 10c***** 54
Bushfire 13a*** 211
Bust a Move 12a** 62
Butt Wipe 10a* 83
Butterknife 8*** 95

C

C-4 Yourself 11a*** 185
C.L.O.T. 10c*** 85
Cabaret 11a*** 121
Cadillac Desert 10c*** 81
Cajun Barbecue 10b** 188
Caldera 11c**** 185
Camping 21
Candy Colored Clown 13a*** 162
Captain Crunch 12a* 191
Carnibiator 10a** 199
Cat in the Hat 8** 181
Catch-n-Release 11d**** 147
Cement Overshoes 12b** 73
Center Court 8* 105
Central Gorge Basics 77
Chaos 10d** 131
Chicken Belly 10a** 189
Child of Light 9**** 115
Child's Play 12b***** 192
Chillin' at the Grill 11c*** 95
China Doll 8**** 115
Chipmunk Pancakes (With Batbrain Syrup) 10a** 165
Chocolate City 11d** 97
Chompin' at the Bit 12a*** 191
Chongin' in the Hood 12c**** 139
Chossman of the Desert 10d**** 211
Chossman's Dessert 12a** 211
Chuckers 10d*** 175
Chuckwalla Wall 221
Chuckwalla Wall 11a** 221
Cinderella 9**** 199
Circo Gringo 12b**** 162
Civilized 12b*** 139
Climate 19
Climbing in the Owens River Gorge 42
Clip Jockeys 9**** 155
Clip Jr. 6**** 98
C'mon Knucko 11b**** 179
Cobbler's Delight 10a*** 133
Cobra 11b** 119
Coffee Achiever 10b*** 153
Coffin Lid 11d*** 159
Come of Age 11a** 133
Coming Attractions 8*** 62
Conduct 42
Confusing Confucius 10d**** 113
Conquistadors Without Swords 13b*** 91
Contagious 10b** 121
Controversial Insert 10d*** 191
Cornercopia 11b*** 115
Corporal Clinger 10b** 165
Corvus Mortis 6• 66
Cowering 13a***** 139
Cracked Towers 207
Crash Landing 11a*** 103
Crater Holds 238
Creaky Hollow Fracture Show 10c** 131
Criss Cross 11d** 104
Crotalulsley Challenged 6** 199
Crotch Pasta 11c*** 191
Crowd Pleaser 9**** 98
Cruella 10c*** 200
Crumb Donut 11b*** 191
Crybaby 12c**** 103
Crystal Corridor 154
Custom Made 12c* 81

D

D. Barbi-onslut A2* 159
D.W.P. 11c***** 73
Darshan aka Ripoff 12b***** 95
Daughters of a Coral Dawn 11a** 65
Dead Crow Buttress 66
Dead on Arrival 11d** 121
Death By Mudhen 10b• 66
Delicate Mechanism 10b*** 211
Dellinger 10d*** 155
Desert Storm 12a**** 103
Desire 13a** 103
Destination Oblivion 10c*** 161
Destiny 11b* 129
Dial 911 10d** 121
Diamond Face 65
Difficulty Ratings 47
Dihedrals 211
Dilithium Crystal 153
Dimples 10d*** 197
Direchossimo 11b*** 119
Direct North Face 11b** 129
Dirt Pile 8* 65
Divine Sculptor 12a**** 157
Disco Inferno 11a**** 135
DMZ 133
Doesn't Anybody Work Around Here? 10c** 133
Dollar Three Ninety Eight 10b*** 81
Done With Spare Change From Mikey's... 10b** 106
Don't Kid, Minibike 9** 174
Don't Look Down 9*** 129
Don't Look Up 10b**** 129
Don't Make Me Laugh 9** 131
Don't Nuke Nevada 11b* 54
Doowutchyalike 11d*** 183
Double Flipper 9*** 203
Double Insulated 10c* 85
Double Take 8* 103
Downward Spiral 12d** 139
Dr. Claw 11d***** 153
Dr. Evil 10a***** 203
Drill Rig 11c**** 191

Drill Sergeant 8*** 165
Drillin' Time Again 12b*** 145
Driving Times *17*
Dummy Up 11a* 183
Dust in the Wind 11d*** 155
Dynamite Face 11d* 81

E

Eastern Sierra Climbing Guides *7*
Easy Enough 10a** 133
Ego Unchained 10a**** 166
El Pollo Grande **219**
Elbow Macaroni 11b** 174
Eldorado Roof - Left Side **143**
Eldorado Roof - Overview **135**
Eldorado Roof - Right Side **139**
Eldorado Roof - Towering Inferno **137**
Electric Kachina 8** 85
Electric Launderland 8** 81
Electric Vex 12c** 71
Elephant Gun 10a** 129
Elephant's Butt 10d** 199
Embrace This 12a*** 91
Emergency Room **121**
End of an Era 12b*** 166
Engorged 11d*** 179
Enraged 12a** 179
Enraged Pixie 11a** 145
Enslaved by the Belle 10a*** 183
Enter at Your Own Risk 10d*** 69
Enter the Dragon 8** 115
Enterprise 12b***** 153
Environmental Concerns *31*
Environmental Terrorist 10c**** 83
Equipment *43*
Escapade 11a***** 149
Excelsior 12d***** 147
Exit Stage Left 9• 185
Exit Stage Left II 10a** 62
Expensive But Worth It 7** 149
Expressway 11b***** 95
Extreme Caffeine 10b***** 153

F

Failsafe 12a**** 191
Failsafe Wall **191**
Faith No More 12c*** 183
Family Man 11d** 197
Fantasia 10c* 133
Fashion Racket 10a*** 105
Faulty Tower **103**
Fear of a Black Planet 10a*** 97
Fender Strat 10a**** 103
Feudal Beerlords 10d**** 95
Fever 11c**** 191
Fight Club 13b***** 147
Fine Dining 7** 199
Finger Food 10d* 103
Fingertip Ledge of Contentment 10c** 133
First Ascent Ethics *40*
Fish Products *241*
Fixings For a Sandwich 10c* 56
Flailsafe 10c** 191
Flakenstein 12b*** 139
Flash or Splash 9* 64
Flashflood 12b***** 73
Flashing With Jeckyl Juice 11b** 56
Flavin Haven **184**
Flex Your Bazooka 9** 105
Flex Your Head 11c***** 203
Flush Twice L.A. Needs the Water 11b** 105
Flying Tigers 11c** 207
Fobes 40 9*** 157
Focus 11b**** 119
Focus Marty 10a** 157
For Patricia 7*** 188
Foreword *12*
Fork it Over 10c** 95
Forkash and Riches 12a** 103
Fortune Cookie 9** 115
Frank 9*** 188
Franklin's Frosty Funeral 10b** 203
Franklin's Tower **200**
Freaks of the Industry 11d**** 196
Free Falling 11d*** 103
Fresh Squeezed 11c* 95
From Chocolate to Chossman 9** 103
From Chocolate to Morphine 11d***** 103
Fun House **149**
Funky Cole Patina 11b*** 73
Further Reading *236*

G

Gangsta Lean 8**** 211
Gape Index 12c***** 143
Gary Gray 10b*** 87
Gecko 10d* 133
Geisha Girl 11c** 113
George Bush 10b**** 91
Get Over It 10c**** 196
Get Your War On 12a** 107
Getting There *23*
Ghengis Khan 11b*** 113
Gila Bender 10a• 174
Gimme the Helmet, I'll Be the Stunt Man 10a* 200
Giveaway 10a**** 179
Global Warming 10c* 67
Go Back Where You Came From 12a** 81
Go For the Gold 10c*** 110

Godzilla Does the Dizzy Tango 12a*** 139
Going Back to Cali 12a** 91
Good Friday 10c*** 211
Good Thing 12d*** 176
Gorge and Purge 12a*** 179
Gorge Corner 9** 181
Gorgeous 10b***** 179
Gorgeous Towers 179
Gotham City 203
Gravitron 12d**** 165
Great Wall of China - Center 113
Great Wall of China - Left 115
Great Wall of China - Overview 108
Great Wall of China - Right 110
Greenhouse Wall 67
Grey Hair 7• 64
Grey Scale 10a*** 64
Grey Wall 64
Grindrite 11b***** 203
Gringuita 13a** 87
Guide Services 236
Gunned Down By Goofy 10a** 184
Gunnin' For a Heart Attack 10b** 64
Guns & Poses 11d* 62
Guy With a Doberman 11c* 123

H

Hacking & Spitting 12a*** 165
Hagar'n'hilti 9** 104
Half Tone 11a** 64
Hammered 11b**** 87
Hanging Garden 11b*** 221
Hard Copy 12a*** 91
Hardly Wallbanger 10c***** 87
Hatchett Job 10b** 85
Have a Little Faith 10b** 163
Head Banger 10c** 55
Health Club 105
Health Club 8** 105
Heart of the Sun 9***** 115
Held Over 10c*** 62
Helga's Holiday 7** 104
Help on the Way 12c*** 200
Herniated Bone 10c*** 189
Hey Amigo 7• 181
Hey Bubba, Watch This! 10c**** 131
Hidden 11a** 179
High Ball 11d**** 87
High Octane 10d** 70
High Seas 7**** 98
High Tension Towers 85
Hip Pockets 11a**** 83
Hireaeth 10a* 66
His Spirit 9** 165
Hocus Pocus 13c** 119
Hole in the Wall 9* 184
Holocaust 10b**** 133
Holy Trinity Wall 183
Home Skillet 10d* 189
Homebrew 11b*** or 11d*** 87
Hook 12a** 197
Hot Springs - North 224
Hot Springs - South 226
Hotcake Flake 10a** 95
How to Use This Guide 46
Hu Phlung Pu 8 A3*** 115
Humbly, Mumbly, Jumbly 10b**** 98
Humdinger 10a** 81
Humjob 9*** 81
Hungover 11b***** 87

I

ICBM Tower 192
Iceberg 12a* 107
Iceberg II 9*** 175
Idol Maker 12a* 81
If I Told You I'd Have to Kill You 11a*** 71
I'm Like This Because I Live in My Van 9** 57
Imprisoned Behind Lies 6*** 97
Impulse Power aka the Trouble With... 10c*** 153
In the Pink 10c** 203
In Your Red Truck 9* 187
Incorncentric 10c** 54
Independent Worm Saloon 12b**** 143
Induced Labor 10d**** 188
Init 10a*** 187
Inner Gorge Basics 127
Insane in the Membrane 12b*** 129
Insanity 11d*** 212
Introduction 17
Inyo Mono Line Tower 56
It's the Gaaazzz 8*** 181

J

James Brown 11b**** 97
Jaws of Life 10b**** 184
Jesus Built My Tri-cam 10a**** 157
Jizz Soaked Action Pix 11a* 181
Joe's Garage 176
Joker's Acid Bath 12d** 203
Jump Start 10c*** 197
Junior Achievement 11d**** 197
Junior Wall 197
Just Under the Wire 10a** 85

K

Kelly's Heroes 10c** 188
Keough's Hot Springs Resort 226
Kicking Ash 10c** 185

Kinder Gentler Arete 10d** 99
King Rat 11b*** 91
King Spud 11a* 196
Kingsnake 11c*** 203
Kirk 10b** 154
Klingon 12a***** 153
Klingon Crabs 9** 154
Know the Drill 10c*** 163
Knucko's Pride of the North 11b***** 179
Kung Pao 11b*** 113

L

L.A. is Burning 9* 71
L. Alien Wall 81
La Chappeau 10a• 207
La Pavoni 11d*** 196
Lalaland 11c***** 103
Land Before Time 10a** 69
Land of the Giants 145
Last Frontier 221
Lat Machine 12a**** 165
Late for Work 10a** 70
Lava Haul 10a**** 185
Lava Java 8*** 153
Leave No Trace 4* 63
Left Barley Crack 10b* 207
Left for Dead 11b**** 54
Letter Bomb 11c** 139
Lieutenant Uhura 11c***** 153
Life During Wartime 10a*** 211
Life in Electric Larvae Land 10b**** 54
Light Rangers 12a*** 219
Light Within 10c***** 87
Liquid Fire 10d*** 153
Little Crack 5* 62
Living Dead 11c***** 147
Local Trivia Tower 157
Lone Star 11c* 166
Longest Yard 12c** 143
Look Out Below 11a** 65
Loony Bar 10a** 187
Loony Binge 12c***** 143
Loony Left 12b*** 143
Loony Tunes 13b***** 143
Louisiana Liplock 10b* 104
Love of Jesus 10a*** 165
Love Over Gold 11b*** 83
Love Stinks 11a***** 83
Low Octane 9*** 70
Lower Elbow Room - Left 174
Lower Elbow Room - Right 175
Lower Gorge Basics 61

M

M.O. 9** 207
Machine Gun Jumblies 10a***** 203
Mad Cat 10b** 65
Main Vein 12a*** 195
Mal a la Gorge 10c*** 161
Malcolm X 12b*** 97
Malibu 11a*** 91
Malt Linker 12b** 161
Malteese Flamoingo 11a** 191
Mammoth Mountaineering Supply 237
Mandarin Orange 11b**** 113
Mandela 11d* 97
Maps 46
Marco Polo's Boys Go Dirty Dancing 8** 110
Marty Party 11d**** 161
Maximus Cauldron 12c**** 139
McCracken Wall 166
Me So Horny 12a*** 91
Megalithic 157
Megalithic 11a*** 157
Megalomaniac 11c**** 159
Melts in Your Mouth 10c**** 149
Members Only 10d***** 129
Membership Has its Privileges 11a*** 66
Menace to Sobriety 11c**** 87
Menace II Society 10b** 119
Mental Ward 57
Meringueutan Arch 11a** 189
Michelin Man 10c** 56
Mickey Mantle 11b** 65
Micro Pete 12a** 166
Middle Elbow Room 187
Mildew Encrusted Shower Stall 10c** 211
Mile High Crack 8*** 63
Mind Meld 12b**** 153
Mini Jones 11b** 211
Mini Me 11d** 189
Mini Buttress 197
Missing Link 11b*** 161
Moat 8* 64
Monkey Bean 10b** 187
Monkey See, Monkey Do 10b** 119
Monkey to Monk Cliff 163
Monsters of Rock 11b** 83
More Than Just Mild 10c* 203
Morning Wood 11a**** 119
Mothership Cliff 147
Mouth T. Dung 10c* 97
Mr. Check-off 11a*** 155
Mr. Freeze 11c*** 203
Mumbles the Guzzler 11b• 179

My Favorite Animal is a Liger 10b** 207
My Mom Can Crank 12a*** 192
My Name's Not Harold 12b** 191
Mystical Tricks Cliff 106

N

Nakin 10c** 159
Narcolepsy 8**** 107
Naked Gun 10c* 63
Narrows East 161
Narrows West 159
Natural Lite 6** 63
Neanderthal 12a** 187
Nectar 11d*** 157
Ned Guy's Proud Pearl Necklace 11d**** 95
Negress Wall 97
Neurotic Waltz 11d**** 212
Next Generation 11c* 153
Nice Jugs 9*** 184
Nicely Displayed But Wrappers Weren't... 10b*** 54
Nirvana 10a*** 95
No Chapas 8** 107
No Fly Zone 11d* 133
No Known Cure 11b** 161
No Lifeguard on Duty 10d** 69
No Mo' M.O. 7• 207
Noble Mouse 11a** 91
North Gorge Basics 217
Northern Lite 7**** 83
Northern Pike 11a**** 147
Nose Ring 11a** 197
Not for Sale 12d**** 153
Not Too Stout 7** 87
Not Proud Enough to Name 8** 211

O

O Henry! 11c*** 199
O.R.G. asm 11a***** 211
Oblique Slanting Dihedral of Death 10d** 162
Oceanside 11d*** 91
Off the Hook 6 A4*** 154
Offramp 10d*** 95
Old & in the Way 10b** 91
Old Fart's Formation 55
One Armed Bandit 10b*** 211
One Holer 10b**** 95
Oompa Loompa 8** 69
Optimator 11c*** 129
Orange Peel 10c**** 95
Organ Pipes 218
Original Gorgeous 9* 187
Out of the Pit 11a*** 162

P

P.D. Time 7*** 175
P.T. Barnum Wall 162
Palm Reader 11d** 175
Paradise 9**** 83
Paranoia 11d*** 212
Party on Sean 8*** 166
Peking Duck 10d*** 113
Peligro 6• 85
Penguin 12b**** 203
Pennywise 13a*** 162
Penstock Rock 73
Penstock Slab 10d* 73
People are Weird 9* 133
Perched 10d**** 103
Pet Trackers 10a*** 175
PG13 9*** 69
Phasers on Stun 12c***** 153
Phoenix 7*** 175
Photon Torpedo 11b***** 153
Pick a Finger 11d*** 56
Pick Pocket 11a**** 183
Pink Face 63
Pippy the Zenhead 9** 179
Piranha 12b**** 147
Pitstop 70
Pistop 12a** 70
Players 227
Please Baby, Baby, Baby, Please 12c** 183
Pop Goes the Weasel 11b**** 195
Pop Tart Towers 99
Pop Tart 11b** 99
Posers on the Rig 11b** 199
Positive Approach 9*** 81
Post Partum 10a**** 188
Power 11d**** 119
Power Surge 10b** 69
Powerhouse Wall 71
Praying Mantle 10b*** 56
Pre-erosive Force 12a*** 197
Preface 13
Pretty in Pink 10b** 165
Probation Violation 11d***** 145
Proctology Exam 12c** 143
Projects 43
Psmead 11b*** 119
Psycho 13c** 212
Pub Wall 87
Pulp Friction 10c** 97
Pumice Facial 10c** 187
Pump up the Trust Fund 11c** 133
Pumping Groundwater 12a***** 73
Pumping the Slots 9**** 211
Pumpkin 11c**** 104
Pyroclasm 11d*** 185

Q

Quail Crack 10a** 175
Quail Trail 10b*** 175
Quality Ratings *47*
Quest 10c* 83

R

R.P. #4 10b** 69
Range of Light 10c** 83
Rap it Up 11c** 179
Rapid Fire 12d** 107
Rapscallion 7** 63
Ratso 10a* 91
Red Circle With a Slash 10c** 69
Redemption 12c*** 195
Release the McCracken 11d*** 166
Results May Vary 10b*** 69
Retrobolting *43*
Return to Forever 12a** 95
Riddler 11d*** 203
Right Barley Crack 10b* 207
Right for Life 10c*** 54
Right Wing 10b** 91
Rim Job 11a** 83
Riverside Island **91**
Roadkill 13a** 95
Roadside Boulders **107**
Rob's Rock **155**
Roberto Clemente 9* 200
Rock, the *42*
Roller Coaster Ride 12a*** 174
Romulan Roids 10b** 154
Romulan Roof 12a**** 153
Route Descriptions *47*
Routes by Rating *228*
Rubber Room *240*

S

Sabado Gigante 8*** 119
Safety Concerns *44*
Safety in Numbers 10c** 54
Sandbag 5.8 10a* 161
Sanitarium **212**
Santana 11c**** 95
Satori 11a• 165
Savage Garden **218**
Savage Garden 11b** 218
Save Mono Lake 11d• 73
Scalded by Spivey 12a*** 207
Scalpel 8** 155
Schitzo 11a** 212
Schneider/Clay 12c** 184
Scorched Egos 11b** 163
Scorpion 10b*** 85
Scratch 'n Sniff 10a*** 56
Scrotal Hotpack 10a*** 105
Scrotal Squeeze 10c* 105
Scrutinized 11c*** 95
Sea Cow 11a*** 179
Seam's Difficult 11b*** 196
Sendero Luminoso 10b***** 119
Serial Driller 12c*** 188
Set Free 10c*** 87
Sex 11d***** 183
Sex Packets 12a***** 183
Shaded Wall **123**
Shadow Catcher 9* 218
Shafted 11c*** 162
Sharptooth 9** 69
Shell of a Man 10b* 63
She's a Man, Man 11a** 203
Shock Treatment 11a**** 212
Shocker 13b** 119
Shogun 10d** 113
Short But Steep 10c** 123
Short Cake 11d** 66
Shout Around 11d* 81
Show Us Your Tits 10c***** 121
Shuttle Craft 11c** 153
Sidewinder 9** 97
Silence of the Poodles 8**** 207
Silent Pillar Wall **54**
Size Doesn't Matter 10b* 192
Skeletons in the Closet 11c**** 95
Skin Tight 12c*** 91
Slab Metrical Illusions 10d** 55
Slacker 12a**** 139
Slackjaw 10a*** 211
Slander Crag **57**
Slander Session 10b* 57
Slip 'n Slide 9**** 175
Slipknot 8• 200
Slot Machine 10a* 103
Sly Little Fart Blaster 11d** 103
Smell the Glove 12a** 163
Smokey the Beer 10b*** 159
Smoothie 12c** 97
Snake Eyes 12a** 119
Snapping Pussy Doll 10a**** 181
Sneak 13c***** 139
Sneak Preview 9* 62
Sneakaroma 9** 105
Sniveling 13a**** 139
Social Platform **95**
Solarium **119**
Solito 10c** 103
Some Kind of Wonderful 11c** 71
Somerot 10c* 87
Soul Music 10b* 179

Spare Change 10d*** 81
Sparky Does Power Tower 10b*** 85
Sparky the Drillhead 10a** 188
Spinal Fracture 11a*** 95
Spivey for Breakfast 11a*** 187
Splashdown 55
Splashdown 11d**** 55
Split Decision 11a*** 119
Spock 10a** 154
Sport Trac 12a* 197
Squeezin' the Buddha's Titty 7• 166
Staging Tower 183
Stardate 9* 153
Start Me Up 10b** 105
Stay Hungry 10b** 199
Staying Power Towers 129
Steel Monkey 12c***** 200
Stella 8*** 188
Stella's Fella 10a** 188
Step Right Up 8** 199
Sting of the Honeybee 12c*** 199
Stonefly 10a* 181
Stowaway 10c*** 163
Stradivarius 8**** 103
Stress Puppet 11a* 73
Stronger Than Dirt 9• 203
Sub Gorge Basics 51
Subdivisions 10d* 66
Sulu 8*** 155
Sunset Sam 6* 188
Sunstroke 9** 104
Super Fine Booty 11b*** 211
Super Pipe 12b* 218
Superfly 10c***** 203
Supergroveler 10d*** 159
Supreme Wizard Formation 165
Surgeon General 10a* 69
Swamp Thing 9* 207
Sweet & Sour 10a** 97
Sweetie 6* 174
Szechwan Bambi 10c*** 199

T

Tall Dollar 10b**** 203
Tempest 10b** 87
Tephra Sampler 10b* 185
That's a Cold Shut, Darlin' 10c** 99
The-Aretical 11b**** 179
Thieves in the Temple 12a***** 129
Thing That Wouldn't Leave 12d** 71
30 Miles to Water 8• 174
3.B.A. 11c* 99
Three Stooges 10a*** 56
Thrill Pig 11d**** 191
Thumbs Up 11c**** 149
Tiananmen Square 10c*** 113
Time Will Tell 10a* 69
Timeless 10d**** 69
Titty Twister 8 A3+** 65
To Knee or Not to Knee 10a*** 129
Too Crazy to Be Gripped 10b** 57
Too Proud to Ignore 10b** 211
Tore Down 11a*** 184
Towel Rack 10d*** 211
Tower Line 12a*** 200
Towering Inferno 11b***** 137
Transcendence 10c** 133
Trestle Wall 195
Tricks in Motion 10a*** 106
Trigger Finger 11c*** 221
Triple Play Cliff 181
Truck Tire Graveyard Tower 56
Trundle of Joy 12b** 199
Tsing Tao 10b**** 115
Tsunami 11c**** 113
Tumbling Dice 10d***** 95
20/20 9** 56
Twister 11b** 155
2 Feet to Hell 11a** 179

U

Unbearable Lightness of Beans 11d*** 91
Uncontrollable Urge 10a** 65
Under the Knife aka Sport This A3**** 97
Underground Cliff 196
Unemployment Line 10a** 149
Unnatural Silence 9* 121
Unrepentant Sinner 11d** 95
Upper Elbow Room 188
Upper Gorge Basics 171
Upwardly Mobile 10b*** 81
Urrr! 11b* 207

V

Valley 5.8 10a**** 71
Venom 11c***** 119
Vital Signs 12a** 121
Volcanic Meltdown Cliff 55
Vulcan Jock Itch 10a** 154
Vulcan Variation 11d** 153

W

Wacked Scenario 10b**** 179
Wafer Thin Mint 11c*** 221
Walk the Yellow Line 11b**** 188
Warm Out Wall 189
Warm Up Wall 98
Warning: Laser Beam 8*** 69
Warning Signs 10d***** 69

Warning Signs Wall **69**
Watch for Rocks 8*** 69
Waterline 11a** 133
Wedge-O 10b*** 83
Weird Al 7*** 131
Weird Corner **131**
Welcome to the Gorge 9*** 97
What Me Worry 12b* 139
What Up? 10b** 98
What's its Face 10b*** 103
Where is the Owens River Gorge? *17*
Whirlpool 10d* 64
White Dwarf 12a*** 104
White Zombie 12c*** 195
Whiteout 11a** 196
Who Knows? 9** 197
Wiggly 11a***** 145
Wilson's Eastside Sports *238*
Win, Lose or Claw 11a** 149
Wired 10d*** 129
Wonderbar 10d** 87
Wonka 10a** 69
Wooly Bugger 12d***** 203
Worst Enemy 9• 81
Wounded Knee 10a* 221
Wowie Zowie 10a***(r) 63
Wrath of Khan 11c***** 113

X

Y

Ya Shoulda' Killed Me Last Year 11c*** 129
Yellow Peril 10c***** 113
Yellowstreak 13a**** 113
You Are What You Is 11a** 176
You Don't Want None 10d** 174
You Have Been Nothing But Trouble... 11c*** 179
You Like it Sideways? 10b** 196
Your Soaking in it 10c* 203

Z

Z Crack 12a* 97
Z Dong 10a**** 97
Zig Zag 10a** 65

The author hard at work field testing **Wounded Knee** 10a* in the Owens River Gorge. ©*Kevin Calder Photo.*

ABOUT THE AUTHOR

Marty Lewis grew up in the Santa Monica Mountains of Southern California, where he showed an early interest in the outdoor world. His father helped cultivate this interest by taking Marty on annual trips to the Sierra Nevada Mountains, to hike, backpack and peakbag.

The author moved to Mammoth Lakes in 1978, where he managed a successful family business.

During the early 1980s Marty climbed in Yosemite Valley and Tuolumne Meadows, which he found a little frightening. He focused mainly on skiing, bouldering and mountaineering. By the mid 1980s he fancied himself a fitness man, spending his time running, cycling and weight-lifting.

In 1989 Marty climbed his first sport climb in the Owens River Gorge, finding it to be one of the most fun, exhilarating and athletic things he'd ever done. From then on, he has spent his free time rock climbing, most of it in the Eastern Sierra. During this time he has made a substantial contribution to the development of sport climbing in the region.

Marty has not climbed El Capitan, Mt. Everest or any 5.13s. He has logged over a thousand days in the Owens River Gorge.

In 2000, after twenty-two years in Mammoth, the author moved out of the snowbelt to a rural area near Bishop, where he lives with his wife Sharon and their dogs Blue and Joe.

About Maximus Press

Maximus Press was launched in 1990 with the publication of the pamphlet "Owens River Gorge Climbs". Garage-style in appearance, this publication was nevertheless accurate, concise and easy to use. Fifteen years later after considerable improvements, Maximus Press continues to strive to produce the most useful and state-of-the-art guidebooks possible. The knowledge base of our editorial staff comes from years of experience climbing, exploring and living in the Eastern Sierra. You can count on our commitment to deliver high-quality books.

I have spent the past 27 years living in this fantastic region. The combination of spectacular natural beauty, a stable climate and an incredible diversity of climbing options, in one of the most wide open and least populated areas in California is hard to beat. Enjoy!

—Marty Lewis
Publisher

Another shipment of books coming your way.

Guidebooks available from Maximus Press

Maximus Press Books can be found at fine outdoor shops or ordered directly. California residents please include 7.75% sales tax. Shipping and handling included in price. Prices subject to change without notice.

maximuspress.com

Maximus Press
P.O. Box 1565
Bishop, CA 93515
Phone & Fax: 760-387-1013
E-mail: smlewis@qnet.com

MAXIMVS PRESS

BIG CHIEF AREA CLIMBS

by Marek Hajek, edited by Marty Lewis

LAKE TAHOE CLIMBING GUIDES VOL. 1

March 2005 - 1st Edition
96 pages - $20.00
ISBN 0-9676116-7-9

The Climbing Guide to the Big Chief Area, Lake Tahoe.

- **Big Chief**
- **Little Chief**
- **Light Deprivation Buttress**
- **Sawtooth Ridge**

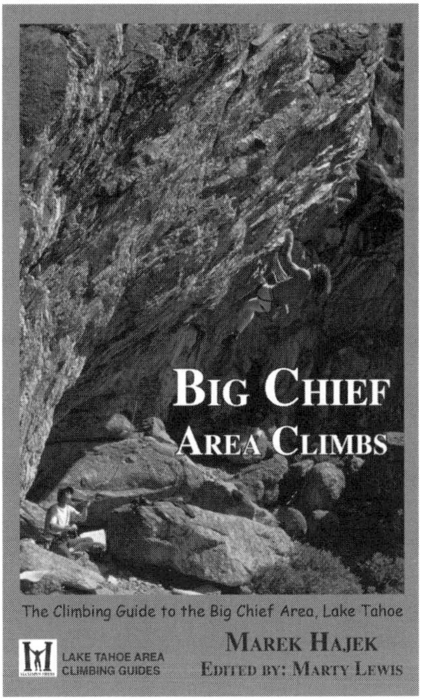

MAMMOTH AREA ROCK CLIMBS

by Marty Lewis and John Moynier

EASTERN SIERRA CLIMBING GUIDES VOL. 2

May 2004 - 3rd Edition
288 pages - $30.00
ISBN 0-9676116-5-2

The Climbing Guide to the Eastern Sierra—North.

- **Rock Creek**
- **Benton Crags**
- **Bear Crag**
- **Clark Canyon**
- **Deadman's Bouldering**
- **Granite Basin**

BISHOP AREA ROCK CLIMBS

by Peter Croft and Marty Lewis

EASTERN SIERRA CLIMBING GUIDES VOL. 3

Spring 2006 - 3rd Edition
??? pages - $??.??
ISBN 0-9676116-?-?

The Climbing Guide to the Eastern Sierra—South.

- **Whitney Portal**
- **Alabama Hills**
- **Cardinal Pinnacle**
- **Buttermilk Bouldering**
- **Tablelands Bouldering**
- **Pine Creek**

Not Yet Released

Spring 2006?

THE GOOD, THE GREAT, AND THE AWESOME

by Peter Croft

EASTERN SIERRA CLIMBING GUIDES VOL. 4

July 2002 - 1st Edition
244 pages - $30.00
ISBN 0-9676116-4-4

The Guidebook to the Top 40 High Sierra Rock Climbs

- **Tricks of the Trade**
- **Whitney Region**
- **Palisades**
- **Bishop High Country**
- **Tuolumne Meadows**
- **Roadside Cragging**

SPORT CLIMBING IN THE SANTA MONICAS

by Louie Anderson

SOUTHERN CALIFORNIA CLIMBING GUIDES VOL. 1

June 2003 - 2nd Edition
250 pages - $30.00
ISBN 0-9676116-6-0

The Climbing Guide to the Santa Monica Mountains

- **Echo Cliffs**
- **Boney Bluff**
- **Malibu Creek**
- **Black Flower**
- **Tick Rock**
- **Conejo Mountain**

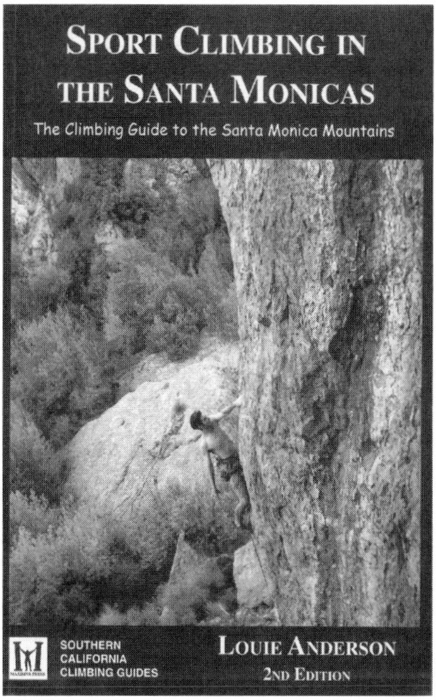